Mastering Weave Structures

Mastering Weave Structures

Transforming Ideas into Great Cloth

Sharon Alderman

Interweave
interweavebooks.com

DEDICATION

This book is dedicated to weavers past, present, and future who go to their looms to weave beautiful cloth . . . and do.

Technical editor: Sarah Saulson
Illustrations: Gayle Ford
Photography: Joe Coca
Photo styling: Ann Swanson
Cover design: Susan Wasinger
Page design: Marc M. Owens

Interweave Press LLC
201 East Fourth Street
Loveland, CO 80537-5655 USA
interweavebooks.com

Printed in Singapore by Tien Wah Press (Pte) Limited

Library of Congress Cataloging-in-Publication Data

Alderman, Sharon D.
Mastering weave structures / Sharon Alderman.
p. cm.
ISBN 1-931499-32-2 (hardcover)
ISBN 978-1-59668-137-8 (paperback)
1. Hand weaving. 2. Textile fabrics. I. Title.
TT848.A64985 2003
746.1'4--dc21
2003001529

10 9 8 7 6 5 4 3 2 1

Contents

Acknowledgments ~ vi

Introduction ~ 1

Plain Weave ~ 3

Twills ~ 25

Satin ~ 63

Waffle Weaves ~ 83

The Distorted Grid ~ 95

Compound Weaves ~ 123

Loom-Controlled Doubleweave ~ 157

Bedford Cords and Piqués ~ 179

Loom-Controlled Pile Weaves ~ 189

Crepe Weaves ~ 201

Some of This, Some of That ~ 207

Inventing Your Own Weave Structures ~ 227

Summing It Up: Where To Go From Here ~ 245

Appendix A ~ 246

Appendix B ~ 248

Appendix C ~ 250

Bibliography ~ 253

Index ~ 254

ACKNOWLEDGMENTS

Many people have been helpful in bringing this book to you. Foremost among them is Linda Ligon who never gave up on the idea. Joe Coca, photographer extraordinaire, makes me look good by capturing the very soul of the fabrics. Ann Swanson was the photo stylist; her accessory-less approach has my overwhelming approval! Marc Owens created a beautiful page design.

There is a large number of people who may be surprised to see their names here but at one time or another, perhaps without consciously setting out to do so, they have encouraged me at a crucial time. Gina Elliot Ziegler, Amy Norris, Cathy Reitz, JoAnn Bachelder, Nancy Steward, Joanne Nissen, Rosemary Brock, Corrie Cushman, Nicky Schonkala, Georgian Franczyk: I am in your debt.

Introduction

When I begin to think about a fabric that I want to weave, I think about how I want it to look, how I want it to feel, and what it will have to do. One of the steps necessary in going from the cloth taking shape in my mind to having a fabric in my hands is deciding what weave structure will provide the characteristics I want.

This book was written for you if you want to know more about weave structures. Its purpose is to explore the structure of various weaves in depth so that you will understand how each one works. I have assumed that you know how your loom works, how to dress and use it, and how to read a draft.

When you understand the underlying principles that govern a particular kind of structure, then you can modify the basic draft to obtain the result you want. For example, when you understand how to write a draft for a Bronson II lace weave, then it is possible for you to write a draft that will produce a cloth with lace where you want it. Likewise, when you understand how a Bedford cord is written, you can write a draft that will make the cords the width or widths that you want them to be. The broader purpose of this book, then, is to provide you with an understanding of weave structures so that you can transform your idea about a fabric you would like to create into a draft that can be used to produce that fabric. The selection or derivation of a draft is, of course, only one of the steps in producing the cloth of your dreams; decisions about fibers and yarns must also be made before you produce the fabric. Although the selection of appropriate fibers, yarn sizes, and styles are outside the scope of this book, some advice on these subjects is also given here.

Every book must be limited in its scope, and this one is no exception. I have set limits in accordance with my personal prejudices. There are no interlacements discussed here that require major loom modifications. (I have included some structures that benefit from the use of a dobby-equipped loom; such a loom offers treadling flexibility that is irresistible.) The structures discussed here are those which do not require manipulations with your fingers; there is no pick-up. Likewise, although there exist threading systems that are interesting from a mathematical point of view, I have not included them unless I feel that they produce useful cloth structures that no other threading system can. In other words, if it can be done on a loom without someone's having to become a carpenter/engineer, and if it can justify its existence by producing sound, beautiful cloth, then I'm interested.

Setting aside twining, split-ply twining, and the like, all weave structures are constructed from a very, very simple fact: *either the weft passes over the warp or it passes under it.* What is marvelous is the wide variety of fabrics we can make based on the combination of which—warp or weft—is on top at a particular intersection in the cloth!

When there is disagreement in standard texts or general usage about nomenclature, I have used Irene Emery's *The Primary Structures of Fabrics* as the standard.

I hope that you will find this book useful. I hope that it will help you as you work to transform your good ideas into good cloth.

Sharon Alderman

This cloth, 2/20 worsted wool with silk stripes, requires just four shafts: two for the plain-weave ground and two more for the navy/white stripes.

1

Plain Weave

Variations on a Theme

Percale, ottoman, faille, bengaline, lawn, batiste, poplin, voile, pongee, taffeta, chambray, limbric, broadcloth, chiffon, cretonne, lingette, muslin, sheeting, organdy, gingham, flannel, calico, cambric, grosgrain, repp, tapestry, dimity, china silk, crepe de chine, challis, madras, rib . . .

What do these textiles have in common? They are very different fabrics: some of them are heavy, some light, some of them sheer, some opaque, some of them stiff, some soft. In spite of their obvious differences, they have one important characteristic in common: they are all woven in **plain weave**, the interlacement, according to *Fairchild's Dictionary of Textiles* "used in about 80% of all woven fabrics."

The best place to begin any discussion is at the very beginning; in a discussion of weave structures, plain weave *is* the "very beginning." Plain weave, when closely set, is strong because its over-one, under-one structure produces the maximum internal friction in the cloth: the warp and weft resist slippage. *Each time the warp (or weft) goes from the face (the side facing you) to the back (the other side) it is said to intersect the plane of the cloth. As it travels to or from the back of the cloth, it forms another point of friction, which helps to make the cloth stable and strong.*

Because intersections occur so frequently in the cloth, the warp threads are held apart by the weft threads; there are never two consecutive warp threads rising and falling together in ordinary plain weave (If they occur, they are considered a flaw, sometimes called a **flat** or a **skip.**) A **balanced cloth**—one in which the **ends per inch (e.p.i.)** equal the **picks per inch (p.p.i.)**—produced in this way is stable and strong, and has a lower **thread count**, that is, fewer warp ends and picks per inch, than would a twill using the same yarns, for instance. The sheerest cloth that can be woven from a given thread is the one woven plain weave.*

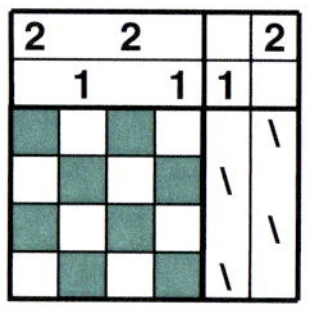

1.1 Plain weave on two shafts.

The draft for plain weave, **1.1**, is the simplest draft of all. It requires just two shafts and is woven using only two sheds.

Though it is possible to weave plain weave using only two shafts, it is a good idea to use more if they are available to avoid crowding. When the heddles (and thus the warp ends) on a shaft are very crowded, it can be difficult (depending on how clingy the yarn is) to open the shed cleanly. The friction of opening and closing sheds when warp ends are crowded contributes to abrasion of tender warps. So use more shafts—four or even eight if you have them—especially if the sett is close.

Plain weave can be woven in innumerable variations. It would be possible, I think, to use only plain weave for a lifetime without running out of possibilities. Let's begin by discussing balanced weaves, any fabric in which p.p.i. = e.p.i. *Fabrics that are woven in this way are said to be balanced weaves, regardless of their structure.*

The first possibility, and one that we see around us all of the time, is plain weave using the same warp and weft: same fiber, yarn style, size, and color. This is the sort of fabric that is easily produced in industry. It is usually woven of unbleached, undyed yarns and then bleached and/or dyed to suit the customer. This **loom-state cloth**, cloth as it comes from the loom, is known as **gray goods**, a fair description of its appearance, too.

Although there may be little point in weaving a fabric that can be purchased, there are many times when we might want to weave a plain fabric with the same warp and weft. For example, suppose that you have woven the fabric for a patterned jacket and want a plain fabric for a skirt to wear with it, or you have woven a fancy weave for an upholstery fabric and want to weave plain accent fabrics for pillows, or cloth woven with your choice of color or fiber or yarn style may not be commercially available. Handweavers usually weave this sort of fabric out of dyed yarns. Care in weaving such a fabric is important: an uneven beat produces crosswise striations in the cloth.

Introducing color variations

A simple variation of plain weave uses warp and weft that are the same except that the warp is one color and the weft another. Chambray and changeable taffeta are two commercial fabrics woven this way. Clearly, this variation must be woven using yarns of the colors desired in the finished cloth; the cloth cannot be piece-dyed unless the fibers chosen for warp and weft take dye differently.

If the chosen yarns are medium to heavy, then the surface of the cloth shows relatively large spots of color; the two colors do not blend visually unless you view the fabric at a distance. If the yarns are fine, then the

---

*An exception is **leno**, which is shown in Chapter 5 and page 20.

colors blend well even under fairly close scrutiny. Colors that may not work well together using heavier yarns can work in finer yarns. Strong contrasts in lightness and darkness (black crossed with white and the reverse are the extreme cases) result in a salt-and-pepper or tweedy appearance when heavier yarns are used; this effect is diminished when the yarns are finer. Both effects are possible; by knowing what will happen, you can select the right yarns to produce the effect that suits your needs.

Handwoven plain-weave cloth that uses one color for warp and a second for weft, just like its mill-woven counterpart, gives the appearance of a color that lies somewhere between those of the warp and weft colors. When the fabric is folded into soft pleats, the eye perceives the cloth as being mostly warp-colored or weft-colored, depending on

ANATOMY OF A STRUCTURAL DRAFT

This draft is a **structural draft**; that is, it shows the structure of the cloth. On the upper left is the **threading**, the order in which the ends are drawn through the heddles; to the right of the threading is the **tie-up**, which indicates which shafts are tied to which treadles. Only treadle looms use a tie-up. On table looms, you lift the shafts directly by levers. On looms with dobby mechanisms, the shafts you wish to lift for each shed are specified by putting a peg in a lag or bar or entering the desired shafts using a computer program written especially for the loom. Each shed must have its own bar and these bars are strung together in the order in which the sheds are to be made, one for each shed in the repeat.

Below the tie-up is the **treadling order**, the order in which the treadles are used.

To the left of the treadling order is the result, the reason for all the other parts: the **cloth diagram**. This diagram is a structural representation of the cloth. Each filled-in square indicates a raised warp end; each empty square indicates a lowered warp end, a place where the weft shows on the face of the cloth. Some of the drafts in this book are written using different conventions, but unless labeled otherwise, all drafts shown are structural drafts.

Structural drafts are extremely useful to handweavers—if we didn't have them, we'd surely invent them—but they have limitations. They assume that all the threads in a draft are of the same size, color, and uniform diameter throughout. They also assume that sett and weft packing are uniform and equal, that there is no shifting in the cloth during weaving or finishing, and that neither the warp nor weft threads are deflected by the structure.

These assumptions are not always warranted, but structural drafts are the place to begin. It is possible to look at these drafts with a knowing eye to find out what you need to know.

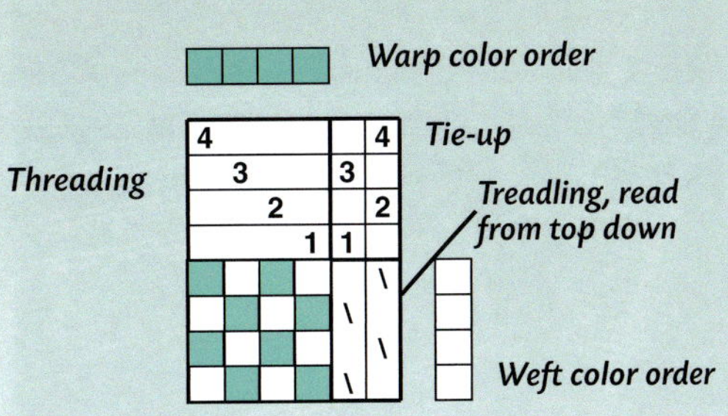

the angle from which it is viewed. This plain-weave variation enables us to obtain colors not otherwise available, but it poses the same technical challenge, only more so, that we face when the warp and weft are the same color: if the beat used to weave such a fabric is not perfect, then the weft striations noted above will be very prominent. It helps to weave a lot of this sort of fabric at one sitting because your weaving rhythm tends to become more even after working for a while. Listening to music that helps you pace yourself and establish the appropriate rhythm can help.

Plain-weave cloth can, of course, be woven with more than two colors. There can be several colors in the warp, in the weft, or in both. Using more than one color in warp or weft produces a streaked or—if the yarns of each color are grouped together—a striped fabric. Using more than one color in both warp and weft can produce a plaid fabric if the colors are grouped into warp and weft stripes, or a fabric in which there is an optical mixture of colors if the contrasting yarns are used singly.

When several colors are used in the warp but not arranged in stripes, the color effects can be rich and beautiful. If smooth color blending is desired, then all the colors ought to be of about the same **value** (that is all light, all dark, or all similarly in between). If the colors are of different values, then the effect is a striated or streaky cloth. The darkest colors in the warp appear more prominent when the weft color is light. The lightest colors in the warp stand out when the weft color is dark; they seem luminous and almost sparkle. When the value of the weft is intermediate between light and dark values in the warp, the cloth shows both light and dark specks, but neither the light nor the dark colors are as prominent as in the two preceding examples. The effect is one of a very rich color with a lot of depth. When the warp colors chosen vary a lot in value, the cloth may look lively or "busy" or speckled, depending on which colors are used. Mills rarely weave this sort of fabric because warping and weaving it requires more time than those with less complex color schemes. Handweavers used to handling each thread individually don't find this a problem (most of the time anyway), and welcome being able to weave a special cloth that we cannot buy.

It is important to know what sorts of effects can be achieved by mixing colors in the warp of a plain weave cloth so that you can use color to obtain the effects you seek.

Plain-weave cotton fabrics. The cloth with the single white stripe is very fine and crisp. The cloth to the right is made of 20/2 mercerized cotton and silky to the touch.

Two fabrics woven on the same worsted-wool warp. To the right is a plain-weave cloth in which very dark blue is woven across a deep bluish-green warp to produce an iridescent effect. To the left, the same warp is crossed by a bluish red, producing stronger iridescence.

These cotton fabrics are woven using a fine, refined, combed pearl cotton (20/2) as principal warp and weft. (The lowest is all 20/2 weft.) Notice how the uncombed, larger (8/2) unmercerized cotton rises up out of the cloth casting shadows. In the middle fabric the effect is heightened by using a slightly lighter color for the accent yarn. Its slight irregularities contrast with the 20/2 cotton.

2/2 basket weave shown in cross section. Two successive wefts will follow the path shown here, followed by two more making the opposite journey: under two, over two, etc.

Adding texture

Texture is another variable that can be introduced into a plain-weave cloth. When the same yarn is used in both warp and weft, plain weave can be given a third dimension by using two or more threads as one. The fabric produced has textural lines in it where the ends or picks are grouped. This plain-weave variation is an easy, relatively inexpensive way to add texture or depth to a cloth without having to buy another yarn. Dimity is a mill-woven cloth that is made this way.

The number of ends or picks that are grouped can be varied in the cloth, too. Stripes consisting, for example, of three ends used as one in some places and five ends used as one in others produce an understated fabric with a lot of variation in its texture. It is amazing how much variation in a cloth can be achieved without changing either the weave structure or the yarns used.

When warp ends are doubled or trebled, they must be threaded in separate heddles if they are to lie side by side in the finished cloth. When grouped ends lie side by side, the ridges they produce in the cloth maintain a uniform width. Warp ends that are threaded double or triple through the same heddle twist around each other as weaving progresses. The heavy warp lines that they produce in the cloth vary just a little bit in thickness: thicker in one place, thinner in another. A cloth that is woven in this way looks a little less formal than one in which a separate heddle is used for each thread. The important thing, as always, is knowing how to achieve the effect you want.

If the grouped ends carried by one heddle are similar in color value but different in hue, a subtle effect almost like ikat can be produced. This is another way to make a cloth that the textile industry is not likely to produce.

Grouping ends and/or wefts in the cloth at intervals in a plain-weave ground is one way to vary plain weave, but there are other ways to group warp ends or wefts; basket weaves are constructed by using such groupings throughout the warp. **Basket weave** is the term used to describe fabrics in which two or more warp and/or weft threads operate as one. The groups of warp ends lie side by side, not twisted together, as shown at left. In order to weave a cloth with this construction, each thread must have its own heddle, as we have seen.

These worsted-wool fabrics (below) are woven plain weave with multiple ends acting as one in the warp to form ribs—five ends for the heavier ribs, three for the finer ones. There is no regular repeat. In the lower fabric, extra picks were thrown into plain-weave sheds to make weft ribs.

This tussah silk fabric (above) is plain weave with an overcheck formed by placing two thicker ends side by side at regular intervals in the warp and the weft. The thicker ends and picks may be formed by doubling the yarn or by using a single larger thread. It feels like tissue paper, except it is very soft.

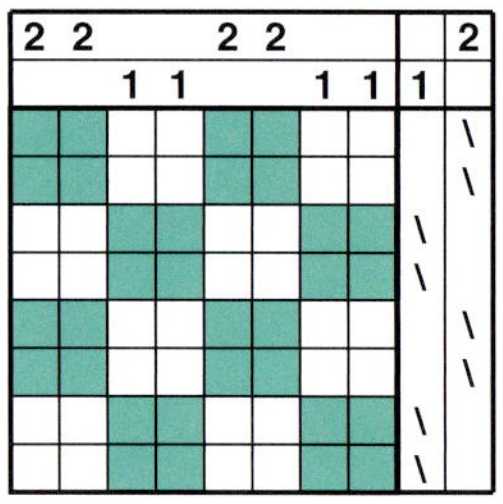

1.2a 2/2 basket weave on two shafts.

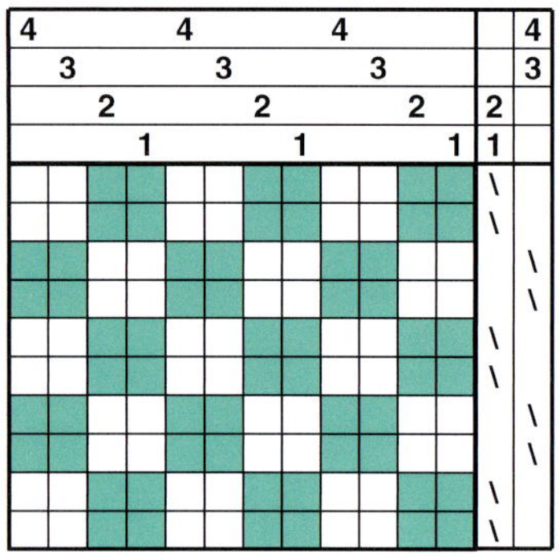

1.2b 2/2 basket weave on four shafts.

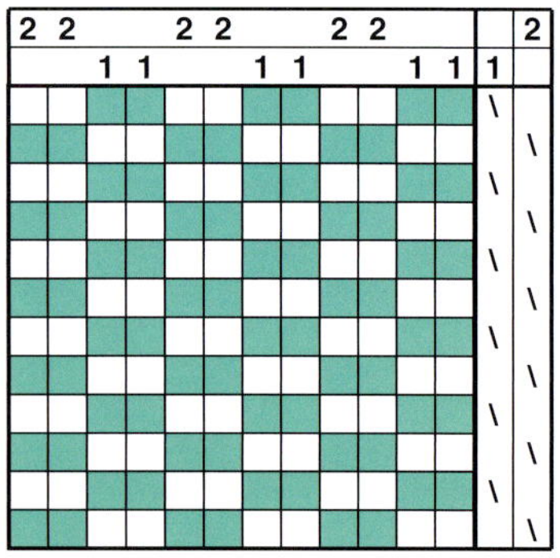

1.3 Half basket weave on two shafts.

These structures are described by naming the number of warp ends that go over and the number of ends that go under a weft in one repeat. Thus, a 2/2 basket weave is one in which two wefts pass under two warp ends and then over two warp ends.

The simplest basket weave, called matt weave in some texts (particularly those in the United Kingdom), is the 2/2 basket weave (**1.2a** and **1.2b**), in which two weft picks pass under two warp ends and then over two warp ends. While it is possible to weave a 2/2 basket on just two shafts, as in **1.2a**, it is usually a good idea to thread it onto four shafts to avoid crowding, as shown in **1.2b**.

As its designation says, this is a structure in which two warp ends move together and two wefts are entered in the same shed, one after the other. Although 2/2 basket weave is usually a balanced weave structure (p.p.i = e.p.i.), the sett will not be the same as for plain weave woven with the same yarn as single elements. In balanced plain weave, the warp ends must be spaced to permit the weft to fit between the ends. In a balanced 2/2 basket weave, there is no need to leave space between the two ends that act together because the weft does not pass between them. A sett that is appropriate for a given warp for plain weave will be too open for 2/2 basket weave, because the cloth woven in basket weave will either be weft-faced if the weft picks are beaten in firmly, or sleazy if a balance between the warp and weft is maintained. The sett that would produce a stable 2/2 twill makes a good 2/2 basket. Likewise, you need to set 3/3 and 4/4 basket weaves more closely than their 2/2 counterparts to produce a stable fabric. In fact, unless the yarns used are very "sticky" or hairy, the structure of basket weave breaks down when more than three yarns are grouped in warp and weft. If the yarns are smooth enough to be free to shift in the cloth, they tend to slide together or "clump" so that the cloth loses its stability. You may depend on it. Weavers can always count on the tendency of yarns in woven cloth to move together if nothing holds them apart (we rely on this tendency to produce lacy effects). It's important, therefore, to weave actual samples of structures that appear to work on graph paper.

When interlacements consist of more than one end or pick acting together, as in basket weave, the cloth is thicker than a corresponding structure woven of single warps and picks. If a given yarn makes an ordinary plain-weave cloth that is too lightweight or too sheer for your need, you may use it in basket weave to produce a heavier, more opaque fabric.

It is possible, up to a point, to cause a fine yarn to behave like a heavier one by using basket weave. One might expect that balanced 2/2 basket-weave cloth would be the same weight as cloth woven in plain weave with a yarn that is twice as heavy. For example, if a balanced 2/2 basket weave were woven with 20/2 cotton and a balanced plain weave were woven with 10/2 cotton, the resulting cloths would weigh the same, as you might expect; however, the basket-weave cloth would be more supple and would drape better than its plain-weave counterpart.

A variation on basket weave, sometimes called **half basket (1.3)**, is usually woven with doubled warp ends but single picks. Vertical lines in the cloth, formed as the weft passes over the doubled ends, are called ribs or **cords**. Technically speaking, the fabric may be described as plain-weave cloth with paired warps and single wefts. Doubling the weft picks instead of the warp ends will also

4/1 basket weave, used as upholstery. The lighter-colored side is the right side because the floats run warpwise—the best direction for upholstery. The use of woolen-spun wool of about 900 yards per pound for both warp and weft makes hearty, comforting upholstery.

Plain weave and 2/2 basket weave combined in one cloth. The interplay of the natural color and deep indigo linen, both 16/2, is pleasing: larger dots of color and smaller dots alternate in squares forming a checkerboard. While plain weave can be woven all across the cloth, four shafts are required where one area of warp alternates plain weave and 2/2 basket weave. There are two such areas, because the structures alternate, requiring eight shafts—four for each area.

The tendency for plain weave to spread out, if possible, causes the deep gray warp ends to "wiggle" a little as they are pushed close together when 2/2 basket weave lies between them, and move apart when plain weave lies between them. 16/2 cotton is used throughout.

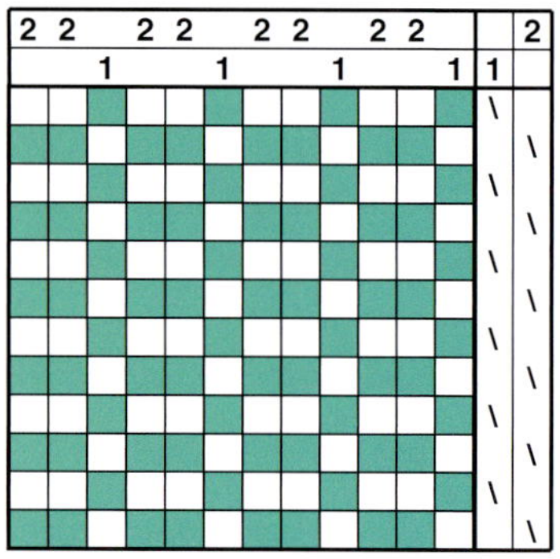

1.4 Haircord, woven on two shafts.

Open spaces form between the pair of heavier ends and the single lighter end. The resulting openness of the cloth makes it ideal for summer wear.

produce ribs but is far less convenient to execute than doubling the warp.

It is not necessary to limit ourselves to cloth in which the number of ends—and/or picks—that are grouped together is constant throughout the cloth; for example, we can design and weave cloth in which two ends act as one followed by three ends as one, twice, and then a single end. Further, there need not be a repeat in the cloth; the only limits have to do with the stability of the cloth produced, assuming that you want a stable cloth. Many variations are possible; one has been used frequently enough to have been given a special name of its own, **haircord**. Haircord has single warp ends alternating with paired warp ends **(1.4)**, and is woven with a single weft pick in each shed. The result is a fabric that has fine ribs or cords running in the warp direction. Using a coarser yarn for the paired ends further emphasizes the cord.

Variations in thread size, fiber, and twist

A similar effect to the grouping of warp ends or wefts can be obtained by using heavier yarns in place of the groupings. The results are different from cloth made up of grouped ends. The heavier yarn may differ only in size or also in color and/or texture as well.

Especially when designing cloth containing a mixture of different yarns, it is important to weave a good-sized sample. A 12-inch (30-cm) square is usually big enough to show how the different yarns interact when woven and finished. Sometimes a heavier yarn will buckle when loom tension is released. Washing and pressing the fabric may eliminate or emphasize the buckling; the only way to find out what will happen is to weave and finish a large sample.

When a combination of yarns puckers or produces unexpected bumps in the sample fabric, don't despair: make a note of it. List the yarns, their manufacturer(s), style, and color in your notes. The time will come when you will want those peculiar yet dramatic effects, and you will know how to produce them if you have paid attention. *Always consider unexpected or unwished-for results to be signposts that point the way in another direction for another fabric at another time.*

If plain-weave fabric is woven with yarns that look the same but are made of different fibers or are spun in two different yarn styles, several interesting things may occur. If you choose two yarns that are the same size and color but one is very shiny and the other dull, you can produce a rich-looking but very subtle fabric by using one as the warp and the other as weft. The fabric will have a luster when viewed from one angle and a matte surface when viewed the other way. You may further capitalize on the

Two ways to produce seersucker fabrics. The bottom fabric (blue, yellow, and green stripes on cream) is made with worsted wool for the cream stripes and 20/2 cotton for the colored ones. The wool shrank less than the cotton. The upper fabric (light coral and blue-green on ecru) is a structural seersucker; the cloth is woven plain weave, but some of the colored stripes are beamed separately and woven under very light tension. The other stripes are beamed under firm tension.

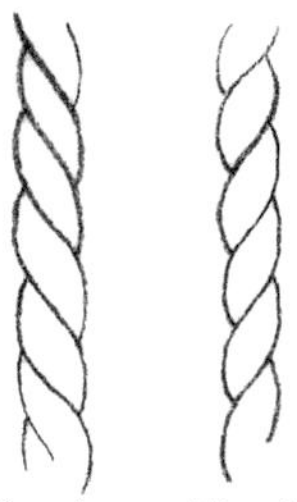

S-twist *Z-twist*

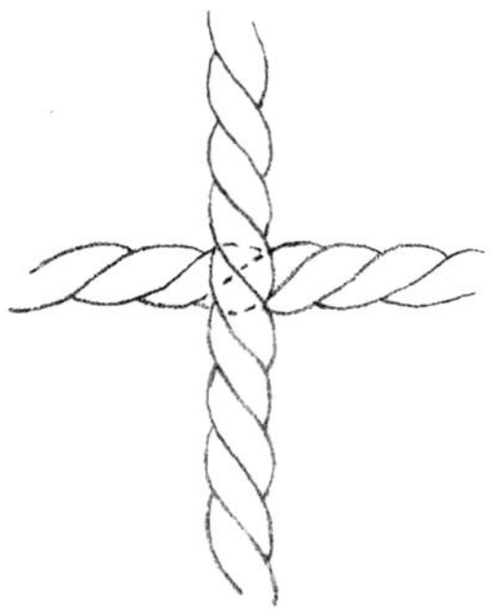

S-twist yarn in both warp and weft

S-twist yarn in warp, Z-twist in weft

extural differences by arranging the yarns in warp stripes and choosing one of them to use as the weft, or use the same arrangement in the weft to weave a very subtle plaid. (Again, be sure to find out how they shrink relative to each other.) The textural differences can be more pronounced, too: consider a smooth wool worsted and a ratiné wool of comparable size to produce a cloth with a more textured surface.

Plain weave may be used to good advantage to show off the differences that the direction of the twist, or of the ply, in yarns can make in cloth. Cloth with S-spun yarns and Z-spun yarns in alternating warp stripes has a subtle sort of patterning that depends not on the color of the yarns but on the way that light is reflected from the two different twist directions. A fabric woven this way is called a **shadow stripe**. Weaving the stripes in the weft, too, will produce a **shadow plaid**. When Z-twist yarn is used for both the warp and weft, (or S-twist yarn for both warp and weft), the yarns mesh with or **bed** into each other. When the warp yarn is twisted in one direction and the weft yarn is twisted in the other, the yarns do not bed but remain more independent; the resulting fabric may feel thicker, crisper, and/or fuller. Although looking at the illustration shown here might persuade you that the opposite is true, a small experiment can demonstrate how bedding works. Find a large-diameter yarn whose twist direction is easily seen (a light-colored plied yarn is a good choice) and lay it across itself at right angles. As seen from the top, the twist directions seem to cross at right angles. Peek under the top yarn to see what happens where the two yarns touch each other; you will see that the twists mesh with each other exactly as the teeth of a worm gear do.

Commercially woven cotton voile gains its crispness from fine, hard-twisted cotton yarns (typically 50 ends per inch and 50 picks per inch and 30 to 40 twists per inch in the yarn) woven Z with S (or S with Z). Using the same fine, hard-twisted yarns 2 S, 2 Z in both warp and weft produces a crepey, crisp fabric called georgette.

The possibilities inherent in combinations of S- and Z-twist yarns are not often considered by the handweaver. Many of us are spinners as well as weavers (or well-acquainted with spinners), so it ought to be possible for us to obtain yarns with the twist direction and number of twists per inch we want.

Mixed warps

One of the simplest variations on ordinary plain weave, one that is a favorite of handweavers, is plain weave woven with yarns in a variety of textures, sizes, and/or colors. The variety may occur in the warp or in the weft or both; the only limit to a varied weft is the number of shuttles that you are willing or able to manage. A "mixed warp" can be threaded either in a regular repeat or **hit or miss** (at random). In the former threading, the ends are taken in the same order every time, for example: a, b, c, d, e, f/a, b, c, d, e, f, etc. In the latter, yarns a through f are used over and over, but their order within the six-end unit varies, for example: a, c, d, b, e, f/b, c, a, f, d, e/f, b, a, c, e, d, etc. When a hit-or-miss warp is being made, the six ends are usually wound together as one on a warping board or reel and then threaded in the order in which they come to hand. When two identical ends fall side by side, tiny random stripes appear in the cloth.

It is worthwhile to note that mixed warps, while not exclusively in the realm of the handweaver, are limited commercially to rather expensive fabrics because they require more care in warping and weaving. For us handweavers, they are a good way to use up odds and ends left over from previous warps. Commercial fabrics woven with a fly shuttle are usually made with two, or a multiple of two, picks of each weft yarn because the fly shuttle can only originate at one side of the cloth and must return before another shuttle carrying another yarn can be used. It is easy for handweavers to use several shuttles in succession for only one pick each if we wish. This is another way in which we can produce fabrics that industry cannot.

There is more good news about mixed-warp fabrics, particularly those that are threaded in a regular repeat. When the yarns are not used in groups, as stripes, any puckering or buckling that they produce when they are woven and finished simply gives the cloth an interesting texture. If one of the colors bleeds a little, it merely helps to blend the colors, (providing that the bleeder is not a dark color in an otherwise light fabric.)

Avoiding and/or dealing with problem yarns

Using a variety of yarns in a single warp presents certain problems. First, all of the yarns must be suited to use as warp yarns. They must all be able to withstand a considerable amount of tension without pulling apart.

Warp yarns must pass through heddle eyes without becoming caught. In theory, it is possible to ease problem yarns through heddle eyes each time the warp is advanced, but in fact, one or more of those yarns is likely to break if you neglect to check the tension of the warp or simply advance the warp too fast or too far. Try passing a representative length that contains at least two of the biggest lumps or bumps through a heddle as fast as possible to see if it gets caught in the eye. If it does catch, you have a choice: you may reserve that yarn for use as weft only, or you may tie a large-eyed string heddle for each such yarn in the warp. If you have to tie only a dozen or so across your warp, it won't be an impossible task; on the other hand, if you will need a hundred or more of them, think it over. Each string heddle must be tied carefully to avoid a ragged, uneven shed and consequent weaving errors.

Warp yarns must also pass through the reed without catching. You can tell when you try to put the yarn through the reed if the yarn is much, much too big for the size of the dents. Test a borderline case by tying one end to the breast beam, threading it through the reed, and tying the other end to the warp beam at the back of the loom. Move the beater back and forth, listening carefully. If the beater doesn't move at all or breaks the yarn straightaway, your question has been answered: no. If when you move the beater you hear a little "ping," the yarn is too big

22/2 cottolin warp and weft. The top fabric is woven using the darkest red as weft. The bottom one is woven using the lightest red as weft. Both results are valid—they are simply subtly different.

for the dents; although it has moved through the dent this time, when you beat it and its fellows repeatedly, breakage will occur. If you hear "shush," then the reed is a tight fit and may cause problems, particularly for a new weaver. Consider using a more open reed (one with fewer dents per inch).

Advancing the warp frequently by small amounts is always a good practice, but it is absolutely essential when weaving a tender or otherwise difficult warp. I routinely weave just 2 inches (5 cm) and then advance the warp by the same amount.

The final consideration is the yarn's resistance to abrasion. Some yarns may have adequate tensile strength and no particularly big loops, lumps, or bumps to catch in heddles or reed but simply fall apart when subjected to abrasion. The friction generated when the shed is changed is enough to cause some yarns to fail; others withstand that pretty well but are scuffed up in the heddles or the reed. To test a yarn for its resistance to abrasion and its stability along its core, hold it firmly in one hand and run the other thumbnail and forefinger back and forth along its length to see whether the loops, bumps, seeds, or other fancy structures shift their position along the core of the yarn. If you find that loose fibers have gathered under your thumbnail, the yarn will abrade during the weaving process. If no shifting takes place, repeat the test a few times and see if the yarn has become fuzzy or ragged through abrasion; if so, save it for use as weft. If the loops or bumps have shifted, reserve the yarn for weft; if you try to use it as warp, the core will be stable, but everything else will slide back behind the heddles and make a big blob that will not pass through the eye of the heddle, and eventually the yarn will break.

It is possible sometimes to use yarns for warp that the simple tests described above suggest are a little too weak; it just takes more care, more work, to do it. For example, if you are determined to use a tender yarn for warp, it is especially important to advance the warp frequently by small amounts. It also helps to change the sheds gently. It is a good idea to use a direct tie-up (certainly no problem with plain weave!) and lift first shaft 1 and then 3 to make the 1,3 shed and then shafts 2 and then 4 to obtain its opposite. Beat gently when you use these tender yarns and keep close watch on the warp ends as they rise. If you see any irregularity in the pattern they make as they rise—for example, if one doesn't rise as high as its neighbors—investigate right away to see if the yarn has become caught or snagged and if so, free it immediately.

Novelty Yarns

Fancy or novelty yarns deserve a few more words on their behalf. Because yarns with unusual colors or textures are so interesting in themselves, it is a good idea to keep everything else about the fabrics in which they are used as simple as possible. In short, plain weave is a good choice for fancy yarns.

Variations in the sett

Plain weave may be varied by the way in which the cloth is set. Interesting and stable plain-weave fabrics may be designed by varying the sett of the warp ends. Cram some dents full of ends and leave others empty. These **skip-dent** fabrics depend for their stability on three things: the texture of the warp and weft yarns, the degree to which

A skip-dent, plain-weave cloth woven in natural 20/2 cotton. The yarn is very silky and smooth, and densely set. The cloth is finished by washing it vigorously in a washing machine, which reduces the size of the open spaces. This cloth was washed twice in the machine with terry cloth towels.

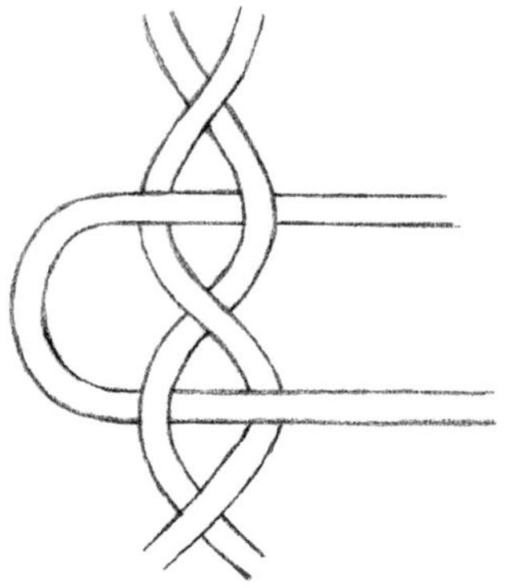

Two adjacent warp ends are given a single twist before each weft is inserted. The result is a clean, stable leno edge.

the ends are crammed together, and the way in which the cloth is woven.

Skip-dent fabrics composed of hairy, clinging yarns or of bumpy, textured yarns are more stable than those woven of smooth, slippery yarns. Slippery yarns rearrange themselves during finishing or even as they are taken from the loom so that the sett is effectively averaged. When that happens, the open stripes in the cloth disappear and the crammed areas become looser.

To some extent, all skip-dented fabrics shift during finishing; the open areas must be wider on the loom than desired in the finished fabric, and the crammed areas must be denser on the loom than desired in the finished fabric. When you want a cleaner, more distinct interface between the open areas and the woven areas, you may either put a more textured yarn at that edge or weave leno at the interface. A leno edging makes it impossible to beat the weft in densely because the twist in the warp ends resists dense weft packing.

Just as dents may be skipped to produce warp stripes of open areas next to dense areas, the same sort of spacing may be achieved in the weft direction, too. It is necessary to beat the weft picks very densely and then leave an open space, held by a spacing device, before beating in more picks. The spacer, which becomes firmly woven into the cloth, permits you to beat in picks firmly while leaving a uniform space unwoven. Since you will want to remove it either before the cloth is advanced or after it has been cut from the loom, the spacer must be smooth. (I don't recommend leaving the spacers in because you will need a lot of them, and the buildup on the cloth beam may interfere with the action of some looms.) I have had the best results using lengths of satin rattail cord, which are easy to store and easy to pull out of even a very wide warp. Satin cords are available in only a few diameters, but several may be used at once, each in its own shed, to create larger open spaces if desired.

A maximum of three spacers (or groups of spacers) is required to weave a cloth with open spaces in the weft: weave in the first spacer, weave plain weave for the desired number of picks, add the second spacer, weave more plain weave, add the third spacer, weave more plain weave, then pull out the first spacer and insert it into the next shed. If the areas of plain weave are large, you can get by with only two spacers used leapfrog fashion throughout.

Another variation on this theme is to vary the size of the spacing in the warp direction, the weft direction, or both. It is simplest, of course, to establish the spaces in the warp direction; weaving varying spaces into the weft requires the use of spacers of more than one diameter or of a greater number of spacers in one place and a lesser number in another.

Skip-dented fabrics must be woven firmly if they are to retain structural integrity. A skip-dented fabric with few picks per inch shifts and slides in finishing and in use. The notion of weaving fabrics that change structurally with time is an interesting one conceptually, but the fabrics thus produced are limited in their practical application.

If a skip-dented fabric is to be used in any practical application, it is necessary to wash the samples very vigorously to establish how much shifting will take place in the finished cloth. I generally machine-wash a sample several times with terrycloth towels—chosen for their gentle abrasive action—to evaluate its structural stability.

Unbalanced plain weave

With the exception of skip-dented fabrics, we have considered only plain-weave fabrics with as many picks per inch as ends per inch. There are many options, however, for creating plain-weave cloth that is not balanced.

Plain-weave cloth may be woven with a wide variety of balances between the number of ends per inch and picks per inch. Poplin is a warp-faced plain-weave cloth in common use. It is said that the original poplin was woven in Ireland using a warp of fine, closely set silk and a weft of coarser worsted wool. These days, poplins are usually woven of cotton or cotton blends. Because the warp covers the weft in poplin, the warp yarns must be hard-twisted if the cloth is to wear well. A silk yarn is still soft and supple even when it is given many turns per inch, so poplin's Irish inventor probably produced a very satisfactory fabric.

The opposite of poplin is limbric, with fewer warp threads and more picks to the inch. Generally speaking, fabrics in which the warp dominates have better draping qualities than those in which the weft dominates.

Structures in which the warp dominates the cloth, essentially covering the weft, are often called **rep** or **repp** weaves. There is a lot of confusion in the weaving literature about the use of the terms "rep" and **rib**, which usually means about the same as rep because the two terms have been used interchangeably for so long. (The term "rib" refers to the ridges that are formed in the cloth.) In *The Primary Structures of Fabrics,* Irene Emery notes that the sometimes contradictory application of these two terms has robbed them of specific meaning and suggests substituting the terms **warp-faced plain weave** and **weft-faced plain weave**. Some older texts, notably Strong's *Fabric Structure,* describe rep fabric specifically as a plain-woven fabric with a coarse yarn alternating with a fine yarn in both warp and weft. The coarse ends are always lifted for the coarse weft picks and the fine warp for the fine picks. Because the coarse warp yarn, traveling further, takes up at a much higher rate than the fine warp, two warp beams are required to weave this cloth with ease.

Strong also describes **imitation rep** fabrics in which there is only one warp and one weft. In this case the warp is beamed in two parts: the warp ends carried on shafts 1 and 2 are wound on one beam and those carried

Rep weave fabric for a placemat, made on eight shafts. The textile is thick and insulates the table surface.

by shafts 3 and 4 are wound on a second beam. The tension on the two beams is unequal; one of the beams is tightly tensioned so that the warp ends lie almost straight in the cloth and the weft bends over and under them while the other is kept as slack as possible so that the warp ends do all the bending.

A modification of Strong's imitation rep structure using a single warp yarn and two weft yarns, one coarse and one fine, combined with color changes in the warp, gives rise to warp-faced plain-weave fabrics that handweavers know as rep. In many of these fabrics, the warp ends alternate colors (A, B, A, B) for a distance, and then the alternation reverses (B, A, B, A). At the point of reversal, two ends of the same color lie side by side. When the coarse weft is thrown, the colors that are up are emphasized; the colors of the warp ends raised for the fine weft are played down. When two fine wefts (or two coarse, for that matter) are thrown in succession, the color emphasis is reversed. This structure is often used for rugs and informal placemats.

Another rep weave placemat. Its four blocks (woven on eight shafts) are plainly visible in this example. The warp is humble cotton carpet warp (8/4). The weft is also carpet warp and three-ply rug wool used alternately.

Although only two shafts are required to weave rep, it is a particularly good idea to spread the warp out over four or, better still, eight shafts. When the warp is crowded, as it must be in this structure, the heddles are packed very closely and it is more difficult to make a clean shed. The loom will work more easily, the friction on the warp ends will be reduced (because they rise into the shed at different angles), and the number of weaving flaws that may be created by ends that cling to each other will be reduced or eliminated.

Plain-weave interlacement can take on the appearance of a much more complex cloth by establishing a color order or sequence in the ends and/or picks used. Such a cloth is said to show a **color-and-weave effect**. Although any structure can be changed visually (but not structurally) by a particular color rotation in the warp and/or weft, some of the nicest examples are woven in plain weave. One of the best known of these has a name of its own, **log cabin (1.5)**. Wherever two dark or light ends or picks lie side by side, the direction of the stripes in the cloth changes from vertical to horizontal or vice versa. The same change takes place where two light or two dark picks lie side by side. The plain-weave structure is, of course, undisturbed by this manipulation of color, but the result is a fabric with a strong, graphic appeal. The weaver/designer decides how far to thread a vertically or horizontally striped area and how often to make the weft

1.5 Log cabin, a color-and-weave-effect pattern woven plain weave. Where two like-colored ends or picks lie side by side, the direction of the stripe changes.

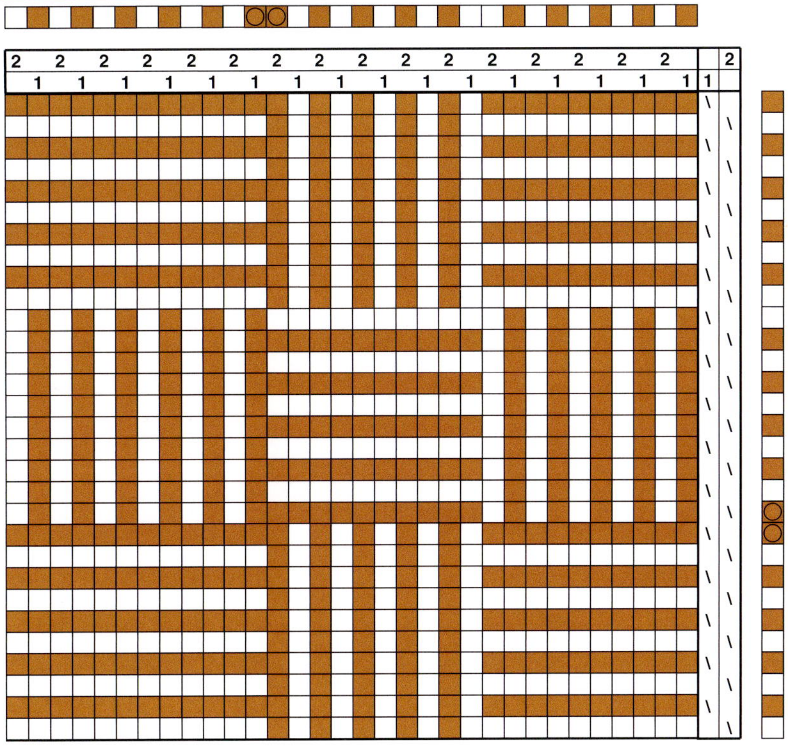

The top fabric is woven in log cabin as shown in the draft. Three strands of 2/20 worsted wool are used as one in both the warp and weft direction.

The bottom fabric, 16/2 linen in natural and deep blue, is woven in a variation of plain weave to make squares of stripes going one way in a ground striped in the other direction.

changes that alter the direction of the stripes. Although any structure may be used when designing color-and-weave-effect cloth, fancy-weave structures may be obscured or simply made confusing by the addition of color to change the visual effect. Fortunately, color-and-weave-effect fabrics may be easily "woven on paper," that is, explored as drafts, either with special computer programs or with pencil, graph paper, and eraser.

Two log cabin color-and-weave-effect fabrics woven with yarns in contrasting sizes. The lower one is constructed of 8/2 cotton (light orange in the warp, raspberry in the weft) and medium blue cotton sewing thread. Here the stripe direction is less obvious than the checkerboard effect of light orange alternated with raspberry.

The upper fabric uses bright pink 8/2 cotton in the warp and red-orange 8/2 cotton in the weft. The high value difference between 8/2 cotton and the 20/2 pearl cotton (the light color) highlights the stripe directions. The wide stripe is three times the width of the narrow in both warp and weft.

2

Twills: A Step to the Left (or Right, or Both)

If plain weave has enough possibilities for variation to last a lifetime, then twills, surely, could provide several lifetimes of study. In plain weave, the warp and weft pass over one, under one in both directions. Both warp and weft may be made up of multiple threads, as in basket or matt weaves, but they always interlace in the cloth as if they were single threads.

When a warp end or a weft pick passes over or under two or more consecutive threads in the cloth, a **float** is created. Twills, by definition, have floats; these typically do not appear in the same place in succeeding picks. The way in which these floats are placed, pick after pick, creates one of the most characteristic features of twills: the diagonal lines that appear in the cloth. In **simple** or **regular twills**, the floats move to the left or right by one warp end with each pick. The number of ends that lie over (or under) any given pick in one repeat varies from one twill to another, but usually does not vary within a particular regular twill.

Twill is the simplest weave structure based on floats and is the basis of many other weave structures, as we shall see. One full repeat of plain weave occurs in two warp ends and two weft picks. The simplest twill, a three-end twill, repeats in three warp ends and three weft picks (**2.1**).

Three-end twill may be woven in two ways: warp-faced (shown) or weft-faced. The back of a warp-faced twill is a weft-faced twill and vice versa. Imagine how many yards have been woven of this particular twill, also called **jeans twill** or denim. In classic blue jeans, the warp is indigo blue cotton, and the weft, undyed cotton. Many of us live a great deal of our lives in jeans twill.

The notation we used for basket weaves is also used for twills. Thus, three-shaft twill

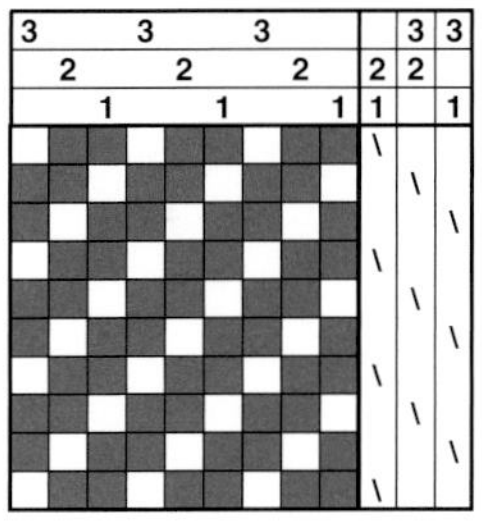

2.1 2/1 twill, jeans twill woven on three shafts.

Figure 1. 2/1 twill. Two warp ends lie above the weft in one repeat.

Figure 2. 1/2 twill. One warp end lies above the weft, and two below, in one repeat.

Figure 3. The warp end in a plain-weave fabric must be set far enough apart to allow the weft to pass between each.

Figure 4. In a 2/2 twill fabric the weft passes between every two warps, so a closer sett is required.

may be written (and woven) as either 1/2 or 2/1 twill. The first number shows how many warp ends lie above the weft picks in one repeat and the second, the number of warp ends below the weft picks in one repeat. The jeans twill of classic dungarees is 2/1 twill, a warp-faced twill.

The warp is dominant because twice as many ends lie over the weft as lie under it; the ratio is 2:1.

In a regular twill, adjacent picks never float over or under the same set of warp ends. If the first two ends of a 2/1 twill are lifted for the first pick, then the second and third ends may be lifted for the second pick and the first and third ends lifted for the third pick. Likewise, if the twill is woven as a 1/2 twill, the first end is lifted for the first pick, followed by the second and then the third if we maintain the same direction. Twills may progress to the left or to the right; the former is called a **left-hand twill**, the latter, a **right-hand twill.** If the direction of the twill movement, the direction of the twill diagonal, remains the same throughout the cloth, it is a simple or regular twill. I think of it as being a **straight** twill because it progresses steadily in the same direction, over and over.

When the number (or sum of numbers) above the line and the number (or sum of numbers) below the line are equal, the twill is said to be an **even twill.** In an even twill, neither the warp nor the weft predominates. Because the number above the line is not equal to the number below it, a three-shaft twill is said to be an **uneven twill:** the warp shows more on one face and the weft more on the other. The **balance** of twill fabrics, on the other hand, is determined by the number of ends and picks per inch which are equal in a balanced cloth, be it plain weave, twill, or any other structure. The rib in a balanced regular twill forms a 45-degree angle with the warp.

Twill sett

The sett of twills woven as balanced cloth must be closer than the sett for a balanced plain weave using the same yarns. Plain-weave cloth is set so that there is enough space between warp ends to accommodate the diameter of the weft yarn (Figure 3). The weft yarns hold the warp ends apart.

Twill cloth works differently. In a 2/2 twill, for example, the two ends that rise together touch each other; there is no need to leave room between them for weft (Figure 4). (In fact, you can't hold them apart short of inserting a weft between them.) The pairings of ends in this twill are always changing (1 and 2, 2 and 3, etc.), but any four ends always work in two opposing pairs—two up, two down. Four warp ends in plain weave require eight spaces, four for the warp ends and four for the weft picks.

For a 2/2 twill, therefore, the sett must be closer than for a plain-weave fabric made from the same yarn (see Appendix C). Fancier twills may be analyzed in the same way to estimate how much more dense the twill sett must be than the plain weave-sett for the same yarns.

Just as the warp must be more densely set in a twill, the weft must be more closely packed for the same reason: there is nothing to prevent the wefts from lying close in the cloth (it will happen automatically). The denser thread count makes twill fabric thicker, heavier, and warmer than its plain-weave counterpart would be.

Because the floats move diagonally in the cloth, simple twill fabrics drape more softly and are more supple than a plain-weave cloth made of the same yarns. They are generally

A simply elegant 2/2 regular twill. The warp is dark brown 2/20 worsted wool with a two-end stripe of medium gray at regular intervals. The color order is reversed in the weft: gray with two-pick stripes of dark brown. The effect is understated and quiet, but very effective.

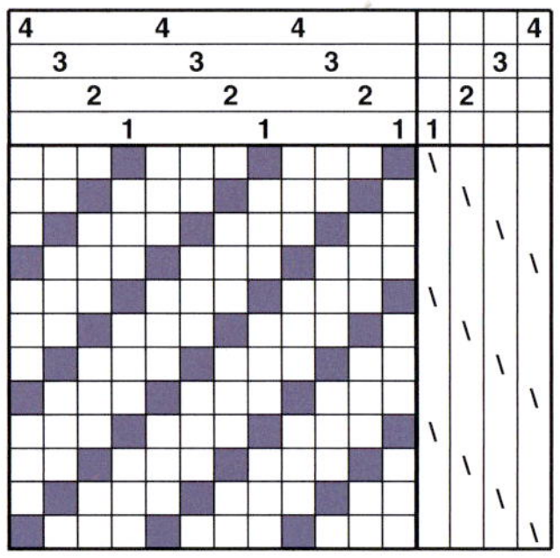

2.2a 1/3 twill, four shafts.

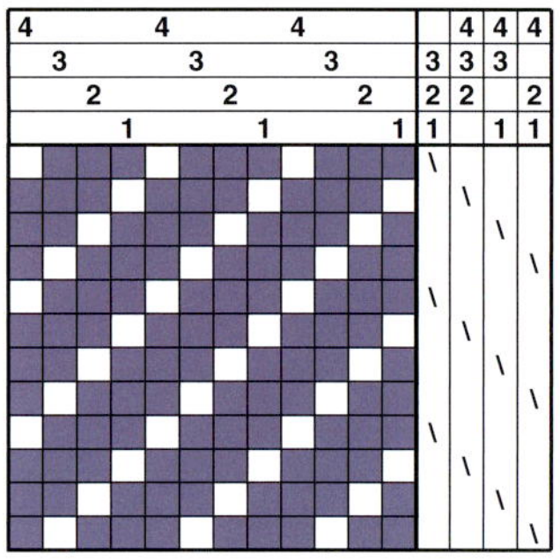

2.2b 3/1 twill, four shafts.

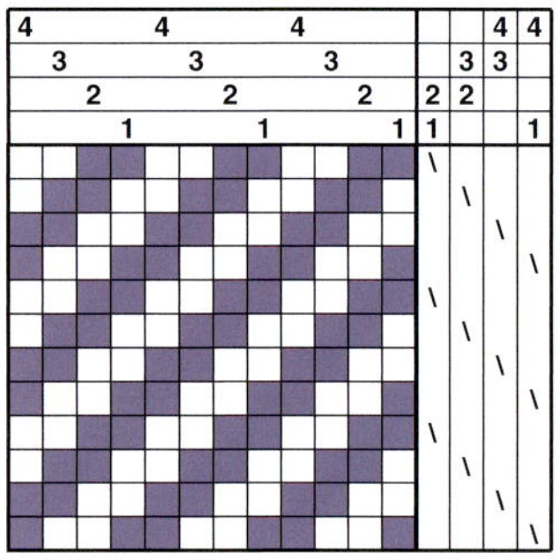

2.2c 2/2 twill, four shafts.

not quite as subject to wrinkling, either (of course fiber content and spinning style are also contributing factors).

As in plain weave, the direction of the twist of the warp and weft yarns in twill weaves affects the qualities of the cloth produced by those yarns. The direction of the twill line reverses from the face to the back of the fabric; a left-hand twill is a right-hand twill on its back, and vice versa. In particular, when the warp and weft show equally on both face and back, the twill diagonal will be more prominent on one side than on the other because of the interaction between the direction of the twill and the twist of the yarns. If the warp and weft are both S-twist, the twill rib is bolder when woven in right-hand twill because the yarns do not mesh as closely. To de-emphasize the twill rib, weave the cloth with the rib slanting in the same direction as the twist of the yarn; that is, left hand twill with S-twist yarns and vice versa. The relationship between the boldness of the twill rib and the twist and twill directions are important in designing whipcords (page 48).

Three regular or straight twills may be woven using four shafts: 1/3 twill is weft-faced (**2.2a**), 3/1 twill is warp-faced (**2.2b**), and 2/2 twill is an even twill (**2.2c**).

Broken twill

There are other ways to weave these twills. They may be treadled as **broken** or **staggered twills.** A broken twill is woven so that the twill diagonal is not continuous. One way to weave a broken twill is to move the diagonal to the left for part of the repeat and then skip one or two sheds *in the regular twill sequence* and finish out the repeat in the opposite direction until all the sheds have been used. For a 2/2 twill the treadling sequence might be: 1,2; 2,3; 1,4; 3,4; repeat (**2.3**). A three-shaft twill cannot be broken because skipping one shed reverses the direction of the diagonal and skipping two sheds brings us back to the first shed again. One four-shaft twill, 3/1 twill, when woven as a broken twill, is called **false satin** because it is warp-faced and the twill diagonals characteristic of simple twills are almost eliminated.

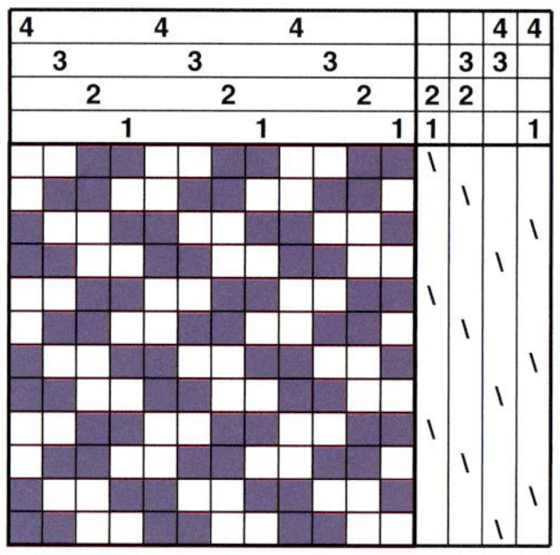

2.3 Four-shaft broken twill, broken in the treadling.

In the treadling given in **2.3** for broken 2/2 twill, the second and third picks lie opposite each other: what is up for the second pick is down for the third pick and vice versa. Because those picks are in opposite sheds, they cannot be beaten in as closely as the first and second picks or the third and fourth picks. The fourth pick and first (which follows it) bear the same relationship to each other. Picks lying next to each other but in opposite sheds stand apart a little bit. (You can see the spaces by looking at the back lit cloth.) A broken twill, therefore, cannot have as high a pick count as a simple 2/2 twill; because the picks oppose each other at such short intervals, this structure provides a way to create a cloth midway between plain weave and a regular twill in weight and draping qualities.

Broken 2/2 twill, woven with a light warp and dark weft (or vice versa), is sometimes called **granite weave** because of its resemblance to evenly speckled granite rock. (A 1/3 twill woven as a broken twill progresses the same way as a broken 2/2 twill: two picks moving one way and then two the other: 1, 2, 4, 3, repeat, or 1, 4, 2, 3, repeat.)

Block twills

Twills may be woven so that warp-faced and weft-faced areas are side by side in both the warp and weft directions. To weave a cloth this way requires more shafts. Where one area is being woven 1/3, four shafts are required. If the warps adjacent this area are woven 3/1 in the same pick, another four shafts are required because a shaft cannot be both up and down on the same pick (**2.4**). Notice in **2.4** that the diagonals move in opposite directions. To maintain a crisp edge to the block, the last end of one block does exactly the opposite of the first end of the new block, creating a **clean break.** Without

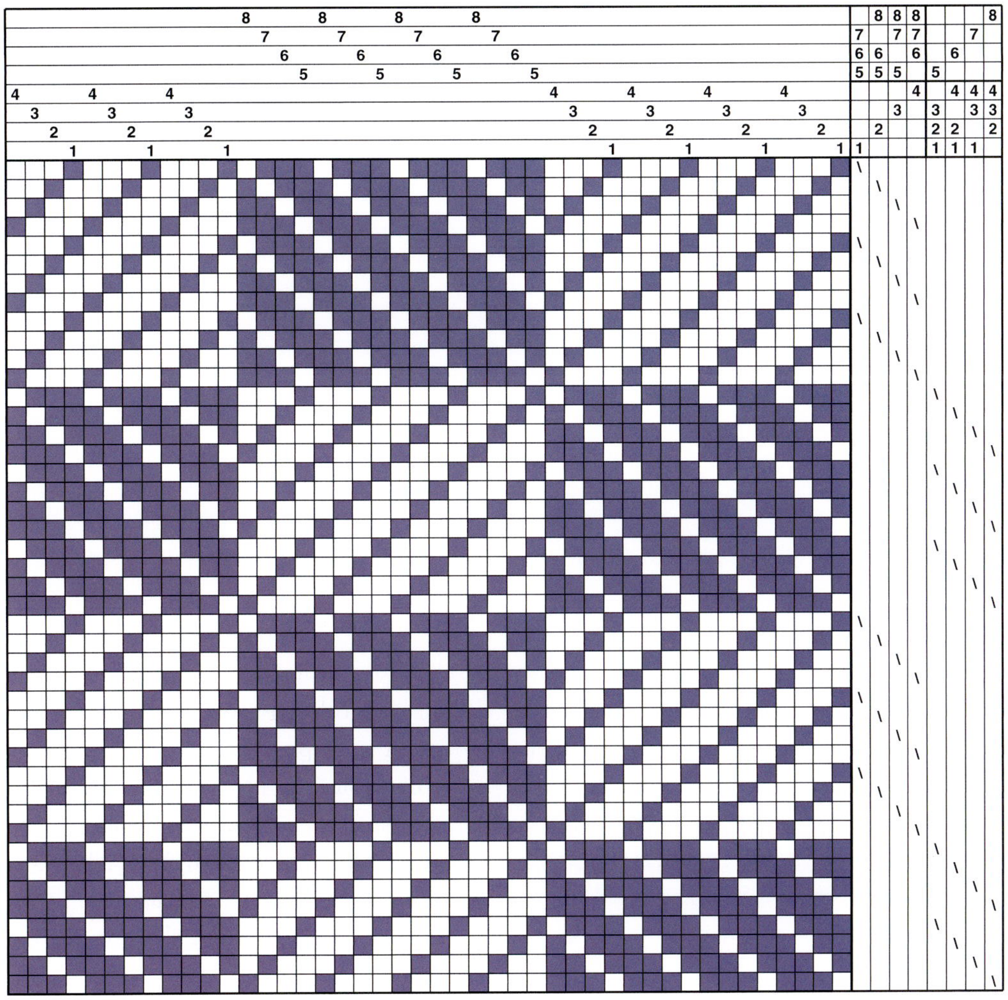

2.4 Two-block twill, eight shafts. Notice that where the blocks meet, in both the warp and weft directions, the threads on either side of the change are woven on opposites.

clean breaks blurring would occur at the edges of adjoining blocks because weft floats would extend into warp-faced areas and floats that were three or four ends or picks long would appear at each interface. We will return to the idea of clean exchanges or breaks again and again.

Think of the four threads that make up one threading repeat for a block as being one **unit.** The area threaded in repeats of one unit is described as a **block;** the draft shown in **2.4** has two blocks, each consisting of four units or repeats in the threading.

Look at the tie-up for draft **2.4.** Think of it as being divided into four quadrants. The lower left quadrant is the tie-up for a 1/3

	8	8	8				8
7		7	7			7	
6	6		6		6		
5	5	5		5			
			4		4	4	4
		3		3		3	3
	2		2	2	2		2
1				1	1	1	

Below, Left: Two-block double-faced twill. The colors reverse on the other side.
Right: Three-block double-faced twill. The reverse of red areas is blue and vice versa. Where two colors are blended, the same blend appears on the other side. This example is woven from a very fine woolen singles.

twill. Just above it is the tie-up for a 3/1 twill. The upper right quadrant produces 1/3 twill and the lower right 3/1, just the reverse of the two left quadrants. The twill diagonals move in opposite directions. Notice that the line forming the interface between the units makes a clean break in the tie-up as well as in the cloth. The last column in the tie-up, the right-most column, is likewise exactly the opposite of the first column. When the cloth is woven the last shot in the repeat (the right-most column) is followed by a shot woven in the shed made by the left-most column in the tie-up.

Twill drafts may be written for more than two blocks. Each block requires its own shafts; a three-block twill based on 1/3 and 3/1 twills requires twelve shafts, four for each of the blocks. To maintain the clean breaks, there are only two choices (setting broken twills aside for the moment): warp-faced and weft-faced twill. The use of three blocks does not introduce a third possibility; rather, it means that the third block may be woven along with block one, with block two, with both of them, or alone. The addition of just one more block greatly increases designing options. The tie-up and treadling must be worked out carefully for each possibility, of course, but a three-block tie-up is no more complicated than the tie-ups we have already considered.

Here is how you go about working out the tie-up. First, decide which blocks will be warp-faced, 3/1, and which will be weft-faced, 1/3. Work out the treadling for one of the blocks first. Keep the diagonal for all the weft-faced sections consistent and do likewise for the warp-faced sections as you write the rest of the tie-up for that treadling block. That is, all 1/3 twill sections will have ribs moving in the same direction and all 3/1

Two two-block twills. The lower one, woven of 20/2 pearl cotton, is threaded and treadled six units per block. Folded, it exhibits exciting iridescence, flashing red and then turquoise. The upper version is woven of 2/8 worsted wool with a single thread of loop mohair at the change of blocks. The mohair softens the edges of the blocks and adds a texture that begs the viewer to come closer.

twill sections will have ribs moving in the same direction—but opposite to 1/3 twills.

If a four-shaft broken twill structure is used in two blocks formed by areas of 1/3 twill next to areas of 3/1 twill, all woven in a broken treadling, then the cloth is called **false damask** or **twill damask.** The twill for false damask may be broken by the way in which the blocks are threaded (**2.5**) or by changing the treadling order (**2.4** to **2.6**). When writing a draft for false damask, clean breaks where the emphasis shifts from warp- to weft-faced or the reverse keeps the blocks distinct. The last shed made in one block will be exactly opposite to the shed made for the first pick in the next block.

Regular two-block twill and broken two-block twill fabrics may be woven on the same warp if the threading in **2.6** is used, simply by changing the order of treadling. If you're using a harness loom, though, there is a good reason for making the treadling as simple to follow as possible: you may spend half an hour tying up the treadles, but you are likely to spend many hours weaving off the warp you have made. Making the actual weaving as easy as possible not only makes good sense—it also makes better cloth.

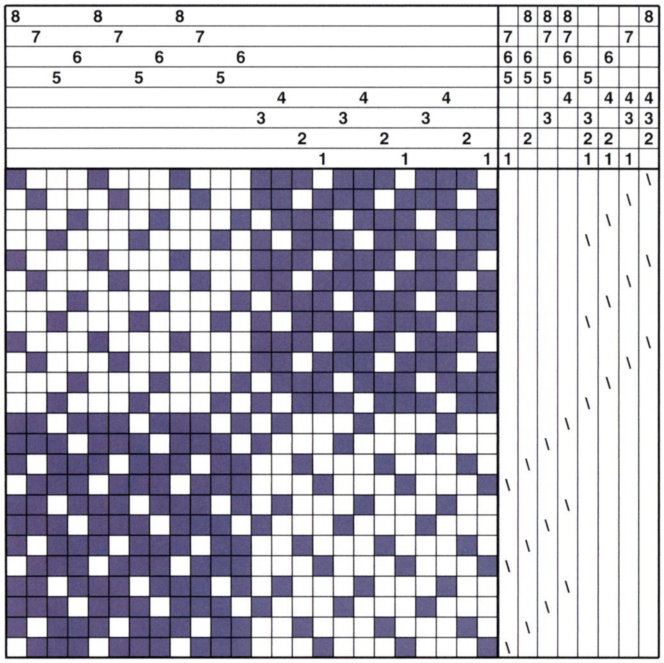

2.5 Two-block broken twill, sometimes called false damask. Note the change in threading from 2.4.

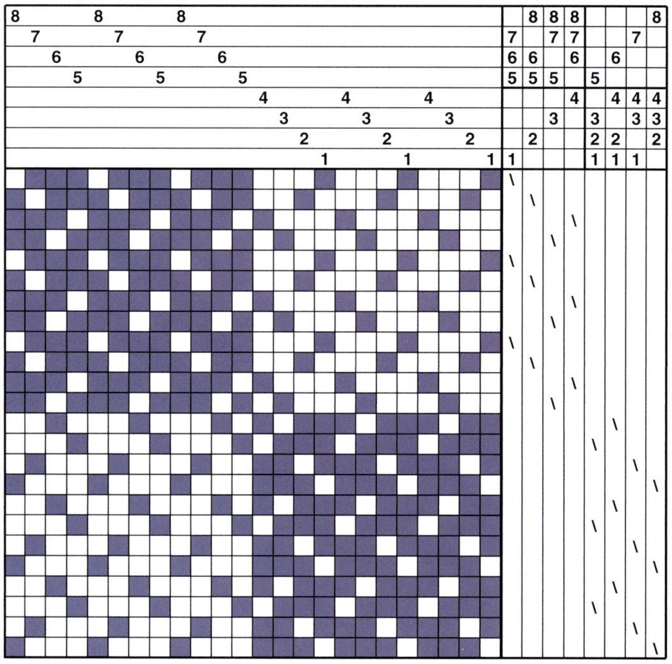

2.6 Two-block broken twill, sometimes called false damask. Here, the threading is straight and the treadling broken.

Below. Two-block broken twill. In this cloth, 8/2 cotton is used to weave a simple two-block twill. The use of three colors has the effect of lengthening the repeat. The color order—tan, light green, lavender—repeats in both the warp and weft directions. Block A is at first tan, the next time lavender, and the third time light green. Thus six blocks are threaded before the same color appears in any given block. The same is true in the weft direction.

Above. The bottom fabric, 2/18 Merino, is a two-block twill. The three colors—blue, blue-violet, and blue-green—follow the color order B, BV, B, BG, repeat, in both warp and weft. The color change occurs in mid-block. For example, block A may begin blue; halfway through it changes to blue-violet, which continues into block B and is replaced halfway through the block with blue-green. The result is a twill cloth with the appearance of a color-and-weave-effect cloth.

The top fabric is also a twill, but it required four blocks (sixteen shafts). The same sort of figure appears in this cloth as in the lower one, but the ground on which the pinwheel shapes appear is a solid color.

Twills that change direction

It is possible to create a broken twill by writing a threading that will produce it with a straight treadling. The threading 1, 2, 4, 3, repeat may be used to weave a broken 2/2, 1/3, or 3/1 twill. It is impossible to weave a simple or regular twill on that threading, however, because the points at which the twill diagonals are staggered are designed into the threading. For that reason, a **straight draw**—a threading that begins with shaft 1 and goes to the highest shaft used—is more versatile.

The direction of the four-shaft twill diagonal may be reversed in many ways. The reversal may be made in the warp direction or in the weft direction. We have examined broken 2/2 twills that reverse after just two ends or picks, but the reversal can occur wherever you like: after two picks, after two repeats, or after 2 inches (5 cm.). *The wonderful thing about weaving is the freedom you have to decide what will happen in the cloth.*

Draft **2.7a** shows a 2/2 twill in which symmetrical reversals take place in the weft direction. This structure is called **symmetrical** or **pointed 2/2 horizontal herringbone.** This structure can be woven on a straight draw on four shafts at any time simply by changing the direction of the treadling progression. Treadle from the left to the right and then at some point use the treadles in the opposite direction. Each time the direction of treadling is changed, the twill rib changes direction without changing the basic structure.

Note, however, that at the points of reversal, some three-pick floats are generated. These longer floats not only catch your eye

2.7a 2/2 horizontal herringbone. Note the warp floats over three picks.

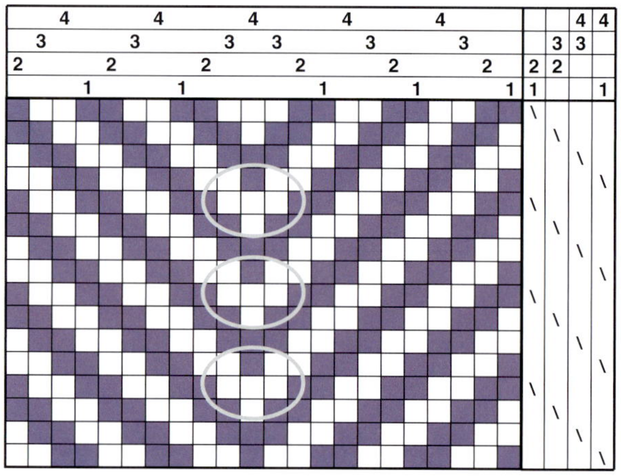

2.7b Symmetrical 2/2 vertical herringbone. Note the weft floats over three picks.

but, depending on the size(s) and sett of the yarns, can also catch and snag.

When the twill is turned 90 degrees to become a **symmetrical 2/2 vertical herringbone (2.7b)**, three-end floats appear every fourth pick. This twill can be woven only on this threading; it cannot be woven on a straight threading, because a straight threading allows the twill rib to move only in one direction, across the warp, just as a regular 2/2 twill cannot be woven on a point threading (a threading that pivots to change directions: 1, 2, 3, 4, 1, 2, 3, **4**, 3, 2, 1, 4, 3, 2, **1**, 2, 3, 4, etc.—the pivots are shown in bold italics).

The treadling may be reversed at intervals on a point-twill threading just as it may on a straight-twill threading. The result is a diamond pattern that shows up in the cloth (**2.7c**). Three-end floats occur at each turning place in the cloth in both warp and weft.

There are ways to avoid those floats. One way is to combine the idea of a broken twill with that of a reversing twill by using a threading that progresses in one direction, then changes direction so that the place at which the change occurs is staggered rather than pointed or symmetrical. This common twill is called a **dornick twill (2.8a)**.

You can see that the break between the two diagonals (one left-hand and one right-hand) is a clean one; that is, where the warp is up on one side of the break, it is down on the other, and vice versa. When there is a clean break between warp ends or between two picks, no floats pass from one side of the break to the other, warp- or weft-wise. Unlike in the symmetrical herringbone twills, in which three-end and -pick floats fall across the point of reversal, there are only clean breaks in dornick twill. There are some places

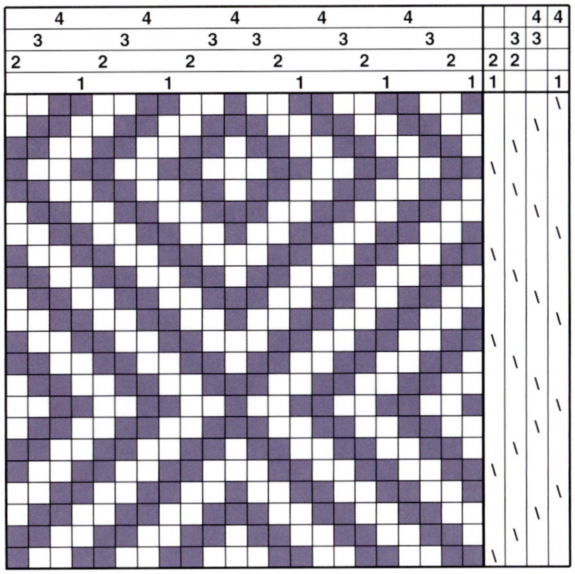

2.7c Symmetrical 2/2 diamond twill. Floats over three occur in both warp and weft.

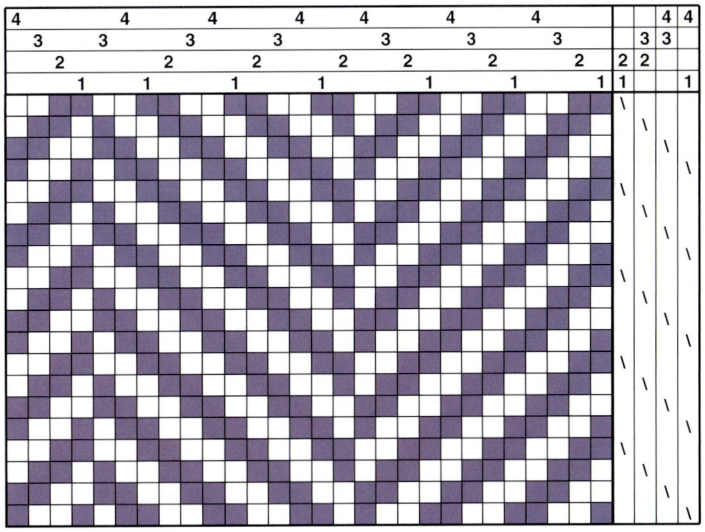

2.8a Dornick twill. Notice that when the twill rib changes direction there is a clean break.

where the weft passes over or under only one end, but those places are neither unsightly nor do they affect the structural integrity of the cloth.

In **2.8b**, the same order has been extended to the weft as well. The changes of direction in the treadling are also staggered so that they make clean breaks in the weft direction. This structure, with each "arm" of the threading and treadling repeated more times than shown here, has also become a classic and is called a **crystal twill.** Irene Emery, in *The Primary Structure of Fabrics,* suggests that the name probably came from a resemblance to some crystalline mineral structures. Both dornick and crystal twills are often used in menswear, particularly woolen or tweed fabrics. Their drape and great structural stability make them especially appropriate for tailored garments.

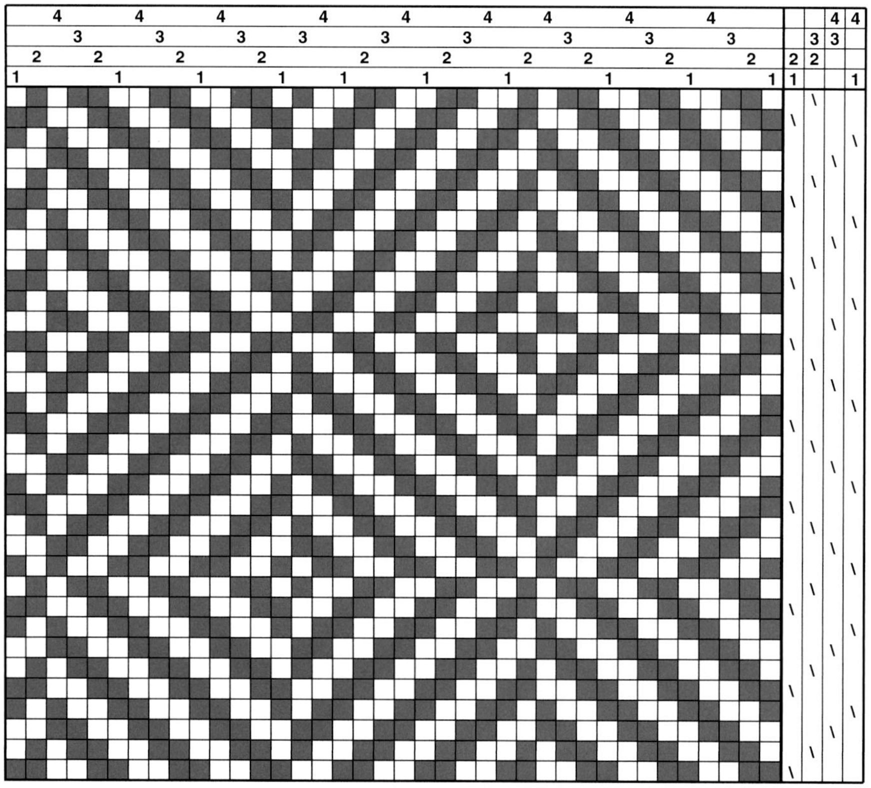

2.8b Crystal twill. Notice that there are clean breaks at every reversal, warp or weft.

The directions of the twill floats change regularly in dornick and crystal twills. The shift from left to right twill (see page 28) changes the way the twill rib lies in the cloth (the twist of the yarn must, of necessity, remain the same over its entire length). The subtle change in rib dominance in crystal twills from the interaction of yarn twists with twill lines serves to emphasize the pattern in the twill. The rib dominance in dornick twill tends to make one side of the break appear stronger than the other; this characteristic may be emphasized or minimized by varying the lengths of the "strokes" that make up the two sides of the dornick "V." The less prominent twill ribs may be shorter to further emphasize the prominent direction, for example. Dornick twills do not have to be symmetrical about the breaks.

Four-shaft twills are very simple, but like plain weave, they may be made to appear far more complex by introducing a color rotation into the warp and/or the weft to produce color-and-weave effects in the cloth. There is always a price to be paid for a new freedom, however, and the price for design freedom in color-and-weave-effect fabrics is the additional time required to dress the loom—to measure the warp and thread the color rotation(s) accurately—and the additional time required to weave the fabric because more shuttles are involved. The results are frequently worth the effort.

Dornick twill on four shafts. The warp is 16/1 natural linen; light tan cottolin is used as weft. The clean breaks between left- and right-hand twills suggest the crispness of the fabric.

More than four shafts

So far we have considered only twills based on four shafts. If we limit ourselves to those, we can design a great many fabrics, but the possibilities increase rapidly every time we add another shaft. Taking the four-shaft limit off a discussion of twills is a lot like opening Pandora's box except that wonderful things come out of the box instead of woes.

Using four shafts, there were only three ways to construct regular or simple twills: 1/3, 3/1, and 2/2. Using five shafts yields more possibilities: 1/4, 4/1, 2/3, 3/2, $\frac{2\ 1}{1\ 1}$, $\frac{1\ 1}{1\ 2}$, $\frac{1\ 1\ 1}{1\ 1}$, and $\frac{1\ 1}{1\ 1\ 1}$.

The conventional notations for these options, as shown here, show the sequence of "up" and "down" warp threads in one repeat. But look at the eight possibilities listed here. The last pair are the equivalent of the pair listed before them. If you begin the notation with a number above the line, you must end with the last number below it. Having a 1 on top first and last is the same as having a 2 on top first (or last). Some of the twill possibilities on five shafts are simply opposites; for example, 3/2 twill and 2/3 twill are the same structure woven with a different sides up. Therefore, on five shafts, the regular twills are 1/4 and its opposite, 4/1; 2/3 and its opposite, 3/2; and $\frac{2\ 1}{1\ 1}$, and $\frac{1\ 1}{1\ 2}$ (see **2.9 a-f**).

Given the choice of weaving a 1/4 twill or a 4/1 twill, I always choose the former because it requires lifting one shaft at a time instead of four; the wear and tear on my knees is reduced by using the lighter lift. But whether your knees are over forty years old or not, it is a good idea to be as kind to them as you can.

With these five-shaft examples in mind, you can see that there are many, many ways of constructing regular twills using six, eight, sixteen, or even more shafts. As in the five-shaft twills, some of the mathematical possibilities are equivalent statements or can be reduced to simpler expressions. For example, for six-shaft twills, the possibilities include 1/5, 5/1, 2/4, 4/2, 3/3, $\frac{2\ 1}{1\ 2}$, and $\frac{1\ 1}{2\ 2}$ (the same as two repeats of 1/2, a three shaft twill), and $\frac{1\ 1\ 1}{1\ 1\ 1}$ (which is plain weave).

Structural considerations play an important role in the design of regular twills on more than four shafts. When the floats become quite long, the cloth will collapse on itself. One of the possibilities for a twill on twelve shafts, a 6/6 twill, looks bold and interesting on paper and might look satisfactory held under tension on the loom, but cut from the loom, the cloth would collapse on itself. That many warp ends that are not held apart cluster to form clumps, making the cloth entirely unsatisfactory for functional applications. Fuzzy, sticky yarns tend to resist slipping better than smoother, slicker yarns, but even a four-end float of a sticky yarn that is not supported by some other structure is likely to be unstable. The insertion of a plain-weave pick between twill picks, however, breaks the warp floats as it stabilizes the cloth. It is no longer a true twill, of course, but it may now be woven with four-end weft floats. The angle of the twill rib is also changed by the stabilizing picks; we will discuss this matter more fully below.

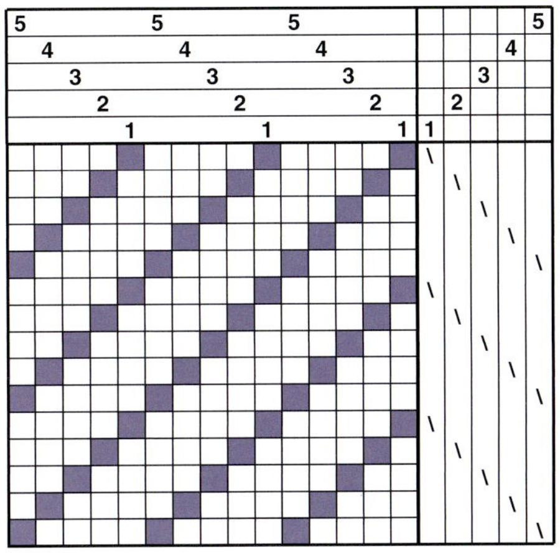

2.9a 1/4 regular twill.

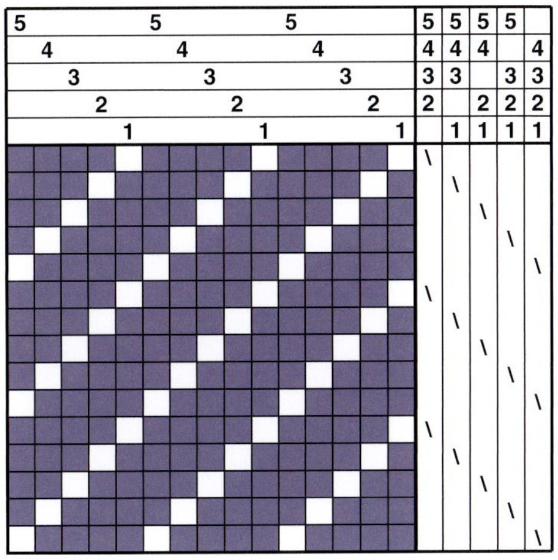

2.9b 4/1 regular twill.

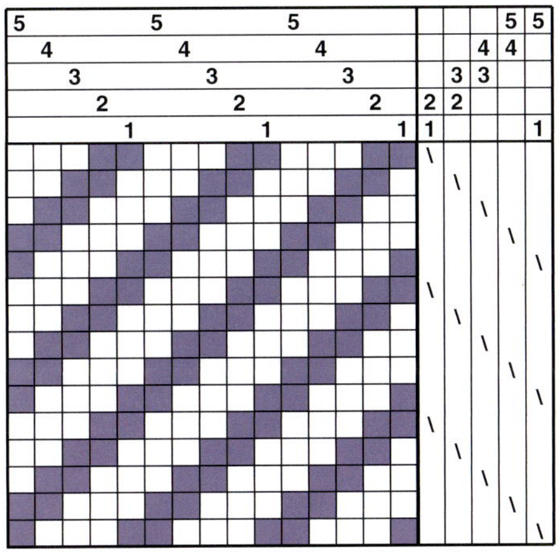

2.9c Five-shaft 2/3 twill.

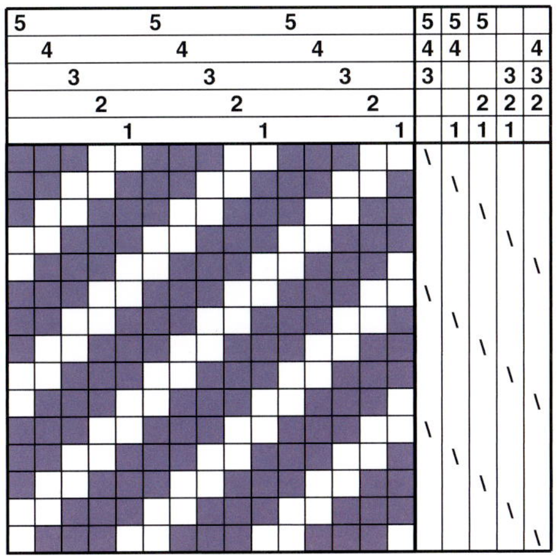

2.9d Five-shaft 3/2 twill.

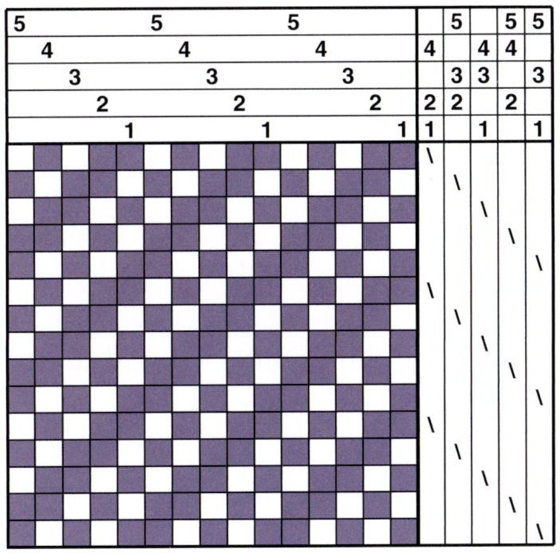

2.9e Five-shaft $\frac{2\ 1}{1\ 1}$ *twill.*

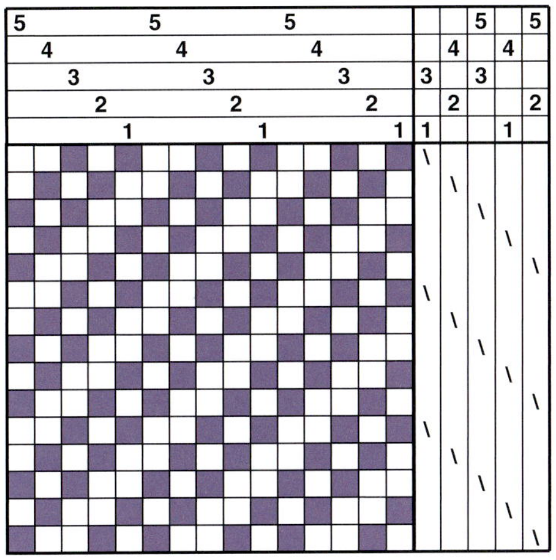

2.9f Five-shaft $\frac{1\ 1}{1\ 2}$ *twill.*

A two-block twill that reverses with clean breaks. This is represented in draft 2.4, with the same number of repeats in the treadling as in the threading so that symmetrical diamonds are woven. The warp and weft are both 2/20 worsted wool in slightly different colors. Using two closely related colors shows off the structure while keeping the cloth "quiet" and elegant.

This eight-shaft twill, woven in 2/18 Merino worsted wool, changes direction in the threading and in the treadling. Does this look like a $\frac{3\ 1}{2\ 2}$ *twill? It is, though not a regular or straight twill. The play of contrasting colors gives it iridescence.*

$\frac{3\ 1}{2\ 2}$ twill and $\frac{2\ 2}{1\ 3}$ twill are combined to make a dornick twill. Sixteen shafts are required because the floats are not the same length on the face and back. For the $\frac{3\ 1}{2\ 2}$ twill, the float on the face is three ends (one end does not technically make a float). For the $\frac{2\ 2}{1\ 3}$ twill, there are two two-end floats on the face.

2/20 worsted wool and eight shafts are used to weave this twill. It is a $\frac{3\ 1\ 1}{1\ 1\ 1}$ regular twill. One side is more violet, the other, more green. The cloth may be used to trim itself by using both sides.

At left, two $\frac{3\ 1}{2\ 2}$ corkscrew twills. Two wefts are used alternately. Each begins at a different place in the treadling sequence and weaves as a regular twill. The bottom fabric is constructed the same way except that at intervals the same shuttle is used for two picks, shifting the color of the twill ribs.

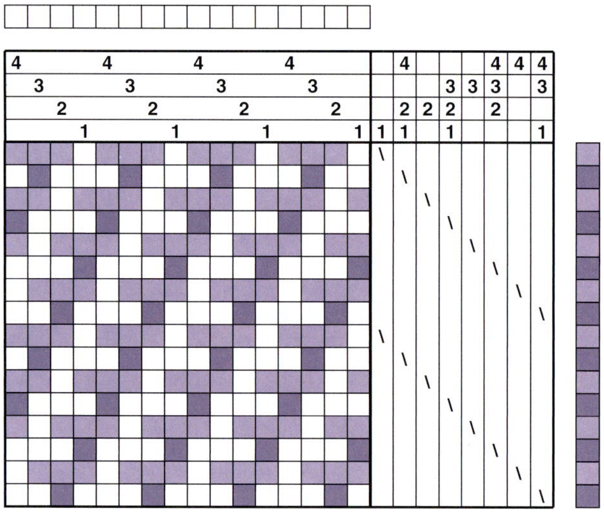

2.10 Double-faced twill. One color on face (weft dominant) and a second on the back (also weft dominant when seen from the back).

Double-faced twill on four shafts. Where this face is red, the other is blue, and vice versa. The mixed colors are achieved by weaving each color for two picks and maintaining the treadling order so that both colors show on both sides. This creates a half-tone, which has the effect of softening the edges of the stripes where it occurs.

Double-faced twills

Sometimes we want to have a weft- or warp-dominant twill appear on both sides of a fabric. A 1/3 twill makes the face of the fabric weft-dominant; a 3/1 twill makes the back weft-dominant. These structures may be combined in the same cloth, in the same place, by weaving the two structures in alternate shots. If two wefts are used, one weft shows on the face, the other on the back. This is a good way to make a thicker cloth. If the draft is written so that the point at which the weft on the face of the cloth passes to the back is covered by the float of the other weft on the back of the cloth, the weft dominating the face of the cloth will not show at all on the back, and vice versa.

The weft makes three-end floats on each side. The end that is lifted for the 1/3 shot is the central end of the three ends that the next shot passes under. In this way, the place where the first weft lies on the back of the cloth is hidden by the weft float (as seen from the back) of the next pick with the second weft. Draft **2.10** shows a double-faced four-shaft twill.

Note that for double-faced twills, the weaving drafts do not produce an accurate picture of the cloth. In the cloth itself, the first and second picks nest together, taking up the space of a single pick, and so it is not possible to see both at the same time even though the draft suggests that we can.

Three shafts may be used to weave a double-faced twill, but the results are not as satisfactory as when four shafts are used. Look at **2.11** for the draft. The space between the same two ends as it travels where both wefts pass from one side to the other becomes distorted. Moreover, the wefts sometimes twist just a little so that a glimpse of the back weft is seen on the face and vice versa. Four shafts make a better construction possible because there are more places for the wefts to pass from one side to the other.

An interesting variation on double-faced twill, although it doesn't beat in quite as well unless the sett is opened up, is illustrated in **2.12**. In this draft, two wefts of the same size but of different colors are used. On each face there is a fine line of the color from the opposite side. In this case, there is more crowding where the wefts intersect with the plane of the cloth, but it is the only way to obtain this effect. A slightly more open sett or the use of wefts that are finer than the warp make it possible to weave the fabric and still maintain a 45-degree twill line.

Any of these double-faced twills except the three-shaft may be combined with plain weave. We may weave a plain-weave cloth with weft-faced twill stripes that look the same on both sides, or are one color on one side and a second on the other, or are one texture on one side and another on the other. Both wefts must be the same size if both of the faces are to be equally weft-faced. On four shafts, the twill stripes will run *across* the cloth, from selvedge to selvedge.

More than four shafts may be used to weave double-faced weft twills. The twills used for each face must be chosen so that the place where a weft passes to the opposite surface can be hidden if the two faces are to show different colors.

Double-faced twills are useful for producing fabrics used in such a way that both sides of the cloth show. They may be used as self-lining, reversible fabrics.

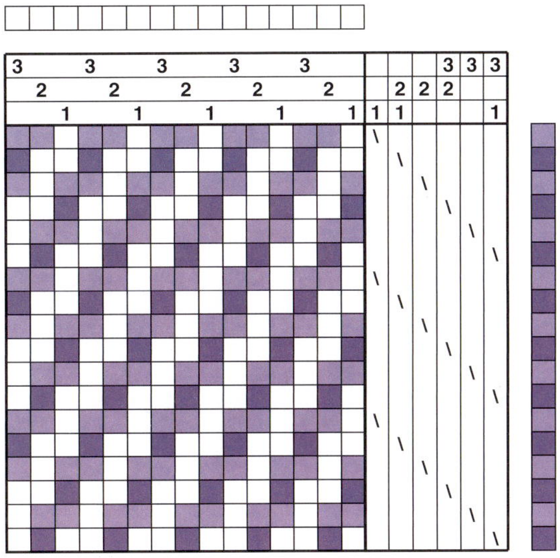

2.11 Three-shaft, double-faced twill.

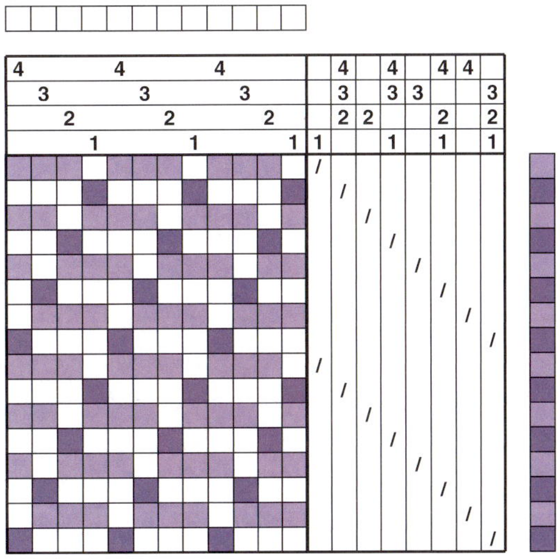

2.12 Four-shaft, double-faced twill woven on opposites. Both wefts show on both sides but one weft is dominant.

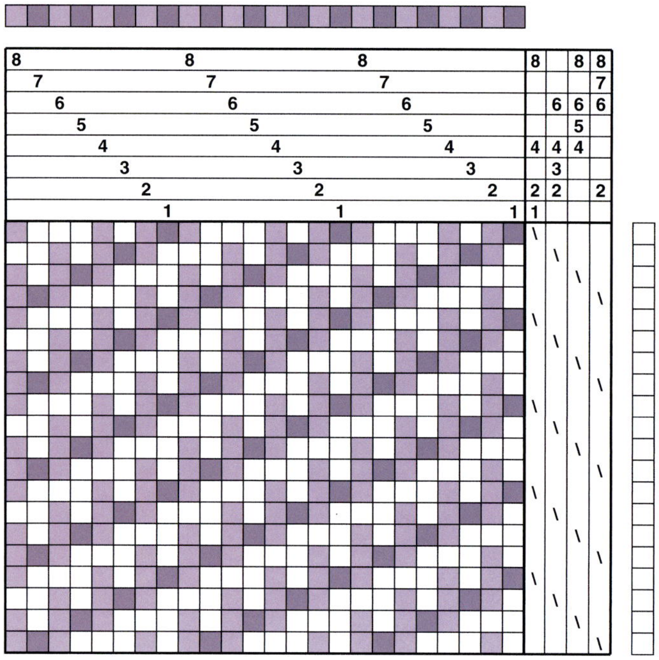

2.13 *Double-faced 3/1 twill.*

Warp-faced double-faced twill requires more shafts than its weft-faced counterpart. The 2/1 double-faced twill structure may be woven on six shafts; the 3/1, on eight. The latter structure is illustrated by draft **2.13**. The draft doesn't produce an accurate picture of the cloth because it suggests that both warp colors show on the face of the cloth. Instead, they nest together as in the weft-faced version described above.

Notice that every other warp end in the draft is up for three picks and down for one; the remaining ends are down for three picks and up for one. The sett for this interlacement is twice that required for a 1/3 twill: in effect, there are two warps woven with a single weft; *each* warp requires the sett for 1/3 twill. These fabrics are well suited for scarves, shawls or reversible garments. They may have different colors and/or textures on each side, striped on one side and plain on the other, or striped two ways—a different warp stripe sequence for each side.

Double-faced twills may be woven with a 2/2 twill on one side so that it may be plaided—a plaid requires that the warp and weft show equally—and on the reverse a warp-striped or plain-colored 1/3 twill (viewed from the back).

Changing the angle of the twill line

The angle of the twill diagonal may be changed in many ways. One way is to cram the warp so that the weft cannot be beaten into place at a 45-degree angle; this produces a steeper angle in the cloth. Another is to space out the warp with a more open sett so that the weft packs in densely, decreasing the angle of the diagonal to less than 45 degrees. (Alternate spacing and cramming produces a changing twill angle.) A third way is to use different yarns in the warp and weft: a weft yarn that is heavier than the warp makes the angle steeper; a finer weft yarn, shallower.

Changing the number of ends on each shaft and/or changing the number of picks in one shed are other ways to alter the angle of the twill ribs. Doubling the warp ends (1, 1, 2, 2, 3, 3, etc.) flattens the diagonal, and threading the warp ends three per shaft (1, 1, 1, 2, 2, 2, etc.) brings the angle of the diagonal even nearer to the horizontal. If you want a well-defined structure, thread each end in its own heddle, because when ends are threaded double in a heddle, they inevitably twist around each other, first one way and then the other, as the cloth is woven. *For any structure, when you want the ends to lie side by side in the cloth, thread each end in its own heddle.*

Inserting two picks instead of one into each shed makes the angle steeper. Three picks per shed produces an even steeper twill line. If both warp ends and weft picks are doubled, a 45-degree angle can be maintained, one way to make a heavier cloth out of a too-fine yarn. If the shuttle is merely thrown through a shed and then thrown back, the pick is unwoven because the weft has not been caught at the selvedge. To avoid this result, you may use two shuttles, one coming from the left and the other from the right (use three if there are three shots per shed). A more practical solution is to use a **floating selvedge**, a warp end (sometimes made of more tightly twisted, stronger yarn) that is beamed with the warp and threaded through the reed but not through a heddle. The shuttle is thrown over it and caught under it each time so that the edge is controlled. Usually, a floating end is used on each side.

There are structural ways to change the angle of the diagonal. As an example, let's start with an eight-shaft twill $\frac{3\ 1}{2\ 2}$ **(2.14a–2.14c)**.

Manipulating the variables can really change the way a particular twill looks, so I've worked out several versions using this one. Draft **2.14a** is the complete draft for the regular version of the twill. It is woven as a balanced cloth: the twill diagonal lies at a 45-degree angle to the fell. The repeat is eight picks long.

Draft **2.14b** shows the same twill woven so that the slope of the diagonal has been flattened to about half the original angle. Every other shed has been omitted. The weaving repeat consists of just four sheds: the first, third, fifth, and seventh of the original twill. The twill diagonal has not been broken or staggered, simply flattened.

In **2.14c**, the diagonal has been steepened by inserting picks between the straight

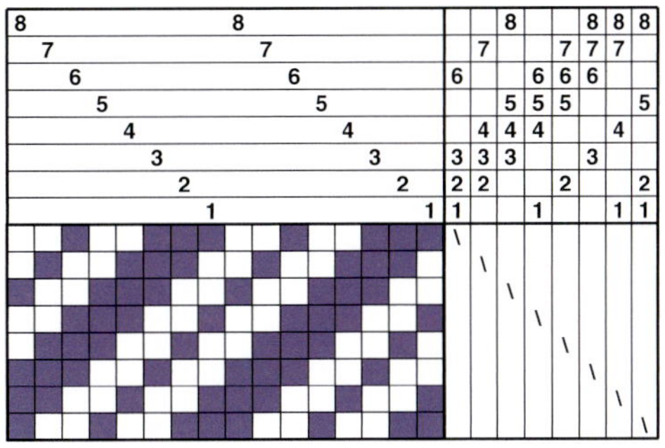

2.14a Regular $\frac{3\ 1}{2\ 2}$ twill.

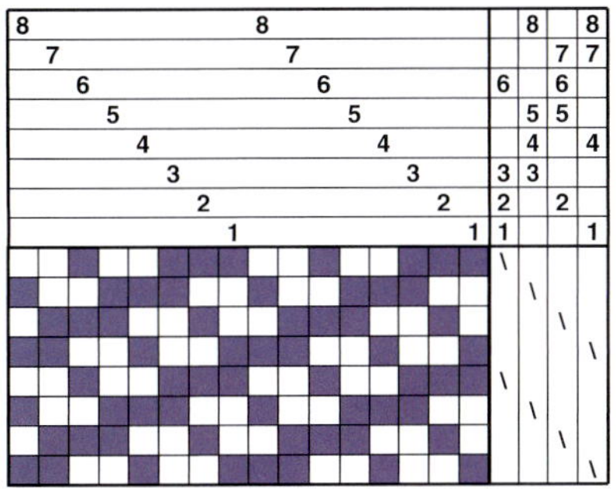

2.14b $\frac{3\ 1}{2\ 2}$ twill, half the sheds of the regular twill.

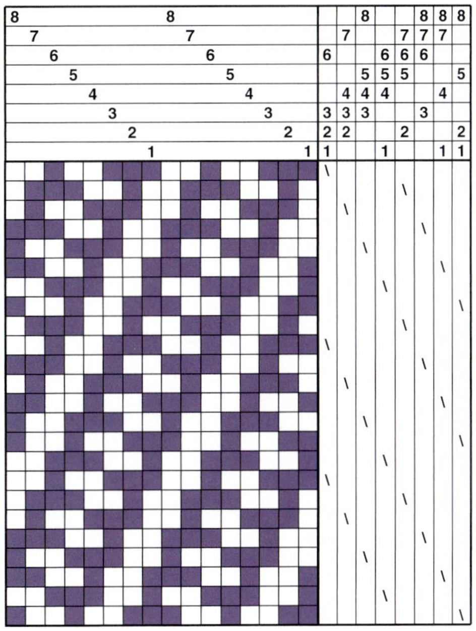

2.14c $\frac{3\ 1}{2\ 2}$ twill. Picks added to treadling.

A white-on-white 2/8 worsted wool upholstery fabric woven by interleaving two twills. Sixteen shafts were used to make this very steep reversing twill. The interleaving made the recessed areas in the cloth very deep, producing wonderful shadows when the light strikes the cloth at a low angle.

sequence of the sheds to retard their progression. In this case, the inserted picks are part of the original twill repeat, but any structure that repeats in two, four, or eight picks may be used instead. If plain-weave shots are inserted to steepen the twill, the fabric will be considerably firmer than it otherwise would be because of the stability of the plain-weave structure.

As we have mentioned, the insertion of plain-weave picks is one way to stabilize areas with long floats in a twill. Although the twill diagonal is altered by such an insertion, you may, if you like, weave the plain-weave shots in a finer yarn to minimize the change in angle. The plain-weave interlacement holds the warp yarns so that they are unable to slip together, causing the fabric to collapse. The warp floats are broken by that insertion, but the weft floats remain unchanged.

Interleaving twills

Interleaving twill treadlings means weaving one pick from one treadling sequence, then one from the second, followed by the next pick from the first, and so on. There are many ways to interleave treadlings on one threading in order to change the angle of the twill diagonal and/or to change the appearance and performance of the cloth. The notion of using one threading that can be woven in a number of ways allows tremendous scope for the imagination. Let's begin with a fairly simple example: a straight-draw threading on eight shafts and the same interlacement we have used before:

$$\frac{3\ \ 1}{\ \ 2\ \ 2}$$

This time, instead of simply treadling the eight-pick repeat, we will double the repeat by interleaving it with itself (**2.14d**). The appearance of the twill is changed a great

Selvedges

If all the time that handweavers have worried about selvedges were given to me, my life would be significantly longer. As we all find out sooner or later, worrying doesn't accomplish much, so what constructive steps can we take to achieve nice straight selvedges?

First, resist the urge to finger, play with, or even touch the selvedges as you weave. Such actions not only slow the weaving to a crawl but interfere with the establishment of a weaving rhythm. It is worthwhile to practice on a cloth where the selvedges do not matter. If you are in the habit of handling the selvedges as you weave, make a warp for something that you will hem or cut and sew. Throw the shuttle without touching the selvedges; it will be difficult to resist the urge to put your fingers on the selvedges, but be brave. You will be glad you were.

Advance the warp frequently. I find the point at which the reed and the cloth are at right angles; that is the ideal place for the beater to strike the fell (the place in the warp where woven cloth meets yet-to-be-woven warp). I advance the warp until it is 1 inch (2.5 cm) closer to me than that point and weave until I am 1 inch past that point; then I advance the warp for 2 inches (5.0 cm) and begin weaving again. This practice also helps ensure that the beat will be even because the beater strikes at the same angle and after passing through the same distance.

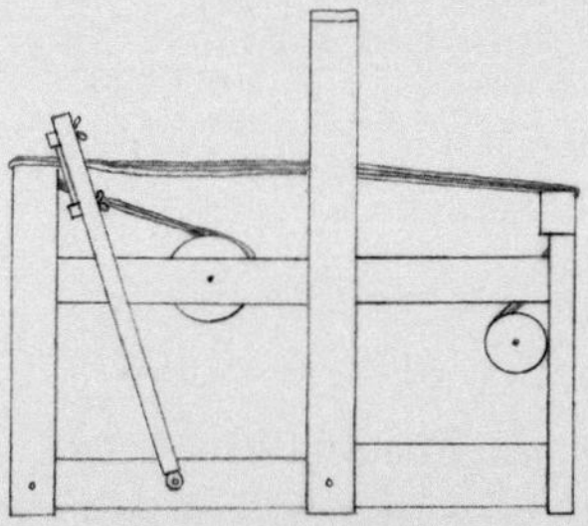

The beater strikes the fell at an acute angle. It is difficult to maintain an even beat when the warp is advanced this far.

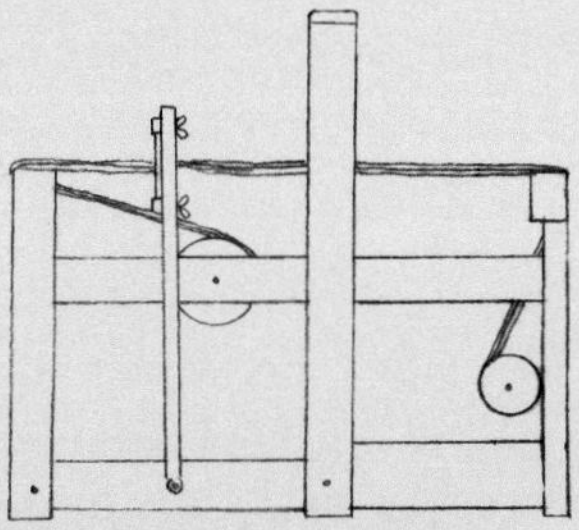

The beater strikes the fell at at a right angle, much better for maintaining an even beat. Advance an inch beyond this point and weave for two inches before advancing the warp again.

The kind of shuttle you use makes a big difference in the quality of the selvedges. A boat shuttle begins with the weft and bobbin at rest, and so the edge threads on the side where the shuttle is launched are pulled inward as the bobbin begins to turn. At the other side of the cloth, the bobbin keeps spinning even after you have removed the shuttle from the shed. To compensate weavers reel out a little weft before throwing the shuttle and brake the spin of the bobbin in the shuttle with a thumb as it is caught at the other side. Using an end-feed shuttle takes care of both starting and stopping problems. The weft begins to reel off the pirn, which is stationary, only when the shuttle moves. When you catch the shuttle, the weft stops reeling off. Moreover, end-feed shuttles are designed so that the yarn tension can be adjusted. The draw-in at the selvedge is therefore reduced, which reduces the wear and tear on the edge threads.

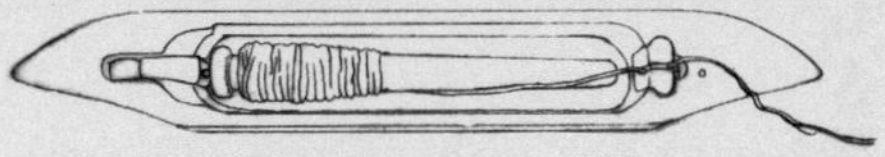

An end-feed shuttle. The weft is drawn smoothly off the stationary pirn as the shuttle travels across the warp. Tension on the weft is adjustable to avoid either loops or draw-in at the selvedges.

Wind your bobbins and/or pirns carefully so that they will unreel smoothly. I have found it best to wind the weft yarn onto boat-shuttle bobbins at a low angle, with respect to the axis of the bobbin by moving my hand rapidly from left to right and then right to left. If you allow the yarn to lie parallel to itself as it winds on, it is possible—likely, in fact—for it to dig into yarn already on the bobbin as the bobbin turns in the shuttle and stop reeling off. When that happens, the shuttle stops and the selvedge ends are pulled sharply inward. They may not break on that pick, but break they will eventually. Keep a good tension on the weft yarn as you wind so that the filled bobbin is quite firm. Insert the bobbin into a boat shuttle so that the yarn comes off the bottom of the bobbin; that way, it will unreel more smoothly.

Here the weft is wound on the bobbin so the wraps are parallel. The weft will tend to bury itself in the wraps, halting the shuttle in mid-pass.

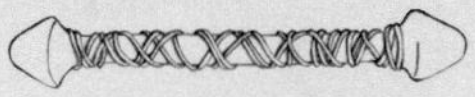

Here the weft is wound on the bobbin at a low angle. The crisscrossing prevents the weft from digging into the wraps, which would stop the shuttle.

If you are using a pirn, wind it in overlapping concentric cone shapes, moving slowly from the flared butt end to the tip. Maintain an even diameter of yarn on the pirn and keep firm tension on the yarn so that the filled pirn is *very* firm.

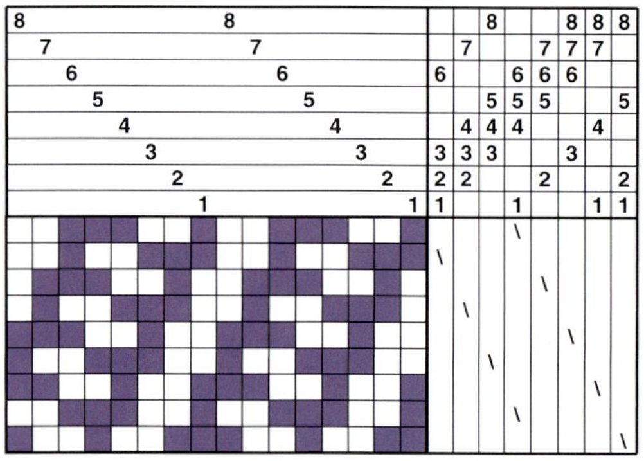

2.14d $\frac{3\ 1}{2\ 2}$ *twill. Extra picks inserted between each pick of the regular twill. This time the same twill was interleaved with itself.*

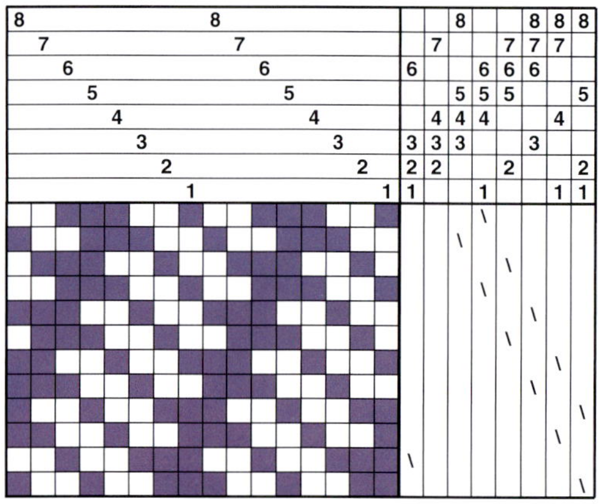

2.14e $\frac{3\ 1}{2\ 2}$ *twill. Extra picks inserted as in 2.14d, but started at a different place. Notice that some ends float over four picks.*

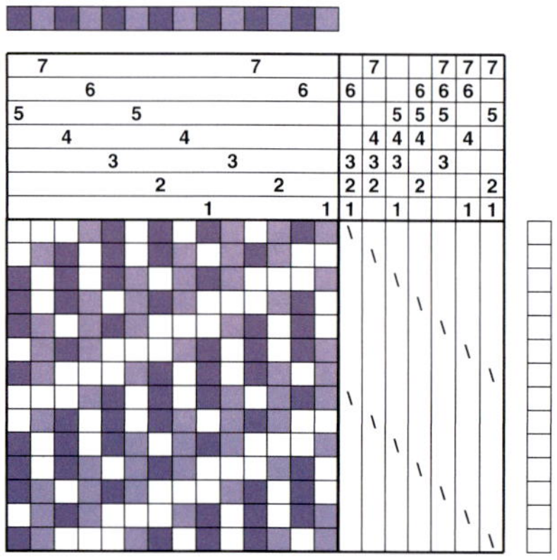

2.15 Seven-shaft corkscrew twill. Two colors in the warp.

deal. This method of interleaving was arbitrarily chosen. The first shot was made using the fourth treadle, the second using the first, third, and fifth, and so on. A different treadling order could as easily have been chosen with quite different results (**2.14e**). When planning interleaved treadlings, be sure to make a drawdown to ensure that unacceptably long floats have not been created.

Whipcords have very prominent, steep twill lines. The twill lines are made steep by rearranging twill treadlings to add sheds, as we have seen, and they are made prominent by weaving them in the direction opposite to the direction of the twist of the warp and weft; for example, a left-hand twill using Z-twist yarns.

A special group of interleaved twills, **corkscrew twills** (which don't look like any corkscrew I have ever seen), are usually woven with an odd number of shafts so that the cloth will be either warp-faced or weft-faced, not an even twill like the examples above.

Corkscrew twills may be easily threaded—for example, in a straight draw, the easiest threading draft of all—but the treadling, although requiring relatively few treadles, repeats in twice the number of picks as there are treadles. The treadling is a little complicated. Many corkscrew twills are woven with two weft colors so that the two **wales** or diagonals of twill floats are of different colors. If we thread a straight draw and weave the cloth by changing the treadling, two shuttles are required, one for each color.

More often, particularly in industry, the draft is turned so that on seven shafts it might be written like **2.15.** Here two colors have been used in the warp (the usual practice,

Three versions of $\frac{3\ 1}{2\ 2}$ twill. The upper one is woven as a regular twill (2.14a). The middle cloth is woven by using only half the sheds (2.14b). The bottom cloth is woven by interleaving the same treadling as 2.14a with itself. Notice how the angle of the twill line is altered just by changing the treadling order. Think of how many variations you could weave on one warp without changing the threading or tie-up!

although that doesn't have to be the case). This time the treadling is straight because the interleaving has been done in the threading draft (note the two parallel "twill lines" in the threading). It is a simple matter to alternate colors in the warp and then throw a single shuttle. The weft color may be the same as one of the warp colors or a different color altogether. In many warp-faced corkscrew twill fabrics, the weft hardly shows. Selection of a weft color that is darker than the warp colors will further accentuate the warp.

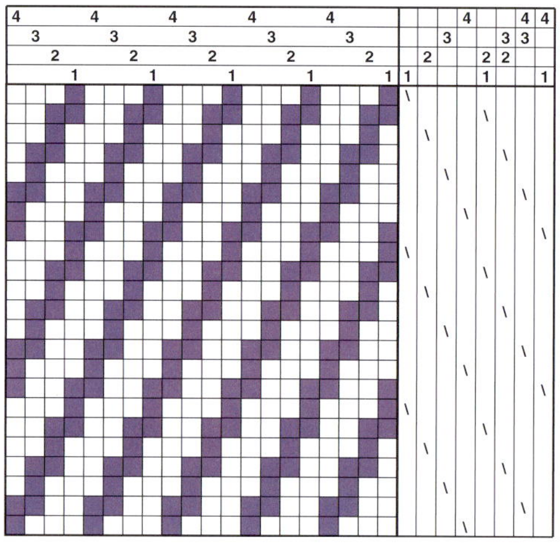

2.16a Two four-shaft twills interleaved.

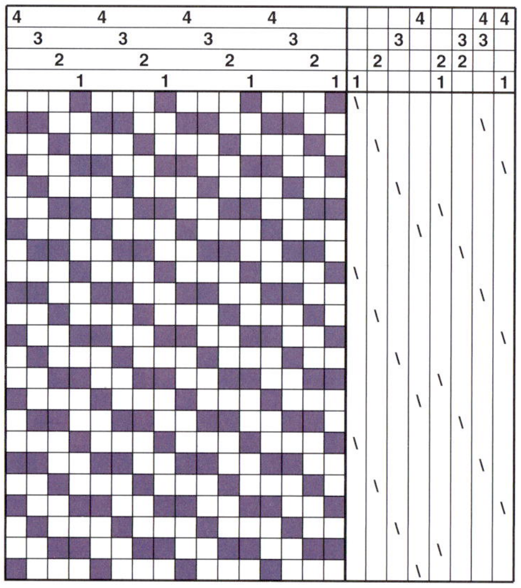

2.16b Two four-shaft twills interleaved, starting at a different point. Compare with 2.16a to see the difference in float lengths and the angle of the twill line.

Just as simple twills may be threaded and/or treadled as straight, pointed, or broken twills, the same manipulations may be performed on corkscrew twills. Usually, these twills are woven straight or with breaks like those in dornick twills in the fabric. The breaks, with the reversal of the twill line, are often marked by a color change as well, especially in warp-faced corkscrew twills.

Although corkscrew twills are woven using *the same interlacement interleaved with itself,* twills based on different interlacements also may be interleaved to create new structures. On four shafts, the treadling for a 1/3 twill may be alternated with that for a 2/2 twill **2.16a-b**. Eight sheds are required: you may use a direct tie-up (one in which each shaft is tied to one treadle and combinations of shafts are lifted by using both feet) or eight treadles, four for the 1/3 twill and four for the 2/2 twill. The pattern of diagonals produced depends on where each twill sequence begins relative to the other. If the 1/3 twill begins with the shed made by lifting shaft 1 and the 2/2 twill begins with the 1, 2 shed (**2.16a**), one cloth results. If the 1/3 twill begins with the 1 shed and the 2/2 twill begins with the 3, 4 shed (**2.16b**), a different cloth is woven. Notice that the float lengths are different. As the number of shafts increases, so does the importance of making a drawdown to check float lengths. As you can imagine, the four-shaft version of this scheme is by far the simplest and looks least complex.

On twelve shafts, two different twelve-shaft twill interlacements could be interleaved, or one twelve-shaft and one six-shaft, or one six-shaft and one four-shaft, or one four-shaft and one three-shaft or other combinations of these. *The two twills may be based on any two numbers that may be divided evenly into the number of shafts.* The number of ways to interleave twills using a straight draw on twelve shafts is staggering. Merely selecting the twill interlacements offers many options; the two twills then must be positioned relative to each other just as in the four-shaft example above. The two interlacements may be woven with a single shuttle or with two colors and/or textures alternating in the weft, which will add even more variety to the appearance of the cloth.

Can three twills be interleaved? Yes, of course. The danger with combining too many twills is that finally the cloth looks chaotic or suffers structurally because warp or weft floats begin to fall together. Usually the float problem can be alleviated by starting at another place in one twill sequence, particularly if only two interlacements are being combined.

Rearranged twills

Besides interleaving twills with each other, we can take a regular twill (**2.17a**) and treadle it in a different way by rearranging the treadling order. If we thread the loom to a straight draw, we can weave many variations of such **rearranged twills** on the same warp *without changing the tie-up* just by changing the order in which the treadles are used. The twills produced by drafts **2.17b–2.17d** each use all eight treadles but look quite different from one another. As we have seen before, a single warp can produce a surprising variety of fabrics.

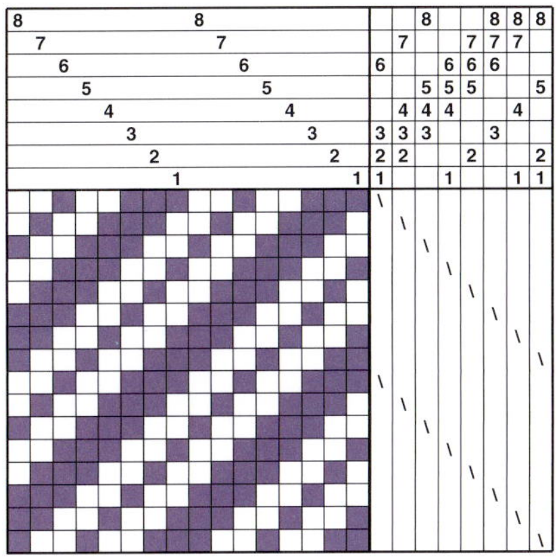

2.17a $\frac{3\ 1}{2\ 2}$ *regular twill.*

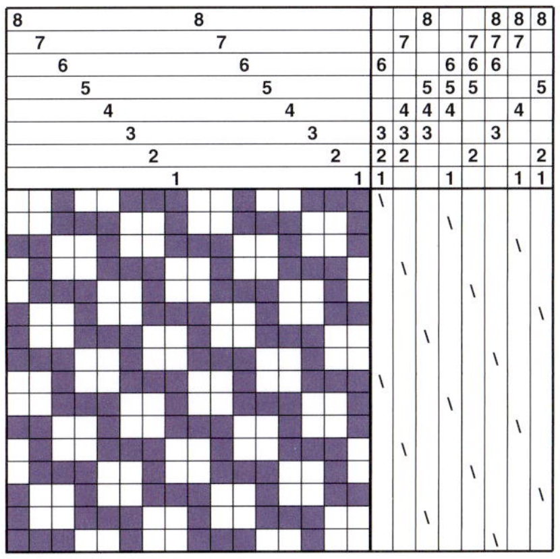

2.17b $\frac{3\ 1}{2\ 2}$ *twill, rearranged (after the fashion of a sateen) in treadling.*

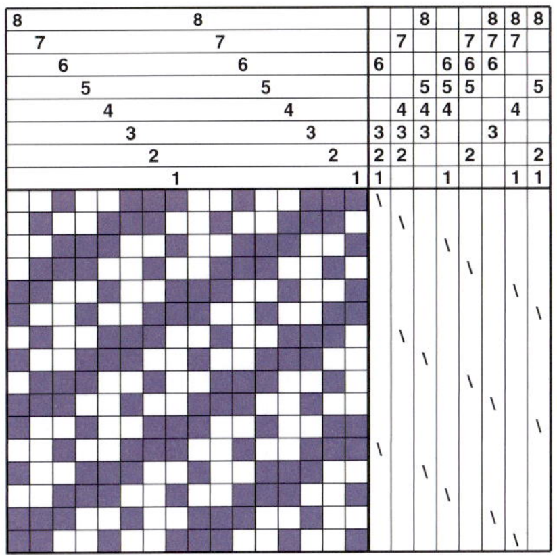

2.17c $\frac{3\ 1}{2\ 2}$ *twill, rearranged in treadling.*

2.17d $\frac{3\ 1}{2\ 2}$ *twill, rearranged in treadling.*

Take another look at draft **2.17a** for $\frac{3\ 1}{2\ 2}$ twill. Compare the first eight ends and picks of the cloth diagram with the tie-up. The arrangement of filled squares in the tie-up also appears, rotated 180 degrees, in the drawdown. This is no mere coincidence. When a straight draw is used with a straight treadling, the structure of the cloth can be read directly from the tie-up. Using this combination of threading and treadling,

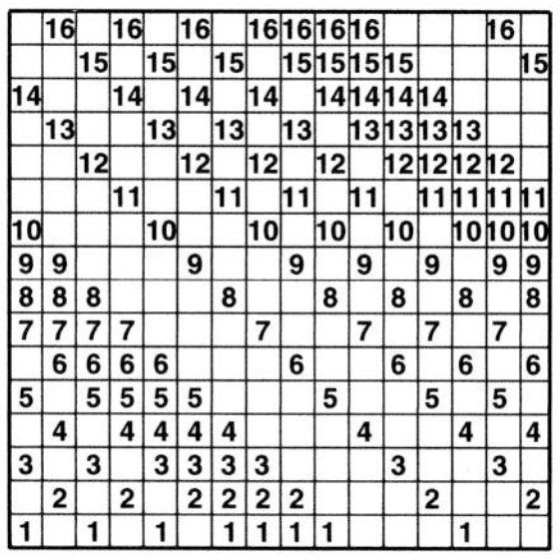

2.18a The tie-up for a sixteen-shaft twill.

working on the design in the tie-up itself, is particularly useful for designing twills, especially multishaft twills. We will return to this idea in Chapter 12, Inventing Your Own Weave Structures (page 227).

In designing twill structures from the tie-up, you are not limited to weaving straight or simple twills. At left is the tie-up for a sixteen-shaft twill (**2.18a**). One woven repeat of the simple twill looks like the tie-up diagram, as we have seen. If you set a mirror on edge in the middle of the edge column at the side of the diagram, you can see how the twill would look threaded as a symmetrical point twill. If you place a second mirror at right angles to the first, in the middle of the top or bottom row of the tie-up, you can see how that twill looks threaded and treadled in a point (**2.18b**). You will be able to see where long warp or weft floats will fall and can decide whether they are acceptable or not. In **2.18b**, the longest weft floats pass under seven ends and warp floats pass over seven wefts. If the yarns are very fine, that might not be a problem—at 50 e.p.i., a float seven threads long takes up only $\frac{1}{7}$" (4 mm); at 15 e.p.i., it would be nearly ½" (1.3 cm) long—but if this creates a problem, the draft could be changed to **2.18c**, in which the longest floats span only five threads.

The twill we just examined, **2.18c**, was written in the usual way as a $\frac{1\ 1\ 1\ 3\ 1}{1\ 1\ 2\ 3\ 2}$ twill.

This is not the only way that such a draft can be written. Drafts **2.19 a–b** were written with the generation of a pointed pattern in mind. As you can see, the floats move diagonally, but not in the same combinations as in **2.18b–c**. Drafts **2.18b–c** can be woven as a straight twill with unbroken twill diagonals, while unbroken diagonals are not possible in draft **2.19a**; that is, when the tie-up in draft **2.19a** is used with a straight-draw threading and treadled as a simple twill, the twill diagonals are discontinuous. The first and last columns of the tie-ups in **2.18a–c** are continuous while those of the tie-up in **2.19a** are not. The change in interlacement

How Long is Too Long?

How long a float is too long? It depends. Because I want the functional fabrics I make to perform well for many years, I do everything I can to make them stable and snag-resistant. For upholstery, I like to keep floats to ⅛ inch (3 mm) long or less. For clothing that I can wear to prune the raspberries, I keep floats to ¼ inch (6 mm) long or less. For dress-up attire—I stay out of the bushes when I go to Utah Symphony concerts—I'll allow floats as long as ½ inch (1.3 cm) for scarves but not for cuffs, or over elbows or knees.

2.18b Sixteen-shaft diamond twill. Both threading and treadling reverse. Notice that there are floats spanning seven threads in both warp and weft direction.

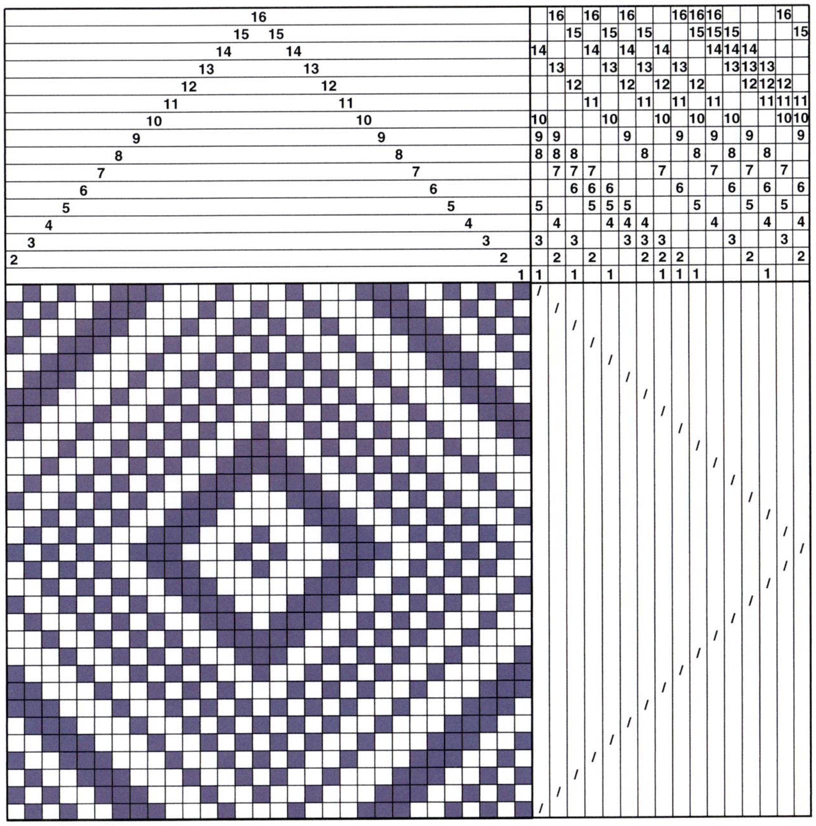

2.18c Sixteen-shaft diamond twill. Floats shortened to maximum of five threads by changing the tie-up.

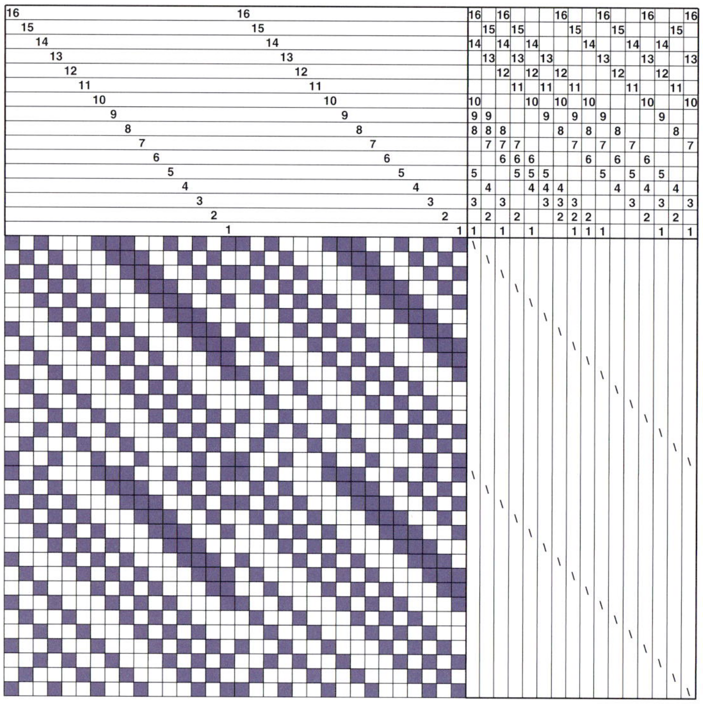

2.19a Sixteen-shaft twill. Notice that the diagonals are not continuous in the cloth diagram.

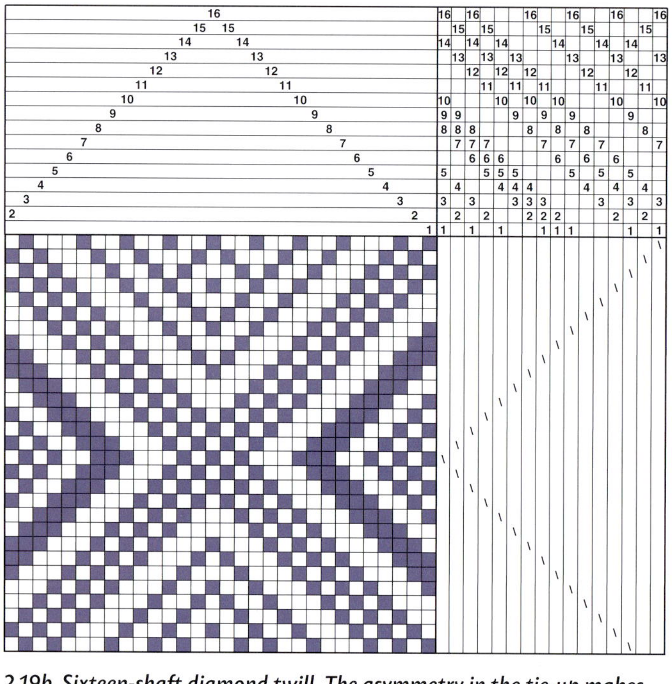

2.19b Sixteen-shaft diamond twill. The asymmetry in the tie-up makes the diamond pattern look more complex and interesting.

in the different quadrants of the tie-up make the pattern more interesting when threaded and woven as a pointed pattern. When it is woven as a point, diamond shapes are generated in the cloth just as in the crystal twill mentioned earlier (page 36), but here there are two different interlacements inside the diamonds. Draft **2.19b** illustrates where the two different diamonds fall in the cloth when a pointed threading and pointed treadling are used with that tie-up.

We have assumed that the treadling order in the preceding examples proceeds either straight, from left to right, or in pointed fashion: left to right and then right to left. But in fact, the order of treadling may be altered almost endlessly to produce rearranged twills.

When you are using four shafts, the rearrangement of the treadles yields very little. The regular twill, a right-hand twill, is shown in **2.20a.** Drafts **2.20b** and **2.20c** show the two broken twills that result from rearranging the treadling. The only other way to rearrange this twill (using all treadles once before repeating) creates a left-hand twill just like the right-hand twill shown in **2.20a** but running in the opposite direction.

Draft **2.21a** is an eight-shaft twill, $\frac{2\ 1\ 2}{1\ 1\ 1}$, woven as a regular twill. Draft **2.21b** (next page) shows one way to rearrange the treadling using all eight sheds, which breaks up the twill diagonal. Sometimes this effect is exactly what we want; we will return to this idea in Chapter 10, Crepe Weaves (page 201).

Two more rearrangements of the twill are shown in **2.21c.** One has strong diagonals and warp floats over five ends; the other, no obvious diagonal and warp floats over four picks.

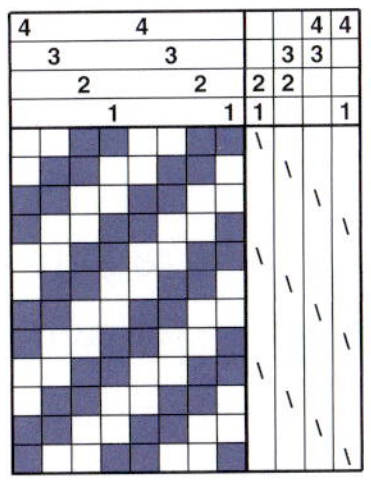

2.20a Regular 2/2 twill—no rearrangement.

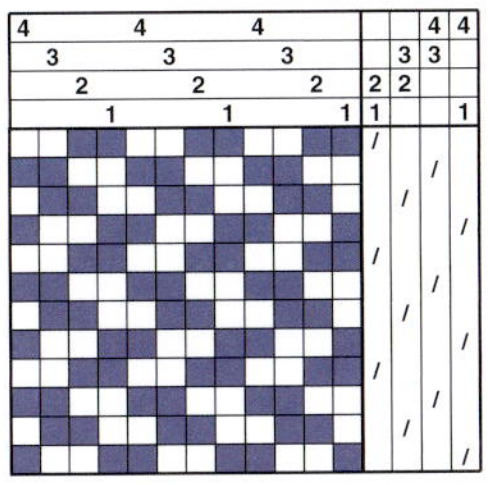

2.20b Rearranged 2/2 twill. Broken twill obtained by changing the order of treadling.

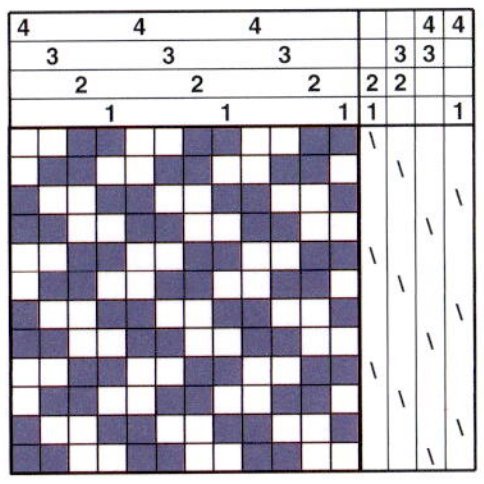

2.20c Another rearranged 2/2 twill.

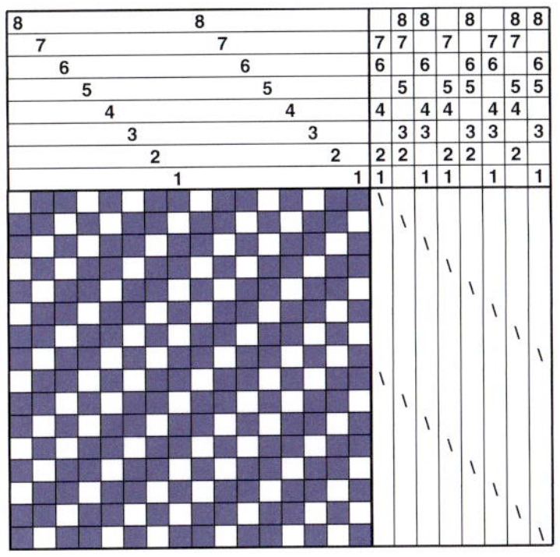

2.21a $\frac{2\ 1\ 2}{1\ 1\ 1}$ *regular twill.*

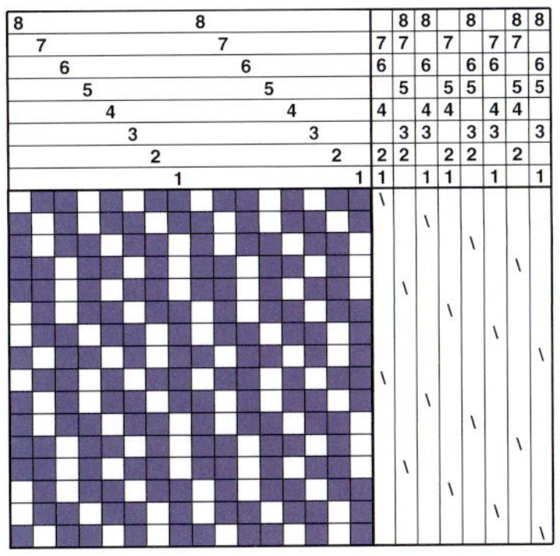

2.21b $\frac{2\ 1\ 2}{1\ 1\ 1}$ *rearranged twill.*

Draft **2.21d** shows a few possibilities using only some of the treadles. Two of these, however, are impractical because warp ends float on the face and/or back all of the time. Examine each rearrangement of a twill with a drawdown of two repeats in both directions so that you can see how the repeats come together. For those of us who are constantly on the lookout for ways to weave many variations on a single long warp rearranging twills permits a lot of variety using a single threading.

The idea of rearranging treadles is also the basis for the writing of drafts for satins and sateens, as we shall see in Chapter 3, Satin (page 63).

2.21c Two more rearrangements of the twill in 2.21a. Both have warp floats over five picks, but one has no obvious diagonal while the other one does.

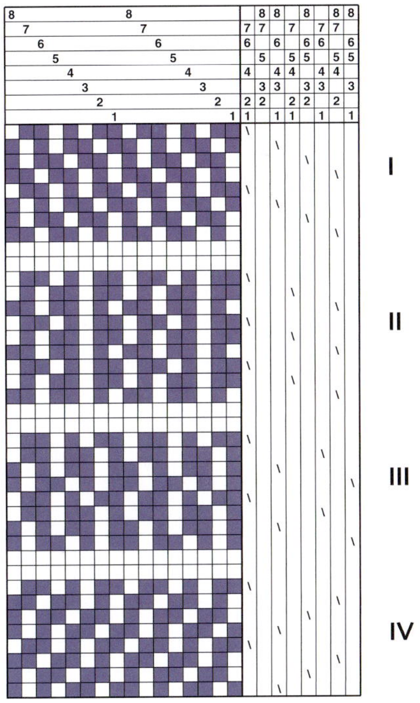

2.21d Two more rearrangements of the twill in 2.21a. Half the sheds are omitted. Sometimes it works (I and IV), sometimes it is a disaster (II and III) because warp ends are up all the time or down all the time.

Undulating twills

We have seen in a general way how the angle of the twill may be altered. We can flatten the angle by decreasing the sett to fewer ends per inch, not always a sound idea, or we can beat the cloth harder—definitely not recommended. On the other hand, using a smaller weft yarn, skipping sheds in the treadling order or threading two or more consecutive heddles on the same shaft are all methods of flattening the angle that will produce a sound cloth structure.

The angle of the twill line may be steepened by cramming in the reed or by not beating as hard (generally inadvisable). A larger weft forces the angle of the twill to be steeper, too. Skipping shafts in the threading causes the twill line to rise but when using four shafts, skipping a shaft looks like an error in the cloth. Make a complete drawdown to be sure you understand how a given change will affect the cloth. The only way to be certain you know how sett and yarn size will change the cloth is to weave a sample. *The proof of the design is the cloth itself.*

Knowing the factors that affect the angle of the twill diagonal with the fell, we can construct twills in which the slope of the twill line is changing almost constantly. Twills with curving diagonal lines are called **undulating twills.** Undulating twills may be made using just four shafts; we'll consider those first.

When we considered the ways to change the angle of the twill, we found out almost all we need to know to construct undulating twills. Recall that the angle is flattened by having more than one adjacent end per shaft or by skipping sheds. The angle is steepened by skipping ends in the threading or throwing more than one pick per shed in the treadling.

When these strategies are combined in the same cloth, the twill line curves. In some places, the ends and/or picks are single; in others, doubled; and in still others, trebled. A smooth curve results only when the transitions are smooth and gradual.

Look at draft **2.22.** The threading progresses as a simple twill for six ends; then there are two ends on shaft 3 followed by a single end on shaft 4; doubled ends continue, to be replaced by four ends per shaft. Look at the twill lines under the different threadings:

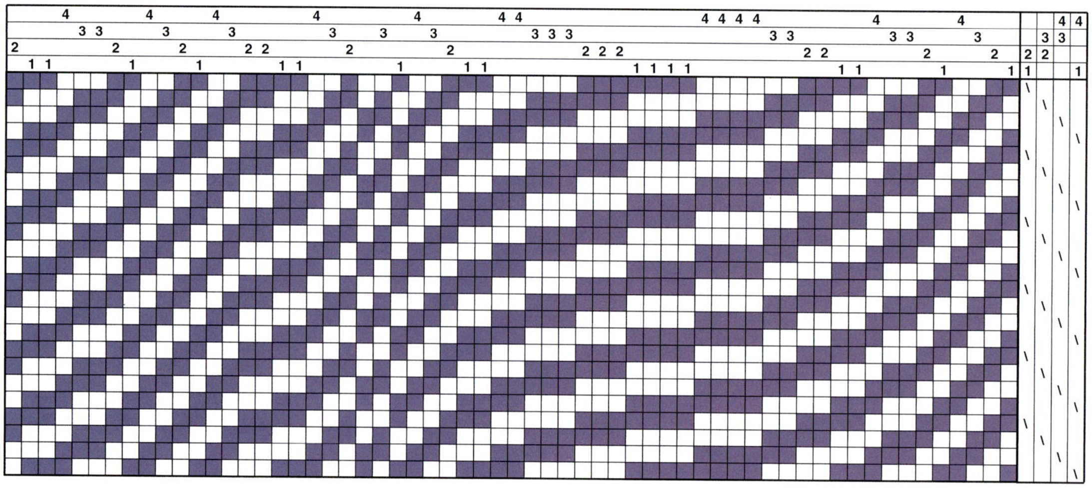

2.22 Undulating 2/2 twill (four shafts). The undulations are not dramatic when fewer shafts are used.

This undulating twill, woven in 2/8 worsted wool, used eight shafts and the $\frac{3\ 1}{2\ 2}$ *interlacement.*

You may have noticed that this particular interlacement has been used for many of the fabrics in this chapter. It's interesting to see how many different "looks" one twill can produce.

under the simple twill threading, the angle is about 45 degrees, and then it progressively flattens as the ends are grouped in larger and larger clusters on the shafts. In the next part of the threading, reading right to left, some shafts have been omitted in the twill threading sequence to steepen the twill line.

Although a fabric woven using this threading and treadling feels nearly flat, it produces an illusion of soft woven folds or pleats—an interesting idea for a drapery fabric. The places where the long floats fall seem to bulge outward a little or a lot depending on the float lengths and their relationship to the floats around them. The cloth is very subtle when woven in a single color and very bold when woven with high value contrast between the warp and weft, black across white for example. When woven for clothing, such high contrast fabrics look fairly flashy; they are not for the faint of heart.

The treadling sequence in draft **2.22** is a straight one. It is easy to use with no technical problems. The twill diagonals may be steepened by doubling or trebling the weft picks; they may be flattened by omitting a shed in the treadling order.

As we have seen before, a gain in design freedom also brings some technical restrictions. Sixteen ends into the threading, there are four ends on shaft 4 and four on shaft 1. Warp ends that fall side by side with no weft passing between them tend to cluster together. The weakness in undulating twills lies in the places where ends or picks lie together. The firmness of the fabric varies; if the firmness is satisfactory in the straight-draw part of the threading, the quadrupled ends will be unstable.

Setting the warp a little closer than for a regular twill will help compensate for, but won't eliminate, the variation. In our example, the float lengths, which are directly related to the differences in firmness, vary from over one pick (where shafts are skipped) to eight (where ends are quadrupled), severely limiting the functional application of the fabric woven using this draft. If fine yarns were used, the float lengths would probably be acceptable, but the variation in firmness is inescapable. If our draft were used to weave drapery fabric, the yarns would have to be somewhat clinging or sticky to avoid weft slippage and resulting sagging where there are long weft floats.

The fabric is noticeably thicker where the long floats appear and thinner where the floats are shorter. This *physical* undulation in the surface of the cloth further emphasizes the visual effects so that in looking at but not touching such a cloth, you can never be quite sure whether what your eyes are telling you is true or an illusion. Visual ambiguity of this sort can be exciting but it can also be rather disturbing; use it with that idea firmly in mind.

If more than four shafts are available, more elaborate patterns may be produced in the cloth as we saw in draft **2.21**.

Undulating twills may be woven with twill lines that move to the left or to the right, as they do in **2.22**. The twill lines may also reverse in the warp or the weft direction as in **2.25**. The changes in direction may be abrupt **(2.23)/(2.24)** or smoothly curved. Smoothly curved twills threaded and treadled to undulate produce ovals in the cloth, see **2.25**.

Steeper twill lines than can be produced with only four shafts are also possible. Remember that the steepest place in draft **2.22** occurs where shafts are skipped in the threading. However, with four shafts, skipping shafts is risky business. Skipping a shaft twice in a row (1, skip 2, 3, skip 4, 1) produces an area of almost plain weave—an interesting idea, something we will return to later—which breaks the diagonals in the cloth. If two shafts are skipped, the diagonal reverses direction. If eight or twelve shafts are available, however, more than one shaft may be skipped without risk of destroying the visual effect—an important fact because creating visual effects is the main reason for using undulating twills.

Draft **2.24** (next page) is an undulating twill that reverses the way a herringbone twill does. The steep sections of the draft occur where shafts have been skipped in the threading. This draft has been woven using a straight treadling. A softer, rounded shape is the result of draft **2.24** (next page).

Compare the threading portion of these two drafts. As you develop your eye, you will be able to "read" the curves right off the draft and see what sort of cloth a straight treadling will produce.

We need not limit ourselves to straight treadlings. By treadling draft **2.23** as drawn in, a pattern of circular shapes is obtained. Treadling as drawn in means that the treadles are used twice (or three times) when there are two (or three) threads side by side on the same shaft, skipping a treadle when a shaft is skipped in the threading. The pattern made by the threading is repeated in the treadling direction: what happens left to right in the threading (repeated ends, skipped shafts) happens top to bottom in the treadling.

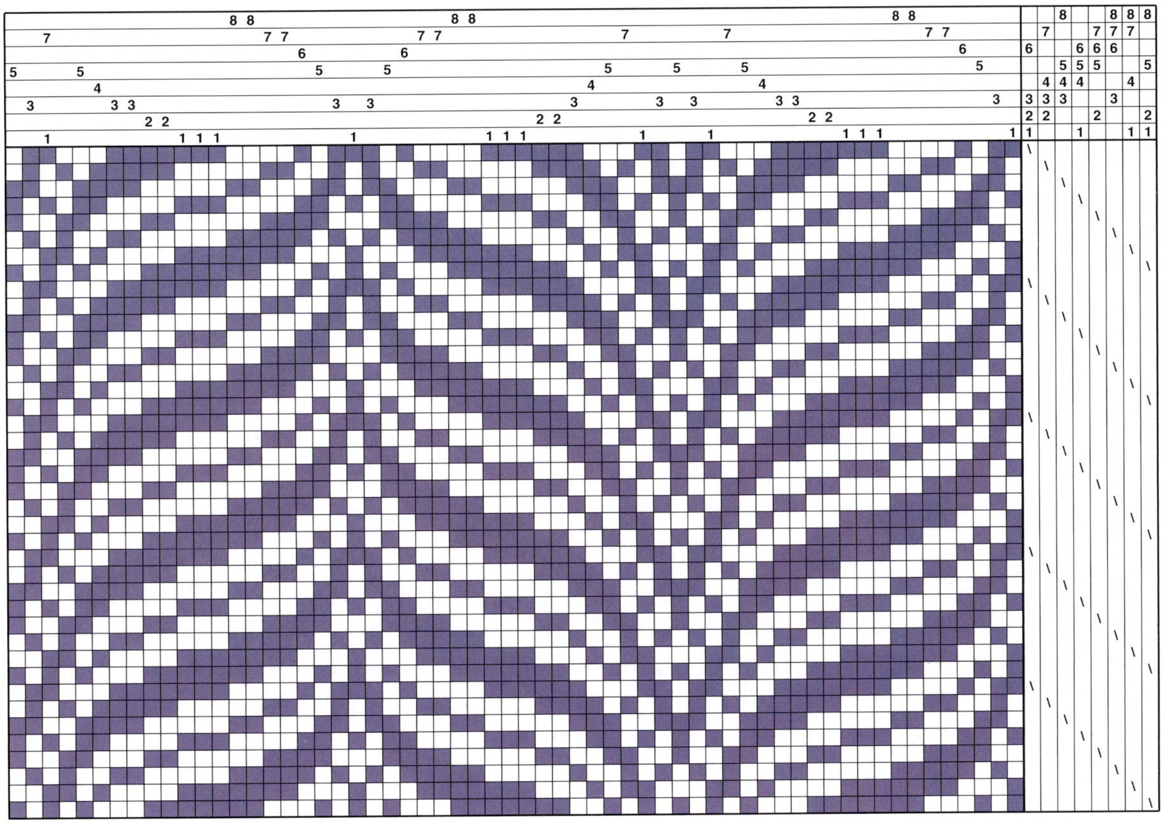

2.23 Eight-shaft undulating twill $\frac{3\ 2}{1\ 1}$.

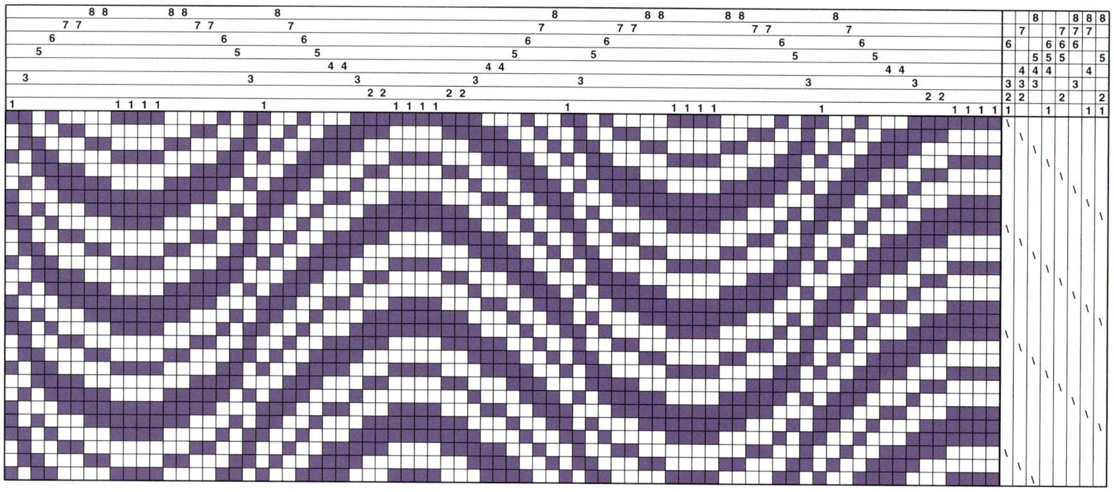

2.24 A reversing undulating twill, straight treadling.

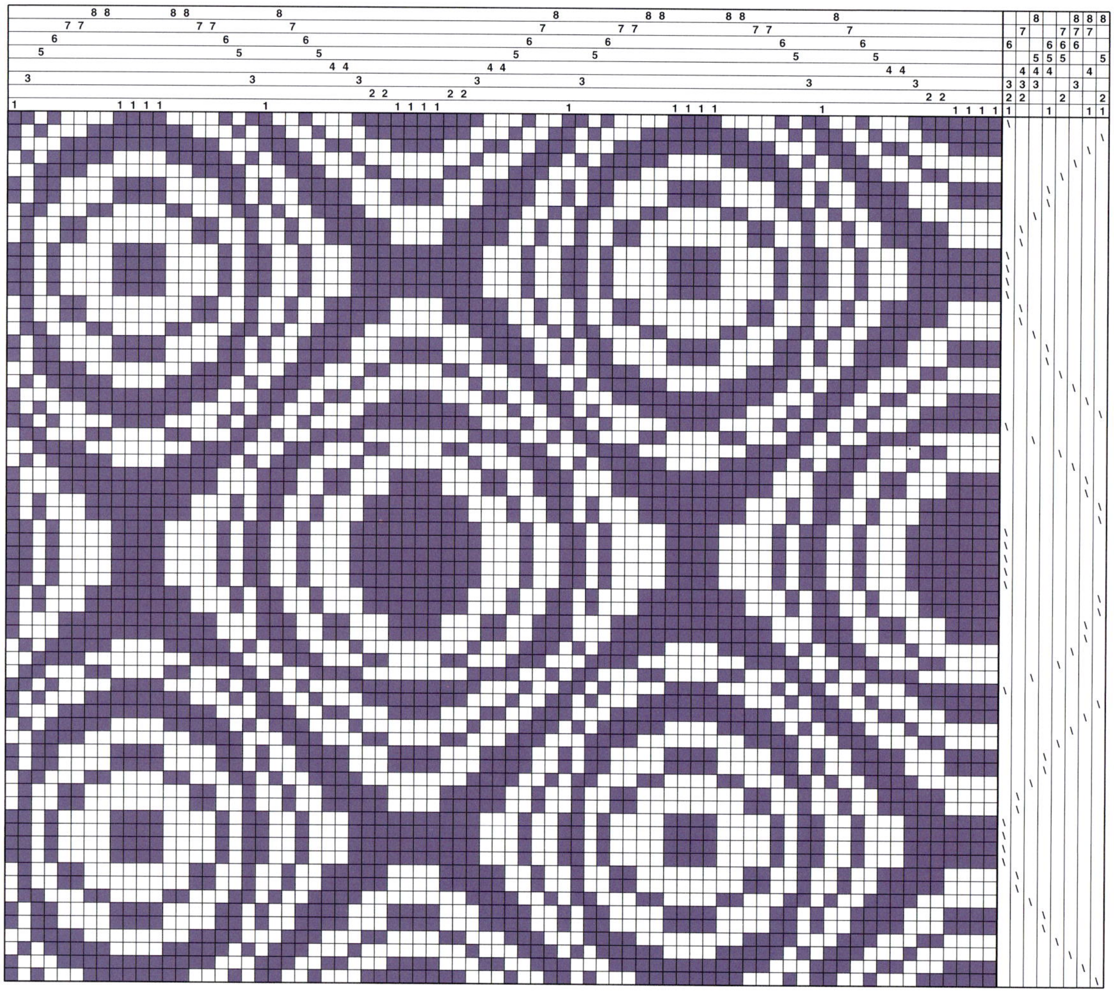

2.25 A reversing undulating twill, treadled in the same curve as that used for the threading. (Note the long floats that make this draft have more theoretical than practical value unless threads are very small, or wool and well-fulled.)

Eight-shaft undulating twill, $\frac{3\ 2}{2\ 2}$. The weft is red woolen-spun wool at about 1,800 yards per pound, which crosses a tweed yarn of the same weight. Fulling helps make this cloth stable. Too much fulling—or felting—obscures the design.

Taming the Wild Pattern

For the most dramatic undulating twills, select colors that are far apart in value, texture, or hue. On the other hand, you can soften the impact of a very strong design by choosing colors that are closer to each other in value. Likewise, a very strong undulating twill pattern might be woven in a shiny yarn using just one color in the warp and weft, allowing the play of light on the shiny surface of the yarn to suggest the pattern by the way the light falls on the cloth. A very strong pattern may be softened by choosing colors quite different in hue but close in value: the undulations show up but they aren't jarring. There are *lots* of possibilities.

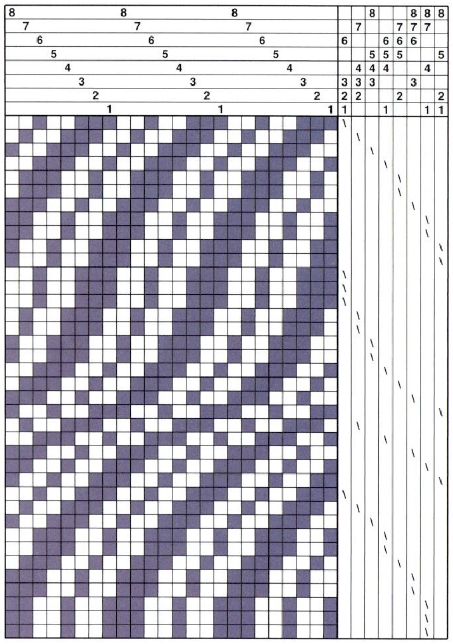

2.26 Straight draw on eight shafts, undulations produced by treadling order.

Although it is always a good idea to draw down two full repeats of a pattern in both the warp and weft direction, the use of a pair of mirrors (described earlier) shows how a pattern looks when repeated several times. The use of a photocopying machine to generate repeats that may be taped together or a pair of mirrors are labor saving methods when working out long drawdowns. Computer weaving software speeds up such repetitive work even more.

Draft **2.26** shows how an undulating twill looks threaded in a straight draw on eight shafts. Here, the undulations occur in the treadling sequence. In a number of places the same shed is used for more than one pick, and you must use a floating selvedge. If you beat differentially, you eliminate the undulations; a firm beat is used everywhere. Using a straight threading has the advantage of permitting us to weave all the possibilities on a given number of shafts; the disadvantage is the complexity of the treadling order, which must be followed strictly if the curves are to look intentional.

Braided Twills

This eight-shaft braided twill, which looks like ribbons interlaced on the diagonal, was woven using a red 2/20 worsted wool crossed with a deep blue green 2/20 worsted wool weft.

Imagine a cloth that looks as though it had been constructed of ribbons interlaced at right angles but placed on the diagonal with regard to the selvedges. Such a cloth, like the one pictured here, is called a braided (or plaited) twill.

I wove my first one in the mid-1970s. I knew what I wanted it to look like, drew out the cloth diagram on graph paper, and worked back to obtain the threading and treadling. My first efforts required more shafts than are shown here.

The draft shown here is constructed by using shafts 1 and 2 to tie down the floats. The "twill ribbons" are constructed as 1/3 twill.

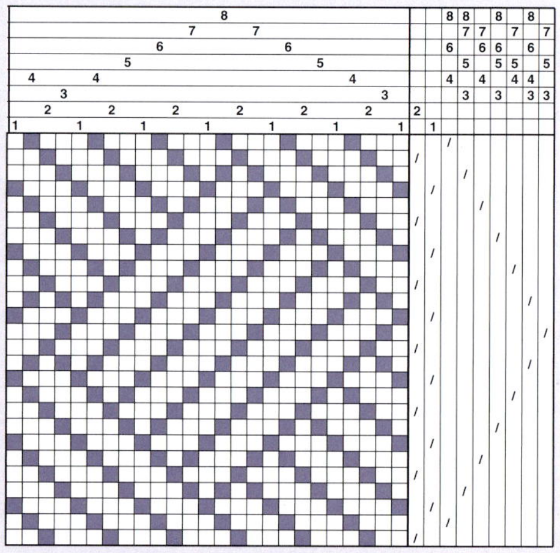

3

SATIN

Have you ever made a warp so beautiful that it seemed a shame to break it up with a weft yarn? That warp was a good candidate for **satin** interlacement. **Satin weaves** have a surface of nearly unbroken warp; their opposite, fabrics woven with a nearly unbroken weft surface, are called **sateens**. Both structures are, like twills, based on floats; warp floats in the former, weft floats in the latter.

Satin has always been considered a luxury fabric. It takes more than four shafts to weave and requires a higher thread count than many other weave structures. The surfaces of satin fabrics are smooth and often lustrous. They look as if the warp had been stabilized somehow without the use of a weft. Our study of satin structures will show how that illusion is accomplished.

In the twill chapter, we discussed a false satin, four-shaft broken 3/1 twill (page 32). That is as close as we can come to a satin using four shafts, but the idea behind the satin structure is very similar: *to break up the twill line so that it disappears from view.* Satins and sateens are almost always threaded as a straight draw, so we will examine ways to use the tie-up or treadling to break up the twill line.

The simplest satin may be woven using just five shafts. Satins are warp-faced, but it is easier to see how they work by studying sateens, their weft-faced counterpart. When a five-shaft sateen is woven, one shaft is lifted for each pick, rather than four, as in satin. In fact, when there is a choice, it is a good idea to weave satins upside down, as sateens, for several reasons. First, it is less physical work to lift one shaft than it is to lift four. Further, jack looms work more easily by lifting one shaft and leaving the others down, particularly when weaving satins using more than five shafts: when treadled as a satin, the single shaft that is supposed to stay down frequently rides up with the others. The problem does not exist on a countermarch loom, whose shafts all are either lifted or pulled down; none is left to gravity as are the shafts on a jack loom.

The following examples are written using sateen interlacements. Draft **3.1a** shows a 1/4 twill; the twill line is very clear in the cloth diagram. To turn this structure into a sateen, we must rearrange the treadling. The points at which the weft comes to the surface in a satin (or to the back in a sateen) are called **stitching points** or **stitchers** because they connect, or stitch, the floating warp surface to the weft back or the weft surface to the warp back. (If the warp did not intersect the weft, there would be no cloth, of course.)

In **3.1b**, the treadling has been rearranged to produce sateen. Although **3.1c** produces the same cloth, the way it is written—using a straight treadling—is more typical of the way sateen drafts are written.

The way in which the rearrangement of sheds is made is important. Look again at the drafts in **3.1**. Draft **3.1a** is made by moving the stitchers in the tie-up up one column to the right and one square (= shaft) up and one column to the right for each succeeding pick. Draft **3.1c** is constructed by moving the stitchers up two shafts in each succeeding column for each pick. The stitchers also may be moved by three shafts, as in **3.1d**. Both **3.1c** and **3.1d** produce true sateens.

The goal of getting rid of the diagonal (while using a straight draw) means that the stitching points may not be adjacent to each other. That is, if we lift shaft 1 for the first pick, we may not lift 2 or 5 next. (Don't forget that 1 and 5 are next to each other in the threading; 1 follows 5 as the next threading repeat begins.) We could lift shaft 3 *or* 4 next (**3.1c** and **3.1d**). If we choose 3, then 2 and 4 are ruled out for the next lift, leaving 5. Only shafts 2 and 4 are left to lift, but 4 is adjacent to 5 so we lift 2 and then finally, 4.

This kind of almost intuitive reasoning works very nicely for a five-shaft sateen, but there is another way to figure out how to distribute the stitchers for satin/sateens using more shafts. Satins and sateens may be constructed by trying out various numbers as **move numbers** or **satin intervals**.*

The move number for regular twills is 1; this means that each succeeding pick is made by lifting one shaft higher than the last. Let us consider the possibilities for a five-shaft satin. A move number of 1 produces a right-hand twill. We have seen the results of move numbers 2 and 3. A move number of 4 produces the draft in **3.1e**, a left-hand twill. If the move number 5 were used, only one shed would be produced; that is called a **degenerate case**: one in which the weft does not interlace with *every* one of the warp ends, producing neither satin nor sateen—or cloth either, for that matter. When we are considering move numbers for satin or sateen, we can always rule out 1, n - 1, and n, where n is the total number of shafts used. The first and second produce twills, and the last is a degenerate case.

Another very useful satin or sateen is constructed on eight shafts. Drafts **3.2a–3.2e** show the tie-ups that result from move numbers 2 through 6. Two, 4, and 6 produce degenerate cases (we automatically rule out 1, 7, and 8). Only move numbers of 3 and 5 produce satins or sateens on eight shafts.

Satins that are constructed with the same move number throughout are called **regular satins**. It isn't possible to construct a regular satin/sateen on six shafts. Move numbers 2,

**Some of this language comes from the textile industry, where satin has been an important class of fabrics for centuries.*

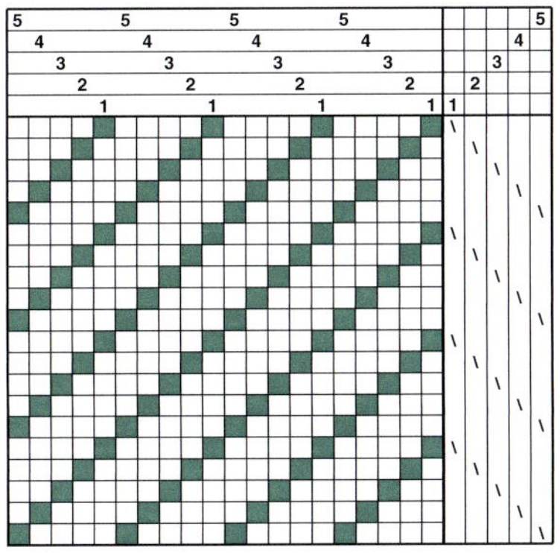

3.1a 1/4 twill shows the twill line we want to eliminate in creating a five-shaft sateen.

3.1b Rearranging the treadling order makes a five-shaft sateen.

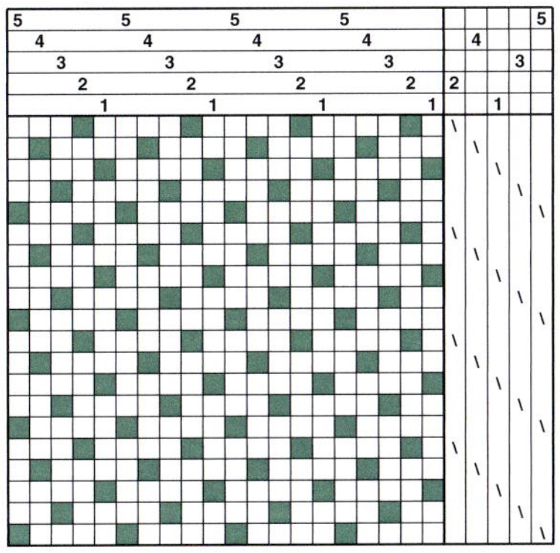

3.1c The tie-up is rearranged to make the treadling easier. The move number is 2.

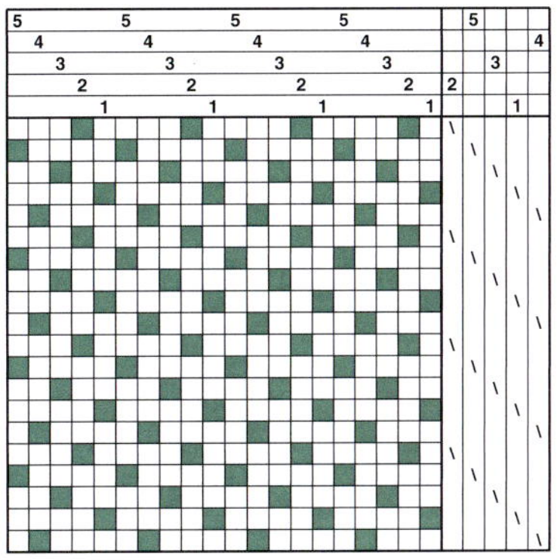

3.1d The move number here is 3.

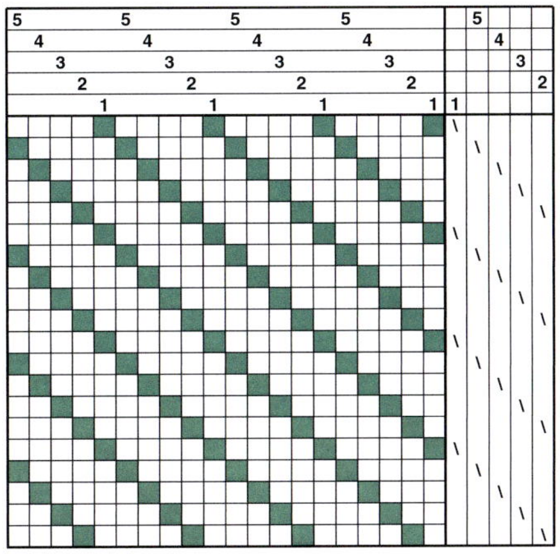

3.1e The move number here is 4. We have returned to the twill, which moves in the opposite direction from 3.1a.

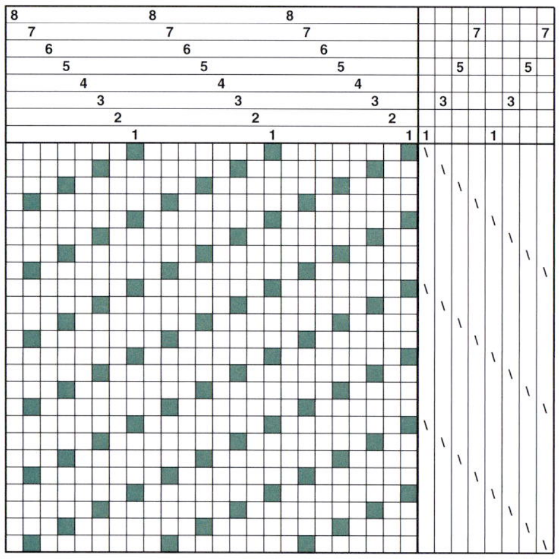

3.2a In the construction of an eight-shaft sateen, here is what a move number of 2 produces; a degenerate example. Half the warp ends are never used.

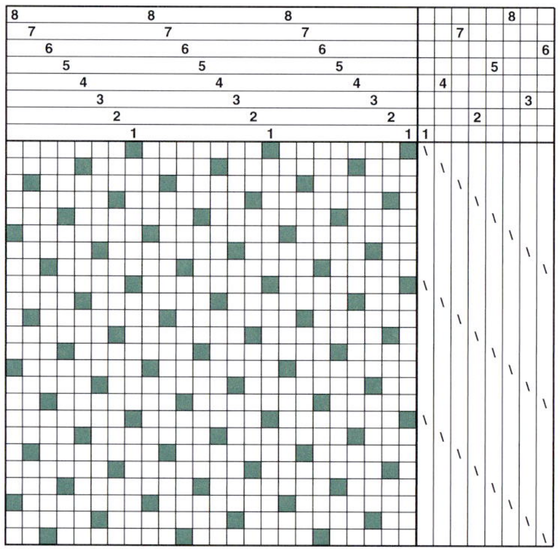

3.2b The use of 3 as the move number produces a satisfactory eight-shaft sateen.

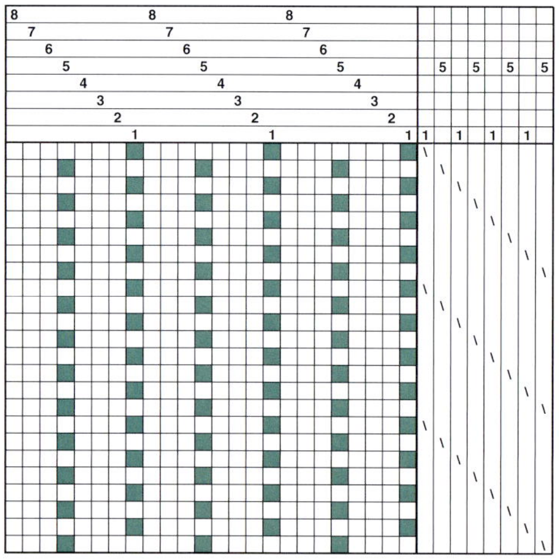

3.2c The use of 4 as the move number is clearly degenerate.

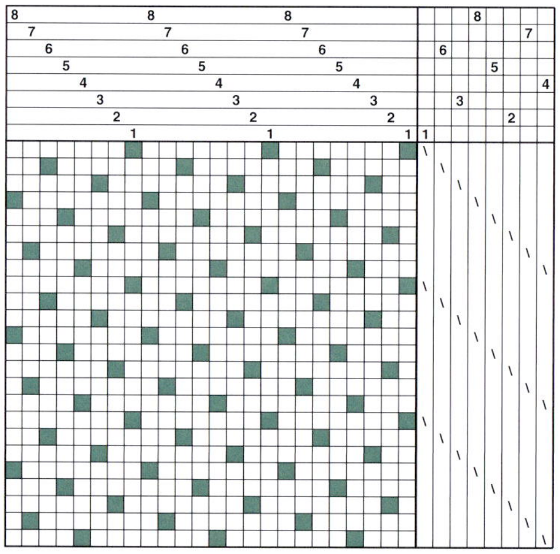

3.2d The use of 5 as the move number results in a satisfactory eight-shaft sateen.

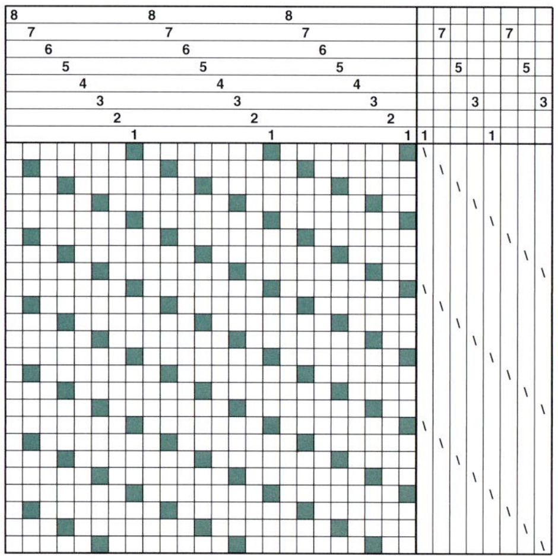

3.2e The use of 6 as a move number results in another degenerate case; some shafts are never raised.

Five-shaft satin woven of 20/2 pearl cotton. The back shows the weft color and was the side facing me as I wove it. This structure is especially good for showing off stripes because the weft shows relatively little.

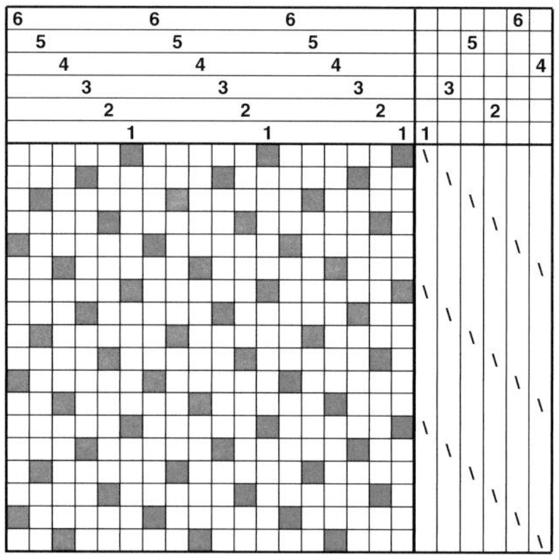

3.3a Six-shaft irregular sateen. Notice that the placement of the stitchers in the cloth diagram doesn't look as smooth as the regular sateens in drafts 3.1 and 3.2.

Two is used for the move number for the first three stitchers, followed by 3 for one stitcher, then 4 for two.

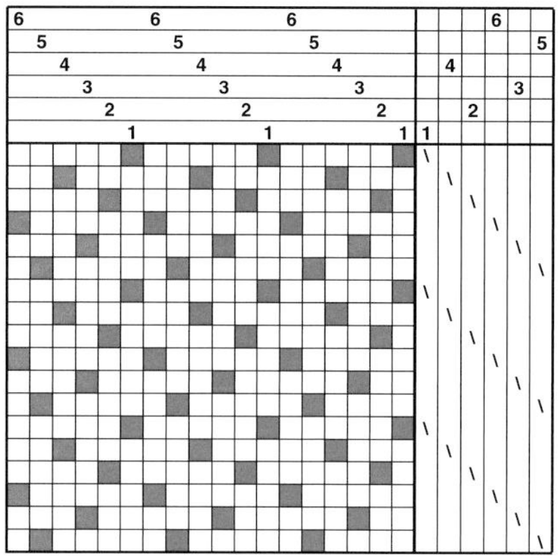

3.3b Six-shaft irregular sateen. Move numbers of 3 and 4 for the first four stitchers leave just shafts 3 and 5. We can't put the next stitcher on 5 because it lies diagonal to the one before it, so we mark 3 next and then 5.

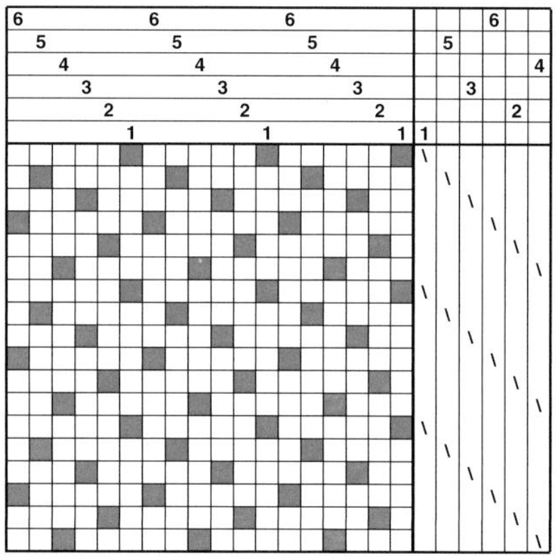

3.3c Six-shaft irregular sateen. Four is used as move number for the first two picks, then 3 for one and then 2 for the remaining two picks.

3, 4, and 6 are degenerate, and numbers 1 and 5 produce twills. When it is important to make a satin or sateen using six shafts, the stitchers must be arranged so that two do not lie next to each other—as they do if you begin with shaft 1 and end with shaft 2 or 6. The structure that is made this way is called **irregular satin** or **irregular sateen**. Drafts **3.3a**, **3.3b**, and **3.3c** show three ways to construct a six-shaft irregular sateen. It produces a slightly "pebbly" look to the cloth, in strong contrast to the smooth, highly refined appearance of regular satins. We will return to irregular satins later. (Six-shaft satin/sateen is often used as the underlying structure on some Scandinavian damask designs woven on drawlooms. The pebbly surface contributes to a "homespun" appearance.)

Satins and sateens are handsomest when woven of relatively fine threads. The visual effects of satin rely on the illusion of unbroken warp; a coarse weft intrudes on the smooth surface, spoiling the illusion, and a coarse warp looks clumsy. Additionally, the length of the floats in satin and sateen fabrics can be a problem if the yarns are coarse. Remember that these suggestions apply to functional fabrics. Art fabrics need only enough structural integrity to continue to deliver the artist's message for the desired lifetime of the piece.

In theory, the reverse side of a satin cloth is sateen cloth. With that assumption in mind, you will be surprised when you examine the back of a mill-woven satin fabric. In fact, the warp usually has been set so closely for satin that the weft cannot be packed closely enough to make a good-looking sateen on the back. The reverse is also true: when a sateen is woven, the sett is slightly less than the theoretical sett (see Appendix C, Calculating Setts, page 250) so that the wefts can be packed in to make the most luxurious sateen. **Damask** is a cloth having satin and sateen areas on the same face. Here a balance is struck and the theoretical sett is used; the satin part shows a little more weft than a plain satin fabric and the sateen, likewise, shows a little more warp.

When a fabric is woven so that one face is strongly emphasized, as the warp is for a satin, the selvedges tend to curl away from the crowded face. In many applications, that is not a problem, but when the selvedges will show in the finished fabric, a separately beamed and threaded basket-weave selvedge can be added.

It is important to tension the special selvedge differently from the main warp because the take-up for satins and sateens is far less than for plain weave or 2/2 basket weave.

If the appropriate sett is used, a five-shaft satin may be turned into a five-shaft sateen at any time simply by changing the way the cloth is woven. Changing the treadling from four up, one down to one up, four down changes the way the fabric reflects light, so that even if one lustrous yarn is used throughout, the perceived color of the cloth changes where the structures shifts from warp- to weft-faced. If the warp and weft

A Second Warp Beam—Who Has One?

If your loom has two warp beams, by all means use them, but if it has just one, you may compensate for the lack of a second by doing one of the following:

First, you may wind the warp requiring a different tension separately from the main part of the warp, thread and sley it, and then hang it off the back beam and weight it either as warp chain(s) or spooled—which may be handier. This method is probably best for adding selvedges; after measuring the little "ribbon" of warp, you can wind it onto a spool or chain it. In the case of selvedges, there will be two such weighted chains or spools, one for each side.

Second, and this is better for warps where a thread occurs all across the warp, not just at its edges, you may beam the entire warp in one piece and then lift all the ends that are likely to sag because they have lower rates of take-up. Put a smooth rod such as a dowel ½ inch (1.3 cm) in diameter *under* the threads that will become slack and *over* the rest of the warp. Work this dowel over the back beam so that it is nearer to the warp beam and tie weights to it at both ends and in the middle. The rod will sink a little as you weave the warp, but the weights will keep it at the tension you have chosen.

Third, and this method is one I have used to *rescue* warps when to my surprise and dismay I find some warp ends becoming looser and looser, you can put a smooth rod *over* the slack ends and *under* the ends making up the majority of the warp by lifting all the warp ends that are behaving well. Weight the rod as above. Finally, tie two cords around the rod and around the back beam—but not too tightly!—so that the rod does not creep forward toward the shafts. The reason for holding the rod back is to ensure that you will make good sheds: if the rod is too close to the heddles, the shed will not open easily or well. As time and warp go by, the rod will sink lower and lower because there is less take-up on the portion of the warp under it. Unless you are weaving miles of it, the rod will not sink to the floor.

colors are different, the cloth will be striped in the weft direction. In the satin sections, the cloth is warp-colored, and in the sateen sections, weft-colored. When we come to damask, we shall consider more elaborate warp and weft colorings and their results.

Double-faced satins and sateens

Designing double-faced satins and sateens involves the same sort of considerations as does designing double-faced twills. Assume that we wish to make the warp (or weft) dominant on both sides, and that the means should not be apparent: both sides of the cloth must look perfect.

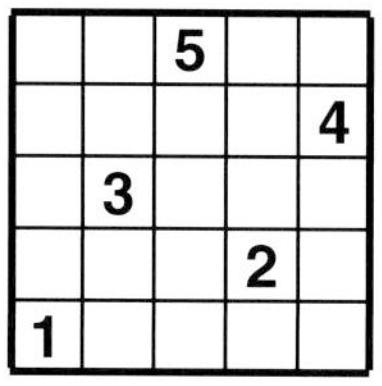

Figure 1. The five-shaft sateen tie-up.

Let us first design a sateen. We'll start by figuring out the sateen interlacement for the face, in figuring out the tie-up and treadling for the side that is up on the loom. See Figure 1.

The weft picks alternate: first one for the face, then one for the reverse side of the cloth; we know what half the treadling will be just by selecting the treadling for the face sateen.

Weaving the sateen on the back is the equivalent of weaving a satin on the face: four ends are up and one is down. To decide what the first shed in the satin lifting ought to be, we look at the first two sheds in the sateen draft. The first shed lifts ends on shaft 1, so that shaft must also be lifted for the satin; otherwise, the second weft might show on the surface. The second weft must nest with the first so that together they take up only one thread width when beaten in. The second shed in the sateen lifts ends on shaft 3, so 3 also must be lifted in the first satin shed. *The end that is lifted is the stitcher for sateen, and in the second of the sateen/satin weft pairs, the end that is* ***not*** *lifted, is the stitcher for satin.*

If shafts 1 and 3 must both be lifted for the first satin pick, then we may lift 1, 2, 3, 5 or 1, 3, 4, 5 for the first sateen pick. Either will do; the former was chosen for this draft. Now that the initial shed has been determined, the rest is easy. The move number for **3.1c** is 2; if 2 is used for the satin treadling that produces a weft-faced fabric on the back, then the back will be a regular satin and the stitchers will never fall on the same end twice in a row. The tie-up and treadling are written in **3.4a** so that the structures generated by alternate picks are clear. In **3.4b**, the treadling order has been rearranged. This interleaving of satin and sateen picks is much like what we did with double-faced twills. The twill/satin connection is quite close. Producing satin fabric on both faces of the cloth requires more shafts than we need for its sateen counterpart because there are really two warp systems being woven with a single weft. It may be done by simply turning the draft in **3.4b**.

As with its twill counterpart, double warp-faced twill, a five-shaft structure requires ten shafts to weave, and a seven-shaft satin requires fourteen. Let us write the draft for this structure.

The first step is writing the draft for the **base satin** structure. It is easier to work out the stitchers for the structure by looking at the sateen version first. Draft **3.5a** shows a sateen structure on seven shafts. Draft **3.5b** is its reverse, the satin.

To weave both of these structures simultaneously requires seven shafts and fourteen sheds. Seven picks are needed for the face and seven for the back, woven alternating one pick for the face and one for the back. If two colors are used, one for each face, two shuttles are used throughout. Weaving the cloth with a single shuttle permits us to weave with a more consistent rhythm and greater speed.

By turning the draft (**3.5c**), we can put the two colors in the warp and throw a single

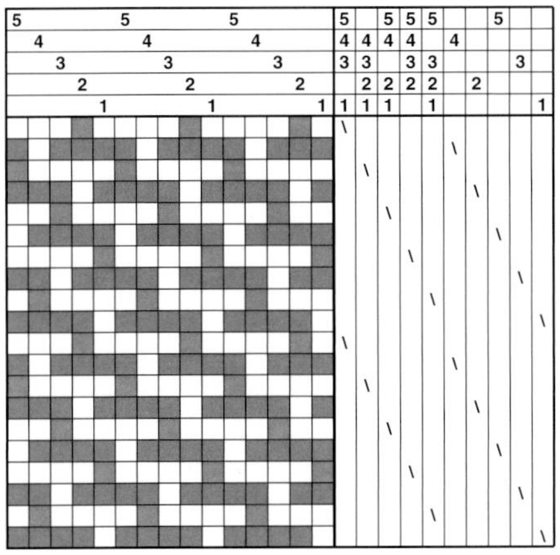

3.4a *Five-shaft sateen, tied and treadled (two wefts) to produce double-faced sateen.*

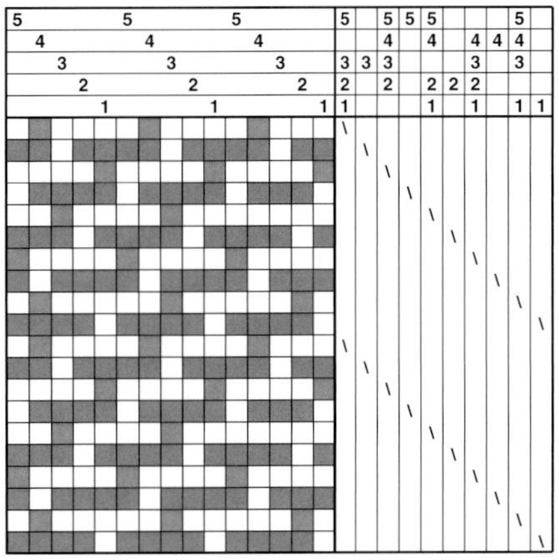

3.4b *Five-shaft sateen, tied and treadled (two wefts) to produce double-faced sateen. Here the tie-up is rearranged to make treadling easier.*

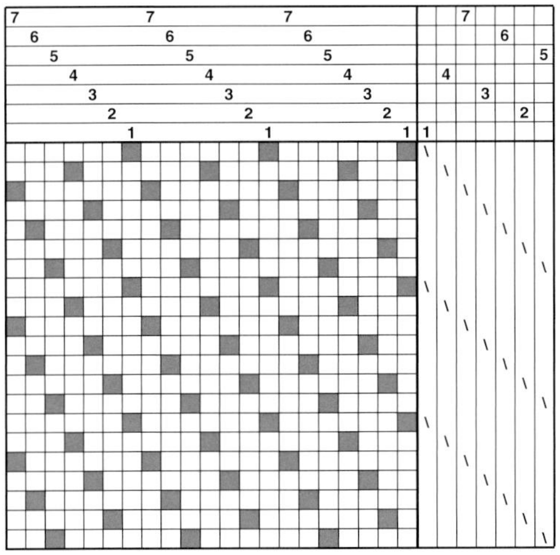

3.5a *Seven-shaft sateen (move number 3).*

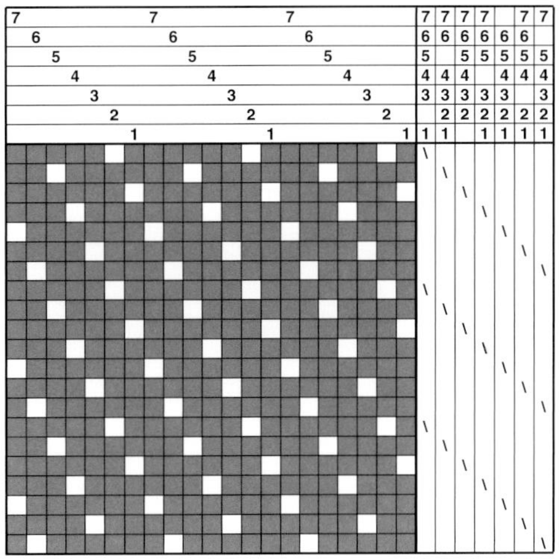

3.5b *Seven-shaft satin (move number 3).*

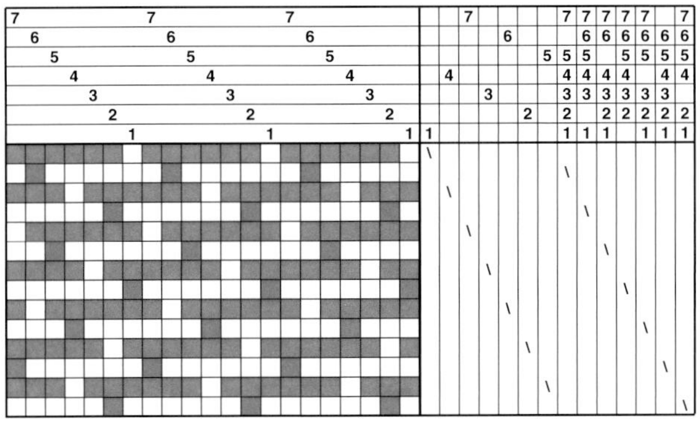

3.5c *The seven-shaft satin interleaves with a seven-shaft satin to make a double-faced seven-shaft sateen.*

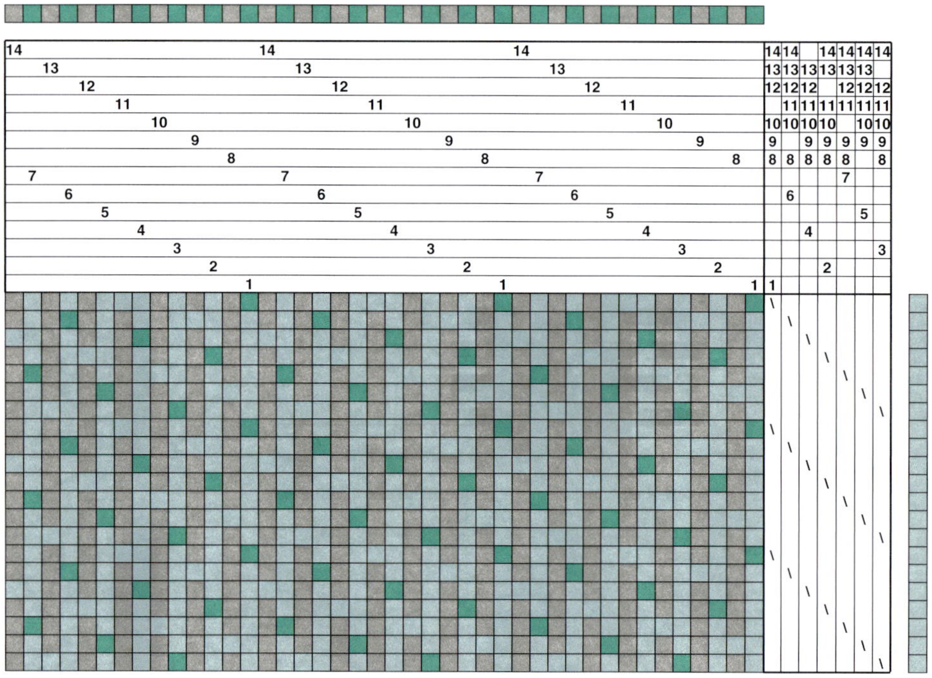

3.5d Double-faced satin, fourteen shafts. This draft is 3.5c turned, so that it may be woven with a single shuttle. The warp is two colors, alternating, and is set at twice the number of ends per inch as a seven-shaft satin, which weaves satin on the face and sateen on the back.

shuttle that interlaces with both sets of warps, one set for the face and one for the reverse side of the fabric. In the most stable construction, the two sets alternate in the threading. In **3.5d**, the face ends are on the even-numbered shafts and the back ends, on the odds. Granted, weaving the cloth in this manner requires more shafts, but it also does away with the necessity of alternating two shuttles—a significant advantage.

A double-faced satin may be constructed based on any satin: First, work out the lifting plan for the base satin. Spread it out on every other shaft. Determine the first stitcher for the back surface and then fill in the other stitchers using the same move number as for the base satin.

Satin and sateen may be woven using more than six shafts. We have seen an example of an eight-shaft sateen, and a seven-shaft satin was used for the base of the double-faced satin. In exploring the principles behind the construction of structures that require more numerous shafts, we'll present the sateen case first—the draft is less cluttered looking than the draft for satin, if nothing else. (The diagrams here have begun with raised ends on shaft 1 for convenience; we could, in fact, begin anywhere.)

A move number of 1 creates the 1/(n - 1) twill; if you are using eight shafts, a move number of 1 creates a 1/(8 - 1), or 1/7, twill. A move number of n - 1, or 7, creates the same twill running in the opposite direction. We could draw all the possibilities for this using all the move numbers between 2 and n - 2, but we can save effort by ruling out those numbers that always yield degenerate cases. Any number that shares a factor with n produces a degenerate tie-up. For example, if n is divisible by 2, all even-numbered move numbers fail to produce satin or sateen: for ten shafts, 2, 4, 6, and 8 fail because they are divisible by 2; and 5 fails because it, too, is a factor of 10. A twelve-shaft satin thus can have only two move numbers, 5 or 7, because 2, 3, 4, and 6 are all factors of 12.

When you examine a satin or sateen structure—as we can do directly in the tie-up without having to touch a thread—you see that the regular structures have a sketchy diagonal line that shows up in the tie-up (and in the cloth itself). Drafts **3.6a** and **3.6b** show the two regular sateens possible on twelve shafts. They are, in fact, the same sateen with the diagonals reversed—they are the mirror images. To generalize: n minus the move number produces the same result, mirrored, as does the move number itself.

For a sixteen-shaft satin, then, we know that move numbers 2, 4, 6, 8, 10, 12, and 14 fail to produce satins or sateens (degenerate cases). Satisfactory viable structures comprise the mirror-image pairs 3 and 13, 5 and 11, and 7 and 9.

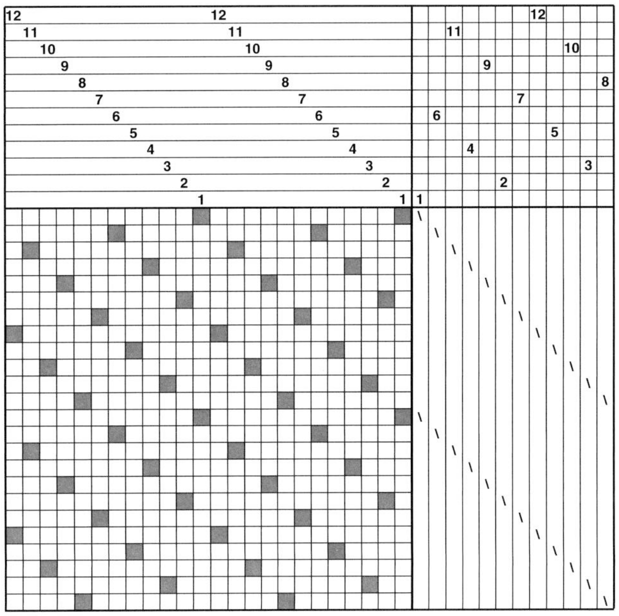

3.6a Twelve-shaft sateen using 5 as the move number.

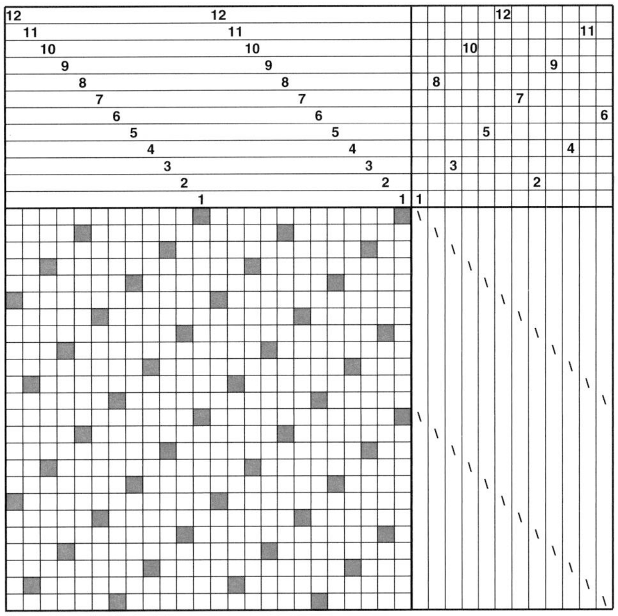

3.6b Twelve-shaft sateen using 7 as the move number.

Satinette

There are times when the very slight diagonals that appear in satins and sateens are undesirable—these seem to show up more in some yarns than others. It is useful in those circumstances to know how to design irregular sateens. From the sateen we can produce the satin simply by turning the cloth over. Irregular satin, sometimes called **satinette**, is the only way to weave a satin- or sateen-like structure on six shafts. In fact, that structure is more like a broken twill than a satin, but that is where the irregular structures begin.

Placing the stitchers in such a way that diagonals are avoided *but without introducing another pattern in the cloth* requires some care. It is an easy matter to work out an irregular

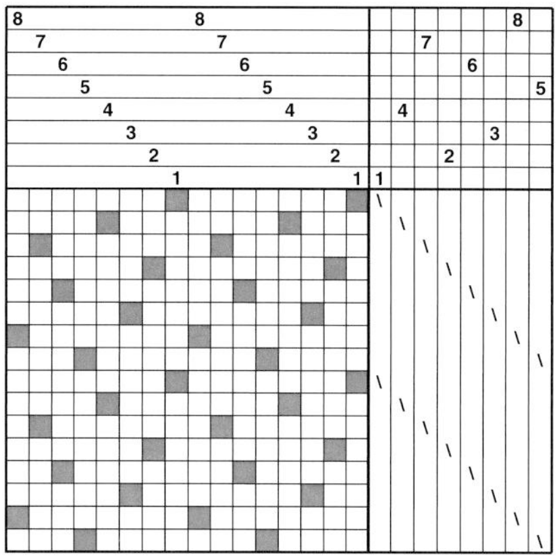

3.7 Eight-shaft irregular sateen. The first four picks are placed using 3 as the move number, the fourth by counting up 4 and the remaining three by counting down 3.

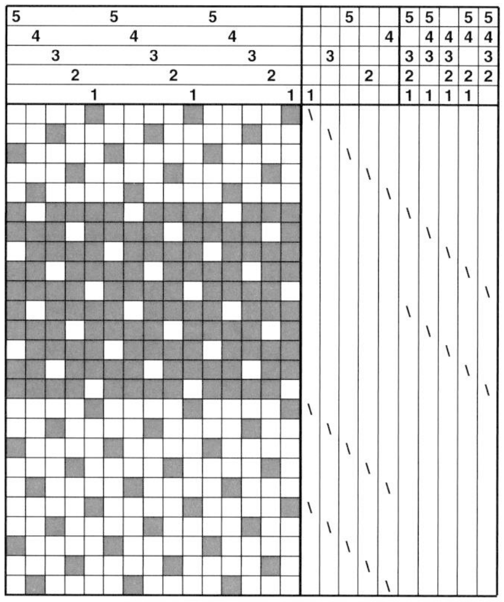

3.8 Five-shaft sateen and satin stripes in the weft direction. The move number, 3 (up for the sateen and down for the satin), is the same for both.

tructure on six shafts because there are relatively few ways of arranging six stitchers, but when ten or twelve are involved, having a few guidelines to follow helps.

Draft **3.7** is the draft for an eight-shaft irregular sateen. Here are the steps that were involved in making it: First the move number was chosen. Only move numbers 3 and 5 (equivalent, really, because they are mirror images of each other) produce regular satin on eight shafts; 3 was chosen. The first four entries use move number 3, counted upward as usual. The fifth was counted four upward; then the last three were placed using 3 but counting downward. Thus a single move number is used throughout except for the placement of the stitcher that breaks the rhythm. Experimentation shows that the number for the rhythm-breaking move is n/2, where n is even. When n is odd, experimentation seems to be the best course; if the move you have chosen places a stitcher on a shaft already lifted, go on by one or drop back one and see how that works. For any satin or sateen, never put two stitchers on the same shaft or diagonal to each other, and keep in mind that the first and last pick of a repeat lie side by side in the cloth because the last pick of a repeat is followed by the first pick of the next repeat.

Stripes

Stripes may be woven in which satin in one stripe alternates with sateen in the next, with the stripes running warpwise or weftwise. Weaving such a cloth with the changes from satin to sateen in the weft direction is simple. Changing from warp- to weft-faced fabric (here, weftwise stripes) involves changing the treadling, as we have seen. The break between satin and sateen must be a clean one: the last satin stitcher, a lowered end, must be

Above, singles ivory silk woven as warp stripes in a five-shaft satin on a plain-weave ground of 20/2 pearl cotton.

Left, another version of five-shaft satin stripes on a plain-weave ground. Warp and weft are the same spun tussah silk.

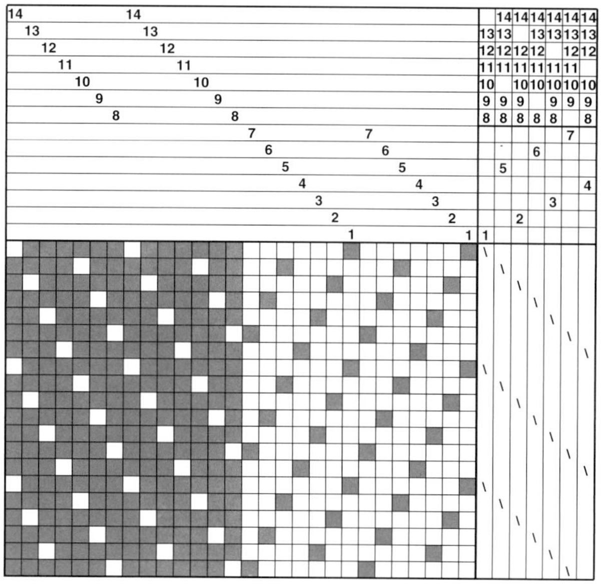

3.9 *Two-block seven-shaft damask. To make satin and sateen appear in the cloth at the same time in one pick, fourteen shafts are needed, seven for each block. Notice that there are clean breaks where the structures change. The move number is 4.*

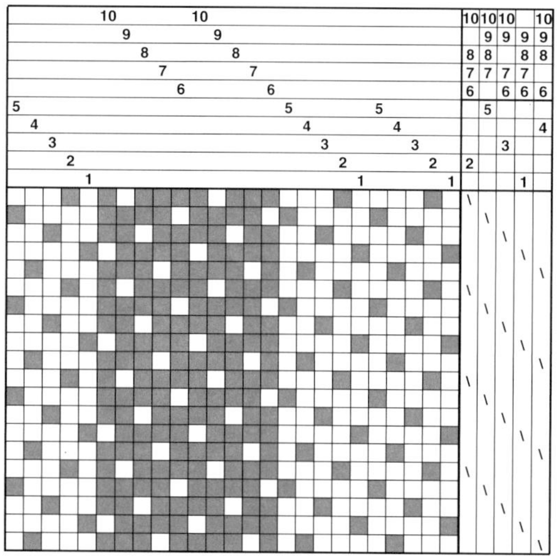

3.10a *Two blocks, satin and sateen, both based on five shafts. Notice that the where the blocks change, clean breaks are maintained.*

followed by a sateen stitcher that is the same end, raised. The reverse holds true for the switch from sateen to satin. The move number for the five-shaft draft shown in **3.8** (page 74) is 3 for both the sateen and satin treadlings. The count is made upward for the sateen and must be made downward for the satin to begin and end in the right places.

The move number must be the same for both structures; there isn't much to choose from when writing a five-shaft satin/sateen, but on seven shafts there are four move numbers, two pairs of equivalents. If the structure is not based on the same move number, then the two structures will not mesh the way they do in **3.8**. And they *must* mesh to avoid unsightly drifting of the sateen wefts into the satin areas. Draft **3.9** shows a satin/sateen stripe based on seven shafts.

Damask

Damask fabrics are those which are woven both satin and sateen in the same weft pick. Writing the drafts for the simplest damask possible, the sateen stripe turned 90 degrees to get the satin stripe, involves more thinking—and more shafts—than for satin or sateen alone. For the five-shaft structures we have been discussing, the satin areas require five shafts, and the sateen areas require five more shafts because in one pick, the two areas are doing different things. *Areas of the cloth that interlace differently with the same pick must be threaded differently.* The result, for satins, is that a two-block damask must have twice the number of shafts that the base satin has.

The area that weaves sateen is said to be in a different block from the area that weaves satin. In the threading draft shown in **3.10a** block A is threaded 1, 2, 3, 4, 5, repeat, and block B is threaded 6, 7, 8, 9, 10, repeat. Satin blocks may be as long as desired: you can thread 10 inches of block A and just one repeat of block B if you wish. True block weaves, or **unit weaves** (so called because they consist of specific threading units), may be repeated indefinitely, granting the designer a lot of freedom.

I prefer to begin writing the tie-up for warp-direction block changes by starting with the sateen structure. The same move number as in the preceding draft, 3, is used here.

Notice that the stitcher on shaft 5 falls in the second column. That means that the stitcher for shaft 6 must fall in the same column to ensure a clean break between the satin and sateen stripes. The same move number is used for writing the satin part of the tie-up, but instead of being counted upward, it is counted downward. Here is a slick way to check your work: if you imagine that the line between shafts 5 and 6 is a hinge, the filled-in squares (think of them as pegs) should fit into the empty squares (think of them as holes).

The changes in warp and weft emphasis may be extended to the weft direction, too, producing a checkerboard of satin and sateen areas instead of stripes (**3.10b**).

In summary, here are the steps in writing a two-block damask: Select the base satin. Write a threading draft with twice the number of shafts as the base. Enter the sateen tie-up for the first block. Leave the square open in the second block of the tie-up that corresponds to the filled-in space in the first block. Using the same move number that created the base sateen tie-up, count down rather than up, starting with that first stitcher, to fill out the satin portion of the tie-up. Proceeding one step at a time, writing a two-block draft is not difficult.

Draft **3.11** (next page) shows the threading for both blocks and the tie-up for sateen in block A and satin in block B. Now we will write the rest of the tie-up so that sateen may be woven in block A and satin in block B. The requirement for clean breaks between the blocks—and in this case *within* the blocks as the structure reverses—stands.

Draft **3.11** presents the possibilities—there are four—for a two-block damask based on a five-shaft satin. The tie-up may be considered to have four sections, each one consisting of five columns. The first section weaves block A sateen and B satin, the second weaves block A satin and B sateen, the third weaves both blocks sateen, and the fourth weaves both blocks satin.

In the first section, the "image" in the 5-by-5 unit written for block A is the negative of that written in the same section for block B. You can apply the "pegs and empty spaces" visualization described above with the "hinge" as the line between shafts 5 and 6.

A. Sateen B. Satin *A. Satin B. Sateen*

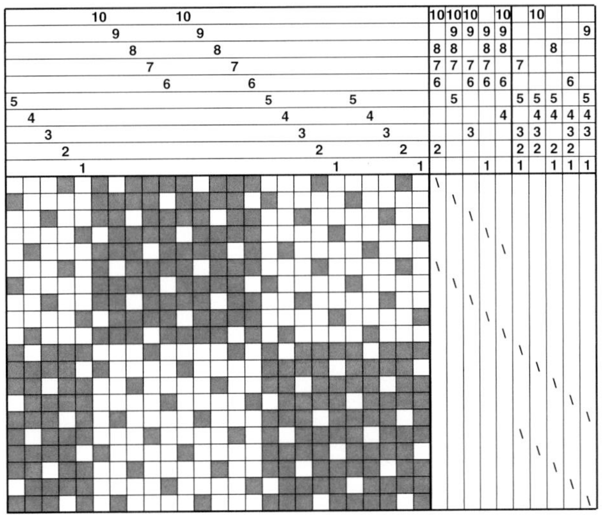

3.10b Two-block damask based on five-shaft structure. Notice the clean breaks where the structure changes from satin to sateen and vice versa. This structure produces a checkerboard when woven in one color for the warp and another color for the weft.

In the next section, the two 5-by-5 units are reversed, *but the organization of those 5-by-5 units is maintained.* You could have a pair of rubber stamps made, one for satin and one for sateen, and simply stamp the tie-ups for the blocks with satin or with sateen, depending on what you want to have happen in each block. Squint at draft **3.11**. The darker areas in the tie-up make satin, and the lighter areas make sateen. The crucial point is that every darker 5-by-5 square is identical, and every light square is identical, too. If either kind of square differed from square to square, we could not make a flawless cloth with satin all across the cloth or sateen all across the cloth, because discontinuities would occur where the treadling changed.

The move number used in **3.11** is 3, counted up for the sateen and down for the satin. Notice that all the breaks are clean. Damask is often figured with flowers, animals, or intricate geometric designs, but without resorting to pick-up or major loom modifications, fancy, figured damask is beyond the scope of ordinary treadle or dobby looms. The minimum number of shafts for two-block damask is ten; for three-block damask, the minimum is fifteen. The numbers rise rapidly beyond the capability of standard handlooms.

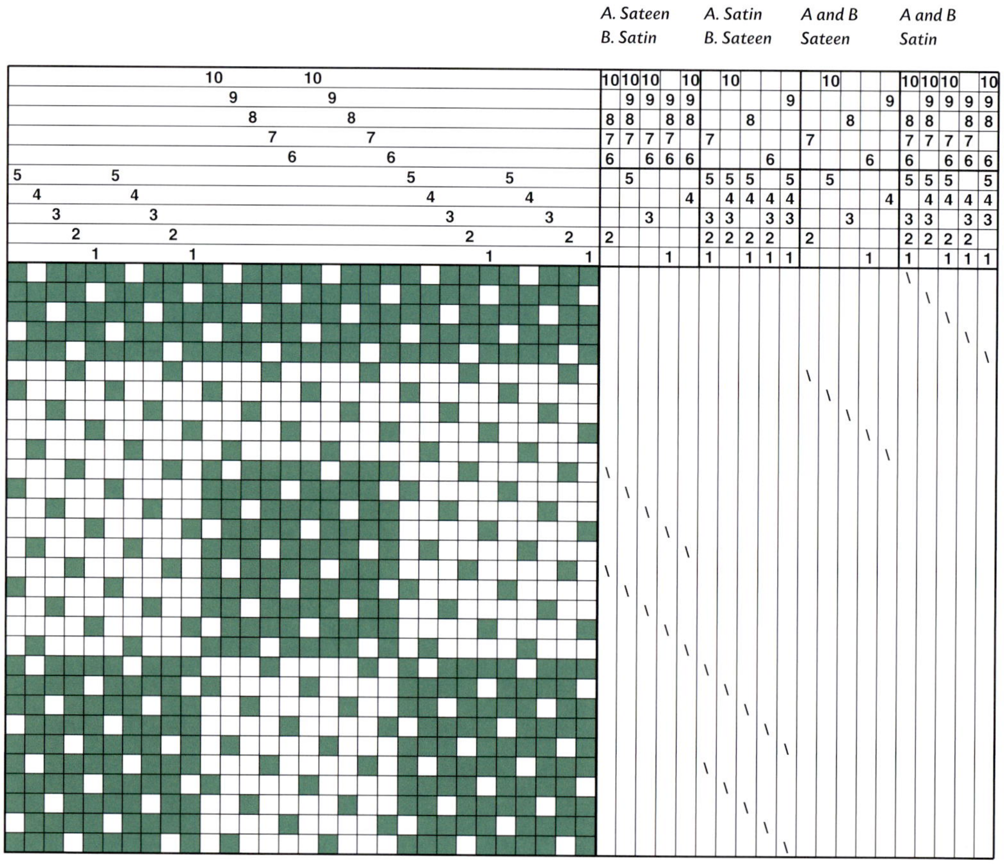

3.11 Two-block damask based on five-shaft structure. Two blocks permit four possible combinations: sateen in A and satin B, satin in A and sateen in B, sateen everywhere and satin everywhere. All of these possibilities are shown here. Note the breaks are clean at every change in the structure.

PROFILE DRAFTS

Satins and sateens, like twills, are unit weave structures. Unit weaves, particularly when more than two blocks are used, may be drafted in a simpler, clearer way to facilitate designing with them. Instead of writing the draft thread by thread, it is written block by block. This sort of draft, called a **profile draft** or **short draft,** shows the proportion and position of the blocks. The profile draft for **3.10b** (page 77) is shown in **3.13a**. The upper part of the draft, where the threading belongs, tells how many repeats of the threading unit there are in each block and how the blocks are arranged. The profile draft must be accompanied by a key showing how each block is threaded: 1 unit of A is threaded 1, 2, 3, 4, 5, etc.

3.13a Profile drafts for 3.10b.

The squares below the profile draft, in the same place where the cloth diagram would be in a structural draft, is the **profile draft development.** This tells us how the units will be woven—how many repeats of A, whether A and B are woven at the same time, and so forth. When you write out what one threading unit of A is, it is a good idea to specify what a filled-in square under a particular block means. For our example, a filled-in square means satin, and an empty square, sateen.

When you define what the parts of the profile draft mean, it becomes more than just a motif—it becomes a sort of blueprint for the cloth.

Drafts **3.13b** and **3.13c** are other two-block profile drafts. They look more complex, but have the same number of blocks as **3.13a.** As they stand, they could be drafts for twill blocks, damask, double weave, or lace weaves.

The power of profile drafting is that it shows us very graphically how the cloth will look. A structural draft can be likened to looking at your lawn on your hands and knees: you see where every blade of grass is. A profile draft is like looking at the whole neighborhood from a helicopter: you can see where grass is, and where pavement is. Once you understand the structure, it isn't always necessary to write the entire draft. A profile draft allows you, the designer, to focus on the placement of blocks in the cloth and the effect their relative sizes have on the appearance of the cloth.

Draft **3.14** is the profile draft for a three-block pattern. In some places the cloth is woven the same way from selvedge to selvedge; there are also some blocks that always weave the same way. A structural draft that looked like this would be nonsensical because it would indicate that there were warp floats that went the length of the cloth, or weft floats that spanned the cloth, selvedge to selvedge.

While it is not useful for weave structures that are not unit weaves, profile drafting is a powerful design tool which makes it easy to plan the "look" or organization of the cloth.

***3.13b** Another two-block profile draft. Notice that there are four possibilities: pattern in A only, in B only, in A and B, and in neither. Pattern in neither block would mean, for our example where we have defined "pattern" means weaving satin, that both blocks weave sateen.*

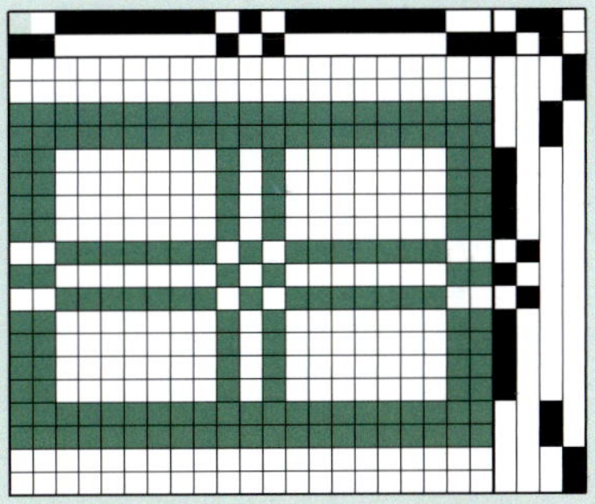

3.13c Another two-block profile draft.

3.14 A three-block profile draft.

16/1 linen woven as shown in 3.12.

Two-Block Damask and Color

Interesting and beautiful color effects may be incorporated into a two-block satin or sateen cloth. Suppose that each block is threaded for 1 inch (2.5 cm) with colored stripes 1 inch wide, and the warp is woven with weft block and color changes that take place at 1-inch intervals to make a checkerboard. Each time a block weaves satin, the warp color shows in an almost unbroken expanse; when the same block is woven sateen, the weft color shows. Using just two colors, one for warp and one for weft, a checkerboard may be woven; the classic red-and-white checked tablecloth is a fancier version of this structure. If this two-block cloth is woven using several colors, particularly colors close in value, a wonderful multicolored cloth results.

Consider what would happen if the color changes occurred at the midpoint of the threading blocks and color changes in the weft direction occurred halfway through the treadling.

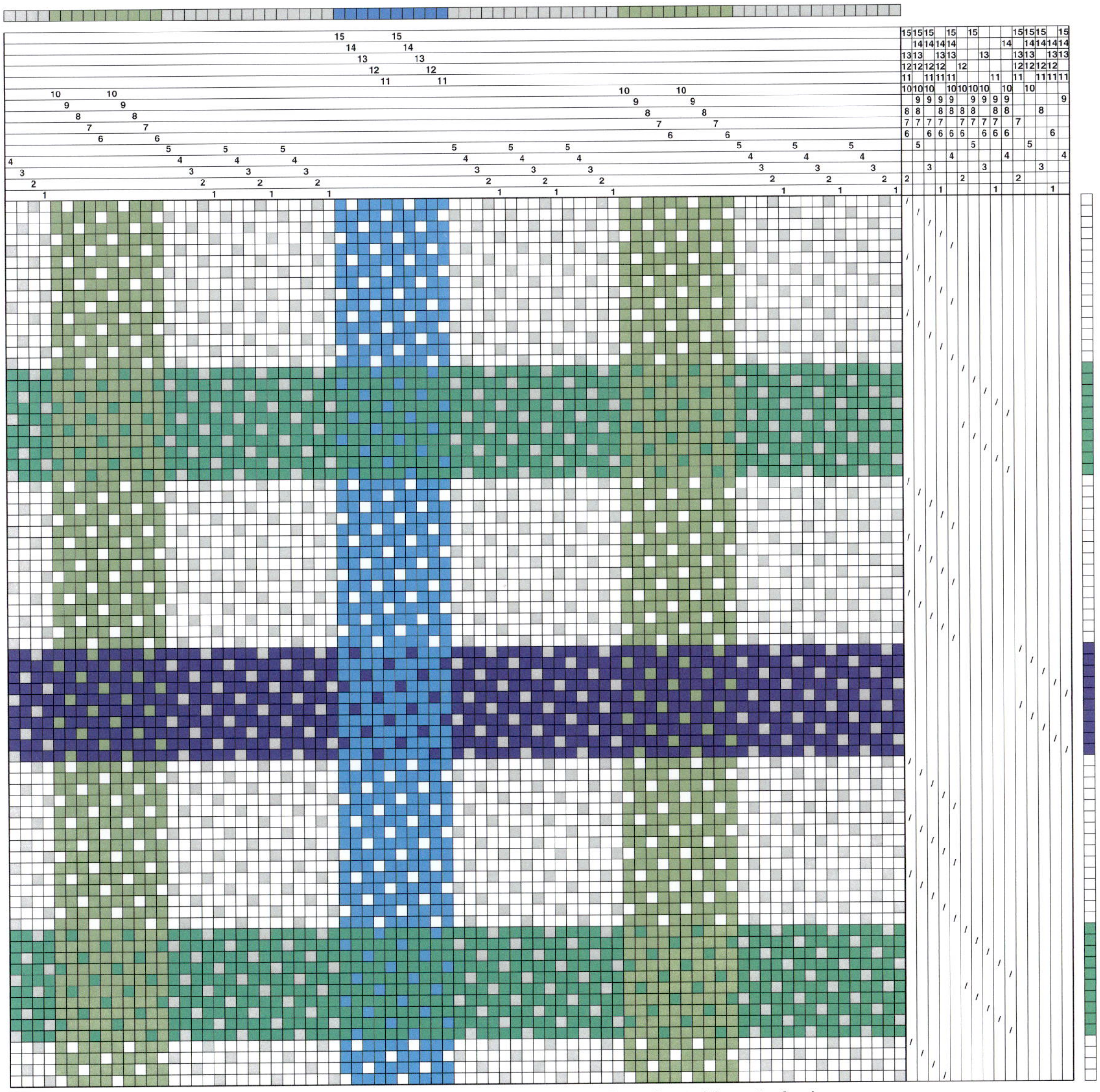

3.12 Three-block damask based on five-shaft satin/sateen. Notice that the "ribbons" of color form a plain-weave-like "interlacement" over the surface of the cloth, like the photo on page 80.

Eight -shaft satin woven of 2/20 worsted wool (each end used singly) for upholstery. The face of the cloth is very smooth and the cloth tailored well.

4

Waffle Weaves
An In-Depth Look

Waffle-weave cloth is one of the most obviously three-dimensional fabrics a handweaver can produce by ordinary loom-controlled means. While it is on the loom under tension, the third dimension is not fully apparent in the cloth. Only after it has been cut from the loom and the threads are free to assume their most stable configuration does the cloth assume the shape that gives it its name. The drafts that are presented in this chapter are all structural drafts and, as such, show which warp ends are up so they cannot hint at the way in which the cloth collapses into a thick, insulating fabric when it is freed from loom tension. In British texts, this structure is called **honeycomb**, a name that North Americans reserve for a different structure.

The structure of waffle-weave cloth is formed by threads that float in both the warp and weft directions, and other threads that are interlaced more frequently, again in both directions. The former lie on the face and back of the cloth while the latter are recessed. Waffle-weave fabrics are of two basic kinds: those that are the same (or nearly the same) on both sides and those with marked depressions on only one side.

Waffle-weave fabrics tend to be bulky because of their structure. This bulk traps a lot of air, making them highly insulating fabrics, very well suited for blankets. The more elastic the yarns are, the deeper the indentations are for a given interlacement. The floats on the surface make these particularly "thirsty" fabrics when woven of absorbent fibers. They are not best suited to uses that put them under a great deal of tension— for example upholstery or cushion fabrics, first, because when they are stretched they flatten out and lose their best feature, their three-dimensionality,

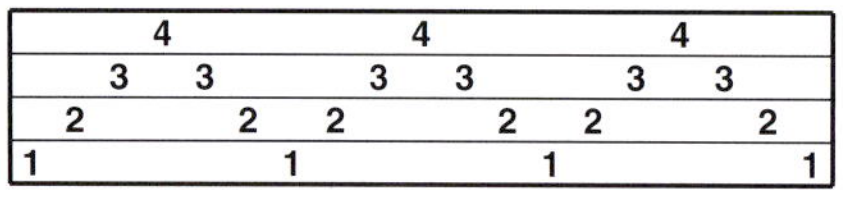

4.1a Threading for a four-shaft waffle weave.

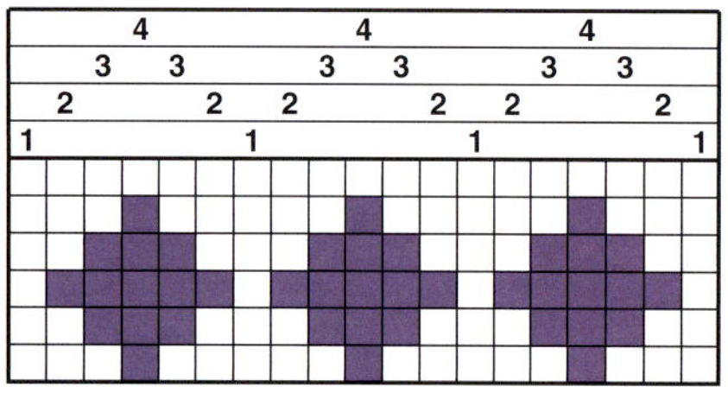

4.1b Four-shaft waffle weave under construction: the diamond shape of warp floats.

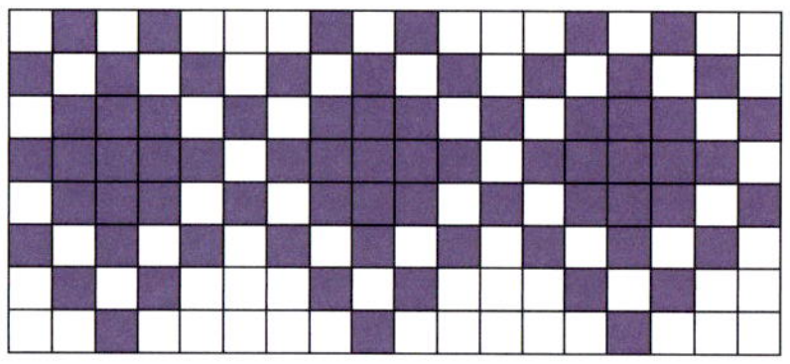

4.1c The structure is stabilized by adding a row of stitchers all around the diamond.

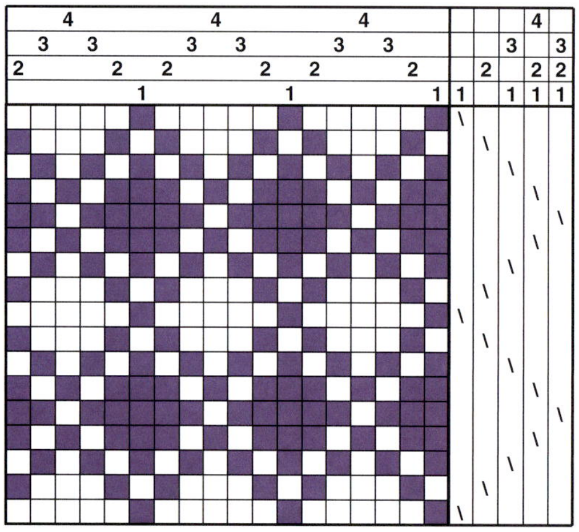

4.1d Waffle weave using four shafts.

and second, because the long floats on the surface have a tendency to snag. (Smooth, slippery yarns snag more easily in any fabric; for that reason, I prefer using yarns with more "tooth" for waffle weaves that will have functional applications.)

Writing a draft for waffle weaves with depressions on both sides is a pretty easy matter. The threading drafts are just like those for symmetrical point twills. Like twills, waffle weaves are based on floats, but they resemble twills in practically no other way. The longest floats in this kind of waffle weave always fall on the same warp ends; they do not move to the left or right as twill floats do.

To write a waffle-weave draft, first decide how many shafts are to be used; four, the smallest number that produces a waffle weave, is a good place to begin. The threading (**4.1a**) begins on shaft 1; one repeat consists of six warp ends.

Next, fill in the cloth diagram. Leave the first weft row empty and then build a diamond shape with its vertical points directly under shaft 4 (**4.1b** This diamond-shaped area of warp floats—there will be a corresponding diamond of weft floats, too—is characteristic of waffle weaves). The structure is stabilized by adding a row of stitchers all around the diamond (**4.1c**). The stitchers are really a little border of plain weave that makes the interface between the warp-float and weft-float diamonds firmer. Note that there are eight picks in one six-end repeat. Now figure out the tie-up and treadling. It is a simple matter to look across the draft and write down which shafts are lifted for any given pick; that information is given in draft **4.1d**.

Examination of **4.1d** shows that the longest floats go over or under five ends or picks. That is an important number, because

Two waffle weaves in 20/2 natural pearl cotton. Seven shafts allowed the option of weaving either a four-shaft waffle weave (in which the longest floats pass over five ends or picks), or a seven-shaft waffle weave (with eleven thread floats).

it has a great deal to do with the depth of the hollows produced in the fabric—the longer the floats, the deeper the depressions in the cloth—and a lot to do with the way the cloth can be used. A five-end or five-pick float is quite short at 30 e.p.i. but would be less than useful for functional fabrics at 6 e.p.i. In general, for a draft constructed this way, *the maximum number of ends in a warp or weft float is twice the number of shafts less three (2n - 3).*

Look at the tie-up. With a little imagination, you can see that the structure of the cloth is evident in the tie-up. The cloth is based on twofold symmetry: that is, it resembles draft **2.18a** (page 52) in that it is meant to be used with a pointed draft and pointed treadling. Place a pair of mirrors at right angles to each other, one across the top of the tie-up and the other at the right-hand edge, and you will see the cloth diagram appear. This is an important concept: for straight and pointed treadlings, taking an educated look at the tie-up in this way can tell you a lot about the cloth.

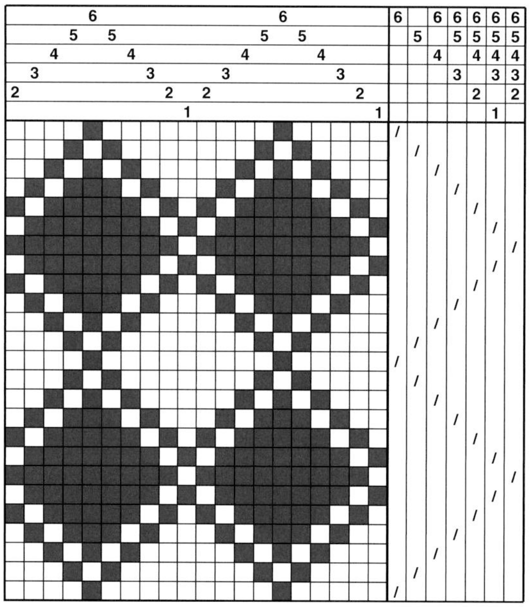

4.2 Draft for six-shaft waffle weave.

The four-shaft draft we have worked out is the simplest but produces the least dramatic effect of any of the waffle weaves. The draft for a six-shaft waffle weave is shown in **4.2**. The longest floats go over or under nine ends or picks. This waffle weave is more dramatic than that on four shafts. The deeper the waffle weave, the more elastic it is. Woven in an elastic fiber such as wool, waffle weaves can be at least as elastic as knitted structures made from the same yarns, and even more elastic on the bias.

These pointed threading drafts are quite versatile. Plain weave may be woven on them at any time. Plain weave at a waffle-weave sett does not collapse when taken from the loom, but the waffle weave does. A plain-weave area woven at the end of a waffle-weave section forms a sort of ruffle when the cloth is taken from the loom. This trait may be used to advantage in designing garments.

Just as plain weave may be combined with waffle weave, several waffle weaves may be combined in one fabric if the draft is chosen carefully. Using a sixteen-shaft waffle-weave threading draft, for example, one may weave a sixteen-shaft waffle (twenty-nine-end or -pick floats, so it will be very dramatic), an eight-shaft waffle weave (thirteen-end or -pick floats), and a four-shaft waffle weave. These combinations are shown in **4.3a**, **4.3b**, and **4.3c**. Instead of showing the usual tie-up and treadling order, **4.4** lists the shafts to be lifted at the side. Such a list is often called a **peg plan** because it shows how the pegs must be inserted into the lags that operate a dobby mechanism. Draft **4.4** shows three waffle structures which may be woven on the same sixteen-shaft threading. Where the floats are the longest, the fabric will be thickest and narrowest.

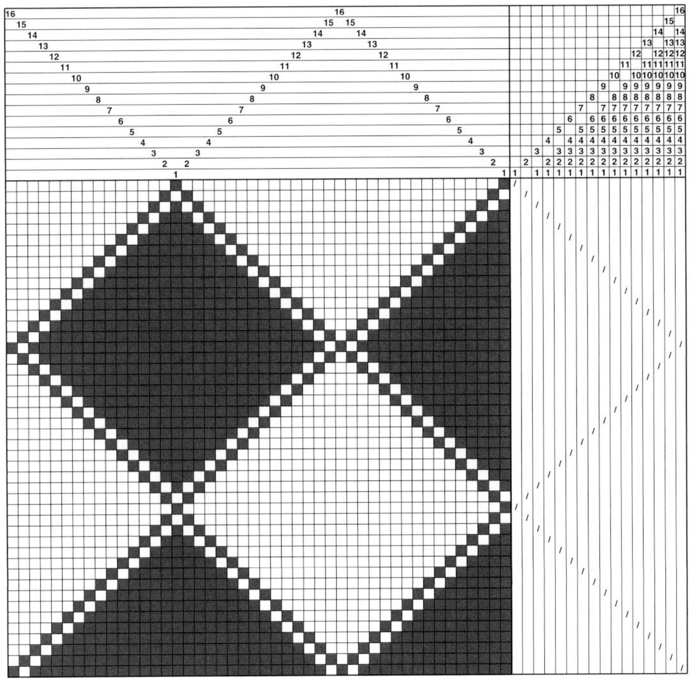

4.3a Sixteen-shaft waffle weave woven on sixteen-shaft point threading. Notice the long floats.

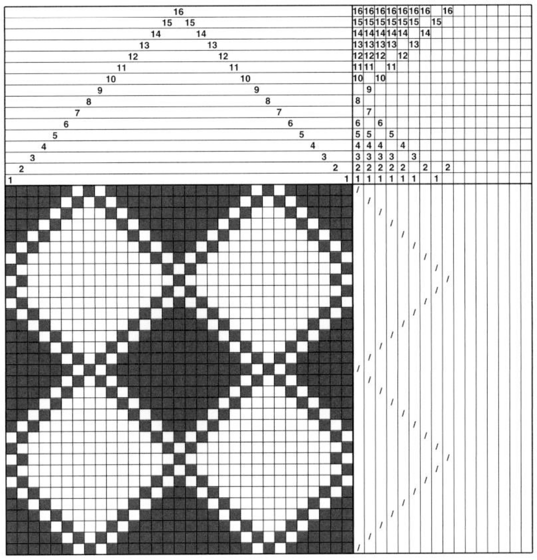

4.3b Eight-shaft waffle weave woven on sixteen-shaft point threading. Notice the long floats.

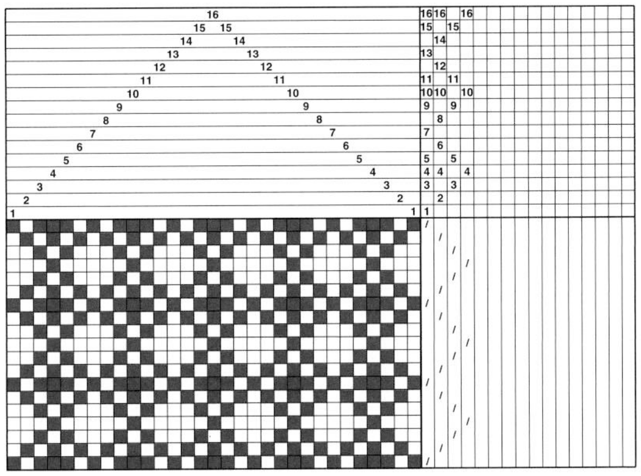

4.3c Four-shaft waffle weave woven on sixteen-shaft point threading.

4.4 Waffle weave on sixteen shafts treadled in three ways.

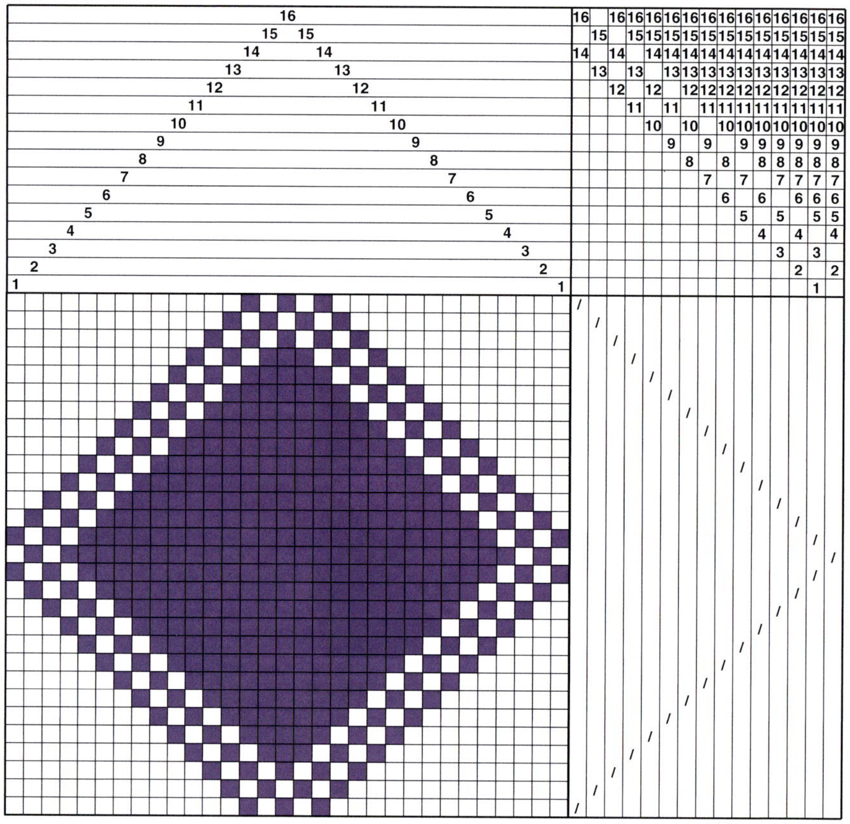

4.5 Sixteen-shaft waffle weave stabilized by double row of plain weave. The longest floats go over/under twenty-five ends/picks. (Still long!)

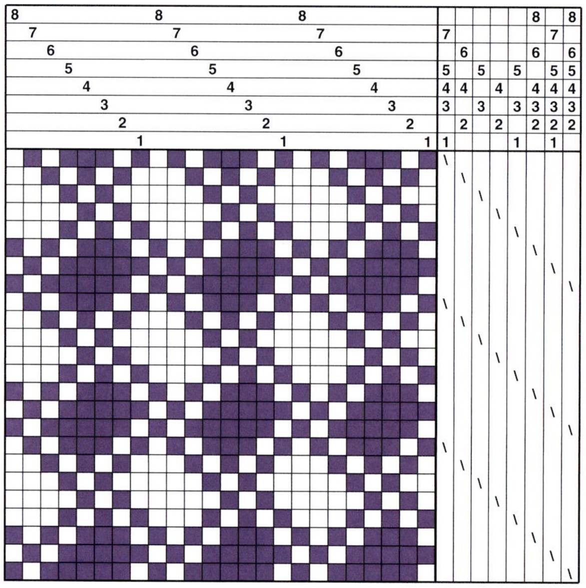

4.6 Eight-shaft waffle weave based on rectangles.

The sixteen-shaft draft with its twenty-nine-end or -pick floats must be set pretty closely, but even with a closer sett, the float length is the weak place in the draft. A sixteen-shaft draft, indeed, any draft of six shafts or more, may be written with a doubled row of stitching to make the cloth firmer. This modified draft is shown in **4.5**.

The above drafts all have floats in a diamond shape. They may also be written so that the floating ends and picks form rectangular shapes, **4.6**. This structure is not symmetrical, however. The threading is a straight draw, and the floats are much shorter (over or under five ends or picks). The waffle thus isn't as dramatic, but it is an interesting variation on the diamonds.

Six-shaft waffle weave. The warps and wefts that float on the face are woolen spun so that they are more secure in the finished cloth. On the back, the blue-violet warps (silk) and wefts (worsted) are not as exposed to snagging, and provide the surprise of a blue-violet dot at the bottom of the depression when viewed from the right side.

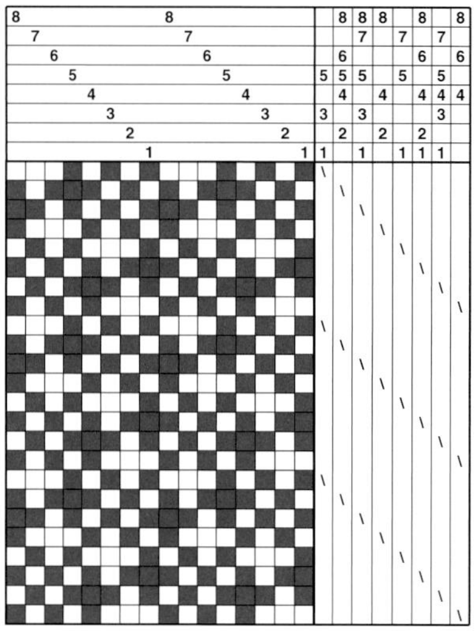

4.7 Eight-shaft Brighton honeycomb. This cloth has small depressions ("cells") on the face, but not on the back of the cloth. The floats are relatively short, just over/under three ends/picks. A minimum of eight shafts are required for Brighton honeycomb. Notice that the diamonds within a repeat are offset from each other. The cloth has a definite diagonal.

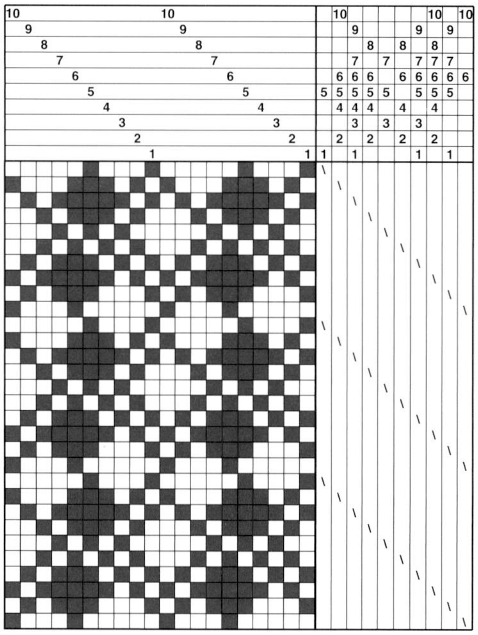

4.8 A Brighton honeycomb on ten shafts, not standard, but interesting.

Brighton honeycomb

The second class of waffle weaves is constructed with depressions that are not lined up. The depressions on the face of the cloth are not matched by equal depressions on the back. This structure is often called **Brighton honeycomb**. The structure is a kind of waffle weave but is generally called by the British name because that is where it originated.

Brighton honeycombs are written on straight-draw threading drafts. The minimum number of shafts on which one may be written is eight. The number of shafts required for a standard Brighton honeycomb is a multiple of four: eight, twelve, sixteen, etc., and one repeat contains the same number of diamonds formed by warp floats as formed by weft floats. See draft **4.7** for an eight shaft Brighton honeycomb.

If ten shafts are used (see the draft in **4.8**), the number of warp-float and weft-float diamonds cannot be equal; in this case, two and three, respectively. This draft is not a standard Brighton honeycomb, since ten is not a multiple of four.

To write a Brighton honeycomb on eight shafts, mark an 8 × 8-square section of graph paper (see page 92). This is the tie-up. Fill in a diagonal of raised warp ends from the lower left to the upper right.

Next, mark a diamond shape of raised warp ends in the upper part of the diagram just to the left of center and another diamond shape in the lower part just to the right of center (on eight shafts, the diamond looks more like a cross). The maximum number of ends in a warp or weft float in a Brighton honeycomb is half the number of shafts less one: (n/2) - 1. Notice that these warp diamonds are offset from each other—they are not lined up. They are adjacent to each other

Brighton honeycomb woven using eight shafts with a very fine woolen singles, violet in the warp and blue in the weft.

with a diagonal of spaces between them and the diagonal you drew first. (*This* requirement *is* met by the ten-shaft example in **4.8**.)

Diamonds of weft floats fit into the draft just over the warp diamond in the lower half and under the diamond in the upper half. Fill in a second pair of warp diamonds—one to the upper left of the weft diamond in the upper half and one to the lower right of the weft diamond in the lower half. Notice that when complete diamonds do not fit into the diagram completely on one side they must be completed by finishing the diamonds on the other side of the diagram. Repeat, forming the weft diamonds. Finally, eliminate any extra weft floats by adding stitching points.

Similar steps have been used to write the draft for Brighton honeycomb using sixteen shafts (**4.9**).

When a sixteen-shaft Brighton honeycomb is woven using a fine woolen yarn, the washed fabric is spongy, stretchy, thick, soft, and very cuddly. It behaves like a knitted rather than woven fabric.

Brighton honeycomb differs from ordinary waffle weaves in that the face and back are not equivalent. The depressions for a given number of shafts are not as deep; it takes eight shafts to weave the simplest Brighton honeycomb, whereas the simplest waffle weave may be woven on four. Why, then, would one weave a Brighton honeycomb when waffle weave is available? Primarily because of its greater visual interest. As in regular waffle weave, the arrangement of warp and weft floats in Brighton honeycomb makes squares, but whereas in a regular waffle weave the cells are arranged directly above one another in a very regular,

Writing Brighton Honeycomb

Here are the steps for writing a Brighton honeycomb on eight shafts. New marks are shown in red. Remember that this structure is threaded in a straight draw and treadled in straight order. What you see here is the tie-up—if it is turned ninety degrees, it will look just like the cloth diagram.

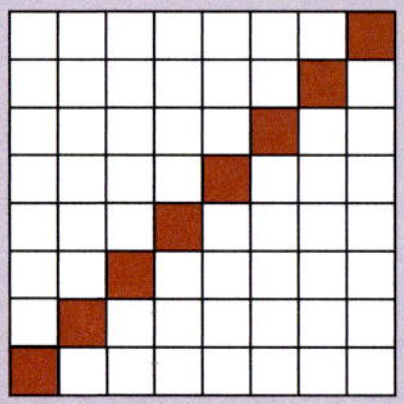

1. Begin by filling in squares along a diagonal from the lower left to the upper right in the 8 × 8 grid.

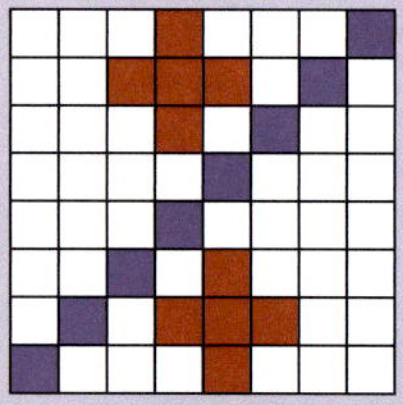

2. Enter two diamonds made by lifting shafts (these are warp diamonds), one to the left and above the diagonal, the other below and to the right.

3. Mark two weft diamonds made by not lifting shafts, one under and to the left of the upper warp diamond, the other above and to the right of the lower one.

4. Add two more warp diamonds (made by lifting shafts), one to the left and above the upper weft diamond, the other to the right and below the lower weft diamond.

5. Add the last two weft diamonds (made by not lifting shafts), and add stitching points to eliminate unwanted floats (so that the only floats are those produced by the warp and weft diamonds).

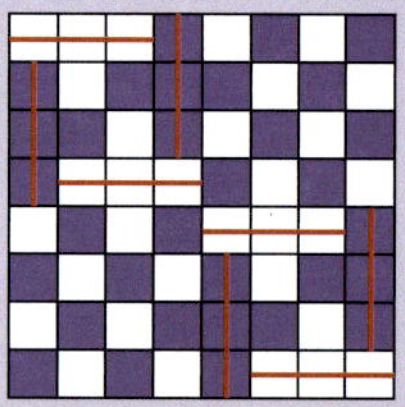

6. The completed tie-up (red lines indicate the positions of the floats in the final fabric). There are four warp diamonds and four weft diamonds. All floats occur on different shafts and with different picks.

***4.9** Sixteen-shaft Brighton honeycomb.*

very square, static-looking array, the cells in Brighton honeycomb are offset so that there is some diagonal movement. The two structures behave similarly; they simply look different. The choice is left to you.

Sponge weaves

Another kind of weave really belongs with the waffle weaves although its construction has a different basis. Few weaving books refer to **sponge weaves**, so called because of the many tiny cells in the surface of the cloth like the surface of a sponge. Unlike ordinary waffle weaves and Brighton structures, whose basis for cell location is the square, the basis for placing the cells in a sponge weave is less regular. Sateen stitching points may be used for their placement. Draft **4.10a** shows the sateen placement (move number 3) for a ten-end, ten-pick sponge weave, and **4.10b** shows the completed draft. Drafts **4.11a** and **4.11b** do the same for fourteen shafts (move number 5).

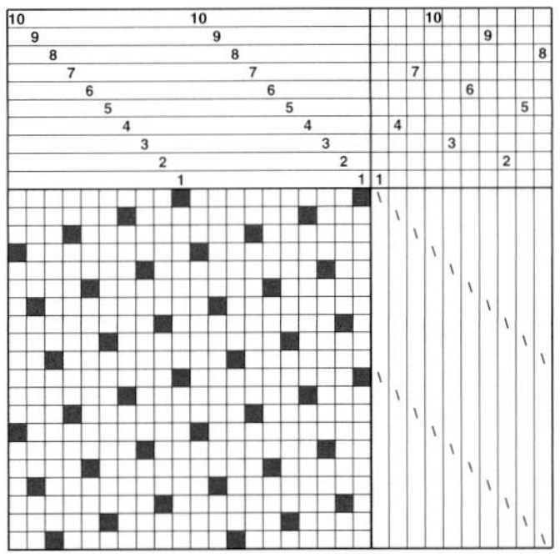

4.10a Ten-end, ten-pick start for a sponge weave. The filled-in squares in the tie-up are placed as in a sateen using move number 3. The remainder is added in 4.10b.

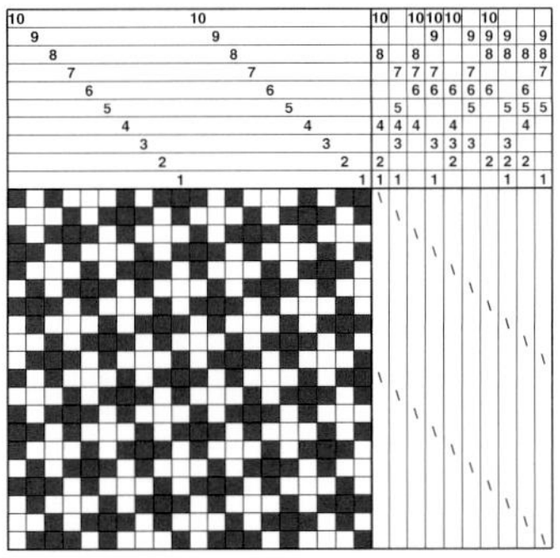

4.10b Ten-end, ten-pick sponge weave. Notice that the points from 4.10a have been formed into little plus signs. When all the warp pluses are marked, the weft pluses automatically appear.

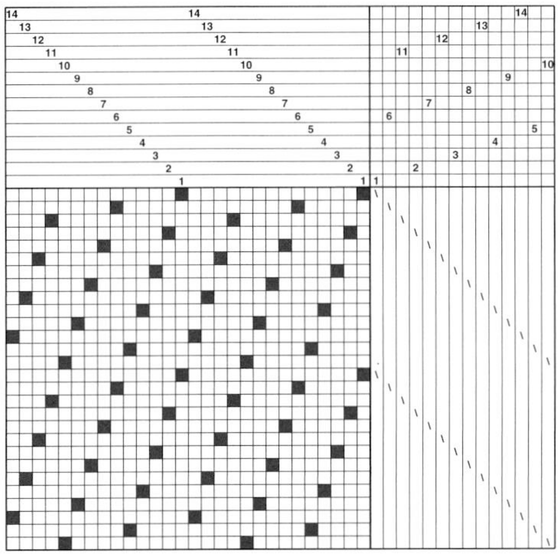

4.11a Fourteen-shaft sponge weave.

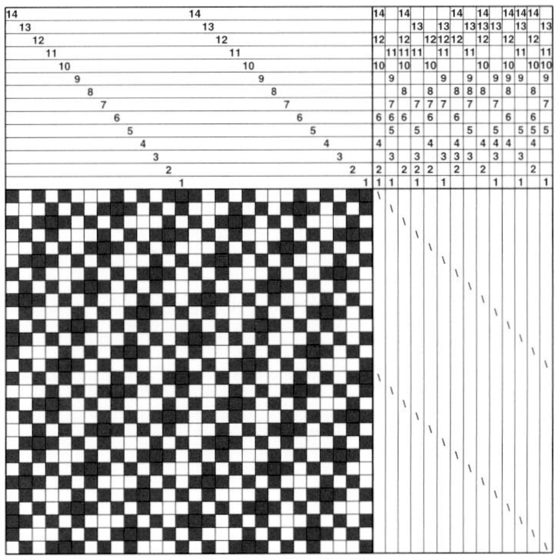

4.11b Fourteen-shaft sponge weave. The sateen stitching points from 4.11a have been turned into warp-faced plus signs and then extra stitchers were added to define the weft-faced plus signs. Notice that they line up in steep diagonals and are not right above each other.

To write the tie-up for sponge weaves, begin with a graph-paper square that has as many units vertically and horizontally as the number of shafts for which you are designing. In both drafts shown here, the cells are three ends wide and three picks high, regardless of whether they are formed of warps or wefts. Notice that when a cell lies up against the side of the square we have drawn for the tie-up, it is completed by finishing the diamond shape just inside the opposite edge. Weft-faced diamonds lie between the warp-faced ones. If lines are drawn to show where the warp and weft floats are, they do not form squares, a characteristic of sponge weaves.

The warp is threaded in a straight draw and treadled in a straight treadling. The cells in this cloth are very, very small, producing a textured surface. Sponge weaves are used mainly to add texture to jacquard constructions. The surface is, however, quite regular, so this is not a **crepe weave**, which will be discussed in Chapter 10 (page 201). Not all sponge weaves are written on a sateen base. In fact, the lack of a single unifying means of arranging the cells characterizes sponge weaves. Draft **4.12** is a six-end, six-pick sponge weave; it was not constructed by use of a move number. Instead, the lower left-hand corner was chosen for the placement of the first little warp diamond; and the next one was placed so that it did *not* line up with the first one, and weft diamonds were sandwiched between. This structure is similar to the three-end huck weaves shown in Chapter 5, The Distorted Grid (page 96). The chief—and very important—difference is that the warp floats are not directly above each other in sponge weave, but they are in huck structures.

Experimentation with pencil and graph paper or computer drafting software yields more examples. Many require more shafts than handweavers have, but those that are feasible are worth considering when you want to make highly textured, relatively thick and spongy cloth.

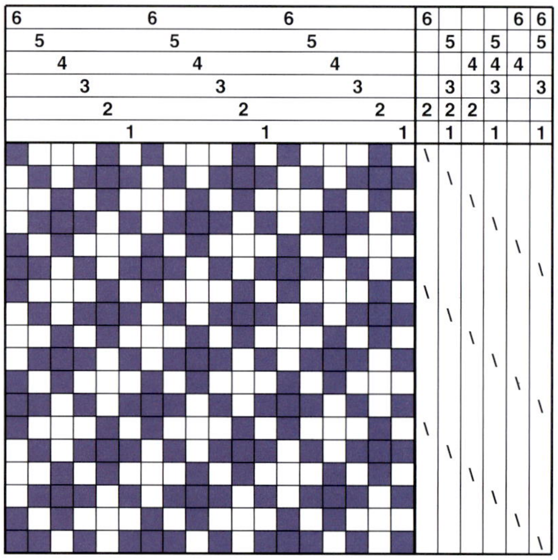

4.12 Six-shaft sponge weave. There is no regular sateen on six shafts (see page 68) so we cannot begin in the usual way. Here the draft was made by entering a straight draw for the threading and a straight treadling first. Then, a 3 × 3 plus sign of warp ends was entered in the lower left corner of the tie-up box followed by another two squares over and two up and then a third two squares over and up (which "wraps"). With those in place, additional stitchers were placed to make an equal number of weft 3 × 3 plus signs. Notice that they appear in diagonal lines.

5

The Distorted Grid

All of the structures discussed so far have been rectilinear or nearly so: the warp and weft lie nearly at right angles, even in undulating twill. That is not the only way that cloth can be constructed. The grid that is formed by the weft crossing the warp may be distorted in a number of ways and to a lesser or greater degree. It is interesting to think of ways to make the warp ends and/or weft picks curve or intersect at other than right angles.

We have already seen how the threads may be forced into curving: when nothing lies between a pair of warp ends or weft picks, they will move together. It is really just as simple as that. We shall see over and over again how this simple fact underlies all structures with deflected warps or wefts. Whenever there are no picks to hold them apart, warp ends will come together. If there are places in the cloth where these ends or picks are first separated and then allowed to fall together, the path they make becomes distorted from the strictly rectilinear grid made by plain weave to form curves.

The smallest distortions occur in a group of weaves that are often used for toweling or linens. The shortest draft is made up of six ends and six picks. Three-pick warp floats alternate with plain-weave areas to form small spots in the cloth. When the floating end is carried on shaft 4, as in **5.1a**, the ends on shaft 3 that bracket it move together. The next three picks, woven plain weave, move those ends apart again. As the ends on shaft 3 are being spread apart by the insertion of wefts between them, the two ends on shaft 1 move together as the end on shaft 2 floats. The distortions are small, particularly when compared with those in structures that follow in this chapter, but there *is* distortion.

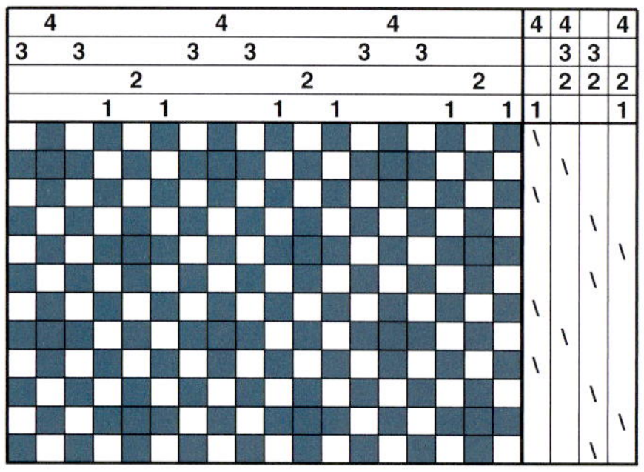

5.1a Three-end huck spot. One side has warp floats, the other weft floats.

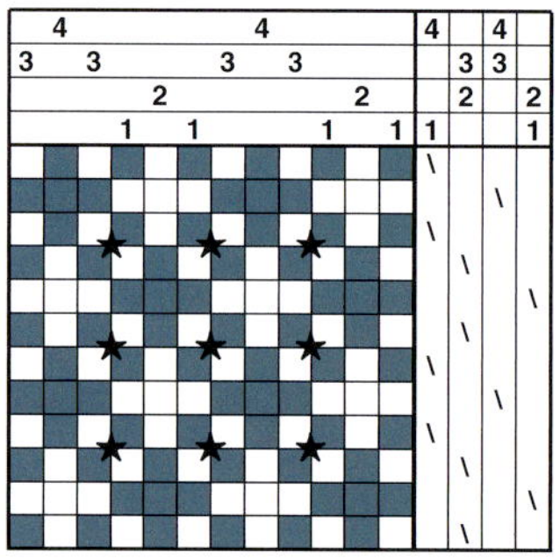

*5.1b A three-end huck lace. Both sides of the cloth have warp and weft floats. The *s show where the openings in the cloth are after it is washed.*

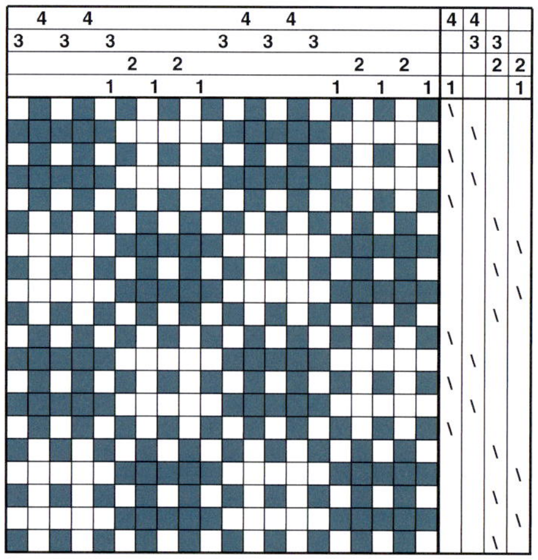

5.1c Five-end huck lace. The repeat is expanded. This draft is like 5.1b but it is based on five rather than three ends and picks.

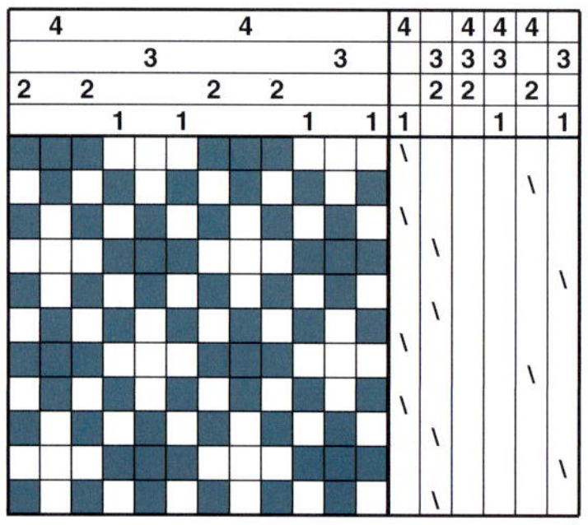

5.2a Huck threading and treadling, which produces the same fabric as 5.1a and 5.1b.

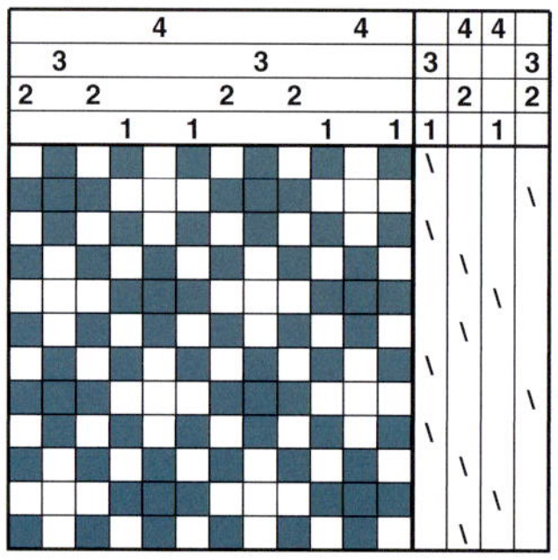

5.2b Another threading for a three-end huck lace.

More distortion may be obtained on the same threading if the treadling is changed so that warp floats alternate with weft floats. The ends carried on shafts 2 and 4 weave three up, three down in the cloth (**5.1b**).

Notice that ends carried on shafts 1 and 3 fall next to each other in the cloth. Those ends are always forced apart because they weave in an opposite way: when one is up, the other is down and vice versa. The third and fourth picks are forced apart in exactly the same way. Sleying the first three ends together in one dent and the second three ends in another may dramatize this structure. In structure **5.1b**, perforations appear in the cloth at the points indicated with *s. The threads making up structure **5.1b** are not deflected as much as those in **5.1a** because there are no plain-weave areas to force ends apart after they have moved together.

The structures shown in **5.1a** and **5.1b** are related to **huckaback**, or **huck** (the nickname for huckaback, and much more commonly used). These structures are based on plain weave with short floats which do not line up (or move diagonally, as twill does) to form ribs. Fabrics woven in huck, particularly those woven using smooth, plain yarns made of linen or firmly twisted cotton, are very lovely. The plain-weave areas nestled between the pattern areas curve outward to form beautiful ovals in the washed cloth, distorting the grid in a very graceful way.

The simplest huck has two alternating blocks: plain weave alternating with a block containing a figure made up of warp floats. In writing a huck draft, it is the structure that is important, not the draft. The draft may be derived from the structure. There are many ways that huck drafts are written in the literature (**5.1b**, **5.2a**, and **5.2b**), but

The two bottom fabrics have rectangles of three-end huck lace surrounded by plain weave. The third cloth from the bottom consists of stripes of five-end huck lace in a plain-weave ground. The three are woven on four shafts in 20/2 cotton. The top fabric, woven of 16/2 cotton, has diagonal stripes of three units of three-end huck, which required eight shafts.

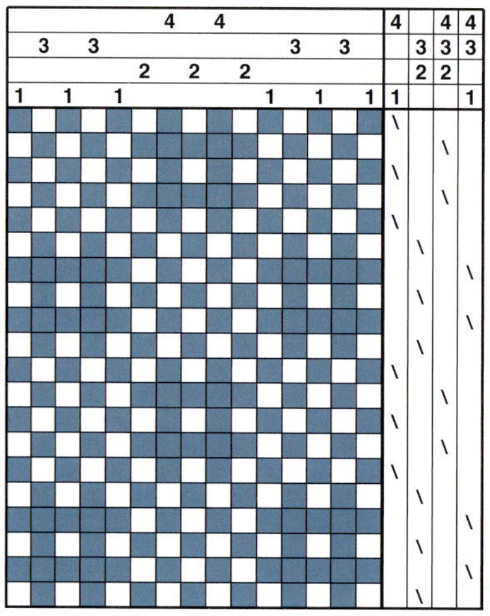

5.3a *Five-end huck spot. The form the draft has taken here is the one I prefer because it allows easy and obvious expansion to more than four shafts.*

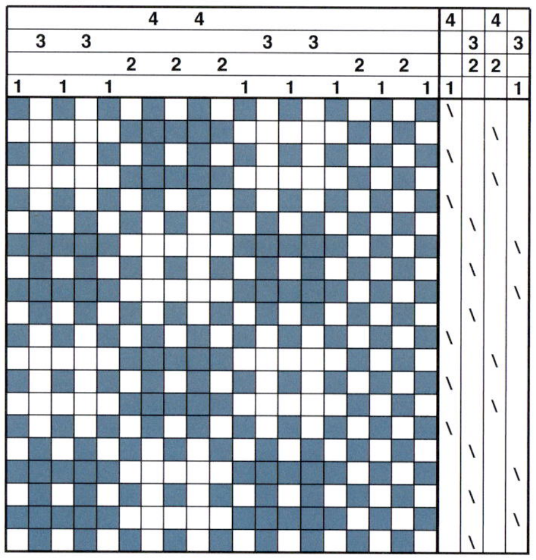

5.3b *Five-end huck lace. Both warp and weft floats appear on both sides of the cloth. At the right (the beginning) of the threading shafts 1 and 2 alternate to permit a plain-weave selvedge.*

all of them yield the same structure. *It really doesn't matter which threading draft is used so long as the shafts are lifted in the order required to produce the cloth shown.*

The structure of huck is based on warp floats in each block (note that there can be one, two, or seven ends that float in a unit) separated by ends that interlace in plain weave. Huck is written in blocks; a five-end huck (**5.3a**) is one in which the block is made up of five ends. Two ends float sometimes and three ends weave only plain weave, forming one block, arranged plain/float/plain/float/plain. In the second block, B, the ends are arranged in the same way except that the plain-weaving ends in block B are up when those in A are down and vice versa. If there is a C block, the plain-weaving ends weave the same as those in the A block; in D, the plain-weave ends weave as in B. Because the plain-weaving ends in alternating blocks must alternate, blocks A and C may not be side by side.

Once it is understood what the basic unit is and what happens in the cloth, a huck draft for more than two blocks is very easy to understand and to write. For a five-end huck, the three plain-weave ends in block A are all carried on the same shaft; those in block B are also threaded on one shaft but not the same one.

When we think of huck woven on more than two blocks, it is simplest to write the huck draft in the form (**5.3a** and **5.3b**); the ends that weave plain weave all the time are, in this scheme, always carried on shafts 1 and 2. Those that float sometimes are carried on shafts 3 and up; those shafts may be thought of as pattern shafts. This method of writing huck drafts is not standard (in fact with such a variety of threading drafts there can hardly be said to be a standard), but it

This cloth is a combination of huck spots and huck lace. An eight-shaft design, its 20/2 pearl cotton cobalt warp and deep turquoise weft are meant to approximate the color of indigo-dyed cotton.

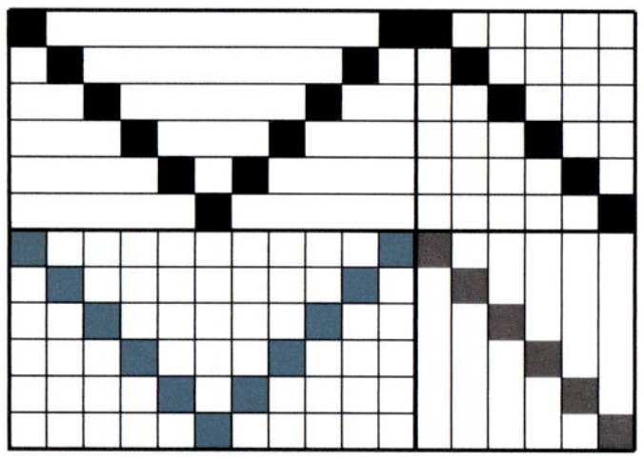

5.4a Profile draft for six blocks where the units are threaded:

A = 1, 3, 1, 3

B = 2, 4, 2, 4, 2

C = 1, 5, 1, 5, 1

D = 2, 6, 2, 6, 2

E = 1, 7, 1, 7, 1

F = 2, 8, 2, 8, 2

makes sense, particularly in light of the way it may be applied to structures using more than four shafts.

This way of writing the basic huck draft makes it clear that for a given number of blocks, n, we need n + 2 shafts: n pattern shafts plus two for the plain-weave ends. Drafts **5.4a** and **5.4b** show the profile and structural drafts for a six-block huck requiring eight shafts.

Notice that in the plain-weave sections of **5.4b**, an unblemished plain weave is maintained everywhere. If block A were followed in the threading by block C, that could not happen; then 1, 3, 1, 3, 1 would be followed by 1, 5, 1, 5, 1. It is essential that the shafts bearing the ends that always weave plain weave alternate from block to block.

When weaving an eight-shaft huck spot like **5.4b**, blocks may be combined in the weaving. That is, blocks A and C may be woven in pattern at the same time, or A, C, and E; or C and E; or B and D; or B, D, and F; or D and F. Blocks A and B may not be woven at the same time. In the first place, the weft floats on the reverse would be ten ends long—too long for fabrics. Second, even if the long floats were acceptable, it is impossible to weave A and B at the same time: when block A is woven in pattern, shaft 1 is raised and 2 is down; when B is woven in pattern, shaft 2 is raised and 1 is down. This contradiction is a very effective deterrent.

Attempts to circumvent this problem do not succeed. Changing the threading so that

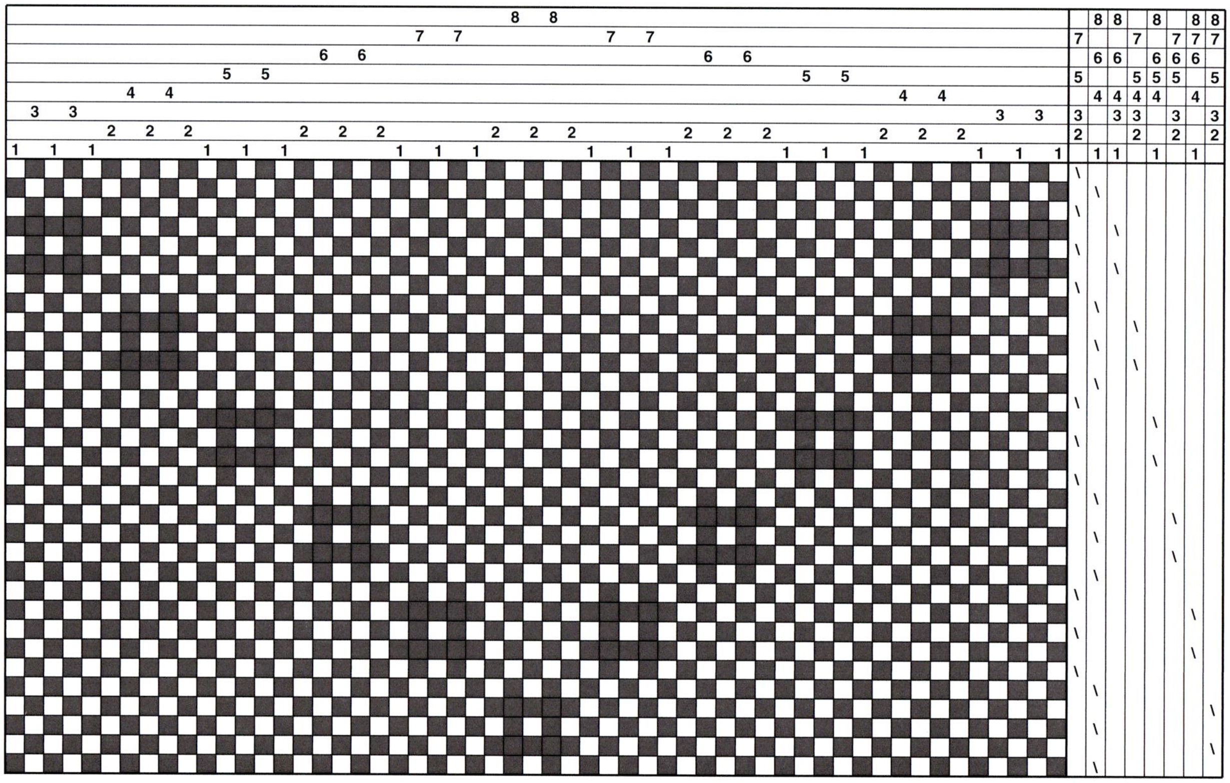

5.4b This is the structural draft for 5.4a.

a block is threaded by pairing the "wrong" plain-weave shaft with a pattern shaft, for example, 2, 3, 2, 3, 2, results in a very peculiar cloth—interesting in its own way, but not huck structure (see **5.5**). The bogus block contains areas of little interlacement between warp and weft. In these areas, the ends and picks will rearrange themselves in the washed cloth, producing gross distortions.

In a nutshell, adjacent blocks use different plain-weave shafts and thus may not be woven pattern at the same time. Blocks that are not adjacent and that use different plain-weave shafts may not be woven together either. Blocks in which the plain-weave shafts are the same may be combined; in any case, they will not be threaded adjacent to each other.

The face with warp floats is generally regarded as the right side for huck spot. Simple huck figures may be enlarged without

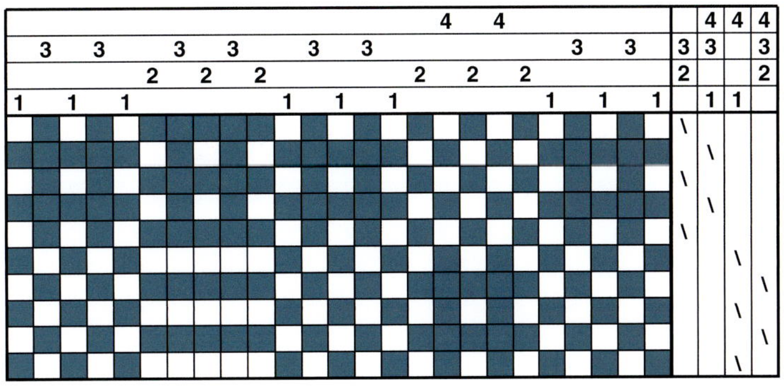

5.5 Pairing a pattern shaft with the "wrong" plain-weave shaft changes the cloth, creating neither plain weave nor huck spots in the affected area.

A sixteen-shaft huck lace woven of 20/2 unmercerized cotton. The cloth has a friendly, velvety feel.

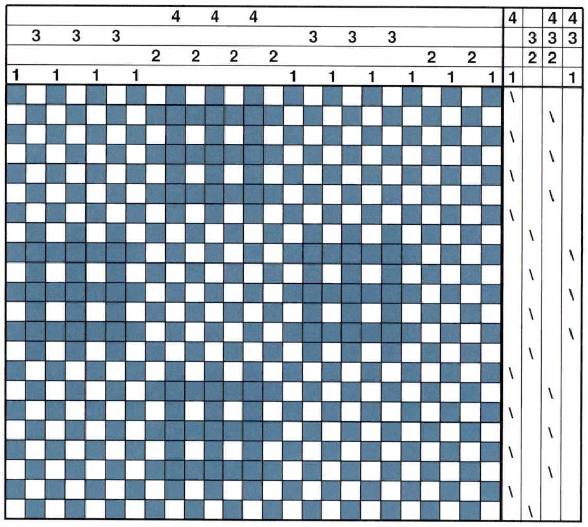

5.6 *A seven-end huck spot. In theory, huck lace can be expanded on and on, but seven-end and -pick floats are about the limit of what I consider prudent. Even so, unless a seven-end huck is woven in very fine threads—where it is dramatic—the floats can snag and the cloth become too unstable for most practical applications.*

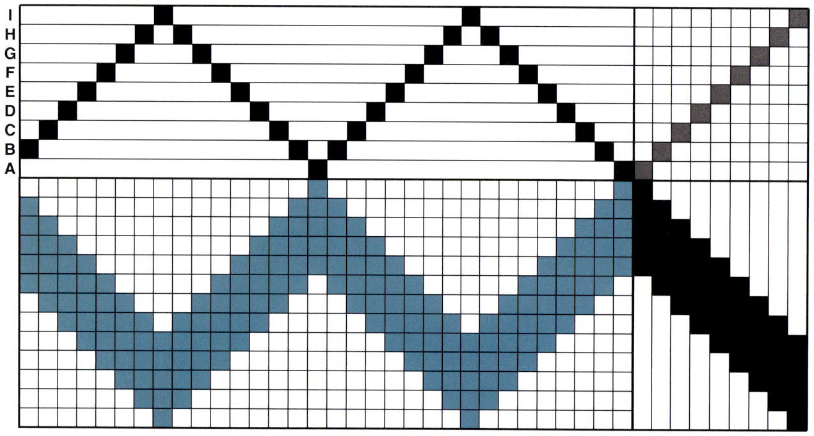

5.7a *Profile draft for a three-end, nine-block huck lace. Two threading repeats are shown and a single repeat of the profile draft development (the order, combinations, and how long each block is woven).*

A = 1, 3, 1	*D = 2, 6, 2*	*G = 1, 9, 1*
B = 2, 4, 2	*E = 1, 7, 1*	*H = 2, 10, 2*
C = 1, 5, 1	*F = 2, 8, 2*	*I = 1, 11, 1*

increasing the number of shafts required, as shown in **5.6**. Simple huck may be increased in this way until the floats become too long for practicality. The floats in **5.6** are seven picks long as opposed to five picks in the preceding drafts. Very fine yarns woven in close setts may be used to create even larger blocks in which float length is not a problem. As the floats become longer, however, the cloth becomes less stable. It is the plain-weave areas that keep it firm and maintain its integrity.

Huck woven without special threading for the selvedges produces irregular edges because the outer ends are not engaged by every shot. Weaving plain-weave selvedges is a solution. For huck threadings following the form shown in **5.3a** and **5.3b**, the selvedge/border threading is 1, 2, 1, 2 until the selvedge or border is the desired width.

Huck is often woven with a border of plain weave on all four sides of the cloth. The plain-weave selvedges are strong, serviceable, and handsome. Plain weave all the way across the cloth at either end balances that in the selvedges and enhances the formality inherent in many huck designs. Plain weave may be woven all the way across the cloth at any time simply by alternating the shed in which shafts 1, 4 (6, 8, 10, 12, etc.) are lifted with that in which 2, 3 (5, 7, 9, 11, etc.) are lifted. There is something very reassuring to the designer about the possibility of weaving plain weave at any time, because it increases the ways in which a particular structure may be employed. Not all weave structures permit plain-weave interlacement everywhere at the same time, as we shall see.

In a huck lace, the floats do not all go in one direction because very long floats would be created that way. Instead, when a block is repeated in the treadling, it alternates

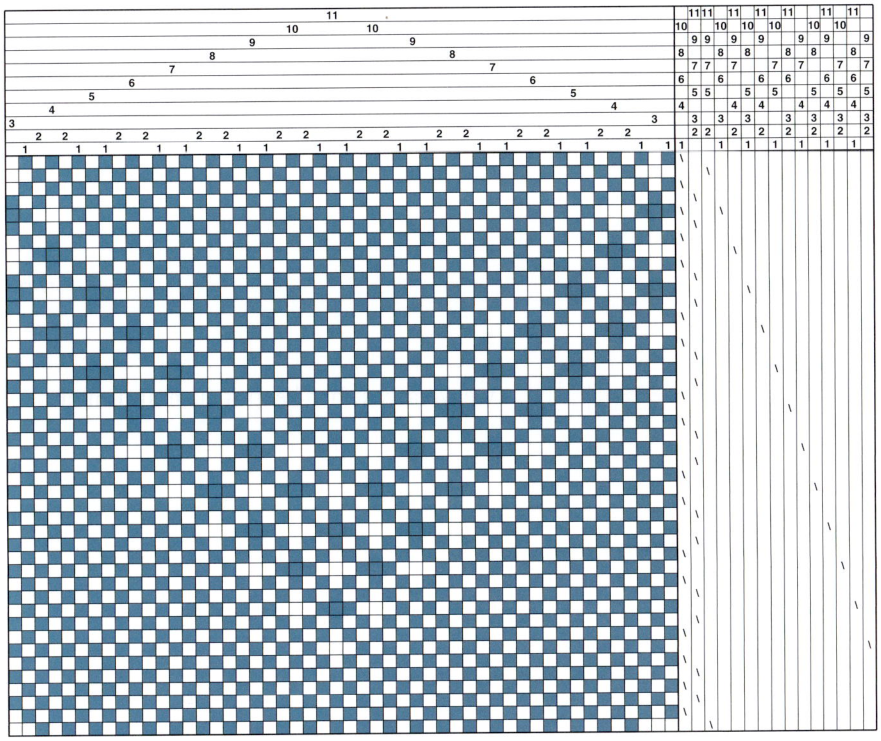

5.7b Here is the structural draft for the profile draft shown in 5.7a. It is a three-end huck lace consisting of nine blocks.

between warp and weft floats. Draft **5.7a** shows two repeats of the profile draft and one repeat of a profile-draft development for a nine-block huck lace. In the profile-draft developments, each block is treadled five times, shifting from warp floats to weft floats and back until all the repeats are woven. Draft **5.8b** shows the thread-by-thread account of what happens in the cloth when a portion of this profile draft is woven in a three-end huck. (Remember that a profile draft shows only the number of units and their order with respect to each other; it says nothing about the specific threading or even the interlacement until the units are defined by a key.)

I have never seen mill-woven multishaft huck fabrics. I have seen huck combined with other structures so that more than four shafts were required to weave the cloth but not huck woven with four or more blocks. Weavers ought to be aware of the structures that they can produce on handlooms that aren't done—or cannot be done—on power looms. It is in these instances that we can feel the power of our craft.

Mock Leno and Canvas Weave

A couple of structures closely related to huck are woven frequently enough to have acquired names of their own; the first of these is **mock leno**.

Leno is the name given to the structure made when the weft is passed between warp ends or groups of ends that have been twisted around each other before the shed is made. Sometimes warp ends in leno structures act singly, sometimes in pairs, sometimes in threes, or one against two, etc., but the twist is always present. This interlacement produces a very open, very stable cloth. The open places in the fabric cannot be shifted, so although the cloth is very open and may be quite sheer depending on the yarns used, it does not sag

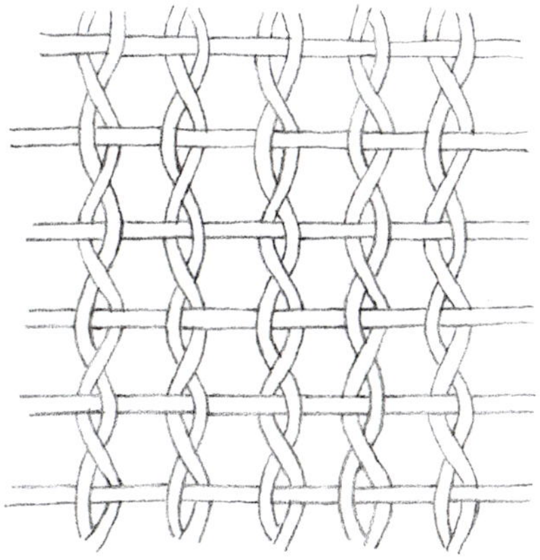

True leno.

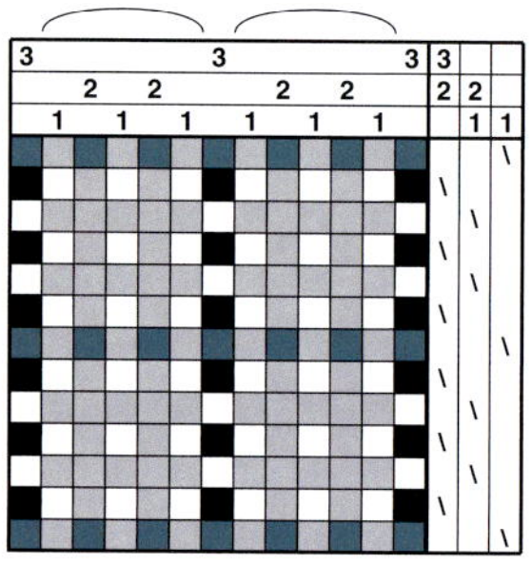

5.8 A mock leno requiring just three shafts. The dark threads in the warp and weft weave plain weave everywhere.

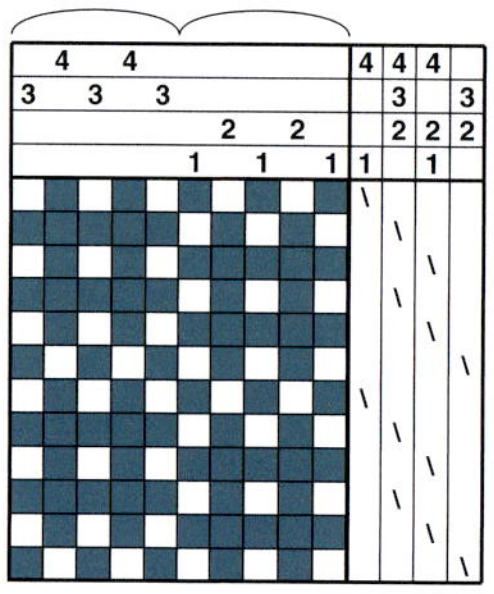

5.9 Another mock leno. Ends carried on 1 and 3 weave plain weave all the time. The weft floats (on the back) are offset to keep them from floating all the time.

Canvas weave (draft 5.10) woven of 36/2 unmercerized Egyptian cotton, then cross-stitched with DMC embroidery floss.

or slip in use. This sort of structure is particularly effective when viewed with light passing through it, as in a screen or curtain fabric perhaps. It sounds like a wonderful structure, and it is, but it requires special preparation or hand manipulation to weave.

An approximation of leno called mock leno may, however, be woven simply and easily in a hucklike structure. The warp ends are not twisted around each other, and the fabric is not as sheer or quite as stable, but it is very fast and easy to weave. Drafts **5.8** and**5.9** are the structural drafts for a mock leno. An examination of the cloth diagram reveals that there is no true plain weave in this structure—although plain weave could easily be woven using the mock-leno threading—so there is actually very little distortion of the grid. The structure is enhanced by grouping the ends in the reed to open up the cloth (shown by ⌒).

Canvas weave is another hucklike structure that handweavers find useful for producing airy fabrics. Canvas weave, **5.10**, is not the structure of artist's canvas nor that of tents and awnings but rather that of the needleworker's canvas. (Think of it: you could

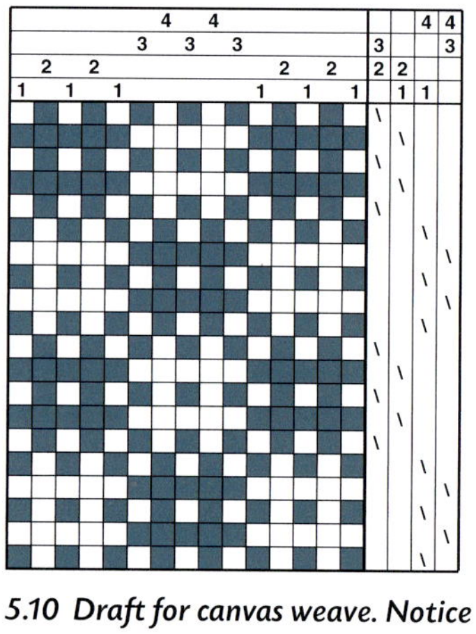

5.10 Draft for canvas weave. Notice that the threading is like 5.9, and is structurally identical to 5.3b (except for the plain weave selvedge, which would be threaded 1, 3, 1, 3 here).

The bottom fabric has little squares of three-end huck lace. The top one has groups of four small squares woven in Bronson lace. Both fabrics are woven of 20/2 pearl cotton on four shafts.

weave your own needlepoint canvas if you wished!) It is often used in summer shirts because its many open places—where the needle goes when working needlepoint—allow air to pass through it so that the wearer can take advantage of every breeze and still be modestly dressed. Note that because warp-float areas alternate with weft-float areas, the cloth is reversible; the faces look the same.

The literature, it must be noted, shows disagreement about the naming of canvas weave and mock leno. One author calls **5.10** mock leno; others consider it a variation of huck.

Swedish Lace

Another set of structures that show distortion of weft and/or warp are the lace weaves, including **Swedish lace** and the **Bronson spots** and **Bronson laces**. We shall first consider Swedish lace, the most restricted of the three.

Swedish lace weave is said to be very, very old. Marguerite Davison reports in *A Handweaver's Pattern Book* that a fragment of cloth woven in this structure "was found in the marshes" in Sweden dating from the time of the Vikings. The distortion of the warp and weft in this handsome structure results from not interlacing some of the threads from time to time so that the ends/picks slide together. As is the case with the huck family of structures, the effect is emphasized by the use of smooth, plain, and particularly hard-twisted yarns and by washing the fabric. The manipulation involved in the washing process allows the threads to come to the most stable configuration: threads not held apart come together. It happens every time. Soft woolen yarns may be used to make warm and cuddly shawls, scarves, and blankets. The structure of the cloth is somewhat blurred when those yarns are used, but the results are still lovely.

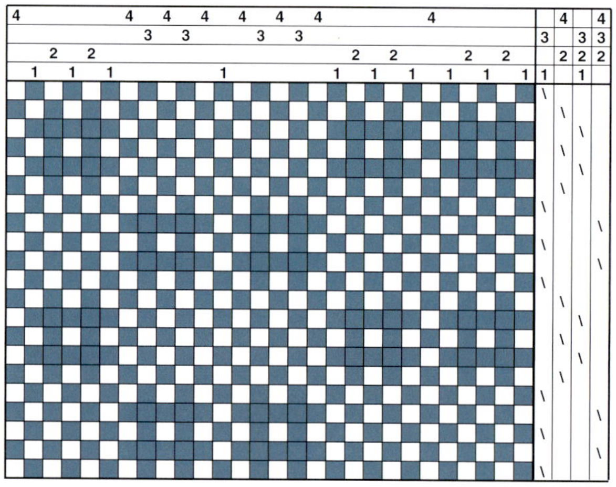

5.11 Draft for Swedish lace.

This structure, like most in this chapter, is woven classically using the same yarn for both warp and weft and a single color, usually light, throughout. The use of different colors for warp and weft attracts attention away from the structure and, depending on the color choices, may produce a chaotic-looking cloth. Generally, the higher the contrast in value, the more confusing the effect is.

Swedish lace requires four shafts. The length of the floats is well defined by the threading unit. Draft **5.11** shows a classic Swedish lace draft. Notice that the ends carried on shafts 1 and 4 weave plain weave everywhere. Within block A, five threads, alternating shafts 1 and 2 (starting and ending on 1), are followed by an end carried on 4 (1, 2, 1, 2, 1, 4). This end defines the float length by breaking it. Frequently, there are three repeats of this figure before the second block, B, is written or threaded. Block B is made up of units threaded 4, 3, 4, 3, 4, 1. In this unit, the end carried on 1 breaks or ties the floats. When these units are used side by side, the end that breaks the last float of block A is omitted because the first thread of block B unit is on that shaft. Likewise, the last end of B is the first end of A. Some ends have a dual role: the final end of block A is the initial end of block B. This sharing of a common end is one of the things that sets Swedish lace apart from Bronson lace, which follows.

Generally, the side with the warp floats is regarded as the right side. The reverse has weft floats. Both faces of the fabric are equally serviceable, and so Swedish lace weaves are useful for fabrics, both sides of which will be seen in use: towels, scarves, shawls, blankets, curtains.

Once I understand a threading system, I look at it with an eye toward adapting it for use on more than four shafts. (That is always a good exercise; it reveals a lot about how the system works so that I can get inside it and see how to manipulate it into doing what I want it to do. Recommended!) Look again at **5.11**. Notice that the draft has the form 1, x, 1, x,1, 4, repeat and 4, y, 4, y, 4, 1, repeat. What would happen if the form were changed to 1, x, 1, x, 1, 4 and 1, y, 1, y, 1, 4? Or, to rearrange it further, 1, x,1, x, 1, 2 and 1, y, 1, y, 1, 2?

When the treadling has been altered to reflect the threading changes, another, similar structure is produced: Bronson lace.

Bronson lace

Like Swedish lace weave, Bronson lace is constructed with warp floats on one side and weft floats on the other. Like Swedish lace weave, within a block, every other end weaves plain weave throughout the cloth. Bronson lace may be adapted to more than four shafts. The form for the draft given above (1, x, 1, x, 1, 2, and 1, y, 1, y, 1, 2) may be extended until the weaver runs out of shafts. The ends carried by shaft 1 weave plain weave throughout the cloth. The ends carried by shaft 2 also weave plain weave (the opposite shed to those on shaft 1) and tie down or break the floats in the fabric. Because these ends are carried on a shaft of their own, they are not shared between blocks as those in Swedish lace are. Compare the cloth diagrams in **5.11** and **5.12**. Notice that an extra plain-weaving end lies between the blocks in Bronson lace; read down from the top of the diagram.

The *form* of the draft (1, x, 1, x, 1, 2 and 1, y, 1, y, 1, 2) indicated just two other shafts, the one called "x" and the one called "y." In fact, the only limit on the number of blocks available is the number of shafts on the loom. Two shafts are used for the plain-weaving ends and the float tie-down; the rest (n - 2) can be used to make the lace blocks. For example, if eight shafts are available, six may be used for lace blocks; six blocks may be woven. The number of blocks possible is always two less than the number of shafts.

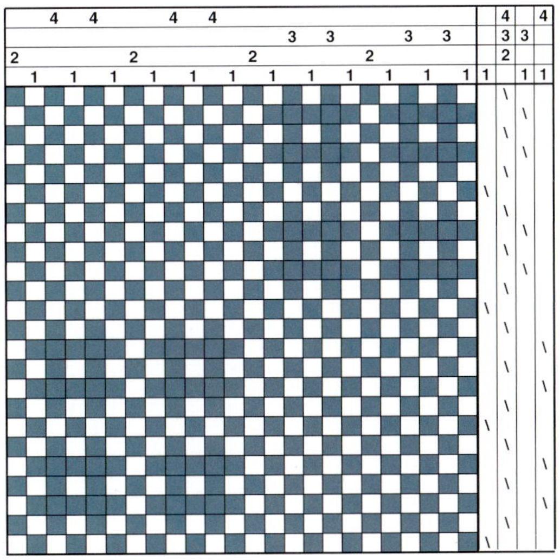

5.12 Draft for two-block Bronson lace. Notice that between each unit of lace there is a thread that weaves plain weave only. Carried on shaft 2, this end cuts the floats and is one of the principal differences between Bronson lace and Swedish lace.

If at least two repeats of a given unit are used to make a block (and at least two repeats of the treadling unit are woven), then little "windows" open up in the fabric after washing, producing a very airy, lacy cloth. In the middle of these windows, a warp end and a weft pick cross each other at right angles like the muntins between the panes of a four-paned window.

If one unit of this threading form is used per block, spots are formed in the fabric. We call this structure Bronson spot or simply spot weave. The effect of spot weave is very dainty, and, of course, it may be combined with Bronson lace if desired.

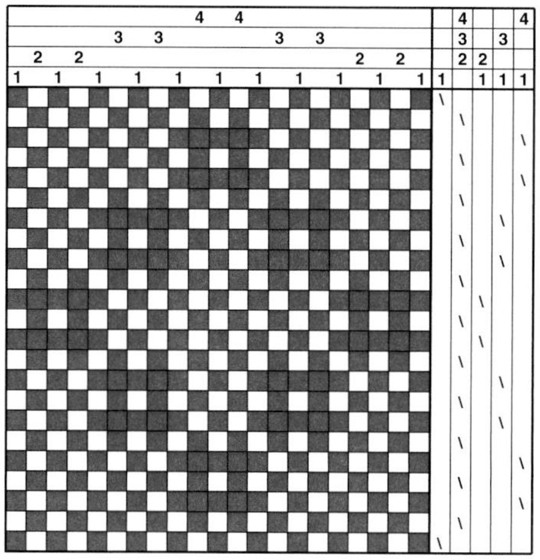

5.13 Spot Bronson. Three blocks are possible on four shafts. They may be threaded in any order. The "spots" share a common thread: 1.

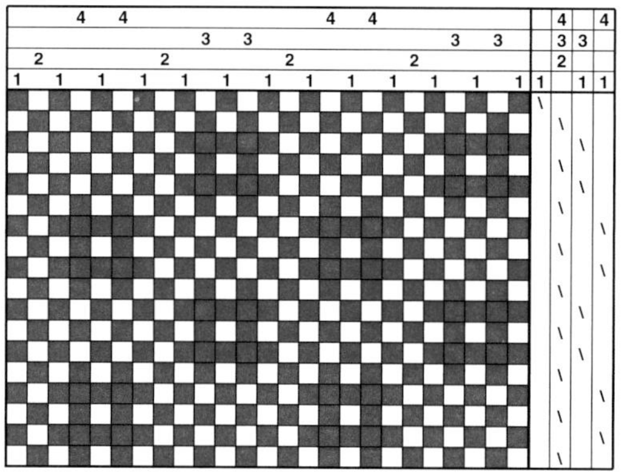

5.14 Spots woven on a Bronson lace threading. The first two treadles weave plain weave.

Spots may be made in a number of ways. A Bronson spot weave is more limited than Bronson lace in that the blocks may not be extended beyond a certain number of ends in order to avoid long floats which threaten the integrity of the cloth. Draft **5.13** is a four-shaft, three-block draft for Bronson spot. (Note that it is possible to weave plain weave all across the cloth.) The unit that makes up block A is threaded 1, 2, 1, 2, 1; the unit making block B is 1, 3, 1, 3, 1; and the unit for block C is 1, 4, 1, 4, 1. Because the units all begin and end on the same shaft, they share common threads as Swedish lace does. The side with warp floats is generally considered the face of the fabric, although the side with weft floats is also very handsome. Warp and weft floats do not appear on the same side in classic Bronson lace.

If Bronson lace is threaded and woven with a single unit and one treadling repeat per block, the appearance is quite similar to **5.14** except that there are no threads held in common (as in **5.13**) and, in fact, the blocks have a thread between them. The results are different; it is up to you to decide which is most suitable.

Do not overlook the fact that Bronson lace requires two shafts in addition to a shaft for each block (n + 2); Bronson spot requires one shaft plus a shaft for each block (n + 1). If you have four shafts, therefore, Bronson spot permits three blocks compared to just two for Bronson lace. On the other hand, Bronson lace may be woven lace in both blocks at once if you like.

The fabric at top is 40/2 ramie cotton woven in ovals of eight-shaft Bronson lace (two ovals in a half-drop arrangement). Below it is 16/2 linen woven in a two-block Bronson lace using four shafts.

The pink/coral fabrics at right are 20/2 pearl cotton threaded on four shafts, one unit of A, then one of B. The cloth on the left was woven to make spots, the one on the right to make an overall lace pattern.

Honeycomb

Honeycomb is the undulating weft (or warp) structure perhaps best known by handweavers in this country. Honeycomb cloth resembles its namesake in that there are little cells, depressions in the cloth, just as there were in waffle weaves, but the threads that outline those cells curve around them instead of remaining rectilinear, as those in waffle weave do.

In honeycomb, small areas woven closely in plain weave alternate across the cloth with areas where no interlacement at all has taken place. In these latter areas, the weft floats on what we regard as the back of the fabric. When one set of these has been woven (two blocks are possible on four shafts), two shots of plain weave are woven all across the cloth, weaving in all blocks. These plain-weave shots are followed by plain weave in one of the other blocks, followed by two shots of plain weave again.

A two-block draft for a modest honeycomb is given in **5.15**. The blocks are just six ends long, and blocks A and B are equal.

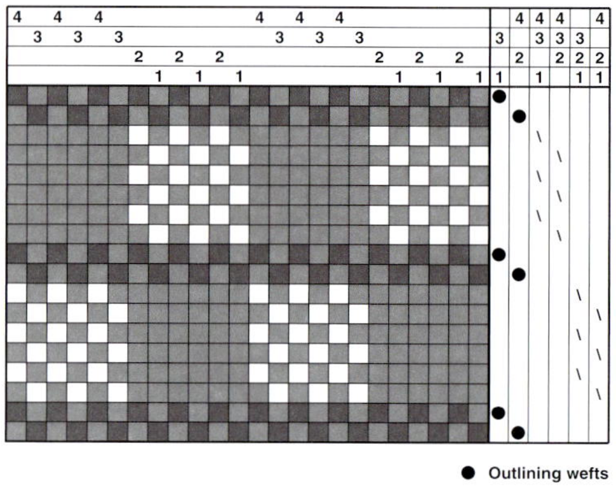

5.15 A two-block honeycomb, woven right-side up. The picks marked in black are plain weave; the "outlining wefts" weave selvedge to selvedge and must be given a lot of slack to allow them to curve around the plain-weave areas in the cloth.

Naturally pigmented cotton in green and brown, plus a natural cream outlining weft, woven as a double-faced honeycomb. Both sides of this eight-shaft fabric—which are identical—are shown here.

Honeycomb drafts may vary considerably. A block may be as few as two ends long—in which case it will be practically invisible, serving mostly to make a break between blocks—or as long as you like. The fabric is regarded as having only one useful face. The weft floats on the reverse or back of the fabric are not typically exposed, but rather than thinking of them as a problem, consider that they are a source of extra padding. As a functional fabric, the floats on the back limit its use to applications in which only one face shows or the back is lined. On the other hand, the lush-looking weft floats on the back of some fabrics are sometimes displayed, float side up, as art fabrics.

A thread-by-thread structural draft fails to reveal what really happens in the cloth when

These two fabrics are very different versions of honeycomb. The one at left is woven of 16/2 linen (natural and very pale gray) with a cotton novelty yarn that follows the curves of the structure. It isn't a classic honeycomb in that cells aren't formed. The structure is used simply to make the curving lines.

The dark cloth at right consists of four blocks varying in length from long to quite short. The two longest blocks are woven together, then the second and third blocks together, the third and fourth, and finally, just the shortest one. Here the warp and weft are 2/20 worsted wool, and the outlining wefts are groups of the same yarn. Wool accommodates the tension problems that build up and then are resolved as all areas are finally woven as cells. This would be a serious problem with linen or cotton.

drawn for honeycomb. The draft shows areas where the warp is lifted to produce what looks like very long warp floats. In fact, if the plain-weave shots labeled "outlining wefts" are given enough slack and the warp is not under too much tension, the plain-weave parts below the unwoven warp move up to fill in those areas, forming lovely ovals in the cloth. The undulations thus produced by the outlining wefts can be dramatic though this effect may not be fully visible until the cloth is removed from the loom and washed.

What happens when cloth is woven this way is really pretty simple: The plain weave, or outlining wefts inserted before and after the plain weave that forms the cells, curve around those cells and touch each other in the unwoven block(s). As you might expect, it is essential to insert the outlining wefts with enough slack for this effect to occur. Sometimes the weft must be generously bubbled, particularly in very dramatic honeycombs—to embrace the cells. At the same time, the warp must be tensioned only tightly enough to produce an adequate shed and to allow the cell wefts to be packed in closely. A highly tensioned warp does not allow the outlining wefts to assume the curved shapes that are the best feature of this structure.

These two honeycombs are woven with 2/20 pearl cotton warps and cell wefts. The bottom cloth uses the same yarn to outline the cells, while the top uses a much larger hard-twisted crochet cotton for that purpose.

The cells in both fabrics are made up of four short blocks woven on eight shafts. In the top cloth the cell weft is darker and the outlining weft lighter than the color of the warp to make the cells look deeper. The lack of a heavy outlining weft in the bottom cloth gives the fabric an embossed look.

The depth of the cells is increased by the use of rather fine threads for cell wefts and heavier threads for outlining wefts. If the outlining wefts are the same size as the warp, the cells will be flush with the surface. The depth of the cells is chosen by the weaver; all sorts of effects are possible. When the cloth is cut from the loom, the relaxation of the warp and weft enhances the cell structure, and washing the fabric completes its development.

Maximum drama is achieved if the outlining weft is soft, squashy, and thicker than the warp or cell wefts. The cell wefts may be finer than the warp and beaten in very firmly so that they cover the warp to produce little ovals of nearly unbroken color. If the outlining weft is velvety, like a plushy chenille, then the warp ends may sink right into the chenille surface and very effectively disappear.

With that general idea about how the structure works, let us consider the sort of draft it takes to create it. As we have seen in **5.15**, two shafts are needed for each block of cleanly constructed honeycomb. (We shall see in Chapter 6 that overshot may be woven as honeycomb with handsome results, although block divisions are not as clear as for regular honeycomb.)

If eight shafts are available, honeycomb may be woven with four blocks. Blocks that do not lie adjacent to each other may be woven at the same time with no restrictions. Adjacent blocks may also be combined to produce longer blocks without compromising the structure of the cloth.

Draft **5.16** is a four-block honeycomb threaded A, B, C, D, C, B, A. Any block may be woven independently of any other block. In addition, A and C may be woven at the same time, as may B and D. Blocks A and B may be woven together to produce a new block that is as wide as their sum. Likewise, B and C or C and D may be combined to make wide cells. It is more difficult to produce deep-looking cells when they are quite wide, but consider the possibilities inherent in the threading given in **5.16**. Draw it as a profile draft and work out the different ways it may be developed.

Honeycomb has one limitation, however, that applies both to two-block patterns and to more elaborate ones. If a single warp beam is used, then the warp will retain equal tension all the way across only if all sections or blocks are woven pretty much equally. Fairly elastic warp yarns are very helpful in maintaining good warp tension.

Cells may be bisected in the weft direction with an outlining weft which is woven selvedge to selvedge; a heavier warp end—or two—in the middle of a block bisects the cell in the warp direction. Bisecting the cells in *both* directions makes crosses

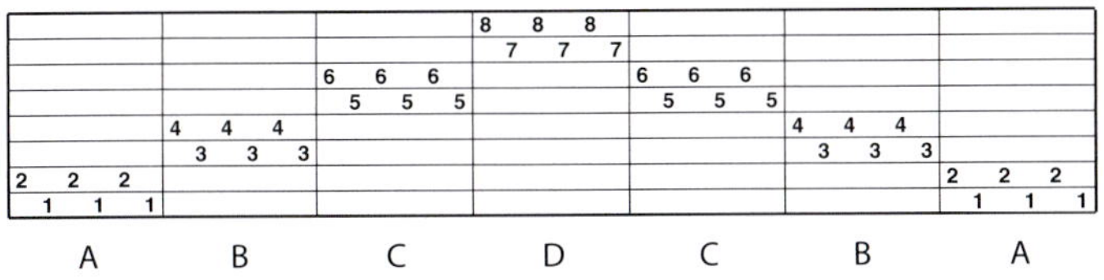

5.16 Threading draft for four-block honeycomb. The length of each block (here six ends) was chosen arbitrarily (see page 112). They can be threaded whatever length is desired.

This 100 percent linen cloth is woven with relatively small (16/2) warp and weft threads in the cells, and large (linen twine) warp and weft that create an outlining pattern. Two heavy ends are positioned between each of two blocks, and two heavy ends mark the center of each block as well. The heavy threads are threaded on separate shafts (four in all). Two heavy picks are thrown before the finer cell wefts, and two more in the center of each cell as well. They interlace between the cells in plain weave to produce the most dramatic feature of the cloth. Care was taken to make the cells as round as possible.

in their centers. Honeycomb may be varied in many ways.

M's and O's

Another structure which depends on distortions of the woven grid is M's and O's. In the four-shaft version, the structure is made up of two blocks, frequently composed of eight ends each. When block A is woven plain weave, the ends in block B make a large rib: over four, under four. As block B is woven plain weave, the rib appears in block A. Draft **5.17** is the structural draft for one full repeat of an eight-end M's and O's. The rib sections of the cloth tend to slide closer than they appear in the diagram, and the plain-weave sections spread out, forming ovals or medallions.

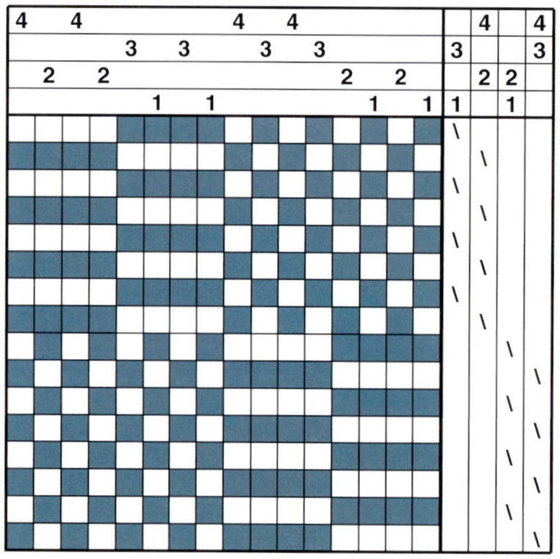

5.17 Eight-end M's and O's. While one block weaves plain weave, the other makes weft ribs.

Floats, in general, make fabrics "thirsty" if they are woven in absorbent fibers. M's and O's is well suited to use in table linens or elegant towels. Because the floats are relatively long, choose yarns that are firmly spun (a flaky yarn continues to flake away each time it washed) and perhaps firmly plied as well to avoid the everlasting shedding of lint in the wash and in use.

Although the blocks in **5.17** are each eight ends long, there is no firm rule about block length. The blocks might just as well be four ends long (in that case, A would be 1, 2, 3, 4 and B 1, 3, 2, 4) or longer. In theory, blocks can be extended to any length, but in practice, a cloth in which the ribs formed are very wide is sleazy and lacks structural integrity. Tightening the sett is not the answer; for a durable fabric, you must often compromise with a block length that produces the desired visual effect without sacrificing the firmness of the cloth.

If a long block of A is desired, instead of making the ribs eight ends wide, the threading of block A may be repeated so that the ribs are smaller but more numerous. The size of a block or the number of times a given block is repeated may be varied within the cloth. You have quite a bit of freedom even within the limitations of M's and O's.

Likewise, treadling may be varied. The blocks may be squared if eight picks are used. (Classically, M's and O's is woven using the same yarns for warp and weft.) The number of picks may be any multiple of 2. As blocks grow in the treadling direction, the cloth begins to soften up and feel mushy in the rib sections; the same balance that is necessary in the warp direction is also necessary in the weft direction. The smoothness and fineness of the yarns are critical to determining how far we may push block lengths. Fine yarns may be woven with longer floats (in terms of numbers of ends) than coarser yarns: An eight-end float is of small consequence in a textile woven of fine yarns at 40 e.p.i. but is a considerable matter in a cloth made of fat yarn woven at 12 e.p.i. Very smooth or slippery yarns tend to move about more in the cloth, so a little "toothiness" in the yarn helps stabilize longer floats.

Four-shaft M's and O's woven of 40/2 half-bleached linen.

Examination of **5.17** reveals that there is no way to weave plain weave all across the cloth. The alternating ends in Block A, carried on shafts 2 and 4 and on shafts 1 and 3, lie side by side in block B, in which the alternating ends are carried on shafts 1 and 4 and 2 and 3.

Look at the tie-up in **5.17**. The treadles that alternate in weaving the cloth produce opposite sheds—not surprising because plain weave and rib, a plain-weave derivative, are both woven on opposites—a characteristic that will help you as you invent other M's and O's threadings and treadlings.

It is possible to add a third block of M's and O's on just four shafts, although the structure is altered a bit. Draft **5.18** is the structural draft for three blocks (plus half of block A again to show the interface between block C and A). The appearance of this cloth is somewhat disconcerting: it would be reasonable to expect plain weave in the places where the ribs aren't being woven, but here we find two-end floats instead of plain weave in some areas; and when block C is being woven rib, there is no true plain weave anywhere.

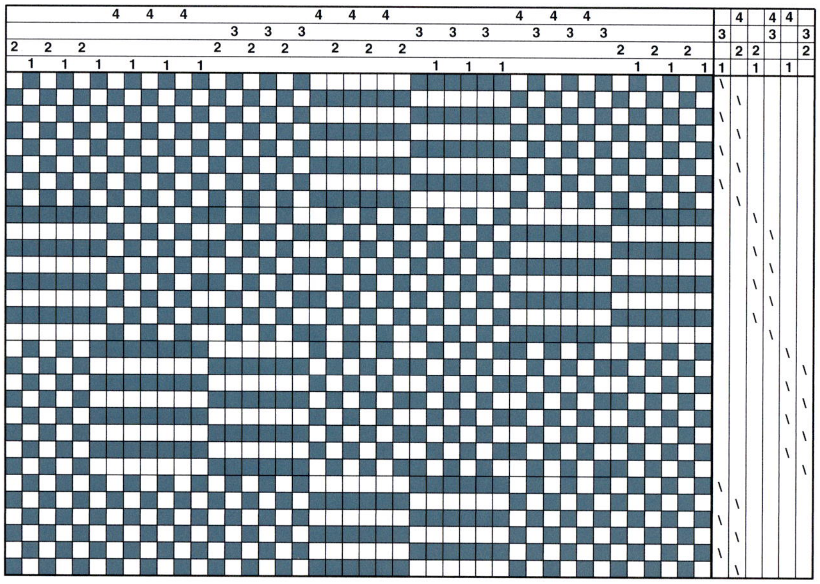

5.18 This is the nearest we can come to three blocks of M's and O's on four shafts. The first two blocks, A and B, are written as they were in 5.17. The third uses the combinations not used before: 1, 4 and 2, 3.

Applying the M's and O's structure to more than four shafts requires further thought. Look again at draft **5.17**. Notice that in both blocks, the ends carried on shafts 1 and 4 interlace in plain weave all the way through the cloth. That suggests that an M's and O's structure could be designed for more than four shafts using two shafts—the same two shafts—for those plain-weave ends. Approaching the structure this way turns it on its head a bit because it means that several more shafts are required, but it turns M's and O's from a quasi-block weave—some sources call it a texture weave—to a true block weave.

Draft **5.19** shows the structural draft for a three-block M's and O's in which perfect plain weave may be woven everywhere and in which the blocks may be woven in any order. This three-block version requires eight shafts; the price of structural design freedom is almost always more shafts.

The same sort of structure may be woven using just six shafts if we are willing to accept ribs that run in the other direction; that is, the draft may be turned. Draft **5.19** requires eight shafts and just six treadles; the same structure turned 90 degrees, **5.20**, may be woven with six shafts and eight treadles. By working this way, with a turned regular draft, each block requires just two shafts, but the number of treadles required is always two more than the number of shafts.

Just as in **5.19**, plain weave can be woven all the way across the cloth at any time using draft **5.20**. That means that the ribs (this time they are warp ribs) may be isolated by plain weave or woven in the order shown in

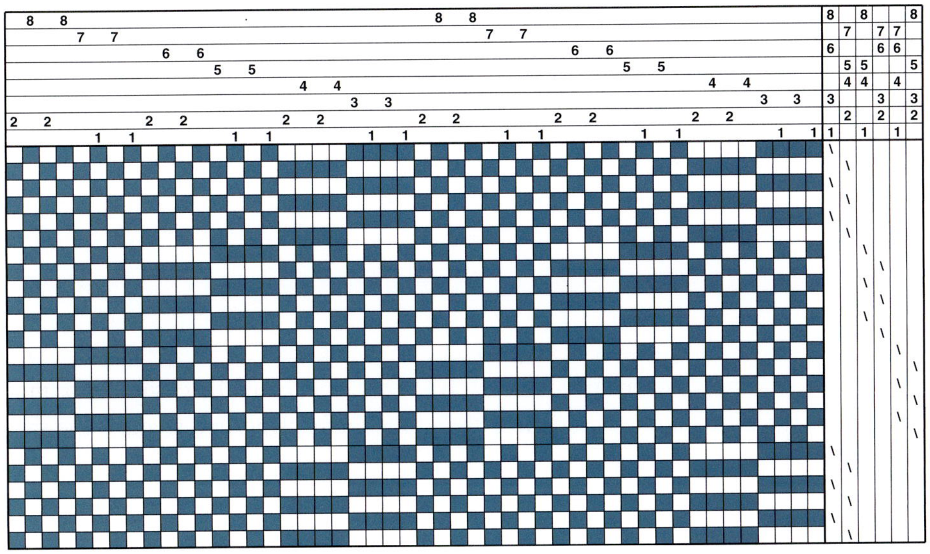

5.19 After recognizing that some ends wove just plain weave, those ends were all threaded on shafts 1 and 2 for this draft and the shafts required to make three true blocks with M's and O's were added. The draft requires eight shafts and six treadles.

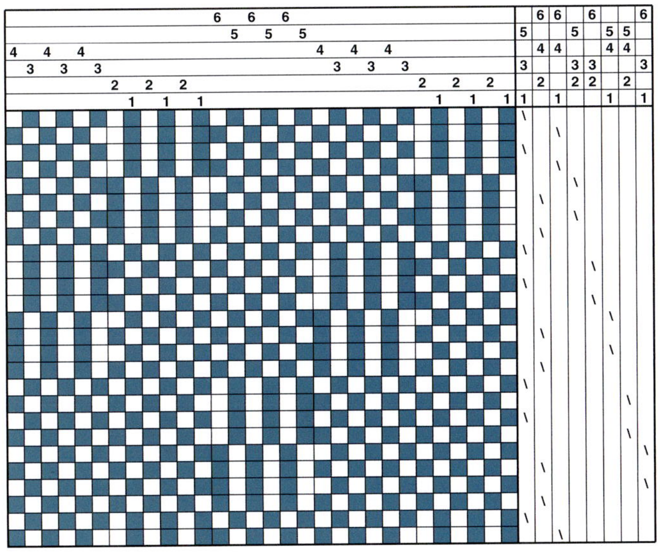

5.20 Draft 5.19 is turned so that now it needs six shafts and eight treadles.

5.20 any time you wish. This sort of structure is particularly effective when viewed with light passing through it, perhaps as a screen or curtain fabric.

Spider Weaves

A very dramatic distortion of warp ends or weft picks occurs in a group of structures called **spider weaves** or **linear zigzag weaves**. At first glance, these fabrics appear to be constructed of a sort of netting overlying plain-weave cloth. Some of the threads, either warp or weft, but usually weft, are shifted in the cloth to give the biggest distortions seen in loom-controlled woven fabrics.

The threads that move in eccentric paths are caught infrequently, first from one side and then from another, so that they zigzag across the cloth or form curves. If these threads are warp ends, they take up at a different rate from the other ends, and so they may be managed more easily if they are carried on a second warp beam. If they appear in the weft, they must be thrown in a wide arc or even bubbled to allow them to undulate or wave in the cloth. These shifting threads move in the direction of least resistance; they move to the center of the floating thread that catches them (warp or weft). If the thread that catches them floats for a long distance, the undulating thread is able to move farther; if the float is relatively short, the weft deviation will be small.

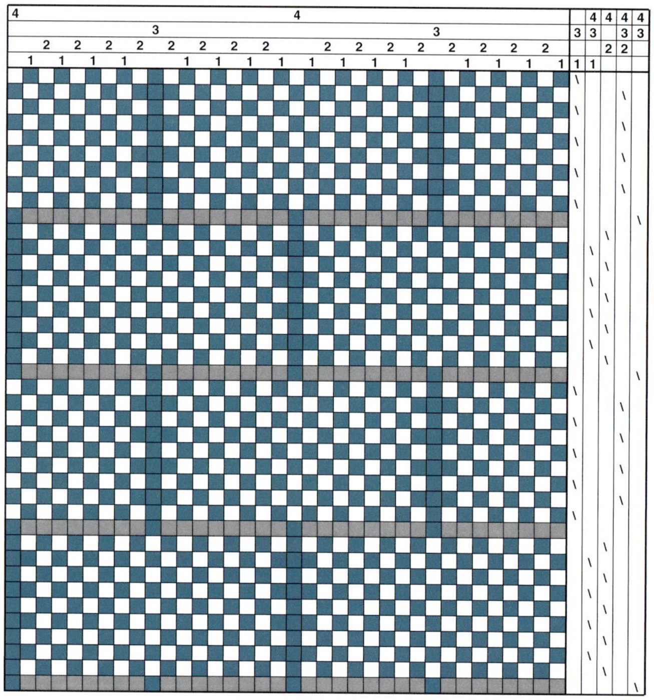

5.21 This draft will produce a fabric with the appearance of a plain weave with a diamond lattice overlay. The threads shown as gray zigzag.

At first glance (at the cloth, not the draft), some of the structures seem to be impossible because the deflected threads seem to be caught in a way that could not happen in one pick. They have shifted so much that it appears that a single weft was thrown partly in one shed and partly in another, a feat that couldn't be achieved without much manual manipulation. The structural draft, **5.21**, however, shows that it is not only possible but also pretty simple. Once again, the structural draft shows the cloth as being perfectly rectilinear, which it is not: the distortion takes place as the cloth is relaxed and even more as it is washed.

The limitation of these fabrics is obvious: the long floats in the ends or picks are sites where the cloth may be snagged or pulled. These fabrics, then, are mainly for decorative use. Note that all spider weaves begin with a plain-weave ground. In designing them, we may begin by marking out a plain-weave structure, leaving blank rows (or columns) for the zigzagging threads.

Let us suppose that the zigzagging threads are in the weft. Mark a plain-weave grid, leaving blank rows to indicate the

V

IV

III

II

I

Spider, or linear zigzag, weaves. The heavier weft threads shift to form what appears to be an overlay on the surface of the cloth. The first and third from the bottom are woven as shown in 5.23 and 5.21, respectively. The fourth, counting up, is 5.22, with two heavy wefts in succession. The second and fifth are different in that the ends that hold the heavy wefts in place change from row to row in a regular way like a twill (II) and in an irregular way (V). Sixteen shafts were used.

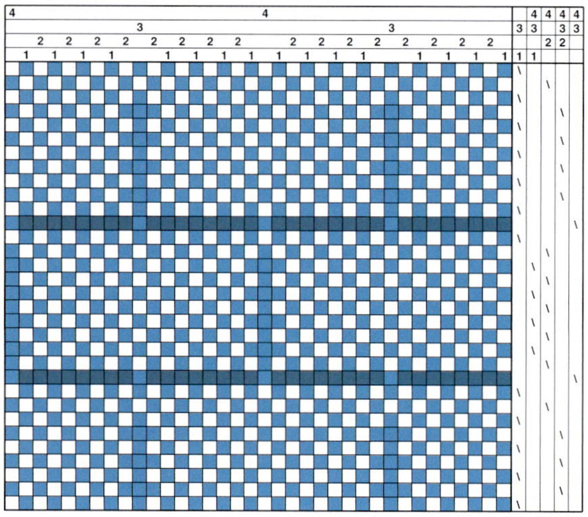

5.22 The zigzagging wefts always move in the same direction. No diamond shapes will be formed. See I on page 119.

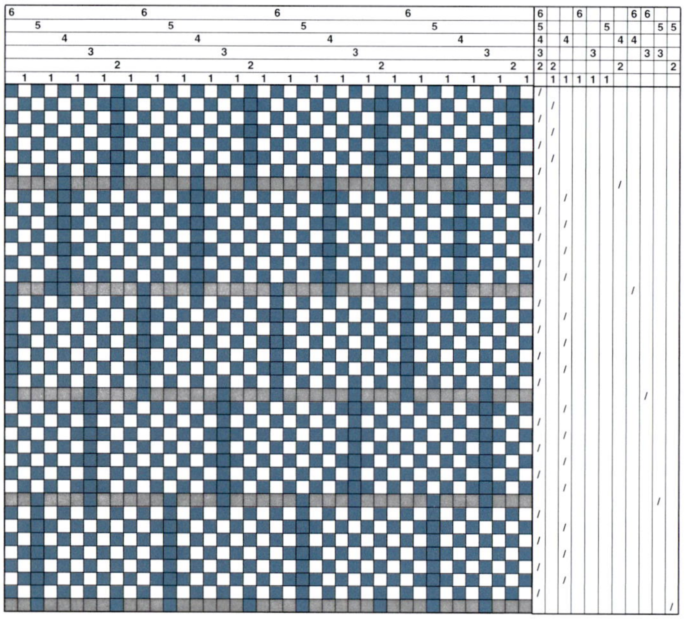

5.23 The warp threads that define the path of the zigzagging weft threads are raised in a diagonal progression, see II on page 119.

position of the weft picks that will lie on the surface. The first decision has to do with the distance between these picks in the cloth.

The next decision has to do with the way the wefts will move at the places it is caught in the fabric. If the pick is to move alternately up and down, the tie must be extended upward in the cloth for upward movement and downward for downward movement. The greater the distance that the tying ends float, the greater possible distortion in the distorted pick. Naturally, there is a limit to how long the tying ends may float, and that limit depends on the size of the threads. When the warp floats tie only one distorting pick, whether these ends float upward or downward, then the distortions take the form of waves lined up under each other. The distorting pick moves into the middle of the warp float, although it is thrown either at the end of the float (just before the end is caught in the fabric) or at its start (just after the end begins its float (**5.22**). If the tying ends change all the time, by moving one or two ends to the left or right, but always extend in the same direction, then the zigzags will fall in a diagonal across the cloth as in **5.23**. If a given tying end extends upward for one zigzagging pick and downward for the next (two distorting picks lying under each tying end), then diamond shapes are formed in the cloth by the distorted pick (**5.21**). The repeat doesn't have to be absolutely regular. Draft **5.24** shows a fabric designed to have great distortions that seem to be rather irregular so they form a longer repeat in the weft direction. (Weaving a cloth with a truly random repeat is difficult, particularly on relatively few shafts. The human eye and brain are very adept at finding the point at which the repeat occurs, as it must.)

20/2 pearl cotton warp and ground weft with 8/2 unmercerized cotton on the surface make an understated and elegant cloth. The floats made by the 8/2 cotton are less than ⅛" (.3 cm). Draft 5.21.

5.24 Linear zigzag where the ends that catch the zigzagging wefts fall in different places that aren't predictable. See V in the photo on page 119.

Each draft was designed following the steps outlined above: starting with a plain-weave grid, leaving blank the weft rows for the distorting pick, and then marking in the lifted ends to move the pick either up or down on the face of the cloth. It's really rather simple when you approach the task one step at a time.

Spider weaves allow the designer a lot of latitude. The zigzagging threads may be single, doubled, heavier than or the same as the ground cloth, and may contrast in color. Novelty yarns, loop yarns, space or dip-dyed yarns are not the best choice because they look confusing. Because the zigzagging threads lie on the surface of the cloth, a fancy, expensive yarn may be used to great effect—every inch of it will be right up front where it does the most good. Likewise, the tying ends may be doubled or may differ in yarn size, style, or color or some combination of these. There are many possibilities for varying the effects obtained with spider or linear zigzag weaves.

All of the drafts in this chapter illustrate the statement made at the beginning: "when nothing lies between a pair of warp ends or weft picks, they will move together." We began with small deviations from the rectilinear, movement of just a few threads over a small distance (huck), and moved through ever more dramatic distortions until we arrived finally at the gross distortions of spider weave. It is interesting to see just how successfully the rectilinearity of the warp/weft grid may be challenged.

Compound Weaves

So far, we have been concerned mainly with structures that are made up of a single warp and a single weft. In *The Primary Structures of Fabrics,* Irene Emery describes structures in which a single weft crosses a single warp as **simple weaves**. Although simple weaves are easier and faster to weave because only one shuttle is used and the warp is made up of only one set of threads, there are many structures that use more than one warp, or weft, or both.

Emery describes structures with more than two elements as **compound weaves**. Several familiar structures fall into this category: overshot, summer and winter, crackle, and beiderwand. Those structures are covered in this chapter, but I would like to open our thinking as well to further possibilities.

Inlay

The simplest way to add another element to a cloth is to begin with a simple weave such as plain weave and add a weft by laying it into a shed with a plain weave pick. Draft **6.1** shows a weft laid in beside the ground weft on the same shed. Such a laid-in weft typically would not run selvedge to selvedge but would be used to add color and/or texture to a particular place in a plain-weave cloth. The fabric looks the same on both sides except where a loop is formed on one face when the laid-in weft turns to go into the next shed.

Draft **6.2** shows an inlay with more visual definition. In this case, the cloth has a well-differentiated face and back because the inlaid weft lies under only one out of every four warp ends. The ratio of 1:3, the balance of warp ends over the inlaid weft, makes the weft more visible. This sort of inlay beats in well, too, lying on top of the ground cloth. Notice that the warp ends under which the inlay lies are raised for the previous ground pick so that when beaten

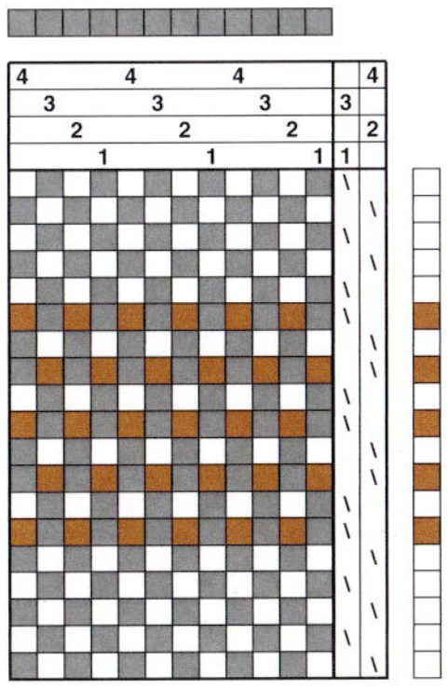

6.1 Plain weave with an inlaid weft in plain-weave shed.

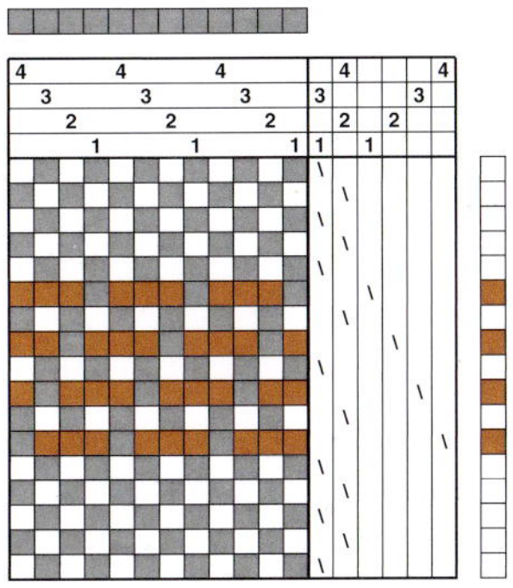

6.2 Plain weave with inlaid weft. The weft passes over three ends and is caught by one.

into place, the inlay will slide over the ground pick.

Theo Moorman, in *Weaving as an Art Form,* refined this idea by putting special warp ends, finer and slightly different in color, into the warp to make the inlay seem to float on the surface of the cloth. The threading she used is shown in **6.3**. The draft shows the tie-down warps in a contrasting color. In practice, they were nearly the same color as the rest of the warp. If the ground cloth were dark and the inlay light, the tie-down threads were a little lighter than the warp. If the ground warp and weft were light and the inlay darker, the tie-down threads were a little darker than the warp. By using finer threads for the tie-down ends and colors that were closer in value to the inlay wefts, the tie-down ends, which may have to be tensioned separately because their take-up is different from the ground, became nearly invisible.

Moorman was looking for a way to construct images as freely as one can with tapestry while using the loom to create the ground cloth on which the images appear. The advantage of her technique is that weaving progresses much more rapidly and the cloth can be more sheer and supple than in traditional tapestries.

Draft **6.4** shows how inlay threads may be added to the surface of the cloth, creating diagonals in the inlay that change direction. If, instead, the same tie-down end is used throughout while maintaining the 1:3 ratio of warp to weft, you will get the result shown in **6.5**. This structure is often referred to as ***dukagång,*** the Swedish name for an embroidery formed by inlay on the same shed throughout. The vertical line (formed by the warp end that ties down the inlay), is characteristic of this weave.

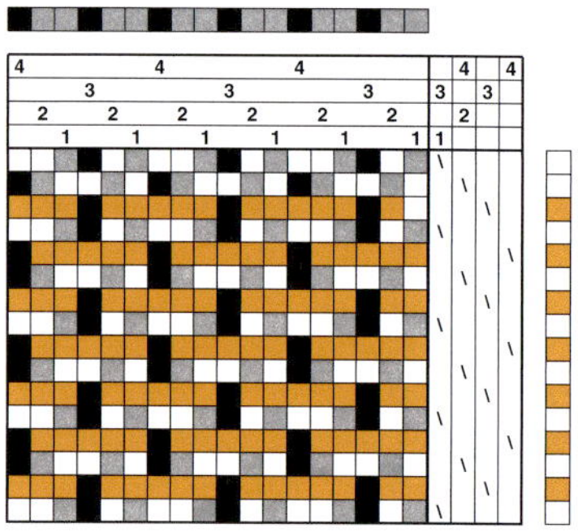

6.3 The Moorman technique. This is the structure Theo Moorman used to weave her images. The ends carried on shafts 3 and 4 (shown as black) are finer than those on 1 and 2. These finer ends tie down the wefts inlaid onto the surface of the cloth (shown as gold). Although shown as continuous here, these wefts were often discontinuous, changing color or stopping, so that the color(s) and texture(s) were placed exactly where she wanted them.

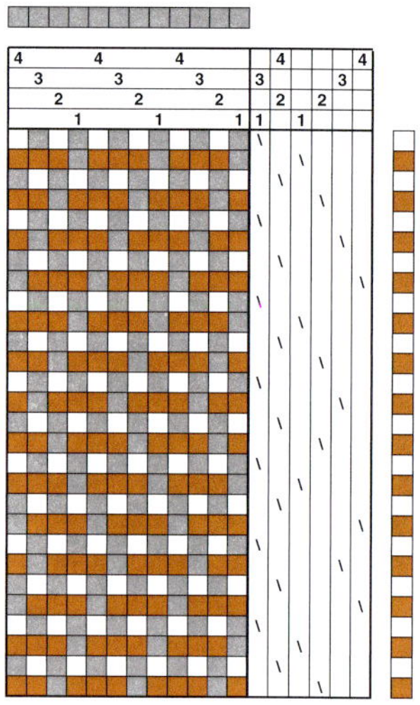

6.4 Inlay wefts added to the surface of the cloth by lifting one end at a time; this time the order in which the warp ends are lifted to tie down the inlaid weft reverses. The inlaid weft is shown as continuous but can be laid in—or not—quite freely.

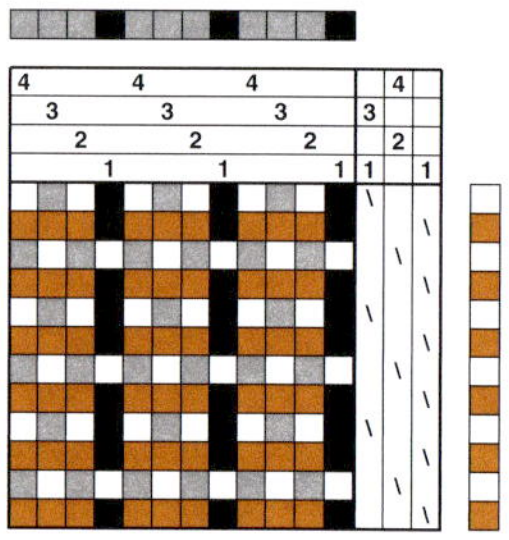

6.5 An inlay technique called dukagång. One shaft is used to lift the ends that tie down the inlaid weft (shown in black), forming a vertical line which is characteristic of the structure.

Two shuttles are used throughout for this fabric (shown in draft 6.6) woven in 20/2 pearl cotton. First, at bottom, pale orange is used to weave the plain-weave ground, and blue-violet makes the weft brocade. In the next area, the colors reverse.

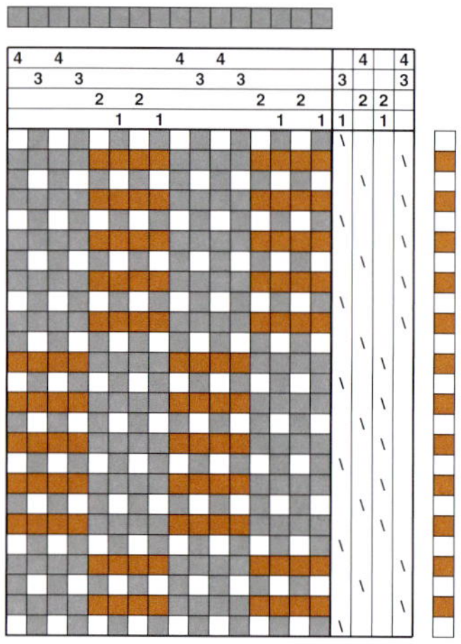

6.6 A selvedge-to-selvedge pick is thrown alternating with the plain-weave ground to form warpwise ribs. Although shown in a contrasting color here for clarity, the weft may be the same color as the ground weft, which permits one-shuttle weaving.

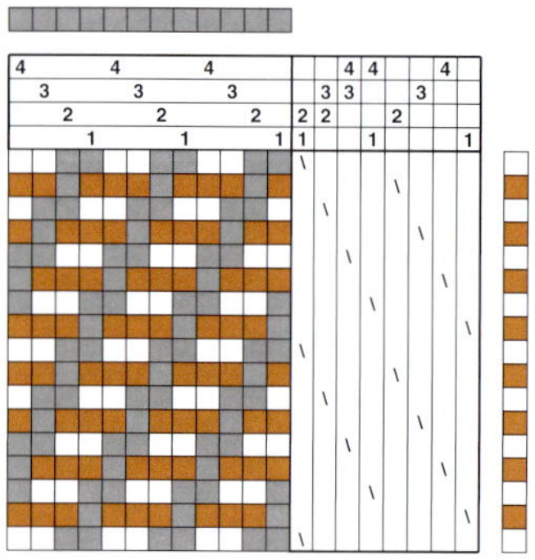

6.7a A selvedge-to-selvedge weft is inlaid on twill ground by lifting the same shaft that is lifted both before and after it. The inlaid weft lies right up on the surface of the cloth on its face, or right side.

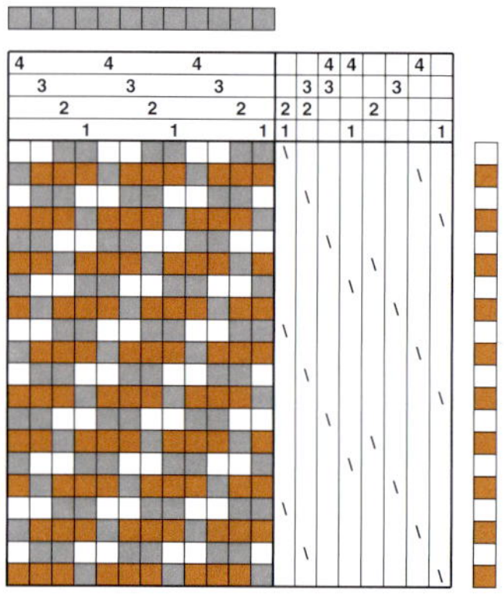

6.7b In this case, a selvedge -to-selvedge weft is inlaid on a twill ground by lifting a shaft that is not lifted both before and after it. The inlaid weft does not "nest" with the ground wefts thrown before and after it.

Typically, the weft to be inlaid is fashioned into a yarn butterfly or wound on a small shuttle. The purpose of the butterflies or little shuttles or bobbins is simply to control the length of weft so that it may be passed back and forth through the sheds conveniently without tangling.

Two wefts, one warp

Draft **6.6** shows another compound structure in which there are two wefts and one warp. In this case, both wefts run selvedge to selvedge and alternate. The cloth may be woven with a single shuttle if the yarns used for the plain-weave ground and the weft floats are identical. The advantage of making a ribbed cloth in this way is that plain weave underlies the weft float ribs, which makes the cloth quite stable. If the weft yarn is lustrous, this structure will allow the luster to show.

Drafts **6.2–6.5** may also be used with selvedge-to-selvedge wefts, producing a face that is different from the back. This sort of construction is a way to add an expensive, scarce, or special-effect yarn to the face of a cloth without hiding any of it in the supporting ground cloth. Thus, a looped or brushed mohair could be floated on the surface of a plain-weave woolen cloth, catching it securely so it ornaments the surface without appearing on the back. The ground cloth can also be woven twill (for its thickness and drape) while floating another yarn on its surface (**6.7a** and **6.7b**).

The extra, ornamental, weft is caught by the same warp end that is lifted before and after the pick. In **6.7a**, shaft 2 is lifted by itself for the ornamental pick, which is thrown after the ground pick is thrown while lifting shafts 1 and 2, and just after the ground pick is woven by lifting shafts 2 and 3. This way of arranging the sequence of shots throws the ornamental weft right up on the surface.

Draft **6.7b** is constructed with the ornamental weft thrown in a shed that is made by lifting one shaft that is not lifted in making the ground sheds that precede or follow it. The cloth will not beat in as easily as in **6.7a**. If your intention is to be sure that the ornamental weft lies upon the surface of the ground cloth, **6.7a** is preferable.

A more dramatic example is shown in **6.8a**, in which a 7/1 twill using an ornamental yarn is superimposed on a 2/2 twill of a ground warp and weft. From the face of the cloth, long, luxurious floats made of the ornamental yarn dominate the cloth. From the back (shown in **6.8b**), the ornamental yarn is scarcely visible, and the longest weft float is over two warp ends.

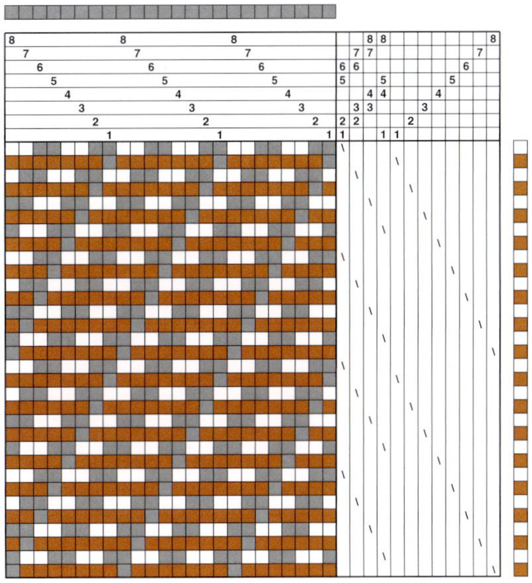

6.8a An extra weft is thrown in the 1/7 twill sheds over a ground cloth of 2/2 twill. The ground is therefore very stable, and the supplementary weft floats are long and luxurious.

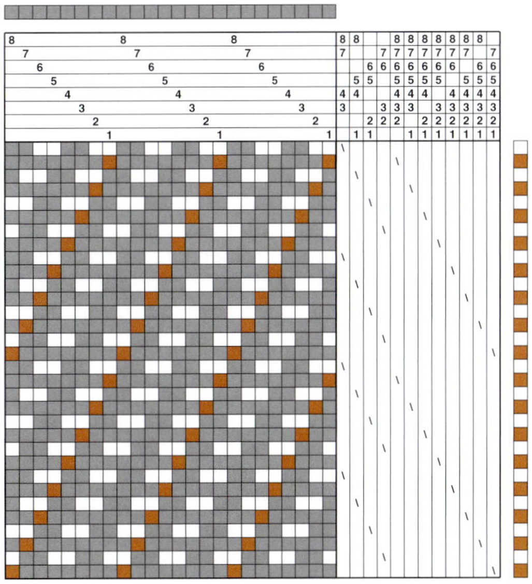

6.8b The reverse side, or back, of 6.8a.

Extra warps

A compound weave in which the ground and ornamental weft yarns are different requires two shuttles to weave. I find that besides being slow to weave, using two shuttles makes it more difficult to establish an even weaving rhythm, which can result in a less evenly woven cloth.

For these reasons, and for design reasons, it is sometimes a good idea to put the extra thread in the warp so that only one weft is necessary. Draft **6.9** shows an example woven using four shafts and four sheds. In this example, the ornamental warp ends are carried on two shafts so that they can be tied to the plain-weave ground in different places. If they were carried on only one shaft, they would all be tied with the same pick, creating a horizontal line in the cloth.

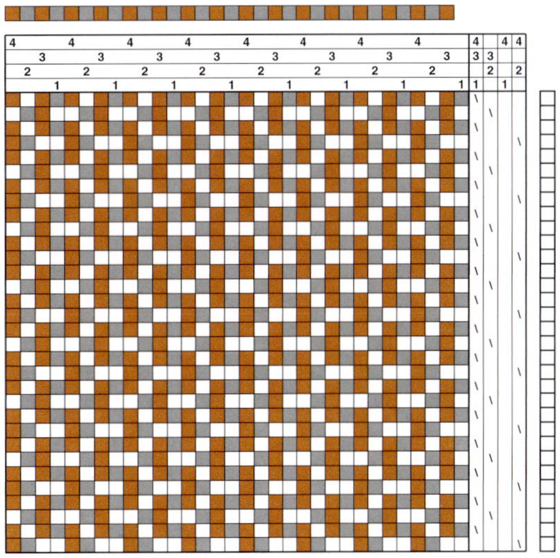

6.9 The ornamental yarn is in the warp so that the cloth may be woven with just one shuttle (carrying the ground weft). The ornamental warp is caught every fourth pick by the plain-weave ground. Because the ornamental warp is carried on two shafts (3 and 4), the places where it is stitched down by the weft are offset from one another.

The light- and medium-gray yarns (8/2 cotton) are supported by plain-weave ends and picks of 20/2 natural pearl cotton. Careful scrutiny of the fringes in those areas reveals them in the warp. The pattern threads are in the warp, so only one shuttle is needed.

These **supplemental warp** ends are not necessary to maintain the structural integrity of the ground cloth but used for decoration. They may be of one or several colors; they may be made of the same materials as the ground cloth or of something quite different. They may experience a different rate of take-up from that of the ground warp. If they are inelastic, they may become loose as the weaving progresses. Indeed, if the warp is longer than 2 or 3 yards, even an elastic warp will sag. The best solution, of course, is to beam the two sets of warps separately. If two warp beams are not available, choose one of the solutions shown on page 69.

This approach can be used in weaving overshot, summer and winter, and the like so that only one shuttle is used. Appendix A (page 246) has instructions for turning drafts so that what was warp becomes the weft, and vice versa.

Some traditional compound weaves

The structures described above consist, for the most part, of a ground cloth comprising warp and weft on which a supplemental or decorative third element lies, tied down inconspicuously by the ground warp or weft. In traditional structures, the supplemental element most often passes from selvedge to selvedge in a repeating pattern sequence. It is traditionally heavier than the warp yarn and is usually more softly spun so that it may be crammed through the holes in the plain-weave fabric when it passes from the face to the back without distorting the ground weave. A yarn that distorts the ground weave will also distort the pattern being formed in the cloth. This sort of distortion may either be avoided or exploited, depending on what you have in mind. *Look at what appears, at first glance, to be a limitation of a structure or yarn as an opportunity to do something you might not have thought of doing.*

Overshot

For American handweavers, the most familiar of the three-element weaves is probably overshot. Many of us actually came to be handweavers because of overshot patterns, intricate-looking, symmetrical, frequently charming patterns that seemed to be available only to the handweaver. North American coverlets were frequently woven using overshot; indeed, they are the most famous textiles woven in this structure.

PUSHING AN IDEA

One of the pleasures of weaving is having an idea—like **6.3**—and observing the resulting cloth, and in this case, liking the idea of a float overlying a ground weave. The warp-to-weft ratio of 1:3 is interesting, but how would it be to increase it to 1:5 or 1:7? Seeing the weft lying on the surface of the plain-weave or twill ground brings up the possibility of using yarns of different sizes. If the ground threads were smaller, the ornamenting weft could dominate or cover the surface, forming a kind of backed cloth. If the ground yarns were larger, then the weft on the surface would look thin and spidery. If it matched the color of the ground but were very shiny, it would add shimmer or sparkle to the face of the cloth. Given all these conditions as well as less shrinkage in the ornamenting weft yarn, the latter might form wavy lines within diagonal floats on the face of the cloth.

Pushing an idea boils down to this: try the idea, notice what happens, and if you like what happens, see if you can exaggerate it. The exaggeration may suggest a new idea or direction to pursue. If you allow yourself time to play with an idea in this way, who knows where you will end up? I've learned not to dismiss the little voice that whispers, What would happen if...?

Double Irish Chain

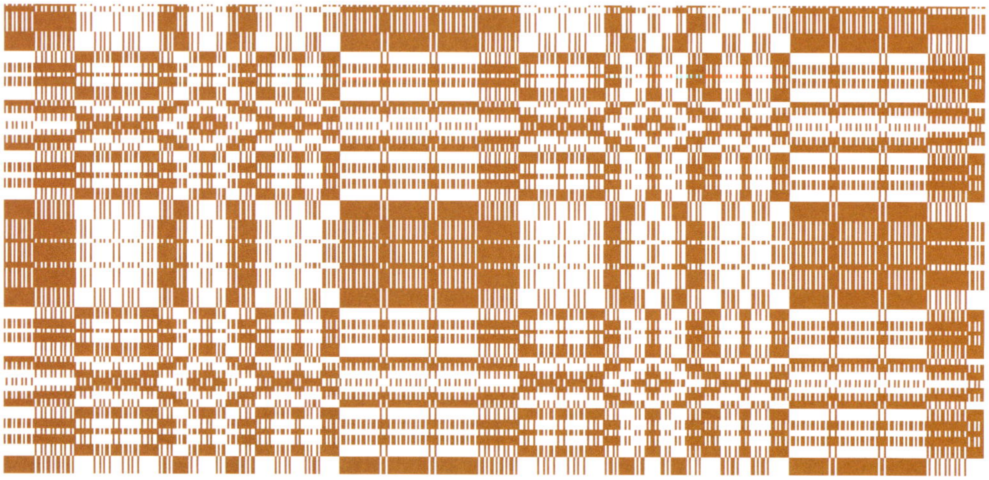

Traditional Roses and Rings, or Whig Rose

Wandering Vine

Overshot is a three-element weave. Classically, the warp for overshot is a plain yarn, most often white or off-white, usually plied. (Plied yarns are usually stronger than singles and therefore a better choice for warps.) The structural weft, the one forming the ground weave, is similar to the warp, usually the same size. In early times, when the yarn for coverlets was entirely handspun, this weft was often a singles yarn because it was less work to make a singles yarn the same thickness as the plied yarn used for warp than to spin and ply a thinner yarn. The pattern weft in these early fabrics is usually about twice as heavy as the warp and weft yarns and more softly spun. The old coverlets were woven with a cotton warp and structural weft and a wool pattern weft.

Overshot requires just four shafts, although more may be used. The structure is based on 2/2 twill. For a four-shaft overshot, there are four blocks: 1, 2; 2, 3; 3, 4; and 1, 4. The ground cloth is plain weave, and so the threading must be written to ensure that plain weave may be woven everywhere in the cloth at the same time. *Drafts, therefore, always alternate ends on even-numbered shafts with those on odd-numbered shafts.*

Look again at the blocks listed above. Notice that each block shares an end with another block; that is, the block written on shafts 1 and 2 shares the end threaded on shaft 2 with the next block, written on shafts 2 and 3. The 1, 2 block also shares a common end, 1, with the 1, 4 block. These ends-in-common are responsible for the flowing appearance of many overshot patterns. One of the standard texts, *A Handweaver's Pattern Book,* by Marguerite P. Davison, is a wonderful compendium of the old patterns. Consider the sinuous curves of Wandering Vine or the interlocked circles of Traditional Roses and Rings, also known as Whig Rose. Both of these flowing patterns rely on the sharing of blocks for the smoothness of their curves.

It is also possible to design very rectilinear patterns using overshot, such as Davison's Double Irish Chain, but they are designed by placing the 1, 2 block next to the 3, 4 block and the 2, 3 block next to the 1, 4 block. Notice that these blocks do *not* share common ends. Each block comes to a full stop where the next block begins. These blocks are said to be **opposites** because when shafts 1 and 2 are lifted, shafts 3 and 4 are down and vice versa. Weaving done this way is said to be "on opposites." We will return to this notion later.

The pattern weft, essential as it is to the appearance of the fabric, is not essential to its structural integrity. In fact, if all the pattern wefts were removed from a well-woven overshot fabric—what a curious thought!—

My Theory About the Origin of Overshot

When the Puritans left Great Britain to settle on the North American continent, they brought with them their weaving technology. This was limited mainly to plain weave, basket weaves, and simple twills on four shafts. It seems likely to me that somewhere along the line a weaver, longing for fabrics with more decorative appeal and large, repeating patterns devised overshot by combining the plain weave that holds it all together with larger, contrasting threads entered on a 2/2 twill shed. Certainly, monk's belt (described on page 140) was woven in Sweden, and rather small overshot patterns were being woven in Germany, too, but the construction of rather large repeats on a simple loom really began in North America. When you think about it, it was an ingenious invention allowing quite a lot of rich pattern using the simple-to-construct four-shaft counterbalance loom.

the remaining cloth would be a regular, even plain weave.

Block length in overshot patterns may vary quite a bit. The minimum block length is two ends (both of which are shared by the blocks preceding and following). The maximum block length depends on how the fabric will be used and the size of the threads that are used to construct it. A ten-end block produces a ⅓-inch-long float at 30 e.p.i.; if the same pattern is used with yarns set at 10 e.p.i., then a 1-inch float is generated. A float that long will snag on paws and claws, little fingers, rings, bracelets and shoe buckles. In some applications, those hazards are not a problem; in others, they may be serious threats. The weaver/designer is the person who must decide.

The flip side of those short, safe, serviceable floats is that they lack drama. The powerful effect you want for a hanging will not likely materialize if all the floats are short. In a fabric that is hung, even though it may never be handled and hence never snag, very long floats will still be subject to the effect of gravity. A long float will sag in time, producing a shallow curve in a once-straight line. If that would defeat your design idea, try some samples to see just how far you can push float length without introducing the sag. A pattern weft that is fuzzy or a bit hairy tends to hold its place better than a smoother yarn. On the other hand, gravity-induced curves may be just the thing for a dramatic hanging.

The threading

Overshot patterns are most often symmetrical (with the notable exception of Wandering Vine, also known as Cat's Track and Snail's Trail, see page 130). That is, there will be two places in the threading in which everything on one side of that warp end is the mirror image of what lies on the other side.

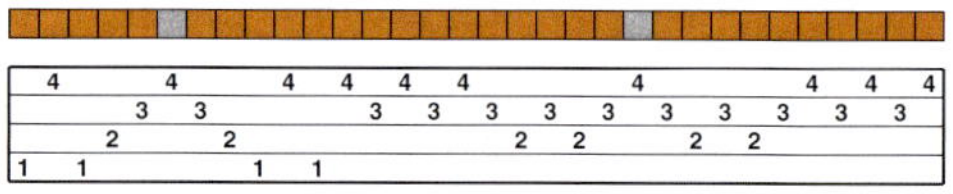

6.10a King's Flower, page 137, Marguerite Davison's A Handweaver's Pattern Book, *threading only. End 11 and end 27, the two centers of symmetry, are marked with a different color.*

Draft **6.10a** is the threading for King's Flower from *A Handweaver's Pattern Book.* The first twenty-one ends form one part of the pattern and the remaining eleven ends, the other. In both these parts, the threading is symmetrical; in the first, the warp end at the center of the section is end 11; in the second, end 27. If you begin threading at one side of the draft and continue to the other, and then repeat, the pattern will not be centered in your cloth. If you draw down the pattern (**6.10b**), you will see that either the wider part or the narrower part of the pattern may be considered the more important. *The portion of the pattern you wish to emphasize should be in the center of the cloth.* If in our example, end 11 of our original draft is considered the center, the result will be **6.10c**. Choosing end 27, the center of the smaller figure, instead gives us **6.10d**. Neither is correct nor incorrect; they are simply different options.

If your cloth needs to be a certain width, calculate how many ends will be required. Choose the end that you wish to have appear in the center of the cloth and then construct the draft from there. It is likely that the section of the draft that is threaded at the selvedges will not contain a complete motif. Draft **6.10e** is balanced for use with fifty-eight ends using the larger part of the repeat as the center.

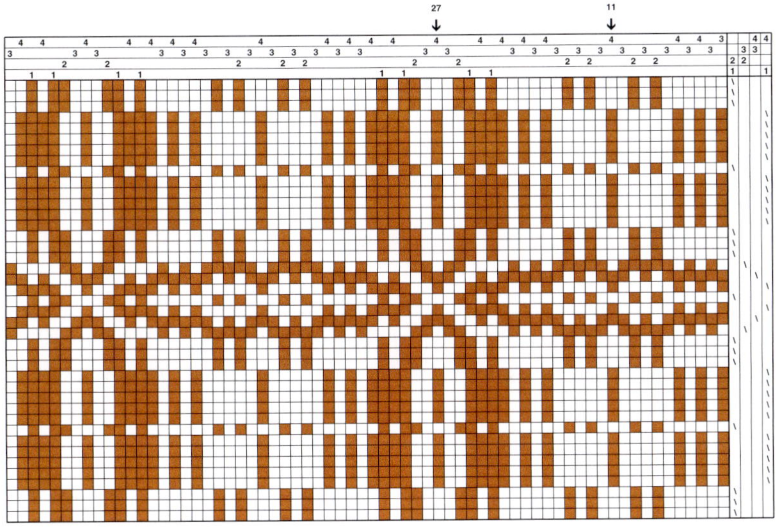

6.10b King's Flower, complete draft. Page 137, Margeurite Davison's *A Handweaver's Pattern Book.*

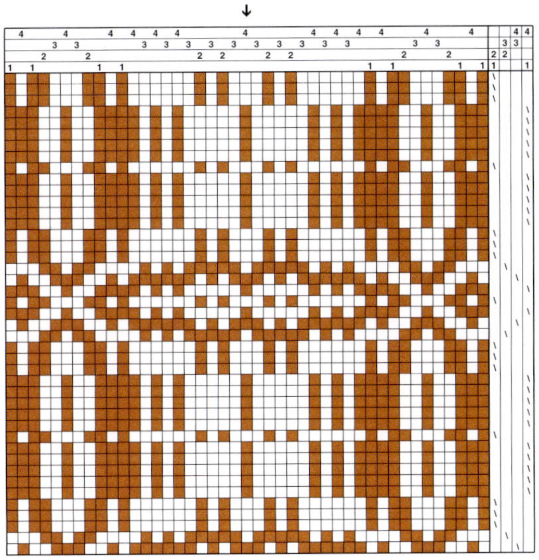

6.10c King's Flower. This draft uses end 11 in the draft given by Davison as the visual center of the pattern.

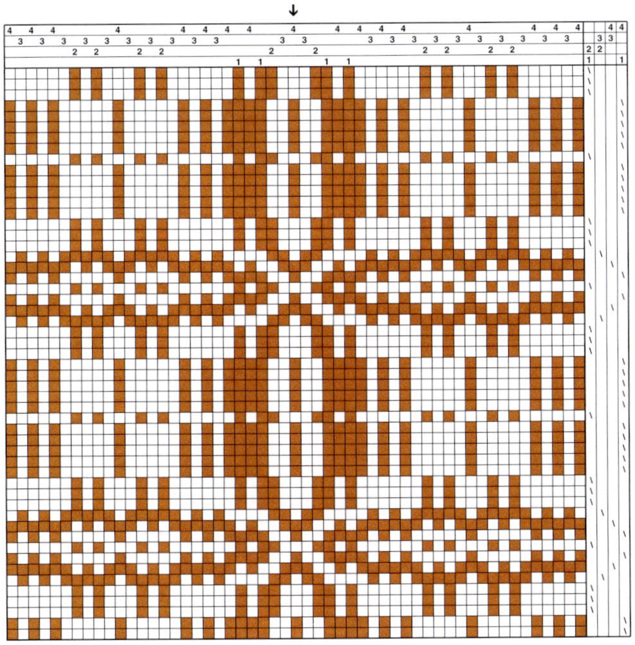

6.10d King's Flower. End 27 is the center of the pattern.

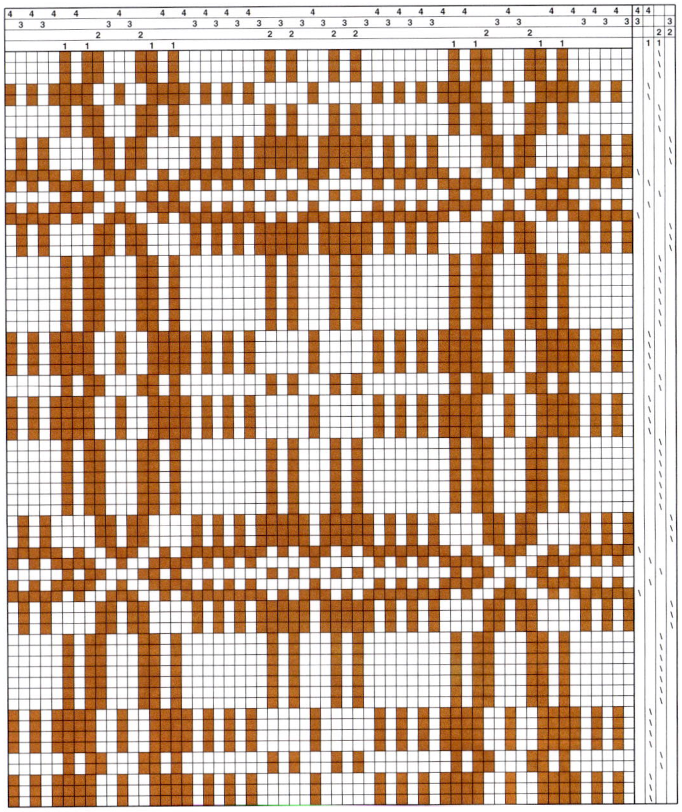

6.10e King's Flower balanced around the wider part of the pattern and woven as drawn in. Tabbies are omitted.

An overshot on four shafts woven in an unconventional way. The ground cloth is 60/2 silk in both warp and weft. The white 2/20 worsted wool pattern weft is laid in, not selvedge to selvedge, but only for isolated motifs or borders that suggest fragmentary overlays.

You can, of course, make up your own overshot patterns. You know what the blocks are and that the threading must alternate even- and odd-numbered shafts. If you have a particular shape in mind, you can, as we did with undulating twill, draw the shape you wish to make and then telescope it down to four shafts.

Follow the sequence of drafts **6.11a– 6.11e** to see how one idea may be worked out.

6.11a Here is the shape I would like to have the pattern take. The pattern moves up quickly at the edges and then is round. The blocks are represented by squares filled in and will be "telescoped" in the next version.

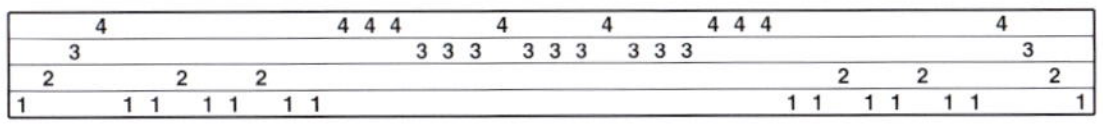

6.11b The shape in 6.11a has been telescoped so that what was on the fifth and sixth shafts is now in the first and second.

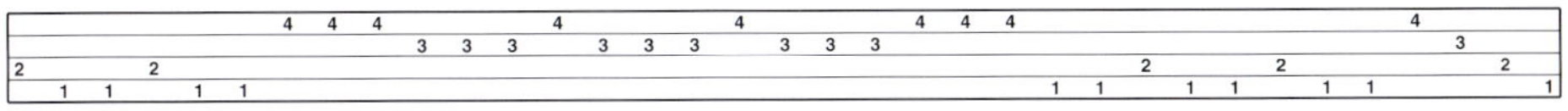

6.11c The form of 6.11b has been expanded by inserting empty squares because each block is made up of two ends. Now we can write the threading (6.11d).

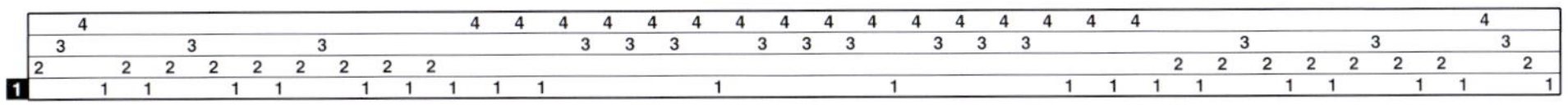

6.11d Our threading draft is complete. It was altered a bit to be sure that symmetry is maintained. The last thread (highlighted, on shaft 1) is omitted when repeats are made.

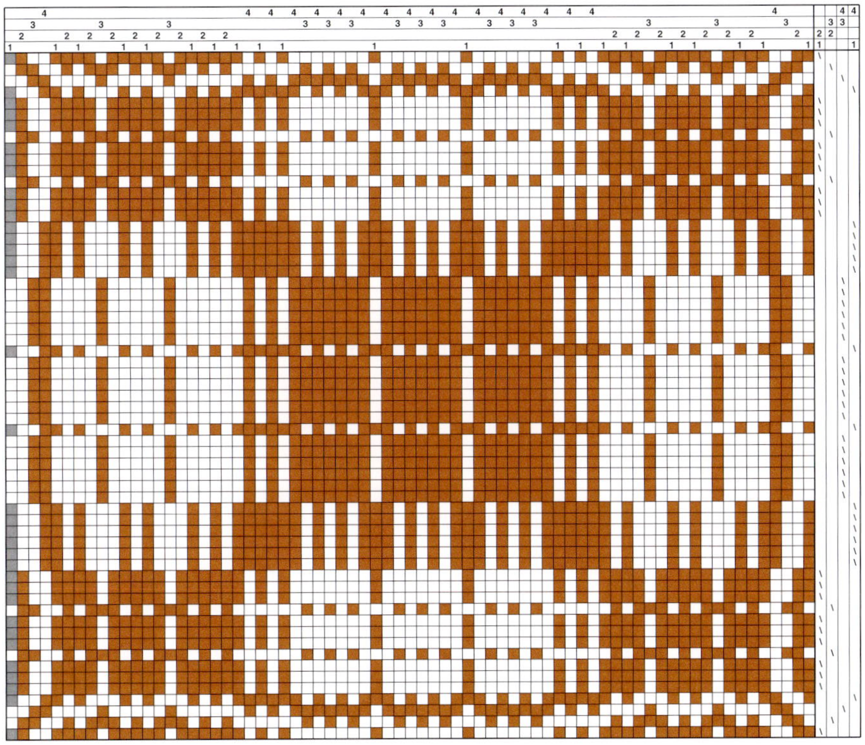

6.11e The treadling has been added making the pattern complete. Only the pattern shots are shown; the plain-weave shots are omitted.

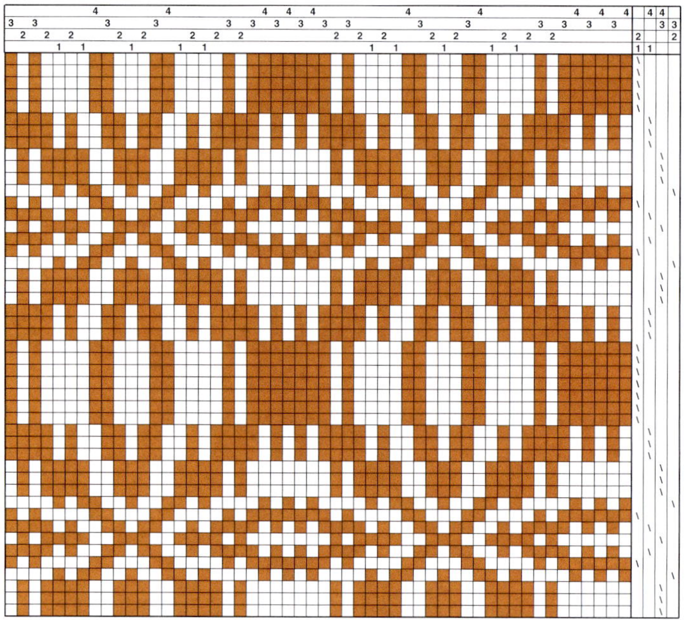

6.12a Johann Schleelein's No. 123, page 131, Davison. Shown treadled as drawn in or star fashion. The pattern weft is shown dark as it usually was in a traditional overshot.

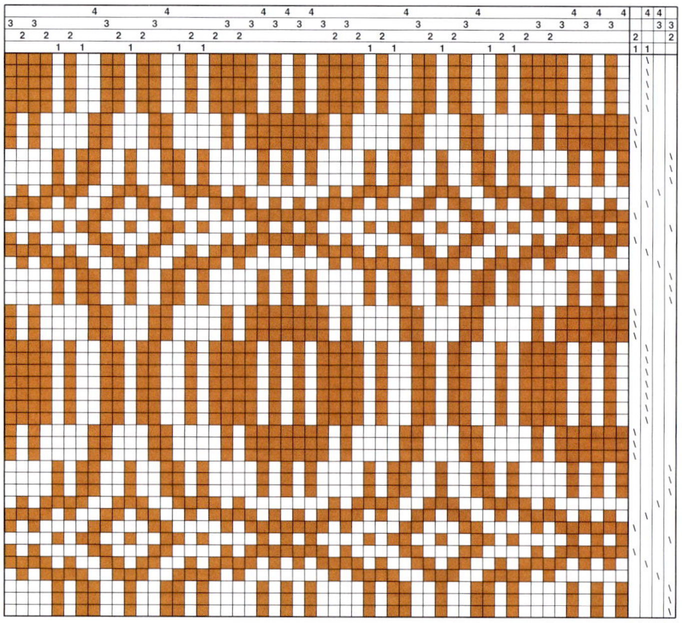

6.12b Johann Schleelein's No. 123, page 131, Davison. Shown treadled rose fashion. Starting with the treadling shown in 6.12a, substitute shed 3, 4 for 2, 3 and vice versa, and 1, 4 for 1, 2 and vice versa. The pattern weft is shown dark as it usually was in a traditional overshot.

Treadling as drawn in

When I first began to weave, I was told of a woman who had bought a warped loom at an estate sale. The loom had been threaded in an overshot pattern which was left on the loom. According to the story, the new owner cut the warp and took it off the loom "because I didn't know what the treadling was." The point of this story is that if we know the threading for an overshot pattern, the treadling is very easy to derive.

Overshot patterns may be treadled in many ways, as we shall see, but the simplest way is to weave it as it was threaded, **as drawn in**, or, to use the archaic but picturesque term, "trompt as writ" (treadled as written).

In traditional overshot weaving, two shuttles are always thrown alternately. The treadling we are working out here is the one followed by the shuttle carrying the pattern weft, the larger, more softly spun, frequently contrasting thread. The plain-weave or tabby weft picks follow a very strict order: 1, 3 versus 2, 4. It is this weft that provides the ground cloth, the underlying grid, over, under, and through which the pattern wefts go, creating patterns in the cloth. Drawing down the structure including the tabby shots obscures the pattern. It is also misleading, because as the cloth is woven the pattern shots "nest" with the tabbies, occupying the space of one shot. A draft that shows the tabby shots as well as the pattern shots also elongates the pattern. The drafts shown in this chapter assume the use of the tabby shots but do not show them.

Look at Johann Schleelein's number 123. Draft 6.12a shows the drawdown of the pattern obtained if treadled as drawn in. Here's how we got there: Look at the draft and you will see that the first six ends are in the 3, 4 block; in the treadling, the shed leaving 3, 4 down (lifting 1, 2) is made five times. (*To have the patterns show in the block threaded on 4, 3, those threads must not be lifted, thus putting the pattern thread* **over** *the warp at that place.*) the next block is the 2, 3 block, containing four ends; 1, 4 is treadled three times so the pattern weft will float over threads on shafts 2 and 3. The next block is 1, 2, containing four ends; 3, 4 is treadled three times. Do you see the relationship? The total number of ends in a block less one is the number of times that the pattern goes through that shed, with tabby shots between. This way of treadling produces diagonals that cross at right angles. In the traditional naming of patterns, these crossing diagonals were called "stars." Sometimes this method of treadling is called "**star fashion.**"

Other ways to treadle a threading

Once we have tried the treadling above, we can begin to play with it. *Note that it is necessary to derive the treadling sequence we developed above for nearly all of the examples that follow.* Draft **6.12a** star fashion or as drawn in. If every time the draft calls for the shed 3, 4 we substitute 2, 3 and vice versa, and for the shed 1, 2 we use 1, 4 and vice versa—the diagonals disappear and rounded shapes, "roses," appear in their stead (**6.12b**). This treadling system is called "**rose fashion.**" Of course, you are free to make any combination of substitutions. If 1, 2 and 2, 3 are exchanged and 1, 4 and 3, 4 are as well, we see a new version of Johann Schleelein's No. 123, draft **6.12c**. A closer look reveals that **6.12b** and **6.12c** (both rose patterns) are the reverse of each other.

If the yarns are reversed, that is, the pattern yarn is used in the tabby sheds and the tabby yarn in the pattern sheds, the pattern of weft floats is wispy or spidery looking,

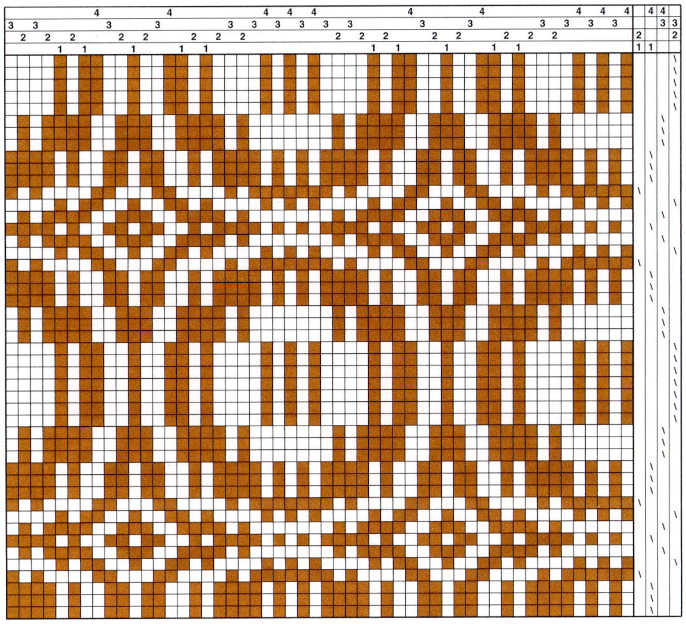

6.12c Johann Schleelein's No. 123, page 131, Davison. Shown treadled rose fashion. Based on 6.12b 1, 2 and 2, 3 switch and 1, 4 and 3, 4 switch. The pattern weft is shown dark as it usually was in a traditional overshot.

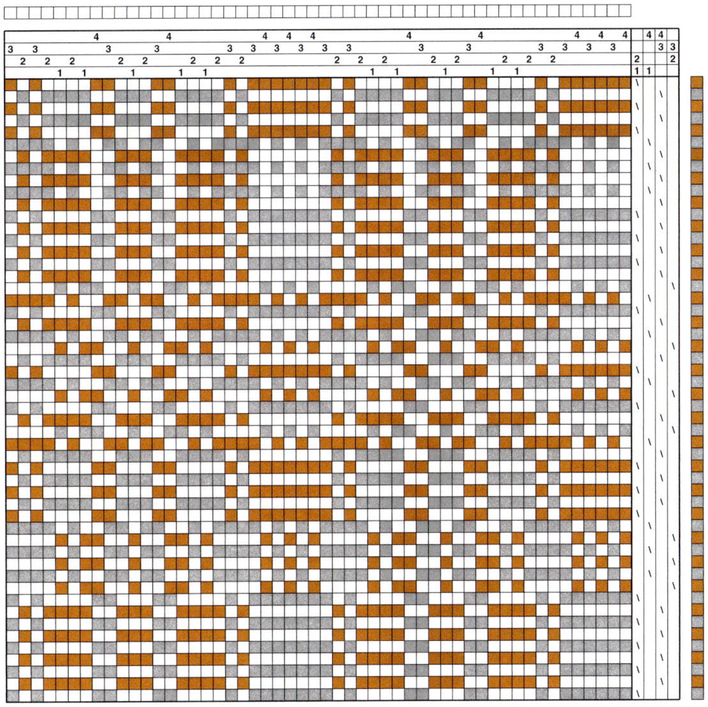

6.13 This is on opposites version of draft 6.12a, Johann Schleelein's No. 123, page 131, Davison. It is shown treadled as drawn in or star fashion. One half of the repeat in 6.12a is shown. Because it does not pack in well, the pattern will be somewhat elongated unless wefts much finer than the warp are used.

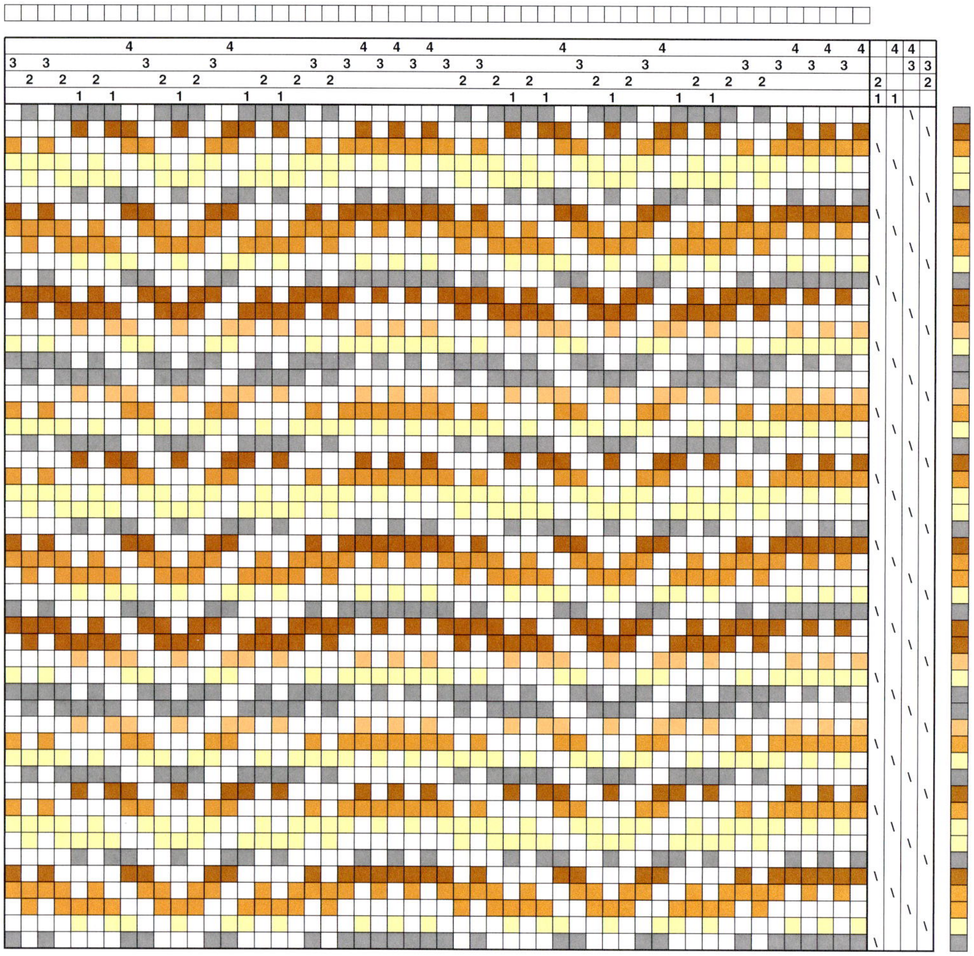

6.14 This is the flamepoint version of draft 6.12a, Johann Schleelein's No. 123, page 131, Davison. The treadling is quite simple, repeating in four sheds. Four colors are used:

Gray	*1*	*1*	*1*	*2*
Dark Orange	*1*	*1*	*2*	*1*
Light Orange	*1*	*2*	*1*	*1*
Yellow	*2*	*1*	*1*	*1*

Repeat all 20 picks

giving rise to its name, "**spider fashion**" or "**shadow fashion.**" Imagine an overshot fabric in which the yarn weights are reversed throughout: heavier yarn for both warp and weft, a fine yarn for the pattern weft.

Overshot threadings may be used to weave honeycomb-like fabrics, too (discussed in detail in Chapter 5, The Distorted Grid). Typically, the plain-weave shots are made with yarn the same color and a little heavier than the warp. The pattern shots are woven, often in another color, sometimes with white, with a thread that is the same size as the warp yarn or a little smaller. For ease of weaving, the cloth is woven *wrong side up*. To produce a cell where the block is 3, 4, we alternately lift shaft 3 alone and then shaft 4 alone, using the colored weft. Davison repeats the sequence three times for each. The reason the block is woven this way is that if all blocks are woven equally, tension problems are avoided. Thus, if we were to weave a particular block treadled as drawn in, we would alternate lifting the single shafts three times each, followed by two plain-weave shots. As is the case for ordinary honeycomb, there will be long floats on the back of this cloth, which is the side facing the weaver.

Another way of weaving an overshot threading is called **on opposites**. There is no plain-weave weft. Two shuttles are thrown, each carrying a yarn of about the same size as the warp or slightly smaller and contrasting in color from each other as well as the warp. For example, the warp could be white and the two wefts, blue and red.

When the draft calls for three shots of the pattern weft in block 1, 2, for example, 1, 2 are lifted and one color is thrown, followed by the other shuttle *in the opposite shed*, 3, 4. The star or rose treadling order may be followed. The fabric produced in this way is generally beaten very firmly to cover the warp completely and so that the cloth is stable (**6.13**).

Flamepoint, a variation with a nod to needlepoint, likewise has no plain weave. Fine, soft wefts that beat in easily are used, sometimes in four closely related colors—often successive tints or shades of a single hue. The first color is used to weave shed 1, 2; then the second color weaves shed 2, 3; the third, 3, 4; and the fourth, 1, 4. This sequence is repeated three or four times, and then the first color is used twice, keeping the treadling order the same, so that the colors now appear in different sheds. This process continues until the first color is back in the shed made by lifting 1, 2. Our Johann Schleelein threading, treated this way, but without repeats is shown in **6.14**.

Overshot using more than four shafts

Why would we need to use more than four shafts to weave overshot? One compelling reason involves a phenomenon called halftones. When we weave a four-shaft pattern, because each block shares a thread with the one before and the one after it, the pattern shows part of the time on either side of the place where the pattern weft shows in a long float. In **6.10b**, the long float formed by the first three pattern picks falls under the 3, 4 block. We have lifted 1, 2 to make pattern appear over shafts 3 and 4; on both sides of that area, the pattern weft will show wherever 3 and 4 appear in the threading. The blocks bordering the 3, 4 block are both threaded on 2, 3, allowing the pattern to show over 3 and be covered by 2. This area, which is neither a pattern area nor an area devoid of the pattern weft (as the 1, 2 block is), is called a halftone.

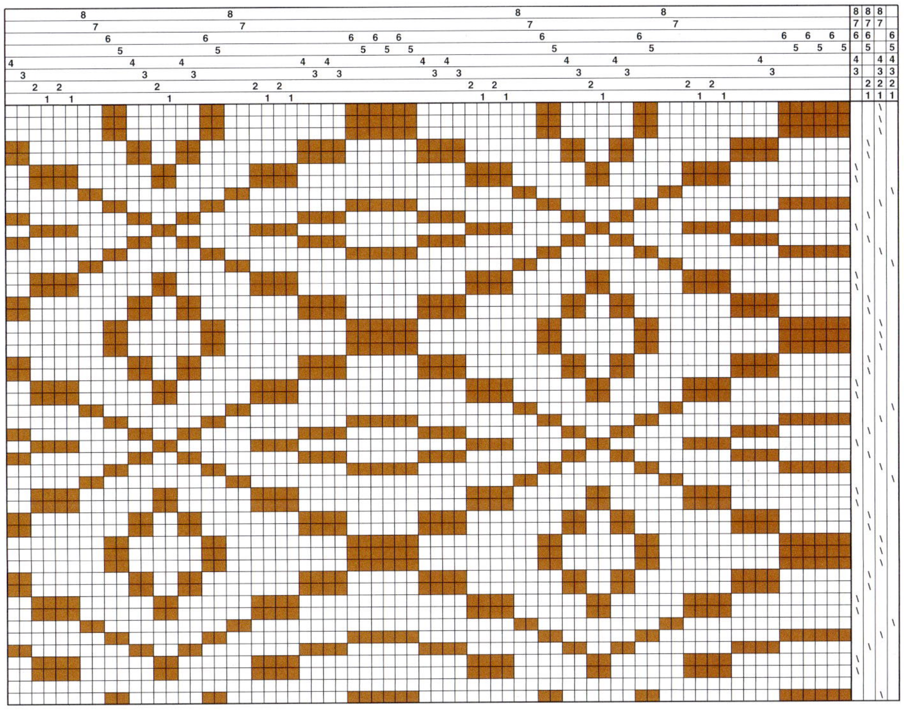

6.15a Based on 6.12a, this draft expands what was a four-shaft threading to eight shafts. In the new threading 1 ,2 stays the same; 2, 3 becomes 3, 4; 3, 4 becomes 5, 6; and 1, 4, becomes 7, 8.

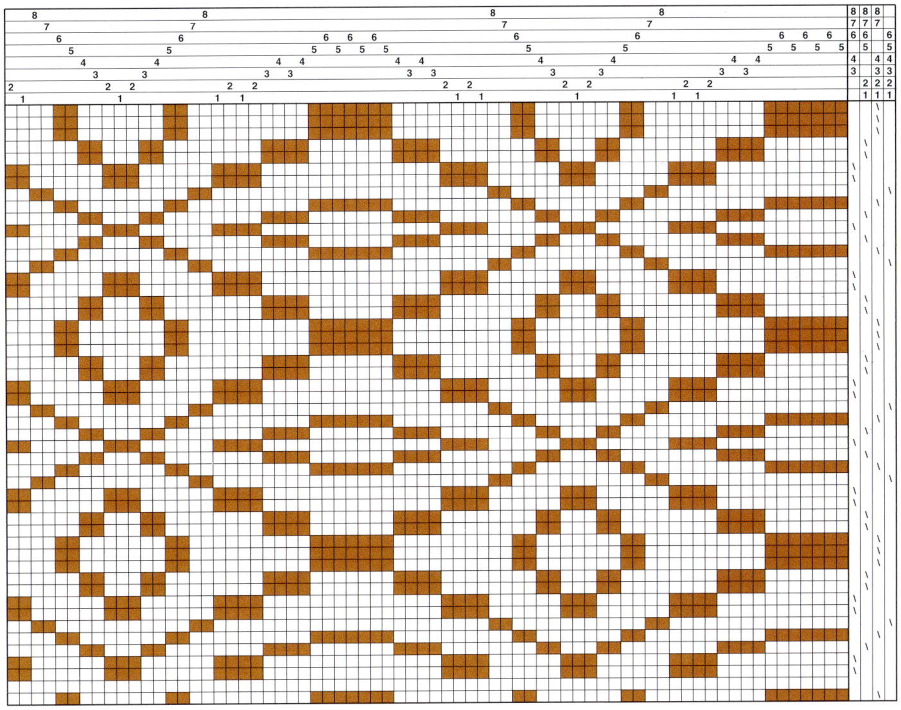

6.15b Draft 6.15a modified so that the transition from block to block is symmetrical.

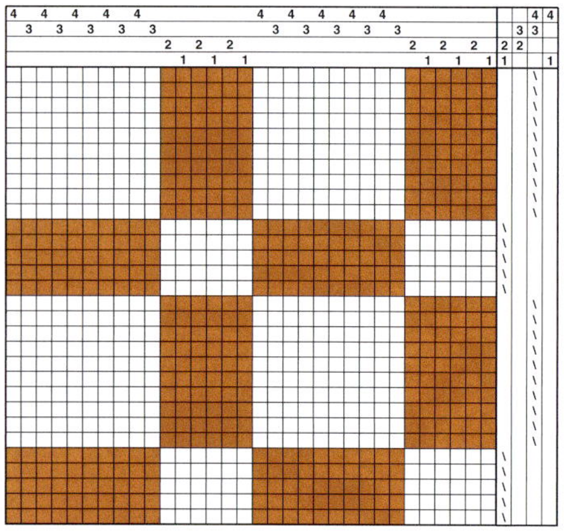

6.16 This threading uses just two of the possible four blocks. It is called a monk's belt pattern and characteristically lacks halftones. Only two pattern sheds are used along with the tabbies, which are not shown.

There are overshot patterns on four shafts which do not produce halftones. Monk's belt (**6.16**) is an overshot pattern that uses only two of the possible blocks (here, 1, 2 and 3, 4). These blocks do not have any threads in common, so there cannot be halftones unless there are halftones everywhere, (as there would be if we lifted 2, 3 or 1, 4). The wefts lie on the face or the back, never interlacing as plain weave. No halftones are produced. This four-shaft method of avoiding halftones reduces the number of blocks from four to two. If we expand a four-shaft overshot onto eight shafts, we can thread 1, 2 (again) as 1, 2; 2, 3 as 3, 4; 3, 4 as 5, 6; and 1, 4 as 7, 8. Draft **6.15a** shows King's Flower expanded to eight shafts and woven as drawn in with no halftones. Draft **6.15b** is made by slightly rearranging the threads within blocks to create symmetry, which **6.15a** lacks. The pattern isn't as smooth looking, because no threads are shared between blocks, but that drawback is minor compared with the long floats on the back that this pattern produces.

The creation of halftones will solve the float problem, and with eight shafts we can choose where they are and what they look like. In the four-shaft version, the halftones show up in the block adjacent to the one in which we see the pattern thread. We can do the same on eight shafts (**6.17a** and **6.17b**): by lifting the same shaft for the halftone in the blocks adjacent to the pattern block, we create vertical lines. Because we have spread the threading out over eight shafts, we can create plain-weave halftones, (**6.17c**).

We can also position the halftone block so that the blocks next to where the pattern appears have no pattern thread showing at all (**6.17c**), making a cloth with crisper pattern areas than those in **6.17a**. Choose the look you prefer.

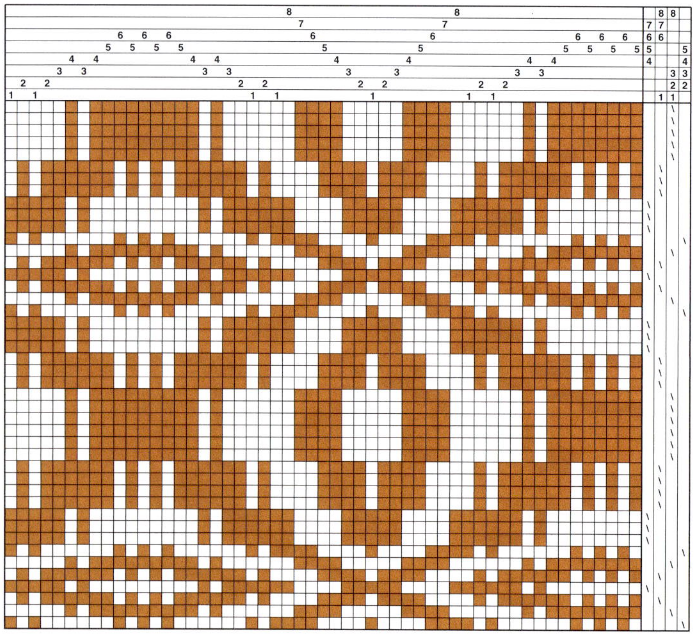

6.17a Draft 6.15b with added halftones to shorten weft floats on the back. Halftones are adjacent to the blocks.

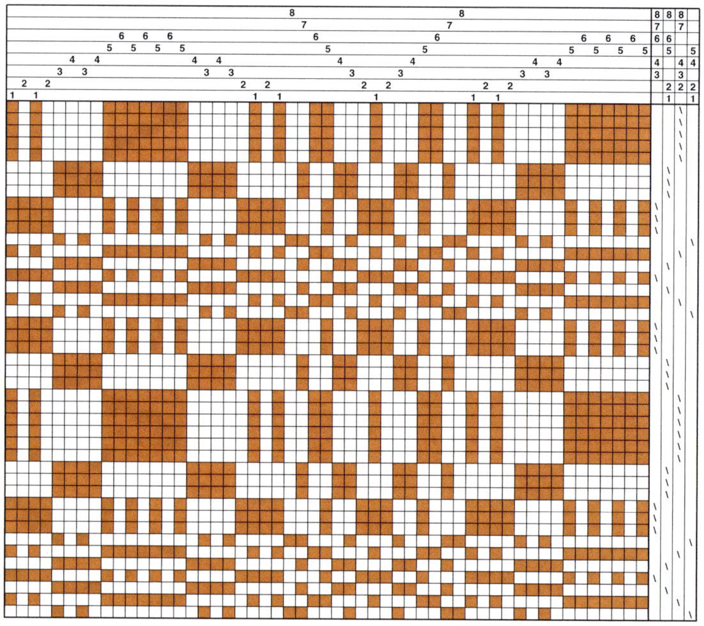

6.17b The halftones have been moved one block over to make a clean edge to the pattern areas in the cloth.

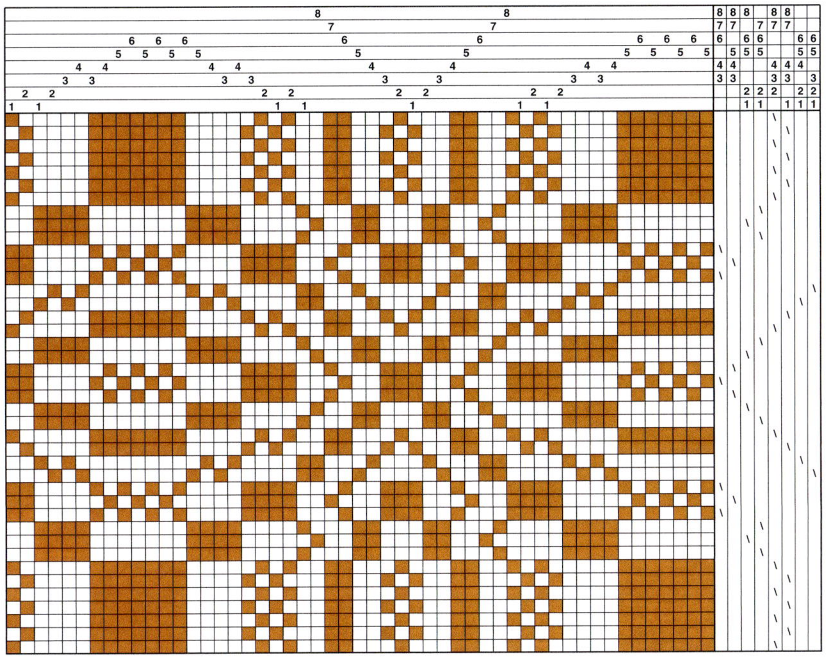

6.17c The halftones are plain weave and moved out to produce a cleaner looking design because the pattern areas are offset by the area with no halftones.

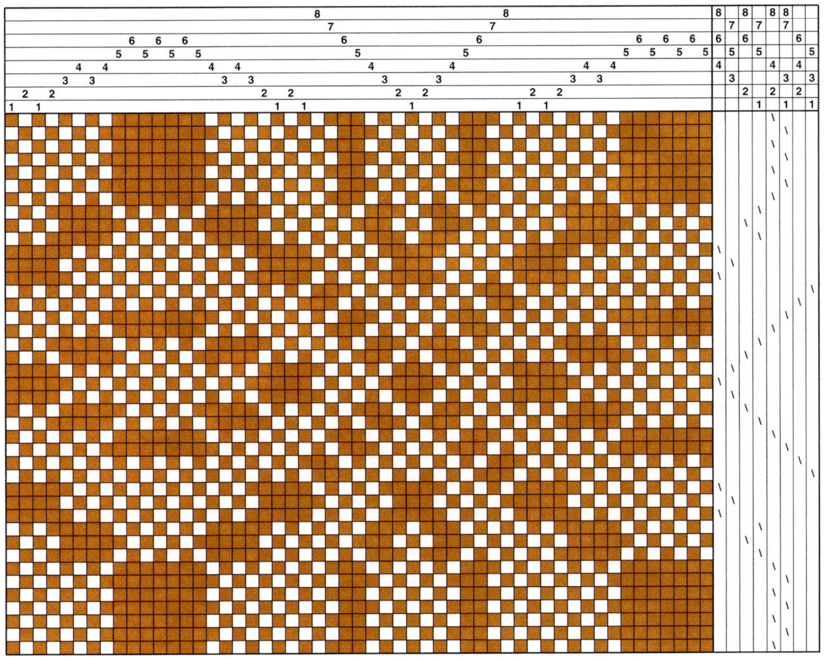

6.17d The pattern weft weaves plain weave in all areas except where the pattern shows. The other side of this cloth never shows pattern floats. This weft plus the tabby wefts could be difficult to beat in well. Choose a smaller, softly spun pattern weft or a smaller tabby thread, or both.

Or, if you like, you can make all the areas *not* weaving pattern weave in a plain-weave halftone (**6.17d**). If you have more than eight shafts, you may allocate two shafts per block as we have done with eight, and expand the pattern produced. Draft **6.18** shows a circular motif that would require twelve shafts and twelve treadles to weave. By adding two more blocks, bringing the total number of shafts to sixteen, a "**table**" (a repetitive geometric area within an overshot formed by alternating two blocks in the threading) can be added (**6.19**) while simplifying the circular area.

In summary, overshot allows the weaver using four shafts to create large, repeating patterns, many of them with curving lines. For functional fabrics, block length must be monitored to avoid creating long floats that will snag and pull. Overshot requires the use of two shuttles, which is slower than weaving with one.

Of course, if you have six shafts, you can weave a four-shaft draft with only one shuttle by turning it: putting the tabby and pattern wefts into the warp.. Because what were p.p.i. become e.p.i. and vice versa, the sett for the turned draft will be twice as dense as the original one. See Appendix A (page 246) for instructions on how to turn a draft.

6.18 A circular pattern requiring twelve shafts. Plain weave halftones have been added to make shorter weft floats.

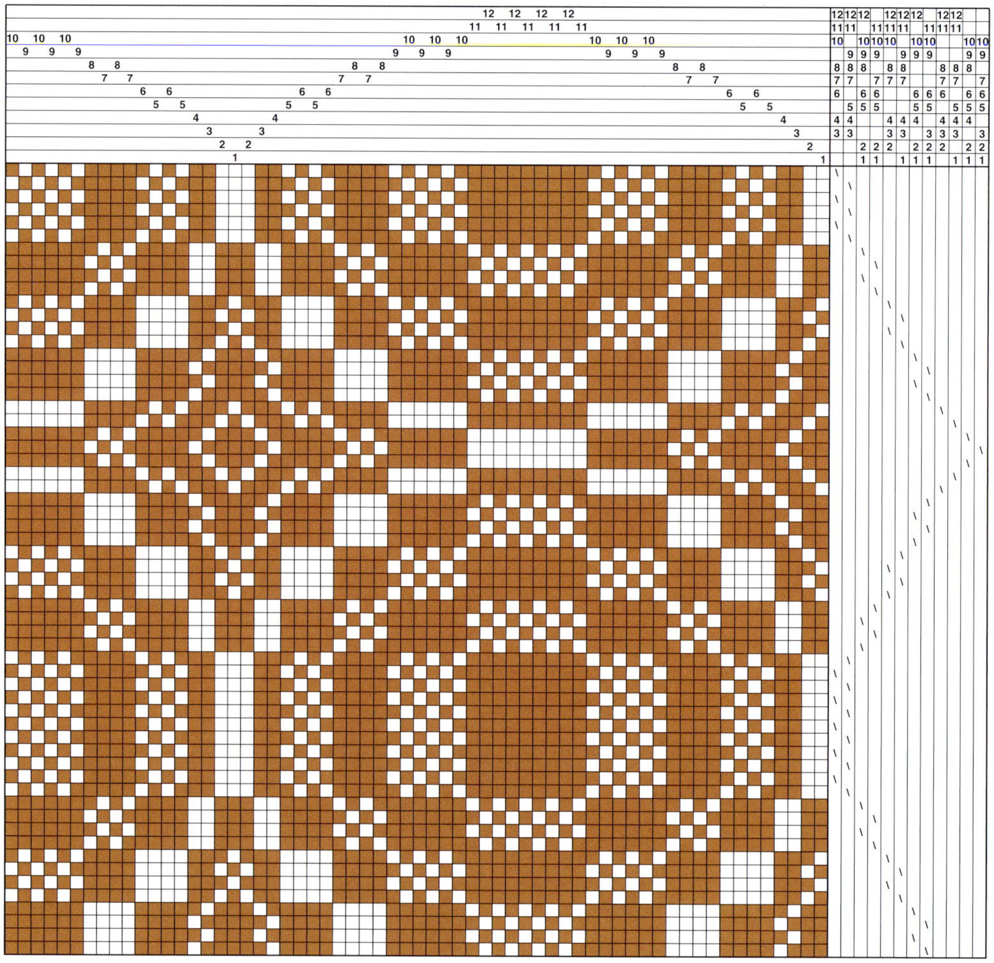

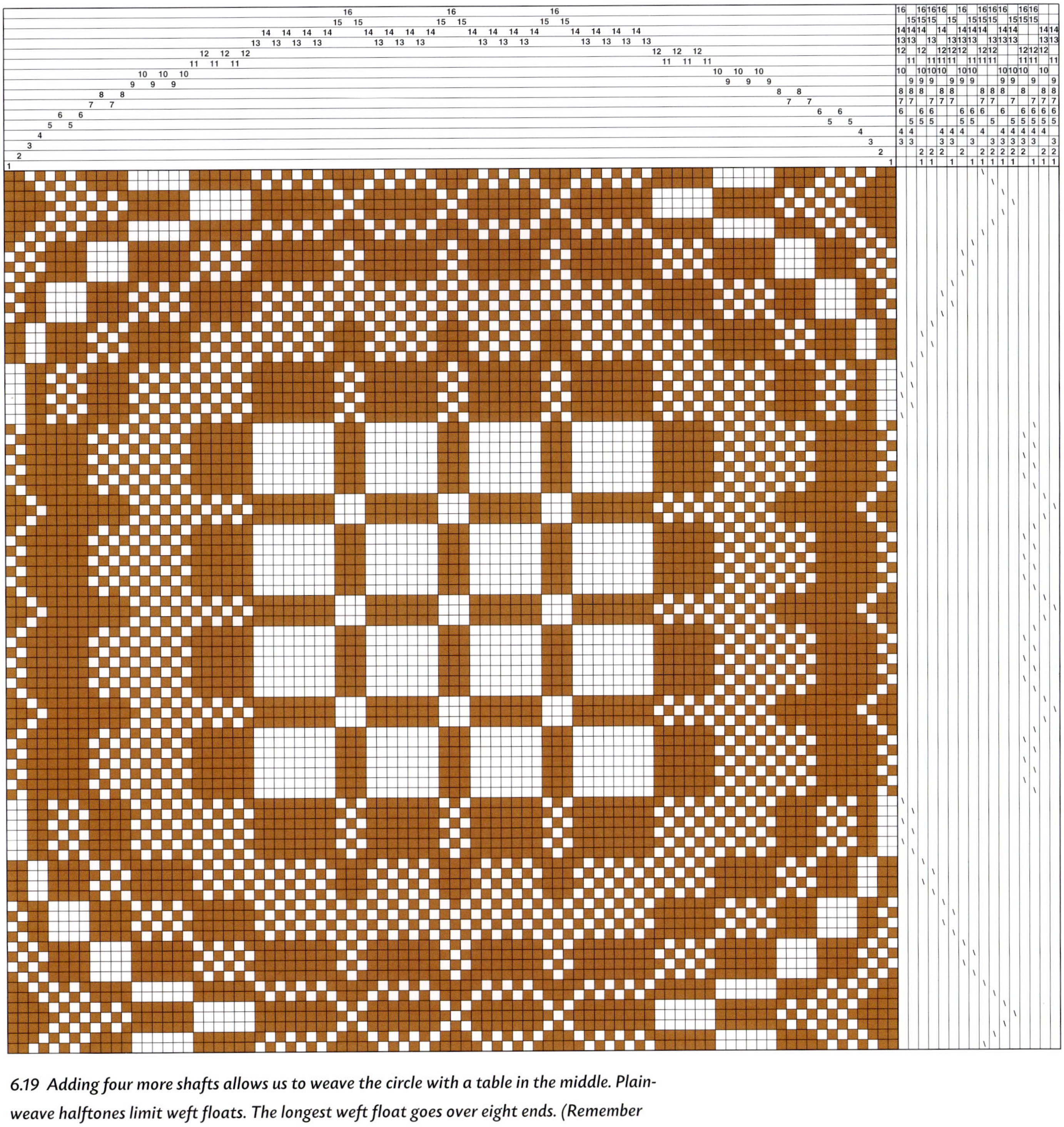

6.19 *Adding four more shafts allows us to weave the circle with a table in the middle. Plain-weave halftones limit weft floats. The longest weft float goes over eight ends. (Remember that a tabby is used so there will be no warp floats.)*

Turned overshot. Six shafts are required when a four-shaft overshot is turned, but only one shuttle is needed. The gray ground fabric is 16/2 cotton. The yellow, yellow-orange and red-orange warps are a softly spun 4-ply cotton.

Summer and Winter

Summer and winter, another three-element weave, has an advantage that overshot lacks: its blocks may be as long as you like without any structural consequences; maximum float length is over three warp ends. It does have a limitation: on four shafts you may weave only two blocks.

Thread choice for classic summer and winter is the same as for overshot: a finer, hard-spun thread for the warp and tabby weft and a larger (twice as large, classically), softly spun yarn, often contrasting in color, for the pattern weft.

The name for this weave structure is said to have arisen from the fact that one side of the cloth—often a coverlet—was predominantly the dark color of the pattern weft and the other side, mostly the lighter color of the warp and tabby. In winter, the coverlet was used dark side up, we are told, and then flipped over for summer use.

In summer and winter, two shafts (the first two) are set aside, with all the others used to create the pattern. The ends carried on the first two shafts ensure that the pattern floats are never longer than over three warp ends. These tie the pattern thread down and thus are often referred to as "tie-downs." If the loom has four shafts, then two of them are available for making the pattern. The draft for this structure is made up of individual units that may be repeated as many times as desired, used in any order in the threading and treadling, and woven individually or in any combination.

The unit for summer and winter consists of four ends and is threaded 1, X, 2, X, where "X" is any shaft other than 1 or 2. From this unit, we can see that the sheds for the plain-weave, or tabby, shots are 1, 2 versus all the pattern shafts. (To make plain weave, we must lift every other end.) For a four-shaft cloth, that would be 1, 2 versus 3, 4. (**6.20**). These sheds alternate with the tabby shots. We will not show the tabbies in the drafts that follow because they distort the pattern in the draw down by elongating it; as in overshot, the tabbies nest with the pattern wefts.

One woven unit of summer and winter consists of four tabby shots and four pattern shots. The order in which the pattern shots are made greatly affects the pattern produced.

First we need to think about where we would like the pattern to be. The pattern weft will show on the face (the side you see while you are weaving) where the shaft or shafts (shaft 3 and higher) controlling that block or those blocks is/are left down.

Draft **6.21** shows four methods of weaving classic summer and winter. Each method of treadling is separated from the others by

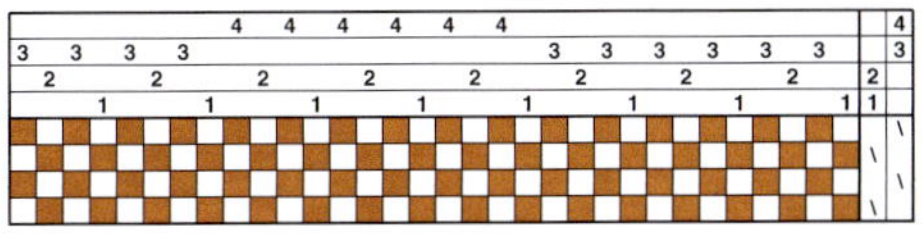

***6.20** Two-block summer and winter. Using the sheds shown here makes plain weave. A plain-weave shot is thrown between pattern shots when weaving classical summer and winter.*

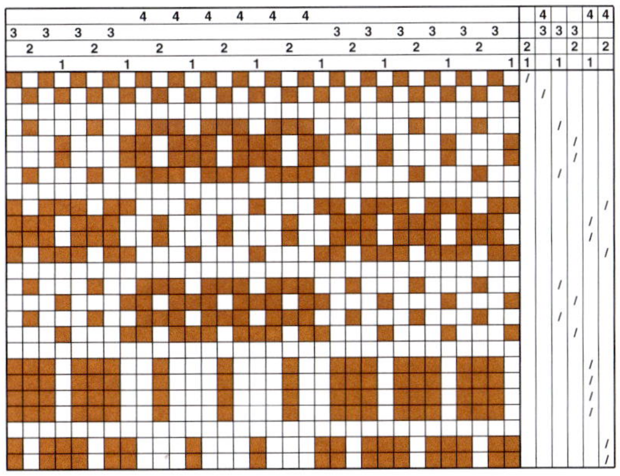

***6.21** Two-block summer and winter pattern consisting of three units of block A (1, 3, 2, 3) followed by three units of block B (1, 4, 2, 4) and then two units of block A.*

The first two picks show the tabby that is omitted in what follows; only pattern wefts are shown in the five sections that follow.

The first section (four picks) is the pairs method that forms O's. The second section is the pairs method that forms X's. The third section is the singles method; the tie-downs are used alternately in the four pattern shots.

The fourth section uses the same tie-down throughout the four picks. The next to last uses one, which produces nice clean edges to the blocks. The last uses two, which breaks the blocks in an asymmetrical way. Using the same tie-down for all pattern wefts is called the dukagång method.

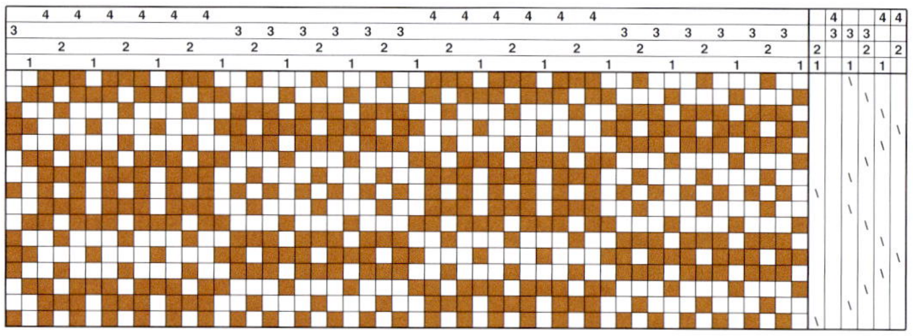

6.22a Two-block summer and winter woven with one shuttle to produce a texture.

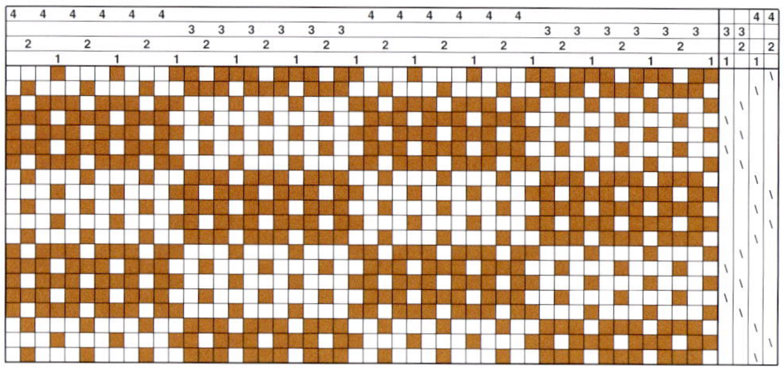

6.22b Another two-block summer and winter woven with one shuttle to produce a texture.

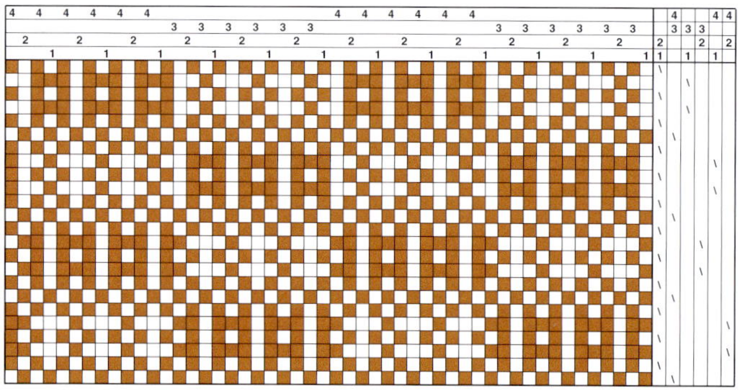

6.22c Two-block summer and winter woven with one shuttle to create another textural effect.

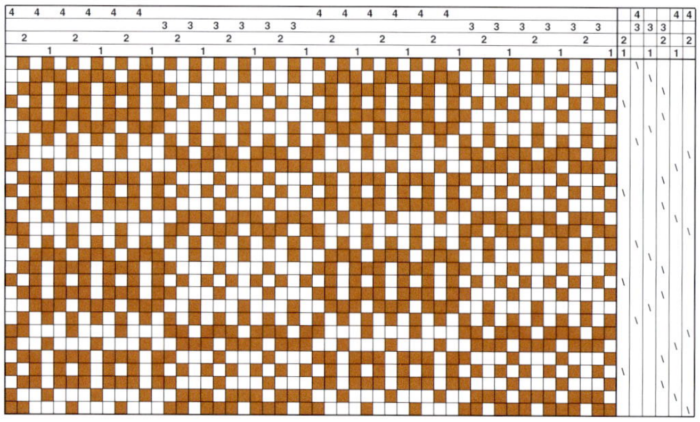

6.22d Yet another two-block summer and winter woven with one shuttle to create another textural effect.

a space in the draft. The first two examples are called "pairs methods" because the same tie-down thread is lifted twice in a row. The first one begins by lifting the tie-down on shaft 1; the edges of the blocks have a rounded shape like the letter "O." When we begin the sequence with the tie-down on shaft 2, as in the next section, the edges of the blocks have the shape of the letter "X." These diagonals connect the blocks in the cloth, whereas the O's method leaves them separate, rounding the edges of the blocks.

The third method of weaving summer and winter uses the tie-down ends alternately. The resulting blocks are more squared off with neither rounded corners nor diagonals connecting the blocks.

The fourth method uses the same tie-down throughout the treadling. This causes vertical lines in the pattern areas because the same shaft (here, shaft 1) is raised for all pattern shots. Because the patterns made in the cloth resemble those of dukagång (page 124), this method is called the "dukagång method." If you lift shaft 2 instead, the edges of the blocks do not line up and the pattern is less clear (the fifth example in **6.21**). Just as there are variations on the ways in which overshot can be woven, the four methods of weaving summer and winter described above are not the only ones we can use. We can also make summer and winter look lacy or like honeycomb, create pile, and incorporate more than two colors.

Drafts **6.22a**, **6.22b**, **6.22c**, and **6.22d** produce textural effects and require only one shuttle. If textural effects are desired, it is nearly impossible to go wrong with summer and winter. The longest weft float will not exceed three ends, but it will be necessary to avoid repeating lifting the same pattern shaft for longer than will produce a reasonable float length.

Summer and winter may be woven as if it were Bronson lace: that is, one tabby, a pattern shed, same tabby, same pattern shed, same tabby and then the other tabby (**6.22e**). Notice that the warp floats appear in one block when treadled one way and in the other block when treadled the other way. In the upper part of the draft shown, we alternate between blocks A (1, 3, 2, 3) and B (1, 4, 2, 4), with one treadling repeat for each. By continuing the same repeat over and over, we may form vertical stripes.

Honeycomb woven on a summer and winter threading requires two shuttles, one carrying larger weft for the plain-weave shots that outline the cells and one carrying a smaller, usually contrasting weft, which weaves the cells (**6.22f**).

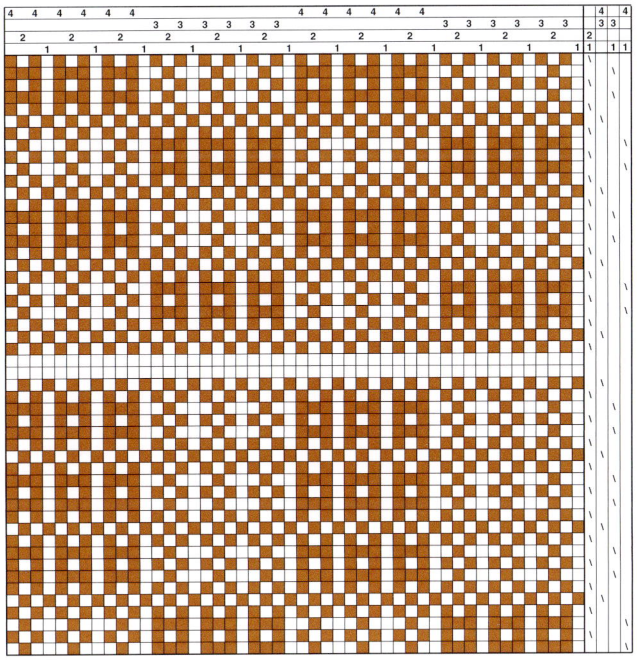

6.22e Two-block summer and winter woven as if it were Bronson lace. Only one shuttle is used.

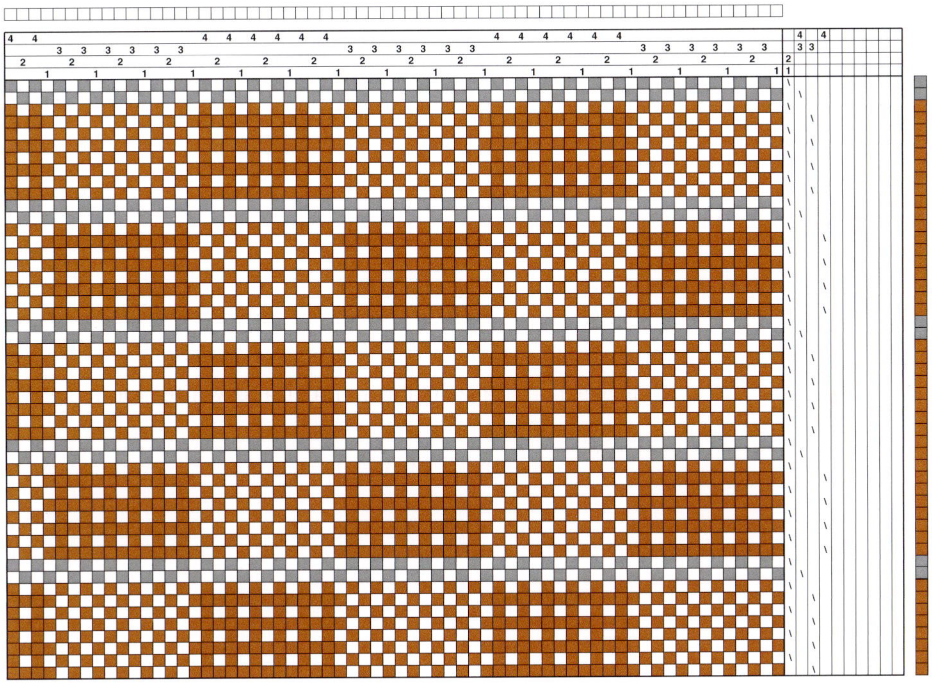

6.22f Two-block summer and winter woven in a honeycomb-like pattern. The wefts weaving plain weave selvedge to selvedge are larger and contrast in color to that used to weave the cell.

6.23 Summer and winter threading used to weave a pile. Dark orange represents the weft. The floats may be lifted with the fingers to form loops or longer pile before the weft is beaten in.

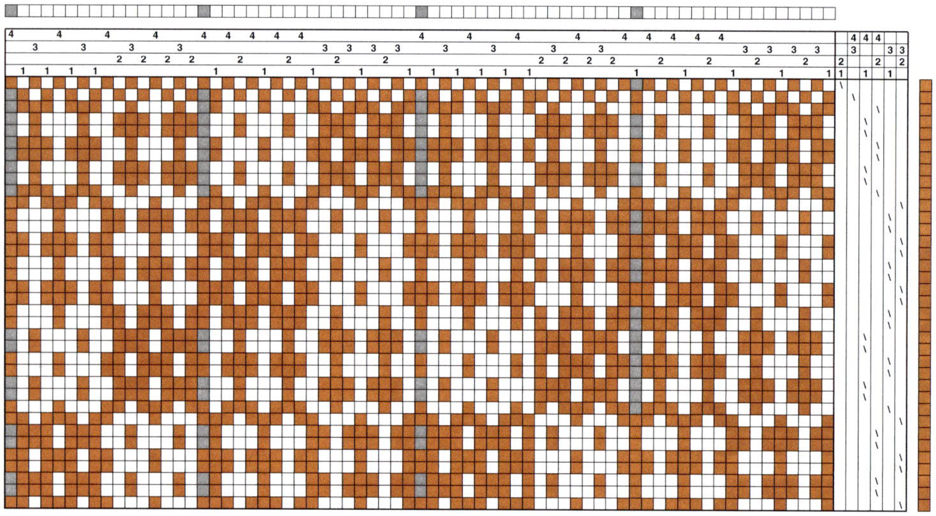

6.24 This four-shaft threading produces a four-block (almost) summer and winter. It requires only four shafts, but needs incidentals between the second and third blocks threaded, and between the first and fourth blocks. They are marked in a contrasting color so they are easy to spot. Is it really summer and winter? Well, no, but it does permit something like summer and winter in four blocks on the four-shaft loom.

Draft **6.23** illustrates a way to use a summer and winter threading to weave a pile weave. The floats are made by lifting the pattern shafts, one at a time, without the tie-down shafts. The floats can be made more dramatic by lifting loops with the fingers before changing the shed. The loops can be cut or not as desired.

If the blocks are narrow, the pile will cover more of the ground cloth. If the pile weft is doubled, the pile will be fuller. Beat firmly to ensure a sturdy cloth. Colors may be combined in one strand, changed at intervals to make weftwise stripes in the pile, or alternated to produce a warpwise stripe. If colors are combined, the pile wefts may be combined in a strand (three yarns, for example) and changed one by one to a new color to obscure exactly where the color change occurs. If the steps in color change are small, the result is a color that seems almost to have been airbrushed onto the pile.

It is possible to squeeze out four summer and winter blocks (almost) on four shafts. The first two blocks are made up of the units we have seen: A (1, 3, 2, 3) and B (1, 4, 2, 4). If we designate the tie-down shafts as pattern shafts, and vice versa, the next two units would be C (4, 2, 3, 2) and D (4, 1, 3, 1). The new units are written so as to maintain the tabby throughout the cloth. When the first extra unit is added to the draft after B, where the last end is threaded on shaft 4 and the first of the new unit is also on shaft 4, an extra thread must be added (on shaft 1) to avoid having two ends side by side on the same shaft *and to maintain the tabby.* The other extra unit also begins with an end on shaft 4, so changing their order does not help (**6.24**). The same problem occurs at the end of the last unit of D: D's last end and the first end of both A and B are threaded

Four-shaft (two-block) summer and winter. The gray warp and tabby are 16/2 cotton; the light yellow pattern weft is 8/2 cotton. This summer and winter is woven the singles method to make the blocks more rectangular (no O's or X's).

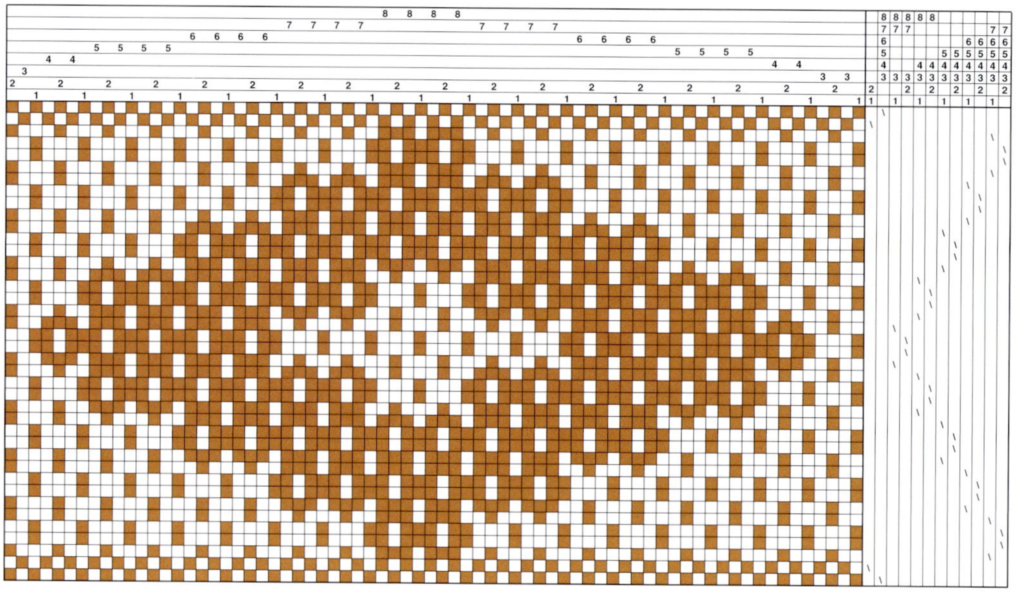

6.25a Eight-shaft (six block) pattern. Twelve treadles (including the tabbies) are required to weave this pattern.

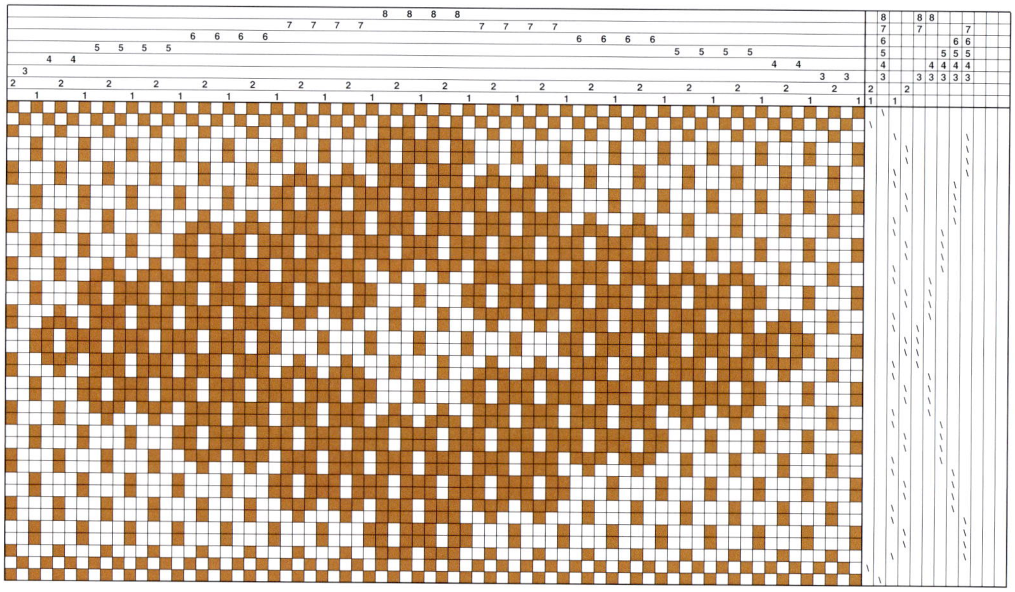

6.25b Eight-shaft (six block) pattern. Nine treadles are required to weave this design. Two feet are required for every pattern shed. Tabbies only shown at top and bottom. This shortened tie-up is called a skeleton tie-up.

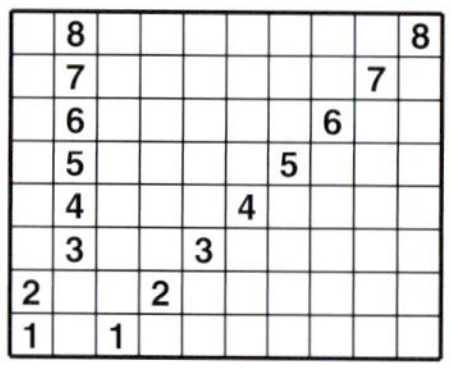

6.25c This would be the most flexible skeleton tie-up, permitting the weaver to combine as many blocks as desired. Both the pattern treadles and the tie-down treadle must be depressed when the pattern weft is thrown. Some combinations can be troublesome. For example, how would you lift 1+3+4+8 at one time?

on shaft 1. In this case, a thread on shaft 4 is added. This variation is not a classical summer and winter, but it is an interesting structure that provides more possibilities for the four-shaft loom.

More than four shafts

Summer and winter lends itself very nicely to adding blocks. For each block that is added, another shaft will be required. The number of shafts required for a given number of blocks is the number of blocks plus two (the tie-down shafts). Thus, on an eight-shaft loom, six blocks could be woven.

The form for the unit remains the same: 1, x, 2, x. So the unit of C in a classical summer and winter is threaded 1,5,2,5; D is threaded 1, 6, 2, 6; and so on. If a lot of shafts are available, then fairly elaborate patterns can be constructed. Remember that blocks may be threaded in any order and may be as long (contain as many repeats of the unit of which they are made) as you like; blocks may be woven in any combination and in any order. Draft **6.25a** and **6.25b** are the same design, woven in an eight-block design. The tie-up requires twelve treadles for the former and nine for the latter.

In the tie-up for **6.25b**, the tie-down shafts are not tied to the treadles that lift the pattern shafts. To weave the pattern, both one tie-down treadle and the pattern treadle are depressed. When the tie-downs are separated from the pattern treadles, the tie-up is called a **skeleton tie-up**.

A skeleton tie-up may also be made by tying each pattern shaft to its own treadle. The desired combination of these, plus the appropriate tie-down treadle, are all pushed at once. Draft **6.25c** shows just the skeleton tie-up for eight shafts.

If we wanted to make a shed lifting tie-down shaft 1 and pattern shafts 3, 4, and 8, then we have a problem. Once I solved that problem by using both feet and a stick to push the treadle controlling the pattern block that was isolated from the others. That is a method I would use only when desperate, which I was. This is a situation in which a dobby mechanism is worth nearly its weight in gold because the number of different sheds possible is large.

Three-block summer and winter. The checkerboard stripes run in the direction of the warp. The white warp and tabby are 20/2 pearl cotton, and the black pattern thread 10/2 pearl cotton. Woven the other way, only two blocks (and four shafts) would be required.

Crackle

Crackle weave is the name that Mary M. Atwater gave to the Swedish structure called *Jamtlandsväv* because she thought that the Swedish term is "to English speaking people something of a mouthful" and "because of the background effect which somewhat resembles the crackle in pottery." Crackle requires both a tabby and a decorative pattern weft. Just as in overshot and summer and winter, the warp and tabby weft are traditionally about the same size with the pattern weft somewhat larger and often contrasting in color.

With four shafts, four blocks are possible, but the threading is more complex that in summer and winter. The blocks are as follows: A: 1, 2, 3, 2; B: 2, 3, 4, 3; C: 3, 4, 1, 4; D: 4, 1, 2, 1. Notice that the last thread of each block is the same as the first thread of the next block in the sequence. Because two consecutive ends cannot be threaded on the same shaft and still maintain the tabby that forms the ground of this cloth, extra warp ends called incidentals must be inserted. It is the need for these incidentals that complicates writing a crackle draft.

Draft **6.26** shows four ways to treadle crackle. For clarity, the sheds of the tabby weft are shown in the tie-up and as the first two picks, but not shown in the rest of the treadling. Classically, the same pattern treadle is repeated for the desired length of the block (first variation). The second variation is treadled as if by the summer and winter singles method.

The third variation does not use a tabby, and is woven on opposites. Two contrasting yarns, finer than the pattern weft used in the first variation, are used alternately. The fourth variation is treadled in an interrupted twill order: 1, 2, 3, 2, 3, 4, 3, 4, 1, 4, 1, 2, and so on.

Although some of the structures shown in these pattern-only drafts appear to have warp floats longer than over three picks, the tabby picks not shown here actually prevent warp floats of any problematic length.

Because of the need for incidentals, crackle is not a unit weave; however, as in unit weaves, a particular block may consist of as many repeats as you like without compromising the structural integrity of the cloth. (Recall that that is not a possibility with overshot.)

Beiderwand

Beiderwand originated in Europe; it was especially used in the Schleswig-Holstein area of Germany, where it was used for coverlets and bed curtains. Beiderwand coverlets were woven in North America in the nineteenth century.

Beiderwand is not commonly used by handweavers, probably because of the number of shafts required to weave it. Historically, beiderwand coverlets most likely were woven on jacquard looms.

Shafts 1 and 2 are reserved for the tie-down ends. Each block in the draft requires two shafts, so a three-block pattern requires eight shafts, six for the three blocks plus two for the tie-down ends.

Drafts **6.27a** and **6.27b** show a three-block design. This is said to be a 2:1 beiderwand because the ratio of pattern ends to tie-down ends is two to one. The form of the threading may appear in a number of different ways with respect to the ends that control the pattern (although usually only one mode is used for a particular cloth). When the ratio of pattern to tie down-ends is 2:1, the pattern-shaft threading can be:

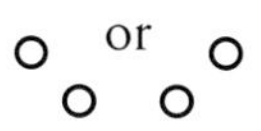

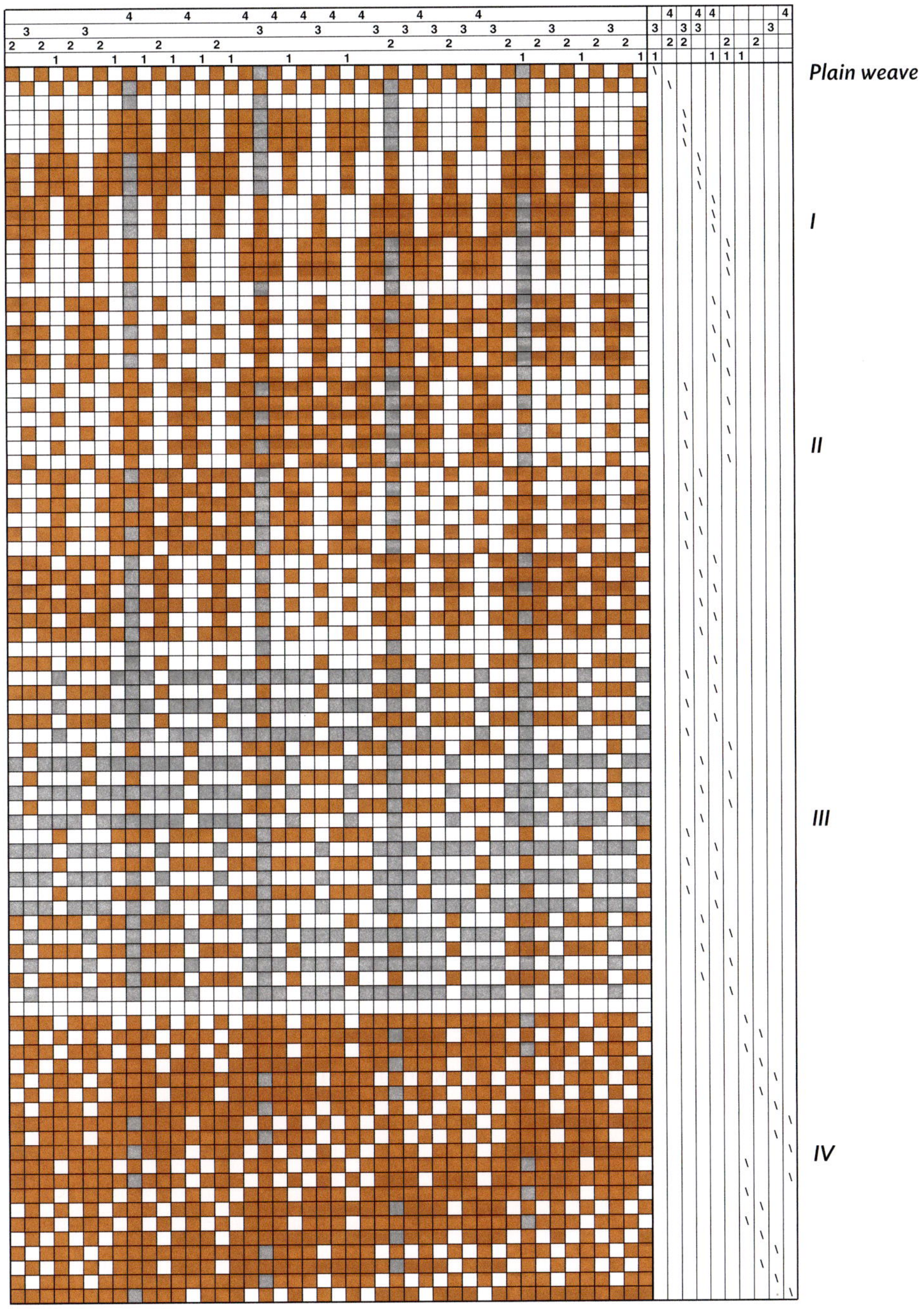

6.26 A simple crackle threading. The incidental threads are marked in a contrasting color so that they are easy to spot.

The first two picks are plain weave, which alternates with the pattern shots except for variation three.

The first variation consists of using the first pattern treadle (alternating with tabbies) until the block is the desired length. In the interest of space, the repeat is only three shots.

The second variation employs the tabbies and alternates two sheds making a pattern that resembles summer and winter singles method.

The third variation does not use a tabby but alternates two colors, both relatively fine, contrasting threads. It weaves on opposites.

The fourth variation uses a tabby and consists of sheds made by lifting single shafts in an interrupted twill order.

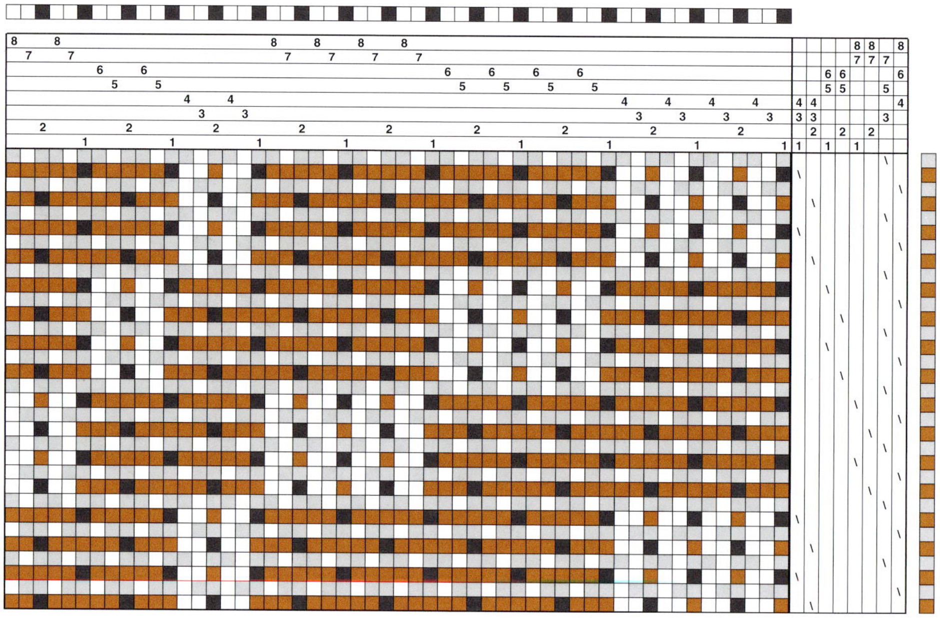

6.27a Beiderwand. This three-block draft requires eight shafts: two for each block plus two for the tie-down ends. The warp threads on the pattern shafts weave plain weave with a weft of the same size, usually cotton (shown here in gray). The pattern weft threads, (dark here), are usually a heavier wool. This draft produces areas in which there are two independent layers of double cloth.

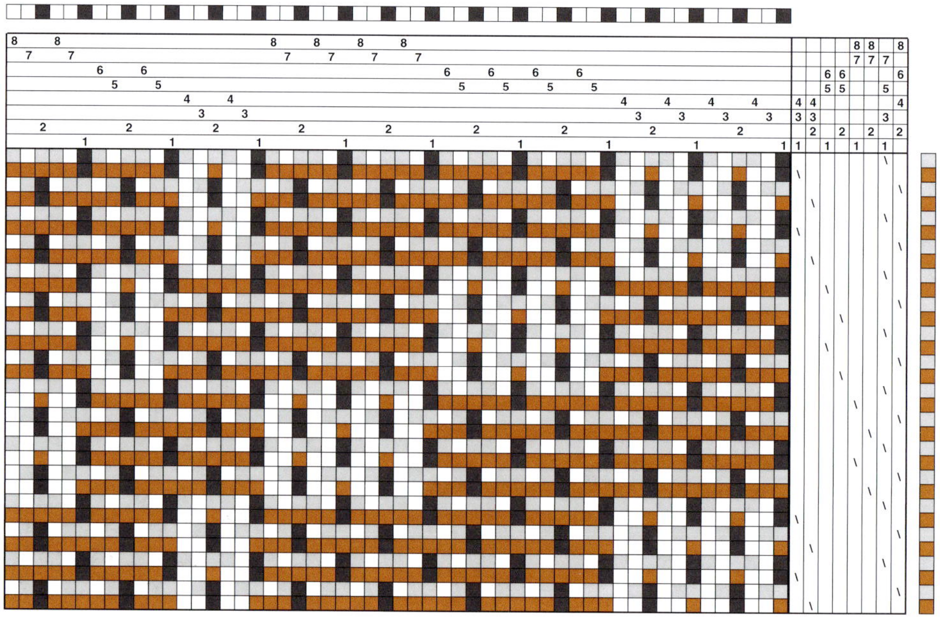

6.27b Another beiderwand. With this tie-up, the layers are stitched together throughout.

Draft **6.28** is the three-block design written for a 3:1 beiderwand. When the ratio of pattern ends to tie-down ends is three to one, there are several threading possibilities:

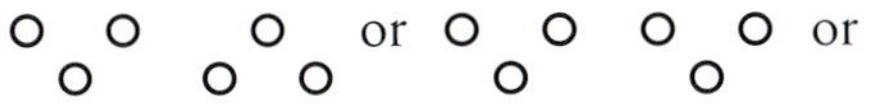

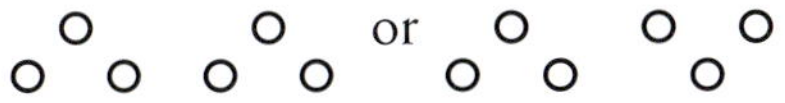

If the 4:1 version is used, draft **6.29**, the pattern ends may be threaded:

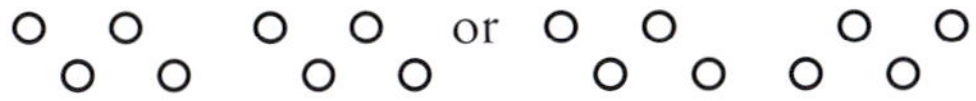

The chief difference between the kinds of beiderwand above is the float length. As you would expect, the pattern weft shows most in 4:1 beiderwand and least in 2:1 beiderwand. Note that "least" doesn't mean that the pattern looks skimpy; the pattern weft floats over nine or five ends, respectively.

Drafts **6.27a** and **6.27b** show two different types of beiderwand. In draft **6.27a**, two independent layers of cloth are produced in the areas where the blocks of plain weave are on the top of the cloth. This does not happen in draft **6.27b**; in this draft the layers are stitched together throughout. The difference is in the tie-up. If shafts 1 and 2 are raised when the pattern shafts weave plain weave (see the last two treadles in **6.27b** and also **6.28**), the layers are stitched together; if they are not, free double cloth is produced in these areas (see the last two treadles in **6.27a** and also **6.29**).

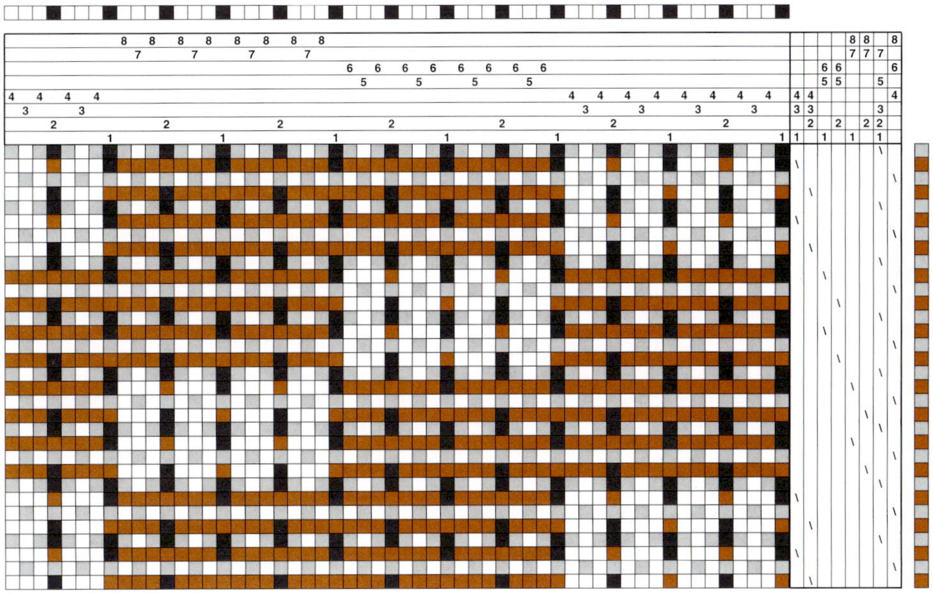

6.28 3:1 beiderwand. This three-block draft requires eight shafts: two for each block plus two for the tie-down ends. With this tie-up, the layers are stitched together throughout; there are no areas of free double cloth.

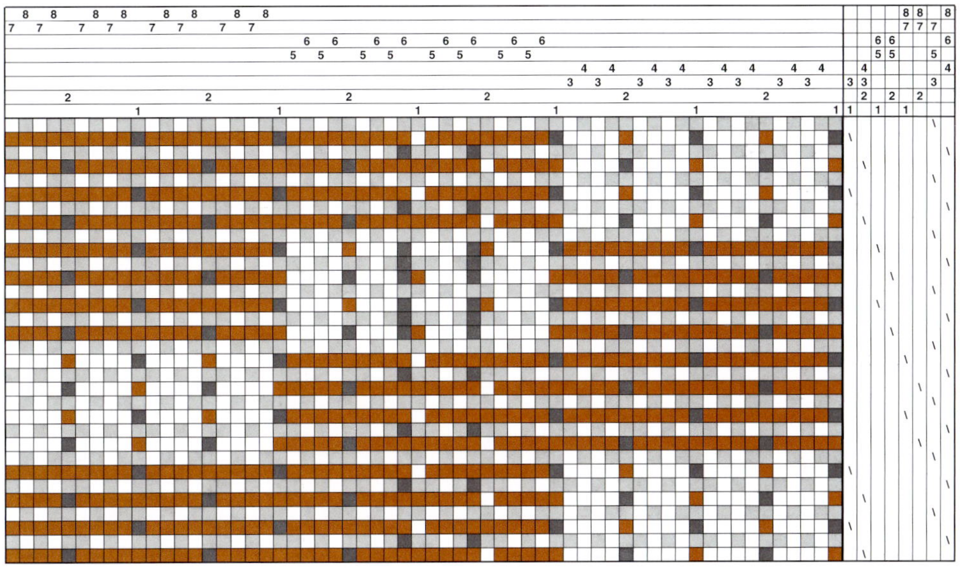

6.29 4:1 beiderwand. With this tie-up, there are areas of free double cloth where the white warp and pale gray weft form plain weave on the surface of the cloth.

The white cotton warp shows in the pattern areas a bit. If you want solid color there, thread the ends on shafts 3 on up with a yarn that matches the pattern weft. The ends carried on shafts 1 and 2 can be smaller and match the tabby wefts.

When the structure is fully tied, large areas of color can be woven with confidence that there will be no snagging or bagging. In general, when beiderwand is tied, both sides are about the same with no clear face or back. When the layers are not tied, the side shown in the accompanying drafts is definitely the face, or right side.

Why weave beiderwand at all? For some of us: because it is there. It does some of the same things that doubleweave does, with far fewer shafts. It adds the possibility of blocks of double cloth where the layers penetrate each other. As we will see in the doubleweave chapter, that sort of intersection requires four shafts for each additional block for doubleweave. Beiderwand requires only two shafts for each block added after the first one.

At right, sixteen-shaft beiderwand. Woven of 2/20 worsted wool, this cloth is shown "wrong" side up, which reveals more about its structure. The opposite side shows blue with the scale outlined in white.

7

Loom-Controlled Doubleweave

Doubleweave has always fascinated me. The thought of weaving two separate layers of cloth at once, not connected to each other, or a piece of cloth that is twice as wide as my warp, is exhilarating. It hardly seems possible, but, believe me, it is.

The advantages of being able to weave two layers at once are many: you can make a cloth with greater insulating power; you can put stuffing between layers as you weave. You can make a cloth that is twice as wide as the weaving width of your loom (with four shafts), three times the width (with six shafts), four times the width (with eight shafts)—you get the idea. You can make a cloth that is self-lining: a cloth that looks different on the face and back. You can mix colors in doubleweave woven in blocks, hiding the color on the lower layer until you want it to come to the face of the fabric.

As with everything else, doubleweave has some drawbacks. To weave two separate layers of cloth or two layers that interconnect with different colors on the upper and lower layers, you must use at least two shuttles (or more, if there are color changes in the layers). For a double cloth, you need twice as many ends per inch as for a single layer of the same width because both layers must come through the reed at the density each one requires. If you are thinking of using a fuzzy yarn (like brushed mohair) for a double-width throw, don't. I once did just that and still recall the frustration of not being able to make a shed. Brushed mohair is an obvious yarn to be avoided, but any other yarn that is somewhat sticky will be much more troublesome when crowded as it must be to make two—or more—layers.

Weave drafts for doubleweave—particularly the cloth diagrams—don't look like what you might expect: the diagram shows the weft that appears on the face with the weft for the back next to it. It is thus difficult to visualize what is happening. Fortunately, there is a way around this limitation, as we shall see.

The last constraint associated with doubleweave is that once you move beyond plain weave, the number of shafts required goes up very quickly. To weave a four-shaft twill

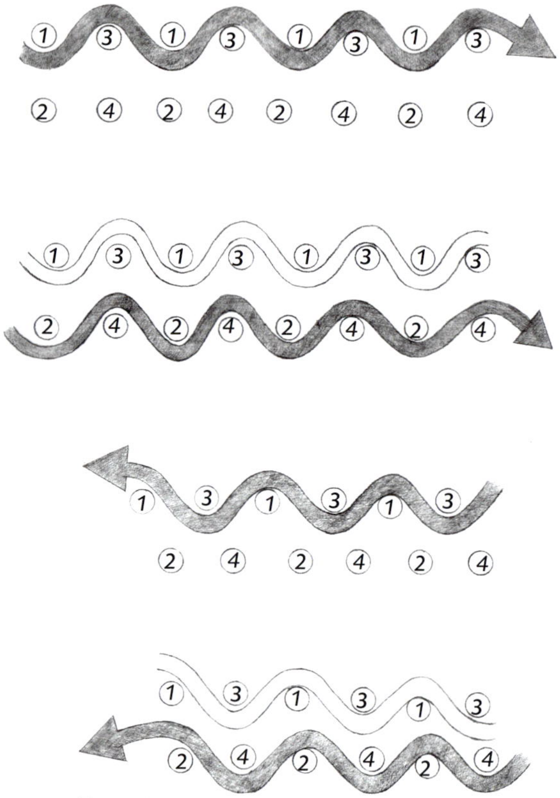

Figure 1

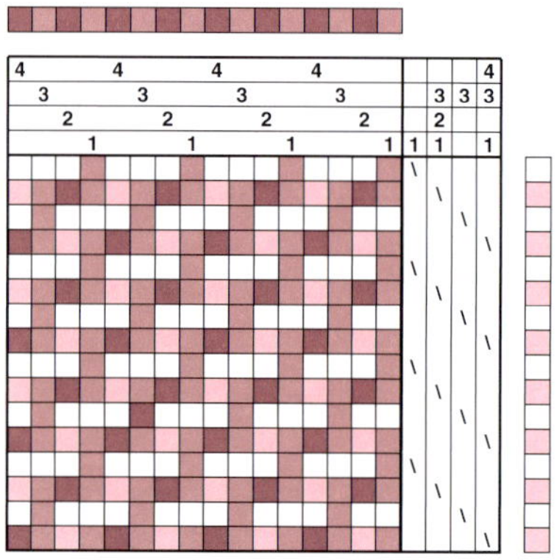

7.1a Two layers of cloth. Light mauve weft weaves in lower layer, white in upper. Notice that the drawdown does not, at first glance, show that there are two layers of cloth. Cross-sectional diagrams are more convincing.

Threads carried on odd-numbered shafts are light. This draft weaves two layers with the threads carried on the odd-numbered shafts on top.

on both layers, for example, you will need eight shafts.

Two separate layers of plain-weave cloth

It takes two shafts to make plain weave: over one, under one, and then the reverse. If your loom has four shafts, you can weave two plain-weave layers at the same time, using a separate shuttle for each: it is as simple as that.

First you must decide which shafts constitute one layer. It makes good sense to assign shafts 1 and 3 to one layer and shafts 2 and 4 to the other. This allows you to thread the cloth on a straight draw (1, 2, 3, 4, repeat) and still have the threads distributed evenly. If, for example, you assigned shafts 1 and 2 to one layer and shafts 3 and 4 to the other, there would be gaps in the cloth if it is threaded to a straight draw—sort of like very bad reed marks. It is always a good idea to thread using a straight draw if possible; it is an easy threading to remember and therefore is easy to thread.

The simplest way to see what happens in doubleweave is to use cross-sectional diagrams in which little circles represent the warp ends coming out toward you and the wefts are shown as they interlace with the warp.

If we want to have the 1, 3 layer on top and the 2, 4 layer under it, the cross section looks like **Figure 1**.

Notice that the wefts weave alternately: upper layer, then lower. When we start weaving blocks in doubleweave, this convention will be even more important.

The first pick goes across in the upper layer with shaft 1 lifted. The second pick weaves in the lower layer, requiring us to lift shafts 1 and 3 (to keep them from being caught) and shaft 2 to interlace in that lower layer.

In the third cross section, we weave first on the upper layer by lifting shaft 3, which finishes the plain weave on that layer. In the fourth, and final, cross section, we weave the weft across the lower layer, lifting shafts 1 and 3 (the upper layer) and 4 (**7.1a**).

If we want to have the even-numbered shafts on top, the cross-sectional diagram looks like **Figure 2**.

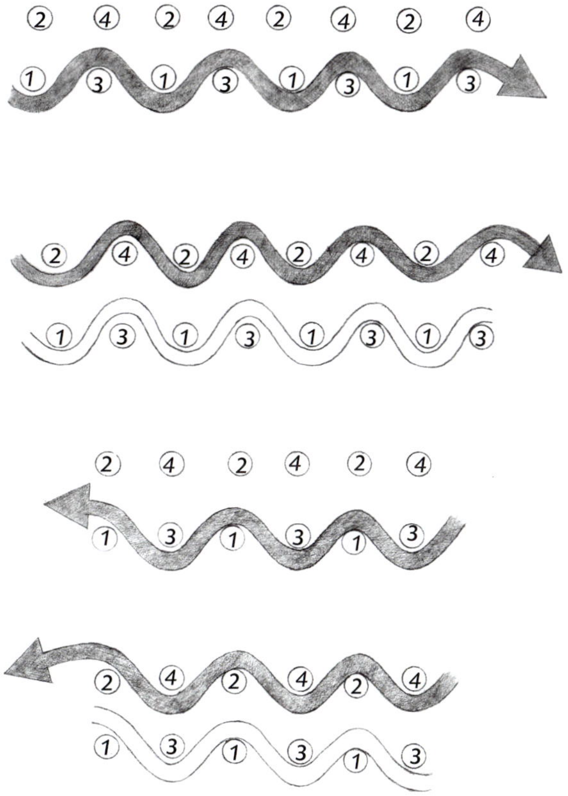

Figure 2

In the first part of the diagram, the weft weaves in the *lower layer.* The reason for starting with the lower layer is that if the order of the shuttles remains the same, you will be less likely to leave out a pick. (That error almost always happens on the lower layer where you cannot see.) To weave in that pick, lift shafts 2 and 4 (to keep the upper layer clear) and shaft 1. The second pick weaves in the upper layer simply by raising shaft 2.

In the third cross section, the shuttles both go back across the cloth *without wrapping around each other* (so that the layers will be unconnected). The first shot weaves in the lower layer, where we must lift shafts 2 and 4 (the upper layer) and shaft 3 to finish plain weave there. The other shuttle finishes the plain weave in the upper layer by passing under ends on shaft 4 (**7.1b**).

Repeat these steps and you will have woven two separate layers of plain-weave cloth. Because it takes four picks to complete the sequence, it will take longer to weave double cloth than it would to weave a single layer.

After you have woven the first sequence four or five times, try lifting shafts 1 and 3 together, and you will find that you can put your fingers under the upper layer and over the lower one. It works. To check the other sequence, repeat it a few times, then, lift shafts 2 and 4.

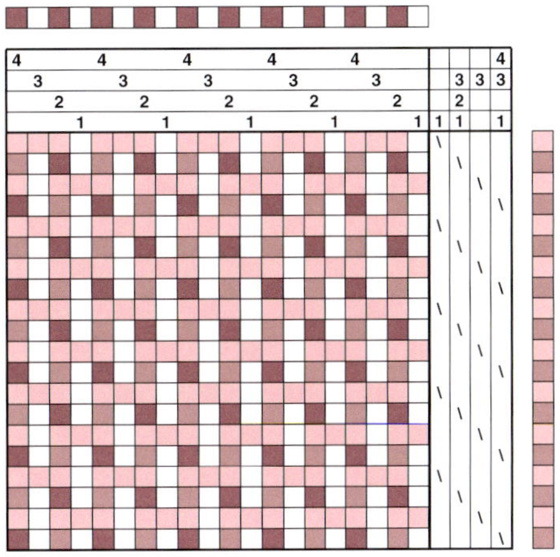

7.1b Two layers of cloth, double plain weave. Layer threaded on even-numbered shafts on top.

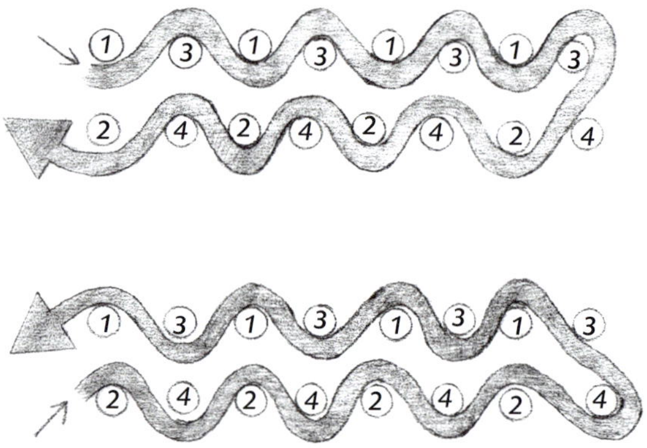

Figure 3

Double-width cloth

With four shafts, you may weave a cloth that is twice as wide as the warp you put on your loom. This doubleweave requires only one shuttle, which makes the weaving go much faster than would weaving two separate layers.

If you wish to have the layer carried by shafts 1 and 3 on the top, weave across the upper layer of the cloth by lifting shaft 1. Lift shafts 1 and 3 (the upper layer, remember?) and shaft 2 and pass the shuttle back to the side where you started, but on the lower layer (see **Figure 3**).

Weave back on the lower layer by lifting shafts 1 and 3 and 4, then across the upper layer by lifting shaft 3. After you have woven a few repeats, if you lift shafts 1 and 3, you can see the two layers, open at one side but joined as a fold at the other side (**7.2**).

The fold presents a technical problem. If you tend to have quite a bit of draw-in at the selvedges, the fold will have more ends per inch than the rest of the cloth when the cloth is taken from the loom and unfolded.

There are many things you can do to improve your chances of weaving a perfect fold. If you are using a boat shuttle, wind the bobbins so that the yarn comes off the bottom so that it will flow more smoothly. I like to hold the yarn at a low angle to the axis of the bobbin and wind it on under hearty tension so that the bobbin is *very* firm. Better still,invest in some end-feed shuttles and use them. You'll find that the weft feeds off them in a smooth and consistent way. See Chapter 2, page 47, for more on selvedge control.

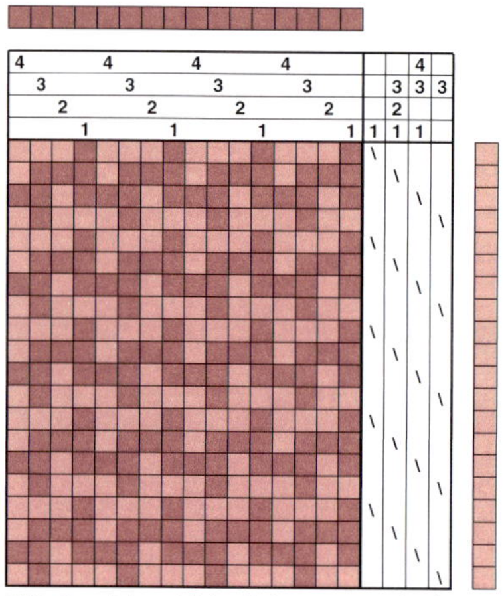

7.2 Double-width plain-weave cloth woven with one shuttle.

Warp yarns that have a fairly soft twist will be inclined to break at the edges—and be sticky, too. Either avoid softly spun yarns for double-width cloth or reinforce the fold with a yarn that is strong, slick, and fairly inelastic. Wind in extra ends of this yarn with the other ends and thread one (as one) with each of the last two ends on each layer at the fold (four in all). These ends will support the fold and resist drawing in (which causes breakage, particularly in a softly spun yarn), and because they are smooth, they will be easy to pull out before the cloth is wet-finished. Sometimes a floating selvedge of stout monofilament fishing line is enough to protect the edge. It depends on how soft the yarn is and how much draw-in you usually have.

If you always weave one selvedge that is beautiful and one that is a little ragged, position the fold on the side with the better selvedge. Better still, find out why your selvedges are different: Chances are, you don't throw the shuttle *exactly* the same with each hand. It's a challenging skill to develop but worth working on if you weave a lot of cloth in which the selvedges will be exposed.

I have seen advice to sley the warp more openly at the fold, but I suspect that this would make the draw-in more pronounced and eventually the selvedge threads would break. If you think that it is a pain to hide the fold, repairing broken ends in the fold so that they don't show is much more difficult.

Some weavers like something cylindrical like a stocking lightly stuffed with polyester fluff put into the fold to provide support.

Tubular cloth

There are times when it is desirable to weave a cloth as a tube. At one time, pillowcases were woven as tubes, seamed at one end and hemmed at the other. Sometimes you can still find cases made that way in an antique shop or at an estate sale. Fire hoses are still woven as tubes because a seam would create a weak place all along the hose where the water pressure would cause it to fail. Weavers sometimes weave decorative pillows as tubes or make toy figures or other novelty items that are tubular.

A tube, like the double-width cloth, requires just one shuttle and weaves up rapidly. For the double-width cloth, you wove across on the upper layer and back on the bottom layer, and then wove on the lower layer and back across on the upper layer to end where you began. The shuttle traced a U-shaped path. When you weave a tube, you weave across on the upper layer and back on the lower one as before but then continue to weave across on the upper layer and back on

Two-block plain doubleweave woven with cotton sewing thread.

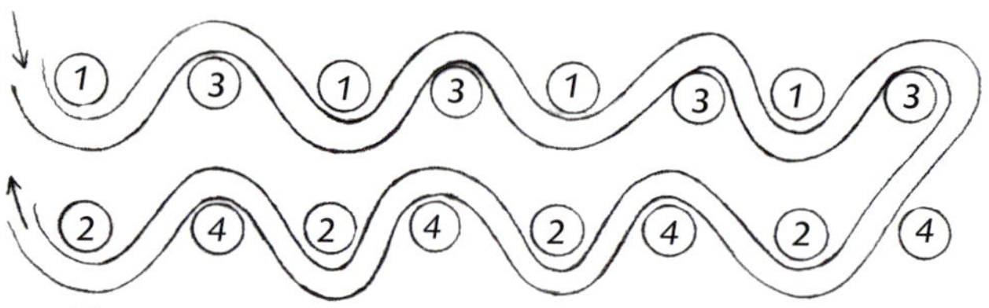

First two picks

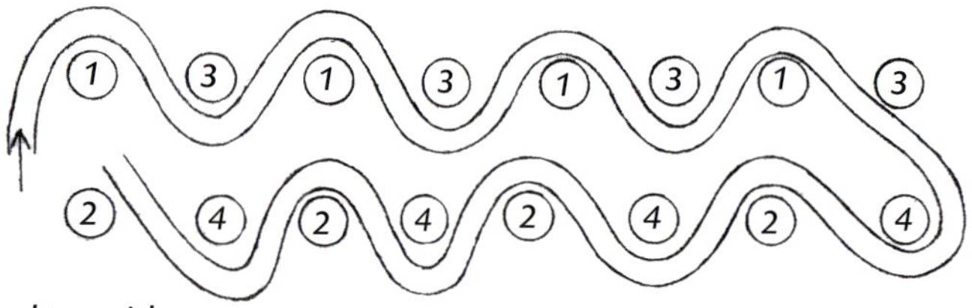

Second two picks

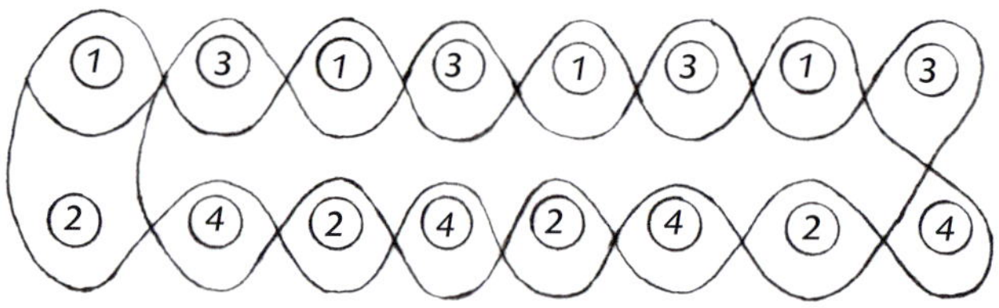

Figure 4 Tubular cloth. Note that two ends are together on left edge.

the lower one. The shuttle travels in a flattened circle.

The same sheds we used to weave double-width cloth are used to make a tube, but their order is changed. **Figure 4** shows what happens:

Weave across the upper layer by lifting shaft 1. Go across the lower layer by lifting shafts 1 and 3 (the upper layer) and 2. Weave across the upper layer again, lifting shaft 3 and then weave back in the lower layer by lifting shafts 1 and 3 and 4 (**7.3**).

Notice that on the left side of our diagram, an odd thing happens: the wefts enclose shafts 1 and 2 as if they were one thread. There are a number of things that you can do about the doubled end: you can love it (as long as the two ends remain together, you know that you have not missed a treadle), you can pull it out at the end of the weaving (which helps because if the doubled end appears right at the fold), you can simply cut that warp end out of the warp, or you can begin threading on shaft 2 instead of shaft 1.

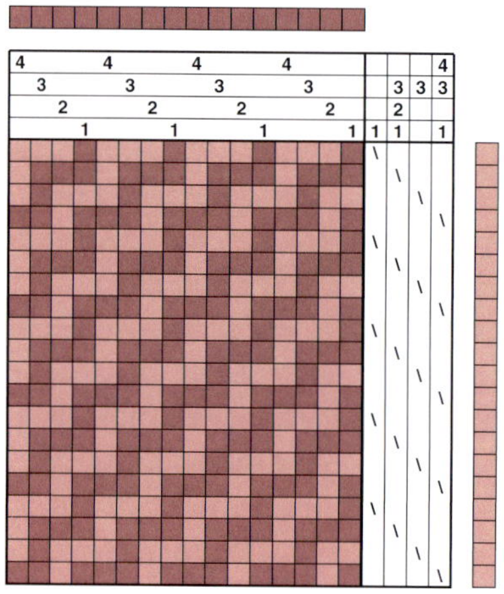

7.3 Double plain weave woven as a tube using one shuttle.

More than one block of double plain weave

On a loom with eight shafts, or any other multiple of four shafts, you can weave blocks of double plain weave that intersect with each other not only in the warp direction—as four-shaft doubleweave will do—but also in the weft direction, across the warp.

The simplest of these possibilities is a two-block doubleweave, which can be used to weave a checkerboard. Because one block requires four shafts, two blocks require eight.

Block A is threaded 1, 2, 3, 4, repeat; block B is threaded 5, 6, 7, 8, repeat. We can weave a black-and-white checkerboard by

Two-block plain doubleweave woven with a fine singles woolen yarn. One side is predominantly red, and the other, a cool brown.

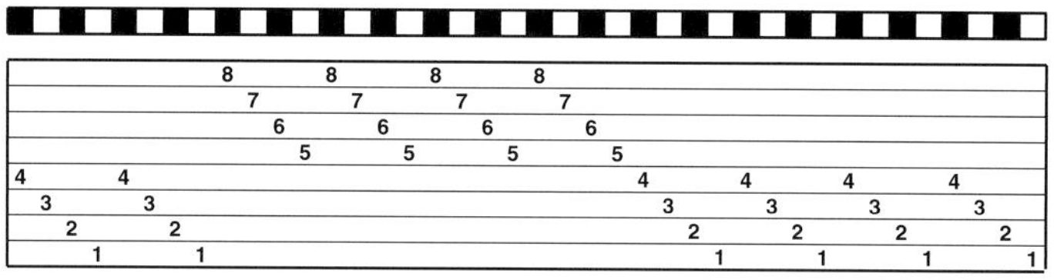

7.4a The threading for two-block double (plain) weave. Light color on odd-numbered shafts, dark on even.

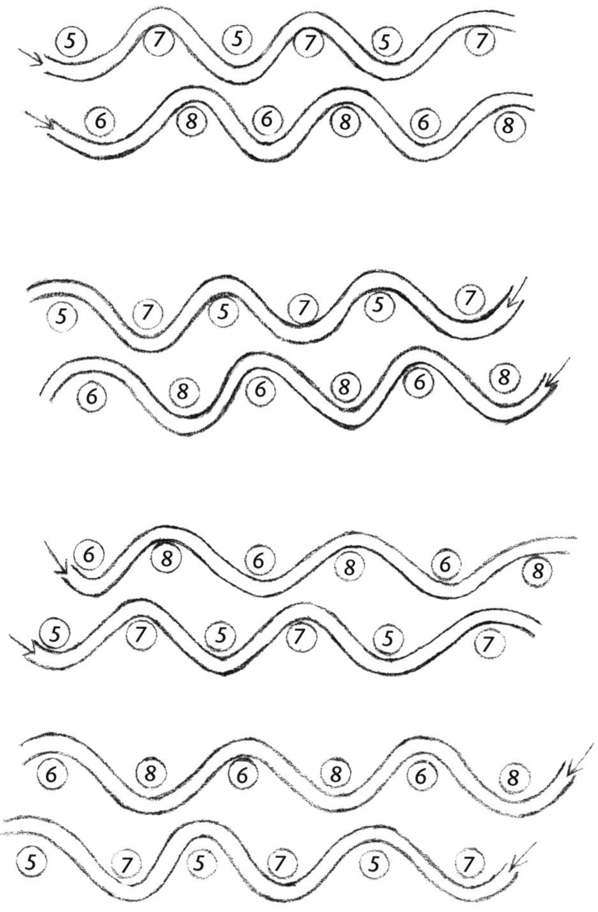

Figure 5 Cross-sectional diagrams for block B.

putting white threads on the odd-numbered shafts and black on the even-numbered shafts. Draft **7.4a** shows the threading.

We have already worked out the structure for threads carried on odd-numbered shafts on top (**7.1a**) and for the reverse (**7.1b**). We can copy the tie-up for those two possibilities into the tie-up for the two-block doubleweave (**7.4b**).

The cross-sectional diagrams at left in **Figure 5** show how to weave with both possibilities in block B: Draft **7.4c** shows the tie-up for block B, evens on top on left, odds on top to the right.

When you put everything together, draft **7.4d** is the result. If the tie-up is seen as a 2 × 2 grid—which it is—it looks like this:

B even on top	B odd on top
A odd on top	A even on top

Look closely at the tie-up. Notice that when odds are on top, the 4 × 4 square in the tie-up looks like the square on the left below, and when evens are on top, it looks like the square on the right:

			up
	up	up	up
	up		
up	up		up

up		up	up
		up	
up	up	up	
up			

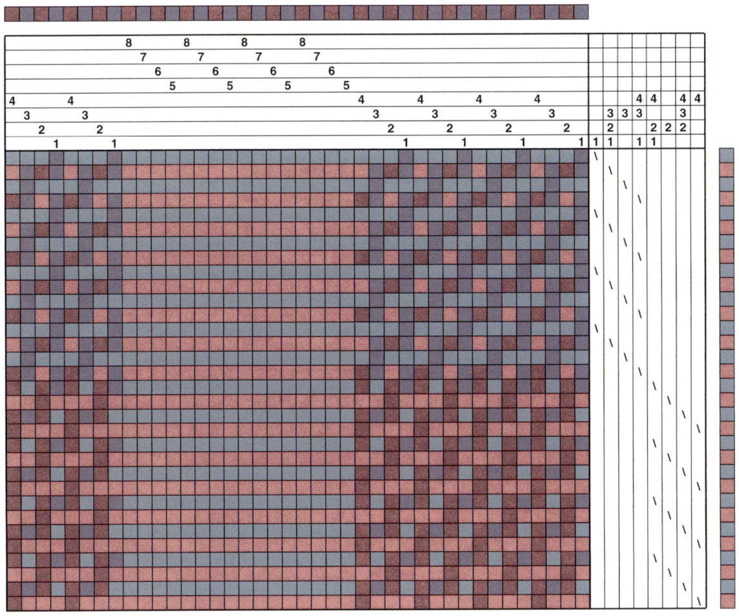

7.4b The tie-ups for Block A are the same as in 7.1a (threads on odd shafts are on top) and 7.1b (threads on even shafts are on top), pages 158 and 159.

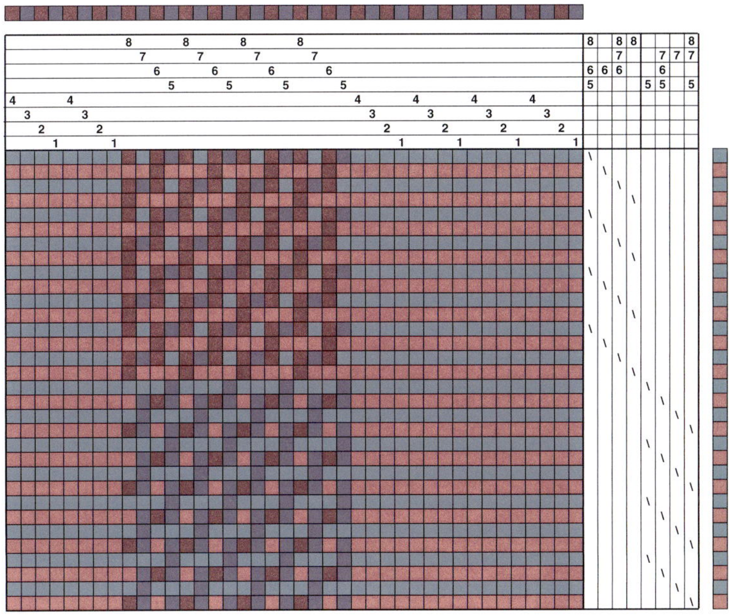

7.4c Here are the two possibilities for Block B (shafts 5–8): threads on even shafts on top (left four treadles) and threads on odd shafts on top (right four treadles).

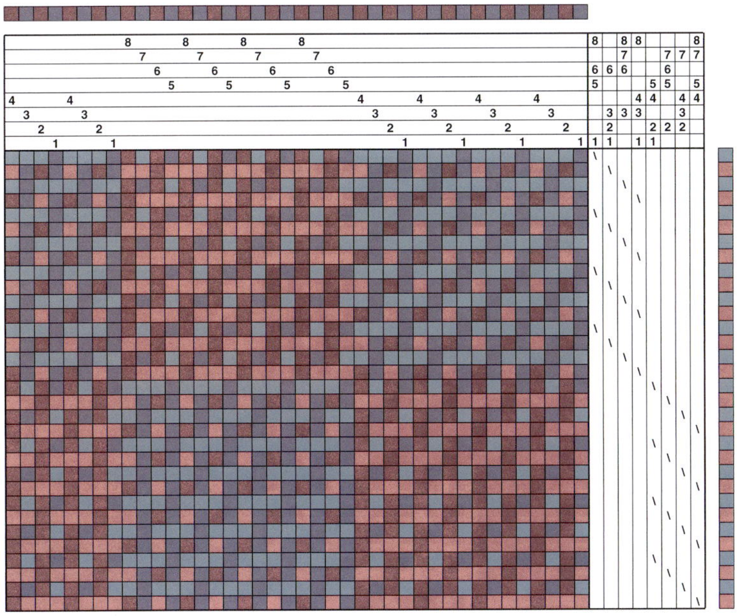

7.4d Two-block double (plain) weave. For the first 16 picks threads carried on odd-numbered shafts are on top in A and threads carried on even-numbered shafts are on top in B. In the next 16 picks, the blocks are reversed: A evens on top and B odds on top.

			O
	O	O	O
	O		
O	O		O

Odds on top.

O		O	O
		O	
O	O	O	
O			

Evens on top.

Figure 6

Once you see that the arrangement of lifts within the 4 × 4 square that represents the shafts to be lifted is the same for odds on top *regardless of which four shafts, 1–4 or 5–8, are represented* **(Figure 6)**, then figuring out the tie-up for double plain weave in blocks becomes a very simple matter. You can use these little modules and assemble them however you choose. Here is an example:

Each block requires four shafts, and so if we have an idea for a four-block double weave, sixteen shafts are needed. The following table shows two full repeats in both the threading and the treadling for a design intended for doubleweave on four blocks. The squares marked "o" indicate that the odd layer is up; those marked "e" indicate that the even layer is up. The tie-up for this draft is shown in **7.5**.

e	e	o	e	e	e	o	e
e	o	o	o	e	o	o	o
o	o	o	e	o	o	o	e
e	o	e	e	e	o	e	e
e	e	o	e	e	e	o	e
e	o	o	o	e	o	o	o
o	o	o	e	o	o	o	e
e	o	e	e	e	o	e	e

Double cloth, but not plain weave

With four shafts, two layers of plain weave is your only option. If you have eight shafts, you can make two layers of cloth with a four-shaft structure on each.

7.5 A four-block doubleweave. A counterchange pattern.

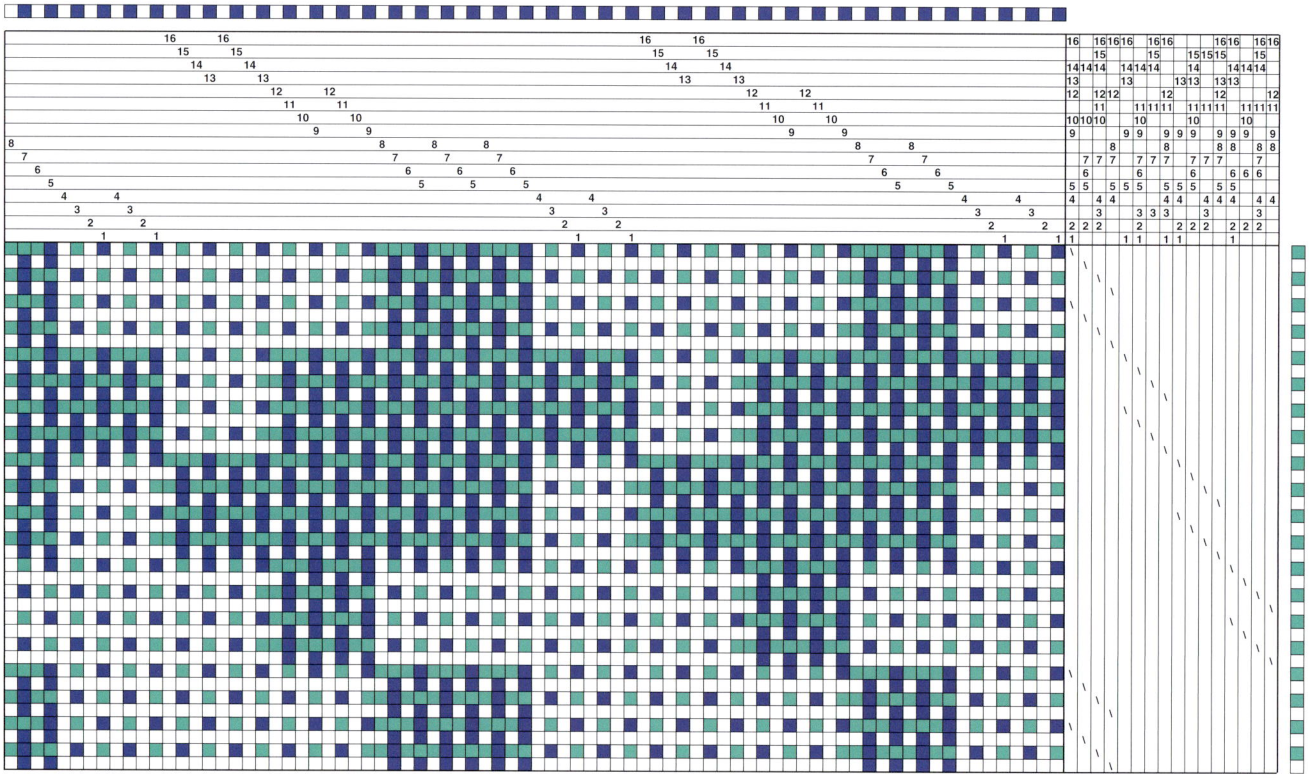

Four-block plain doubleweave woven with 2/40 worsted wool. The turned-back corner at the top shows how the colors reverse on the other side.

Two-block plain doubleweave woven with cotton sewing thread in deep muted colors.

The warp runs left to right in this image, a two-block plain doubleweave color study woven with cotton sewing thread. Silk threads were inlaid as a weft brocade.

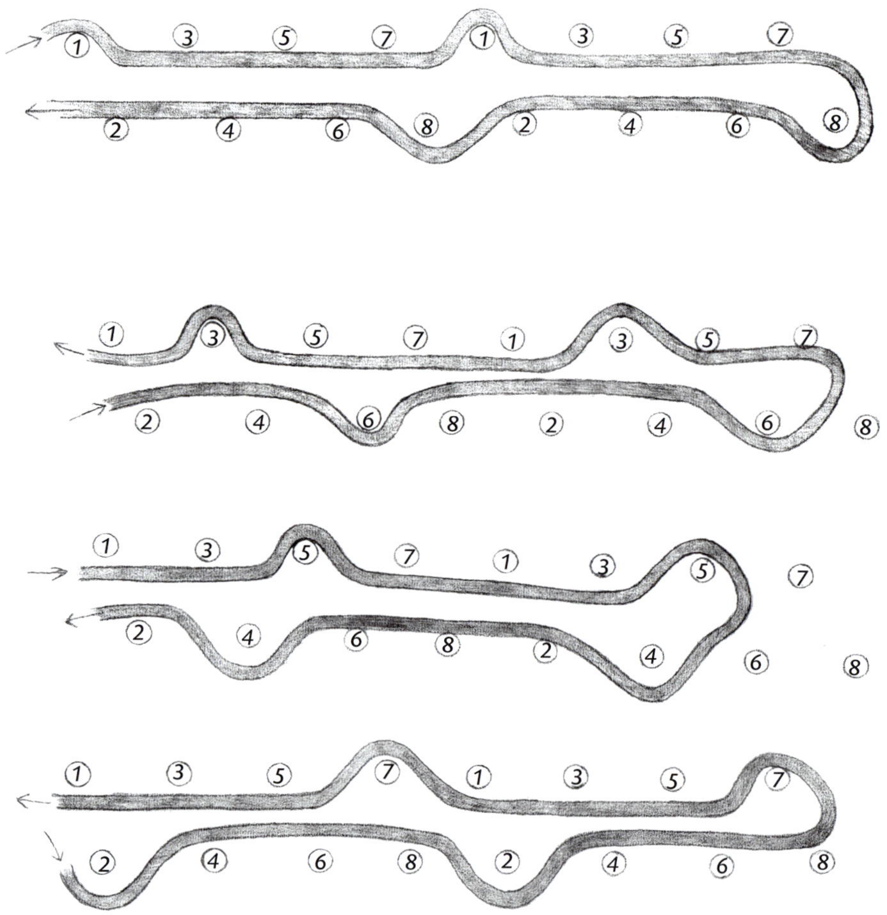

Figure 7 Cross-sectional diagram for draft 7.6b.

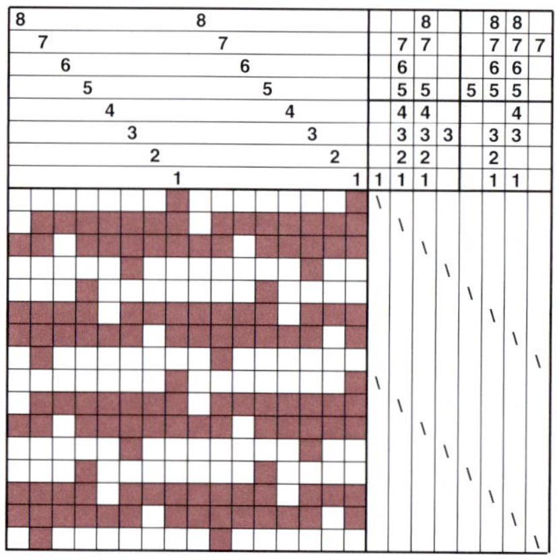

7.6a Double-width cloth for 1/3 twill. When the cloth is opened, after it is cut from the loom, there will be a smooth continuation of the structure across the fold.

Let's start with the double cloth made up of two layers, each using four shafts. For the sake of example, let's say that we want to use a 1/3 twill to make a blanket twice the weaving width of the loom.

First, we decide how the shafts will be allocated. For the reason discussed above, it will be helpful to use the threads on the odd-numbered shafts for one layer and the even-numbered shafts for the other. Let's arbitrarily put the odd-numbered shafts on top. (We could as easily do the reverse, but we need to make some decision.)

As we did before with double-width cloth, we will start by weaving over in the upper layer and back in the lower one, then over in the lower layer and back across the upper one. For two layers of twill, four picks are required for each layer, so we will need to weave six more picks, three in the upper and three in the lower layers, to complete the treadling sequence.

The top layer will be weft-faced (1/3), and the bottom layer will be weft-faced when seen from below. Imagine a cloth shaped like this: >, a sideways vee; the outside of the > is warp-faced. If the > were opened—as our cloth surely will be—one side would be 1/3 twill and the other, 3/1 twill (the inside of the >). The cross-sectional diagrams at left show the sequence of events, **Figure 7**.

Treadles

Thinking ahead, I could see that if the upper layer were woven 1/3, then only one shaft would be lifted for the left-to-right pick, but on the way back *in the lower layer,* seven shafts would have to be lifted. Technically, there is little problem with weaving the structure in this way—although it is possible that lifting seven will cause the ends on the eighth to ride up with them, particularly if the yarn is at all sticky. The more serious issue here is the *effort* required to lift seven treadles versus only one. I find that it's usually better for ergonomic reasons to tie the treadles to about the same number of shafts, when that is possible.

The resulting draft is shown at **7.6b** and **Figure 7**. Notice that the structure is threaded on a straight draw. Even if extra effort is required to figure out the treadling sequence, it is worthwhile to use a straight draw if at all possible.

Threading a double-width overshot

Not every structure will lend itself to the above treatment. What if, for example, we wanted to use an overshot threading for a double-width fabric? Clearly, a straight draw won't work in this case. Our example in Chapter 6, King's Flowers, is the basis for the work that follows.

The first step is to write the four-shaft draft on the first four shafts on graph paper, leaving one blank square between entries (**7.7a**). Write the draft to where you plan to have the fold in the cloth. In the example here, I have positioned the fold with the pattern in mind. The threading forms a point: 1, 2, 3, **4**, 3, 2, 1 in a small section of this threading. I have chosen to put the thread on shaft 4 on the edge so that any narrowing of the pattern that naturally occurs at

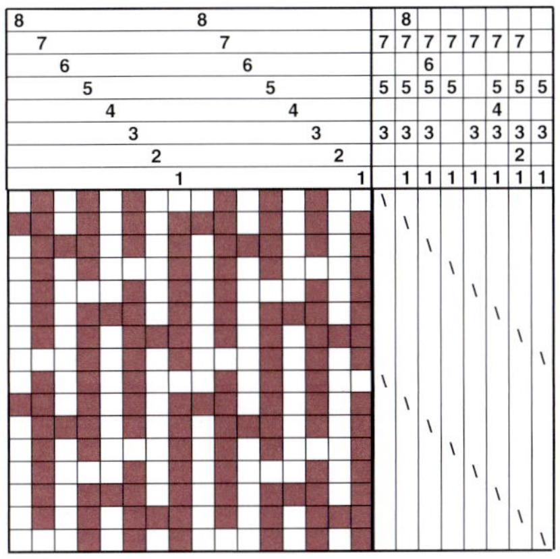

7.6b Double-width cloth for 3/1 twill. The twill will continue smoothly across the fold when the cloth is opened. This version alternates treadles tied to three shafts with treadles tied to five shafts. In 7.6a treadles were tied to one shaft or to seven.

Two-block plain doubleweave woven of cotton sewing thread.

the fold will be hidden and will not distort the flower part of the pattern. It isn't necessary to weave a folded cloth so that the fold is in the center, but if one layer is to be narrower, I make it the upper layer so that I can keep an eye on what is happening.

Once I have the threading worked out with spaces between, I continue to write the threading *by moving backward across the draft, lightly penciling the threading in the blank spaces I have left.* This intermediate step in the threading is temporary and not shown here. When the entire pattern is marked on graph paper, go back to the penciled numbers. Where you have 1, rewrite it as 5 (1 + 4). For 2, write 6 (2 + 4); for 3, write 7; and for 4, write 8. The original threading (**7.7a**) is not changed, *only* the ends you put in pencil working in the opposite direction. The result is shown in **7.7b**. What you have just accomplished is to thread the lower layer on the second set of four shafts.

Treadling for double-width overshot

The treadling is pretty easy to figure out. First think about where the tabbies will be.

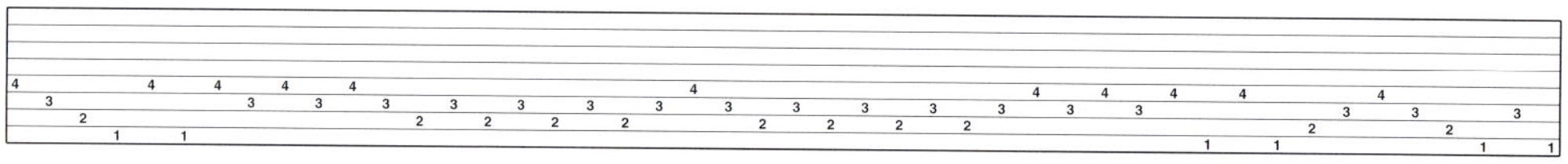

7.7a The beginning of the draft for double-width overshot. First enter the original overshot pattern (King's Flower) in every other square from right to left on the first four shafts.

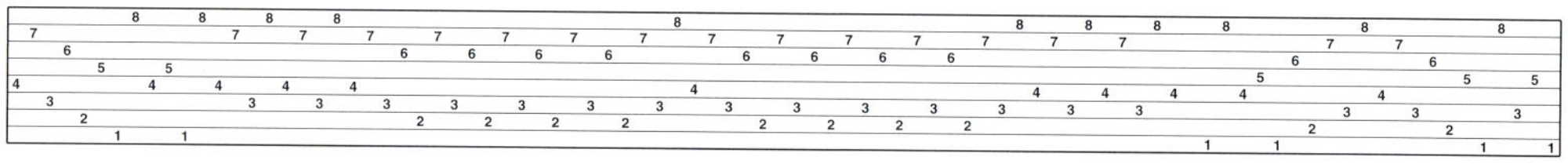

7.7b Now enter the threading for the lower layer on shafts 5–8. This time, work from left to right. Note that the fold is on shaft 4 of a point in the threading.

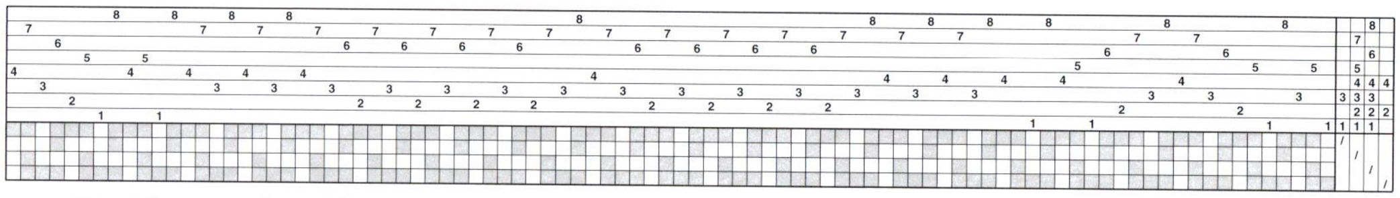

7.7c The tie-up for tabby in both layers is used so that the tabby shuttle first weaves in the top layer, then in the bottom layer, then back across the bottom layer, and then back across the top layer. When the pattern shuttle is added, the sequence is: tabby across the top and then the bottom; pattern across the top and then the bottom; tabby back across the bottom and then the top; pattern back across the bottom and then the top.

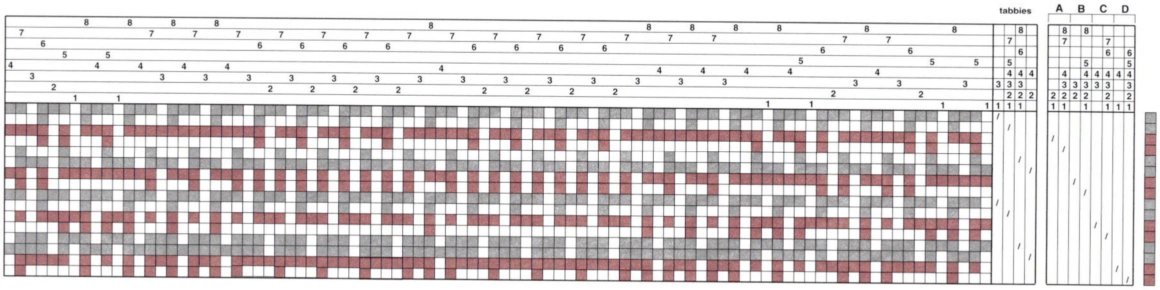

7.7d Here is the complete tie-up for double-width overshot (the first four treadles for tabby, the last eight for the pattern weft). The actual treadling for each block is not shown here, but will follow the order: tabby top layer, then bottom layer; pattern top layer, then bottom layer; tabby bottom layer, then top layer; pattern bottom layer, then top layer. You'll use the treadling for the blocks as derived on pages 136–138 with this order.

When we throw a tabby, we have to weave across in one layer and back in the other: two shots. The first shot will be in the upper layer and the second in the lower. If we have decided to lift the odd-numbered shafts first, we will lift shafts 1 and 3 from the upper layer and throw the shuttle. To continue the shot to the other selvedge, we will weave back from the fold by lifting 1, 2, 3, and 4 (the upper layer), and 6 and 8 for the lower layer. After we have thrown the two shots that will comprise the first pattern weft, we will weave back with the tabby shuttle by lifting 1, 2, 3, and 4, and 5 and 7 for the lower layer and then 2 and 4 for the upper layer. The tabbies are shown in **7.7c**. I have left a space between the first and second pairs to remind you that you treadle *both* pairs between the pattern shots.

You know how to derive the treadling sequence for a four-shaft overshot (see page 136). Write down the sequence that you plan to use.

To weave the overshot in the 1, 2 shed in the upper layer, simply lift 1, 2, the first half of the first pattern shot. To weave the second shot, lift 1, 2, 3, and 4, and 7 and 8. Remember that we lift the opposite—just as we did with the twill example above—so that the pattern follows the > shape we are weaving. The continuation of the shed 2, 3 will be, by the same reasoning, 1, 2, 3, and 4, and 5 and 8. See **7.7d** for the complete tie-up.

Backed weaves

Backed weaves are just what their name implies: fabrics that are different on each side. The difference may be in color or color sequence, yarn texture, or structure, or any combination of these. The thread count may be the same on both layers or different. A backed weave is a good solution for a fabric that is unstable for its intended application; weaving a more structurally sound backing to which it is attached can give it better performance qualities. A true backed fabric has both a warp and a weft comprising the face and another warp and weft for the back. (A double-faced twill—see Chapter 2—has either one warp and two wefts, one for each side, or a doubled warp and a single weft, so it is not a true backed weave.)

The cloths forming the two sides of a backed weave must be "stitched" together as they are woven if the fabric is to have stability. Unstitched, the face and back tend to separate, and one may "bag" relative to the other. The method for joining the two layers depends on a number of variables. Backed weaves may be stitched together by dropping one shaft in the sequence, allowing the weft from the back to weave over the warp ends carried on it so the stitching doesn't show (back to front); by lifting an extra end from the back to be caught by the weft weaving the face (front to back); or by using a third element, a weft that does nothing but weave into both face and back, tying them together. We will look at all of these possibilities.

First, let's look at a backed weave in which there are as many ends and picks on the back as there are on the face. A simple example of such a structure would be a blanket that is one color (or colors) on the face and another on the back. To define our idea further, let us make a tartan on one side and a plain color on the other.

It is sensible to put the plaid on the face so that you can keep track of the color sequence as you are weaving, and the solid color—which doesn't require changes of shuttle—on the back.

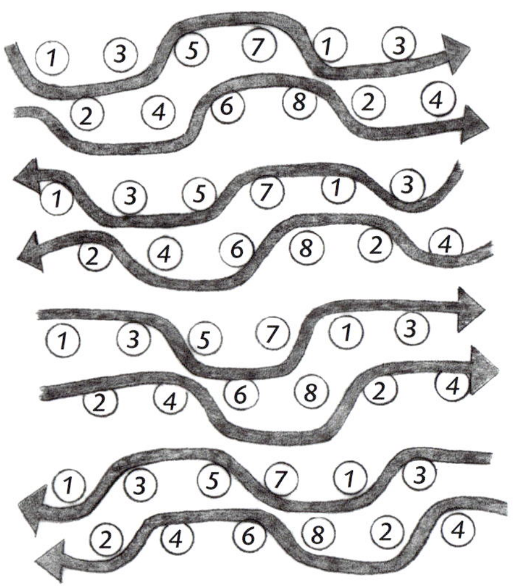

Figure 8a Two separate layers, both 2/2 twill.

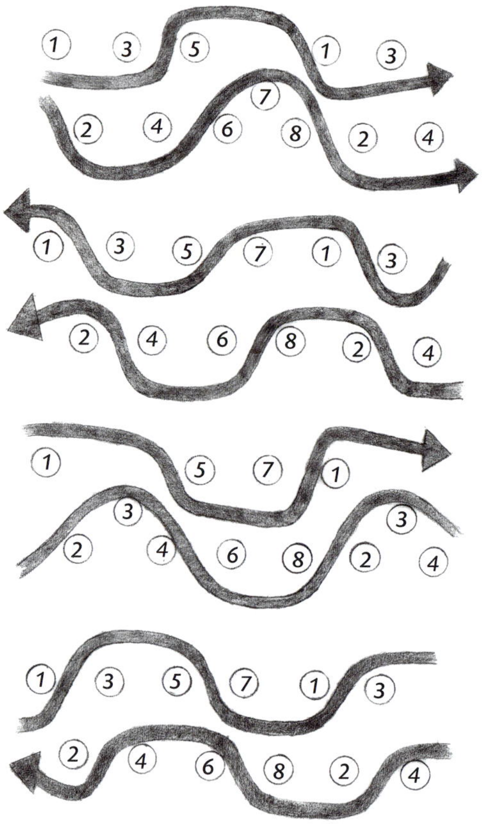

Figure 8b The layers are stitched together.

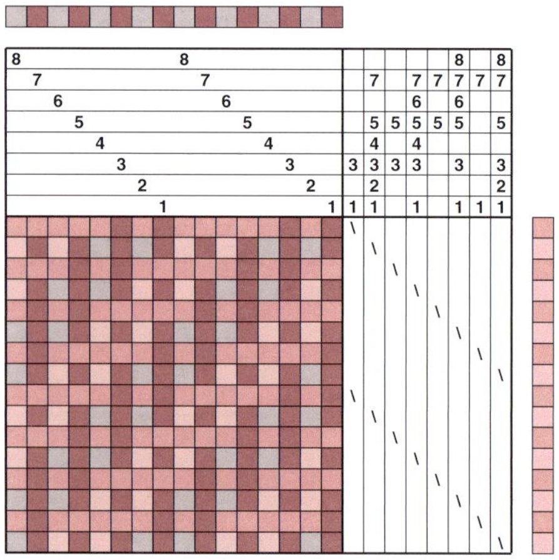

7.8a Double cloth woven with a 2/2 twill on both sides of the cloth. As the draft is given here, the two sides are not stitched together.

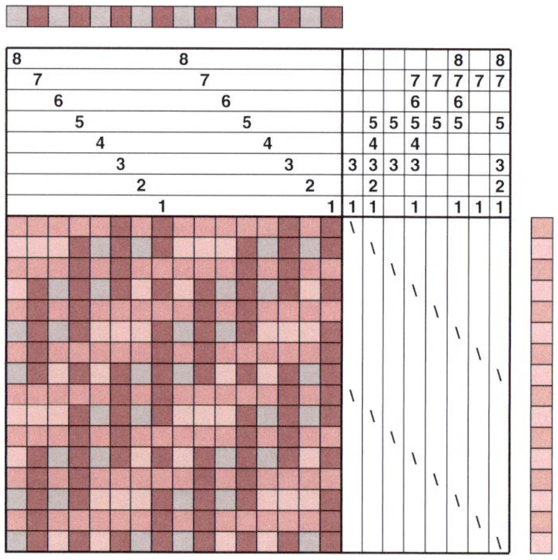

7.8b Double cloth woven with a 2/2 twill on both sides of the cloth. This draft differs from the other in that in the second pick of the sequence, shaft 7 is NOT lifted. And in the sixth pick, shaft 3 is NOT lifted.

If we assign the face to the odd-numbered shafts, an arbitrary decision, and the back to the even numbers, the draft would be **7.8a**. As shown, the two layers of the cloth are not connected unless the shuttles are taken around each other at the selvedges—in which case it isn't actually stitched but just made into a tube.

To stitch the layers together, we will alter a couple of the sheds so that the weft from one side catches warp ends from the other side. Because it is easier to lift fewer shafts than to add a shaft to the lift, the weft from the plain-colored side will do the stitching.

Draft **7.8b** shows how the two layers are stitched together at two places in the eight-pick repeat: the second and sixth picks. I chose those places almost arbitrarily, but several considerations led to the decision. First, I prefer lifting fewer rather than more shafts, so that helped me select the weft that weaves the back for the stitching. I am reluctant to stitch the two layers in just one out of seven picks or by using warp ends on the same shaft all the time, so I chose to have the cloth stitched in two places and by threads from two different shafts. The stitching picks are separated by three ordinary picks so that their frequency is equal throughout the cloth. Finally, the thread that is "dropped" so that the weft passes over it lies *between* the two threads that are lowered in the lower layer and is one of the ends that the face weft passes *over*, which minimizes the chance that the stitching will show.

The next example is made using a warp and weft on the face that are different from those used for the backing and without adding a separate weft to tie the two layers together. Heavier threads in pairs weave plain weave on the surface of the cloth to form an overcheck. Without being tied to a backing cloth, they would not stay put. The warp is made with slightly separated pairs of ends. This arrangement is used in the weft as well. Without some way to keep them close together, the warp ends in each pair would move apart, and the weft yarns would, too.

The trick, then, is to tie them down so that movement both vertically and horizontally is prevented. The simplest way to stabilize them is to catch the warp ends that comprise the face of the fabric with the picks just before and after the two face wefts. We have accomplished that by *not* lifting half the face warp for one pick woven in the back layer before the face wefts and by *not* lifting the other half for the pick that weaves the back for the pick after the face wefts. Draft **7.9a** illustrates this.

This structure is a good way to use a very expensive, showy, or otherwise scarce yarn so that every inch of it shows. By choosing the color of the back warp and weft so that the colors of the fancy face yarns are emphasized, the cloth can be fairly dramatic without creating long floats. The warp and weft for the back are finer and quite plain to further contrast with the face. The effect is more pronounced if the color(s) used in the upper layer are lighter in value than those in the backing cloth.

Sometimes it is desirable to make a backed cloth in which the two layers can be separated. By cutting the layers apart so that seams may be made in each layer separately, garments can be made that are completely reversible with no hint on one side that the other side looks different.

If the previous examples were cut apart, one layer would be destroyed because the two layers were stitched with an element of

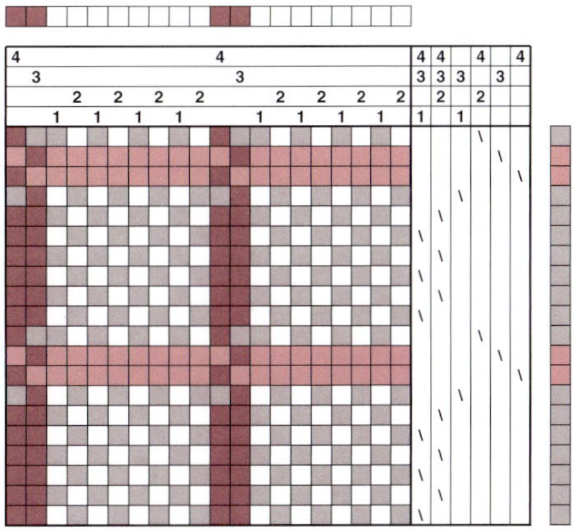

7.9a Plain weave on both layers—except for stitching—the upper layer is made of heavier and fewer warps and wefts. Because both sides are plain weave, the stitching shows on the back. It shows on the face, too, but the weft that does the stitching is smaller and is less obvious.

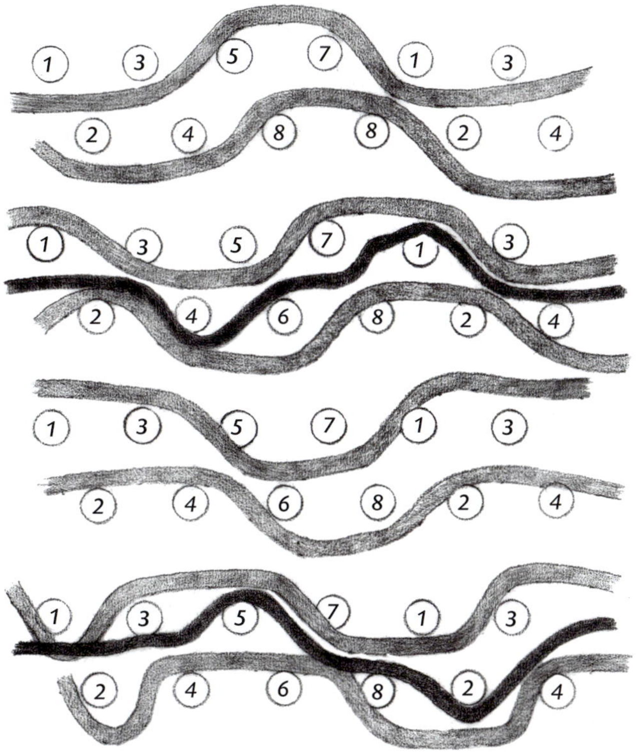

Figure 9 Stitched double cloth using a separate, stitching weft.

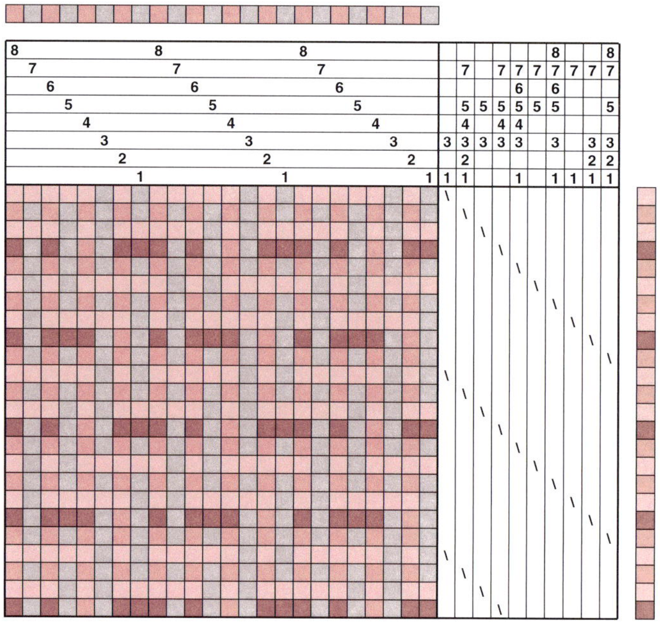

7.10 Stitched doubleweave using a separate stitching weft. This structure allows the two layers to be separated for seaming invisibly (the darkest wefts are the stitching wefts).

the face or the back. To make a backed fabric that can be cut apart, on the other hand, we must stitch the layers together with a separate weft that is used only for that purpose. By cutting this stitching weft, we can separate the layers if we like. The disadvantage, obviously, is the need to use a third shuttle. If you have enough shafts, however, you can turn the draft so that ten shafts and only two shuttles are required.

The stitching weft travels like a little mouse inside a wall, darting from the face to the back, catching a thread from each. This weft should be fine—I like to use sewing thread because it is fine, strong, and available in lots of colors. The diagram that follows shows how such a stitching weft (fine and dark-colored to be unobtrusive) would work. The draft is **7.10**.

Other Stitching Considerations

Sometimes the two warp yarns are of different sizes. When the back warp yarn is finer, using it as the stitcher is easier and less obtrusive. One of the examples that follows is made this way. If the face warp is made of finer yarns than the back warp, then dropping one of the face shafts, chosen so that it falls where a face weft float will cover it, works better. It is risky to give a hard and fast rule about which way to stitch: front to back (by dropping a face warp end) or back to front (lifting a back warp end), so each case should be thought out individually.

Matelassé

Matelassé is a backed doubleweave that is padded by putting **stuffing** or **wadding** threads in either the warp or the weft. If placed in the warp—a method that requires a greater number of shafts—the stuffing threads lie above the warp threads that form the back and below the warp threads that make the face. If the stuffing threads are placed in the weft, the face warp threads must be raised so that the stuffing weft lies under them and over the backing threads. They are not meant to show, and they are often softer and coarser than the face or back threads so that they take up more space. It is important that they not bleed color during wet-finishing, nor be of such a high color contrast that they show through the face or backing cloth.

Frequently the face and back threads are of different sizes. The face and back cloths may be woven in the same or different interlacements. The two layers are stitched togeth-

Two doubleweave fabrics. The striped one requires six shafts, four for the doubleweave stripe (solid navy) and two more for the plain weave on either side. The other doubleweave cloth is made with two blocks (eight shafts) and has one tweed singles and one 2/18 worsted wool in each block. Three combinations of tweed/worsted wool make the repeat look more complex: it takes six squares for the same color to be up again in the same block.

er as well as padded by the stuffing warps or wefts. Drafts **7.11a** and **7.11b** show two padded, stitched, backed doubleweaves. In **7.11a**, which requires eight shafts, the warp contains the stuffing ends. In **7.11b**, which requires six shafts, the stuffing threads are in the weft.

The matelassé fabrics woven by mills are usually figured, often very elaborately, using jacquard mechanisms. Handwoven matelassés are simpler in structure by virtue of the equipment available to us, but they can nonetheless be lovely and interesting.

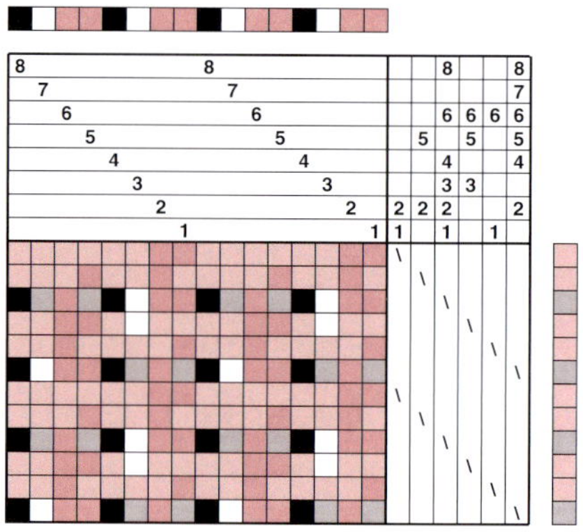

7.11a This draft makes a stitched, padded doubleweave. The structure on the face of the cloth is 2/2 twill with a finer yarn than the back, woven plain weave. The plain-weave yarn is twice the size of the twill yarn.

The fourth and eighth warp ends (black) are the padding or wadding ends (softer spun and larger than either the face or back ends and picks).

The two layers are stitched with every plain weave, (back) pick by NOT lifting shaft 5 for the first plain-weave pick and 1 for the second.

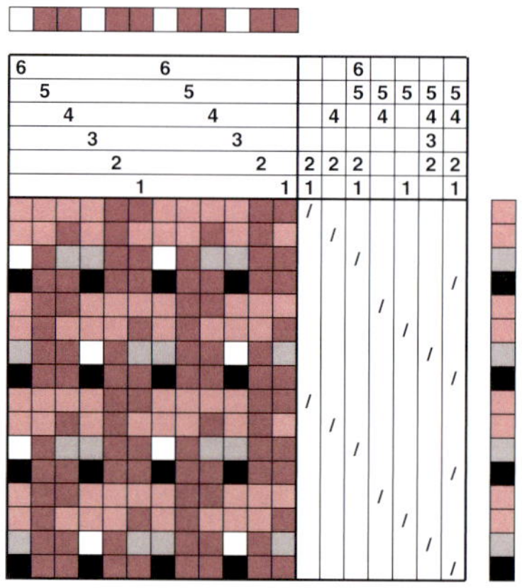

7.11b A padded, stitched doubleweave or matelassé. The wadding or stuffing is in the weft (black).

The face is 2/2 twill (rose/pink)and the back plain weave (white crossed with gray).

The ratio of face ends and picks to back ends and picks is 2:1 (the face yarns are half the size of those weaving the backing).

The first and second picks weave the face and the third weaves the back. The fourth pick is the padding.

8

Bedford Cords and Piqués

Bedford cords and piqués are similar in that raised areas are formed in the cloth in each, they are often padded, and floats on the back (with an exception) are part of the structure. They differ in that the ridges in a Bedford cord run warpwise while those in a piqué run weftwise.

Bedford cord

The simplest Bedford cord is plain weave on the face with floats on the back. If two colors are used in both warp and weft, the face appears similar to a two-block plain doubleweave with plain-weave warp stripes of two contrasting colors. To weave this arrangement as doubleweave requires eight shafts, four for each block. To weave it as a Bedford cord, however, you need only four shafts.

A glance at the diagram reveals what makes the Bedford cord different from the two-block double plain weave: the back has floats. When a Bedford cloth is woven and washed, the floats on the back shrink a bit so that rounded cords are formed on the plain-weave face. To produce more prominent cords, use the sett for a very firm plain weave. If the sett is a bit crowded, the wefts cannot shrink in the plain-weave part of the

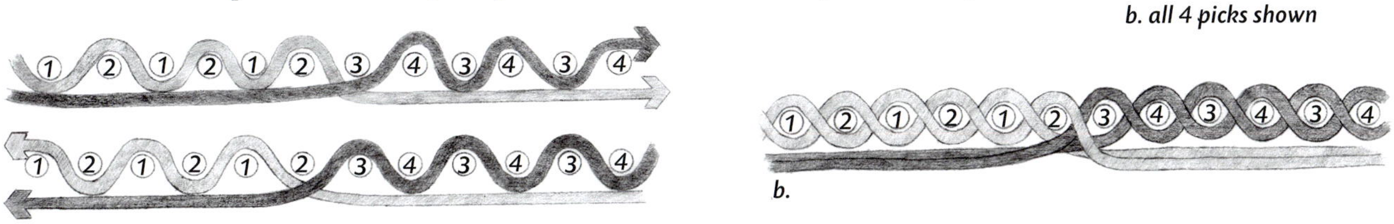

a.

b.

Figure 1 Four-shaft Bedford cord shown in cross section
a. 2 picks shown
b. all 4 picks shown

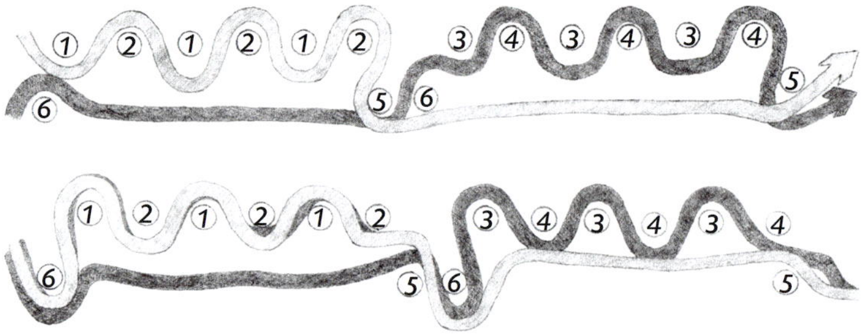

Figure 2
Bedford cord with cutting ends (5 and 6) added. Notice that both wefts go under the same end as they move left to right and both go under the other, moving right to left.

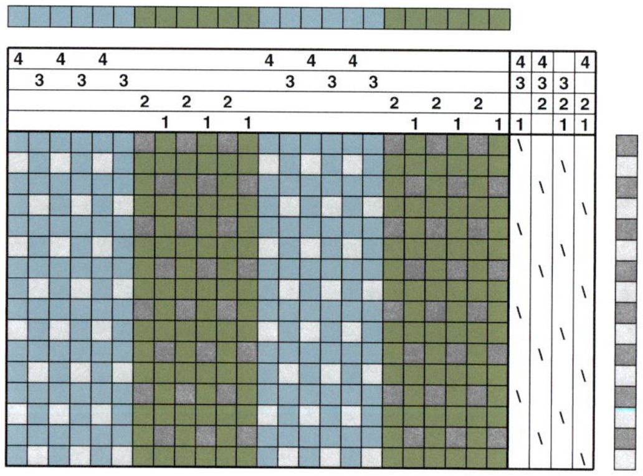

8.1 Four-shaft Bedford cord. The shuttles are used alternately, for one pick each. The face of the cloth is plain weave (no floats) and the back has floats the width of the cords that are not usually exposed in use.

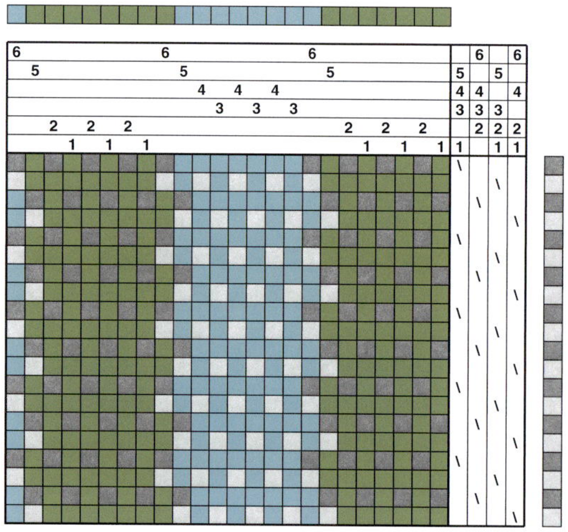

8.2 The same Bedford cord with cutting ends added. The cutting ends, on shafts 5 and 6, keep the slack wefts on the back from working back into the face structure. The ends on 5 are lifted for a pick in each cord (two picks) and then 6 is lifted for the next two picks.

cloth because there is no place for them to go. The weft floats on the back, on the other hand, are free to shrink, thus rounding out the cord. The draft for the structure diagrammed at left is **8.1**.

Bear in mind that the cords may be any width you like; however, very wide cords will flatten out in the cloth, and very tiny ones (made of two ends) don't have enough width to round out. Sampling will help you determine an optimum width for your yarn that will be pleasantly rounded unless stretched in use, as upholstery would be. You must keep in mind that this structure is not suited for uses where both sides are exposed.

Draft **8.1** works well for hairy or sticky yarns; I find woolen-spun yarns especially suitable. Smoother yarns—even 2/20 worsted wool, which I don't usually think of as slippery—are too smooth for this draft: the slack in the floats on the back of the cloth works its way into the edges of the cord, making them loose and flaccid.

Fortunately, it is possible to stabilize the edges of the cords so that the weft yarns do not slip. You need two more shafts (**8.2**). The ends carried on shafts 5 and 6 are called the **cutting ends**. The next diagram shows how they are used: **Figure 2**.

Bedford cord with cutting ends may be woven successfully even with slippery yarns. Notice that both the weft yarns go across the cloth under the ends on shaft 5, and return under the ends on shaft 6. They follow the same path so that the take-up on the cutting ends is the same as those that make up the respective cord. The threads on shafts 1 through 4 interlace with *every other* weft pick. The first shuttle weaves in the cord threaded on 1 and 2 and the second in the cord carried by 3 and 4. The cutting ends interlace

Bedford cord woven of 2/18 worsted wool. The cutting ends are visible where the back of the cloth is shown, at top. Unlike many Bedford cords, only one weft was used so that the face shows violet and violet crossing green.

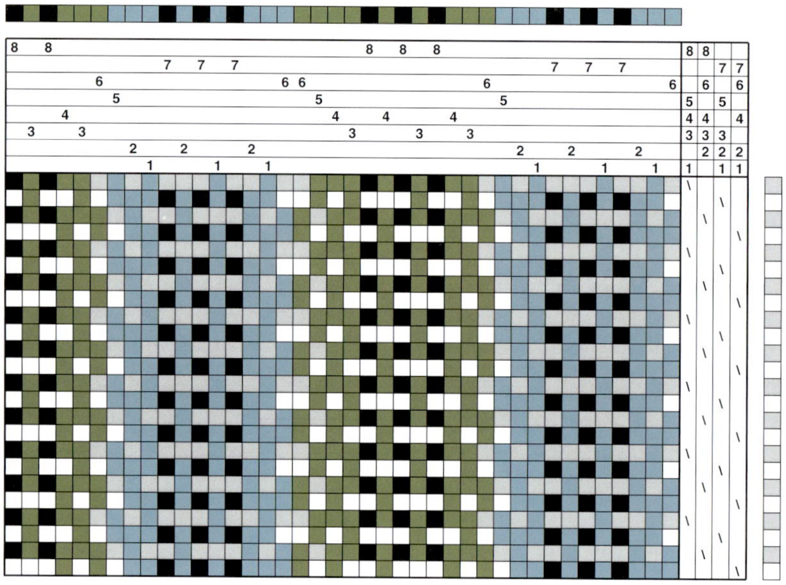

8.3 Bedford cord with cutting ends (on 5 and 6) and wadding ends (on 7 and 8). Notice that the wadding ends (black) are spread out through the cord. Because they are passive—they never interlace with the wefts—they have practically no take-up. They must be beamed or weighted separately from the rest of the warp.

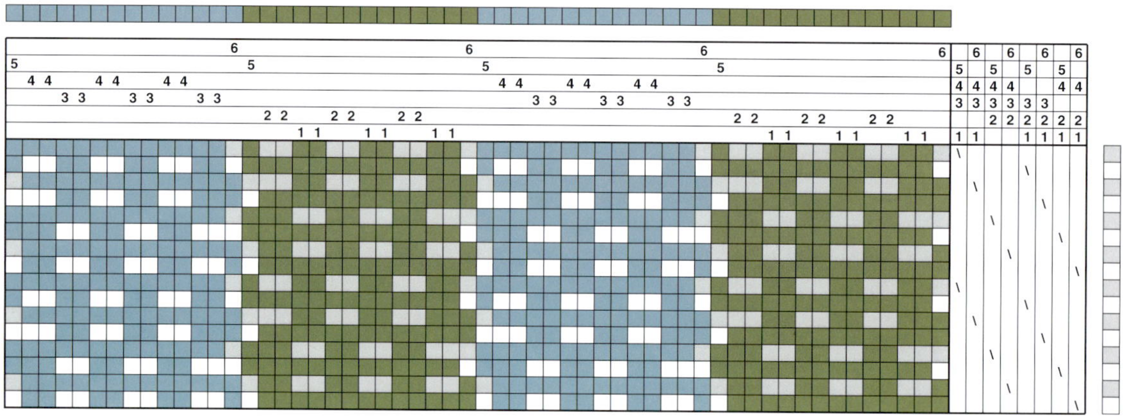

8.4a Bedford cord with 2/2 basket weave cords. Notice that each cutting end is lifted twice in a row, which requires eight treadles in all.

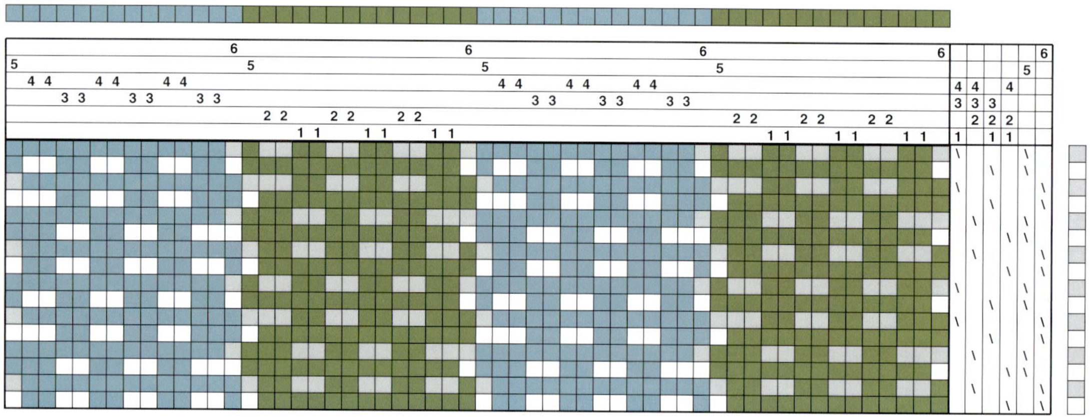

8.4b The same structure as 8.4a. By depressing two treadles at once, the cloth may be woven using only six treadles.

in the same way for both shuttles as the weft yarns go across and back. Lifting shaft 5 for both shots going across in one direction and then shaft 6 for both coming back causes the take-up on those ends to be the same as for those carried on shafts 1–4.

If we want to support the ridges that the cords make, we must put something inside them. Padding them is accomplished by using wadding ends. Those ends cannot be carried on shafts 1–6, which are otherwise occupied. They will be carried on shafts 7 and 8. Both shafts are required: shaft 7 carries the ends padding one cord, (the other weft passes *under* them); and shaft 8 carries the wadding ends for the other cord (**8.3**).

The ends used to pad the cords do not interlace with the weft yarns at all. They lie above the weft yarns that weave in the other cord; shaft 7 is raised when the weft yarn weaving the cord carried on shafts 3 and 4 is used, and 8 is raised when the weft yarn weaving the cord carried on shafts 1 and 2 is used. Because these ends do not interlace with the weft picks (they are said to be **passive**), there will be practically no take-up in the wadding ends. The wadding ends must be beamed on a separate beam, or weighted separately if a second beam is not available. Furthermore, the wadding ends are added to the sett for the face. They aren't given their own dents because that would produce a gap in the face of the cloth.

Two Bedford cords woven with woolen-spun wool (about 1,900 yards per pound). The one on the left uses just four shafts; the cord widths vary. The one on the right has it all: light gray cutting ends and two sets of wadding ends in the white cord which are lifted to the surface from time to time to decorate it.

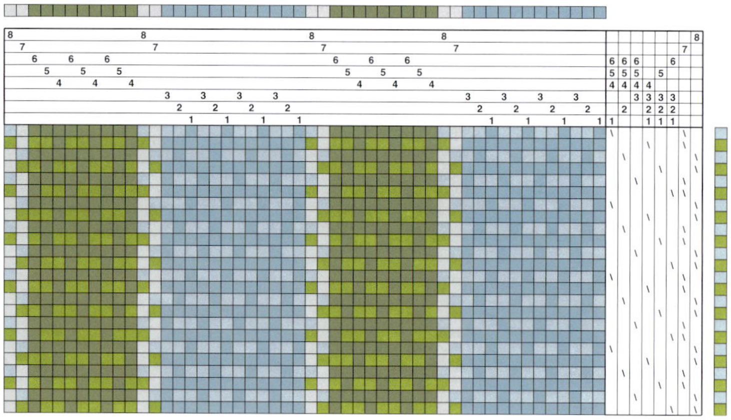

8.5a Bedford cord woven with 1/2 twill on the face of both cords. The twill ribs in both cords move in the same direction. The cutting ends are shown but the wadding ends (which would be threaded on shafts 9 and 10), in the interest of clarity, are not shown.

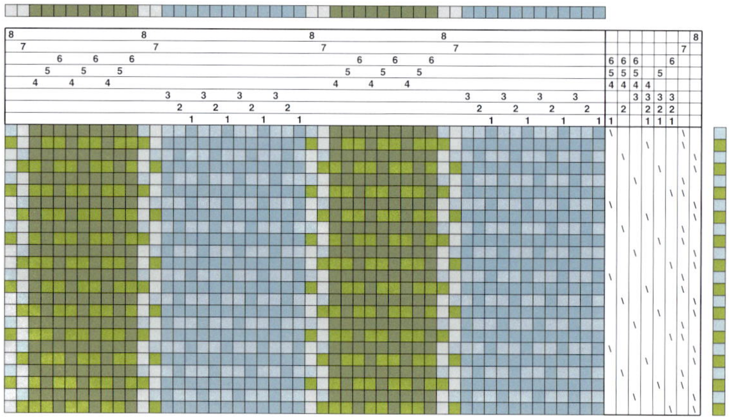

8.5b This is the same structure as shown in 8.5a except that the twill ribs reverse from cord to cord.

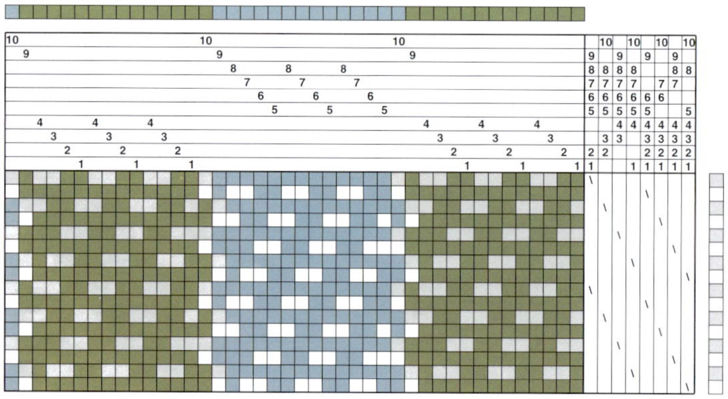

8.6 Bedford cord woven in 2/2 twill. The diagonals in both cords run in the same direction. (Changing the threading as we did for the 1/2 twill would reverse their direction.) Because the twill repeats in four picks, an even number, the cutting ends don't require their own treadles.

Bedford cords may be woven with weave structures other than plain weave. A 2/2 basket weave may be woven without increasing the number of shafts required, but the handling of the cutting ends will be slightly different (**8.4a** and **8.4b**). (Wadding ends may be added as before if desired.) The sett for this cloth will have to be closer than for plain weave because 2/2 basket requires it.

The number of shafts rises rather quickly if other structures are chosen. A three-shaft twill calls for six shafts for the two cords and two more for the cutting ends. Draft **8.5a** produces an unpadded cord in a 1/2 twill. The cutting ends have their own treadles because the twill repeats in three picks per cord. Lifting the cutting ends as well as the ends for the cord on one treadle requires twelve treadles.

If wadding ends are added to this structure, they will be carried on shaft 9 for one cord and shaft 10 for the other. I have omitted them from the draft **8.5a** because it is easier to see the twill structure without them.

The same structure can be used but threaded slightly differently so that the direction of the twill line reverses in every other cord (**8.5b**). These twill cords will require a closer sett than plain weave, about the same as that used for the 2/2 basket-weave cords (remember that, given a range of setts for a particular yarn, it is best to use a closer sett for Bedford cords).

To weave a four-shaft twill in Bedford cord, you'll need four shafts for each cord plus two for the cutting ends, a total of ten shafts (**8.6**).

Piqué weave

Piqué weaves are usually woven so that the face of the cloth is plain weave. A second warp, more heavily tensioned, is used to stitch the plain-weave face at predetermined intervals. The plain-weave face is woven at a moderate tension for up to ¾ inch (1 cm) in plain weave, and then the stitching warps are raised for the next couple of picks; these picks are beaten in firmly, forming a furrow. The plain-weave part of the cloth slides along the stitching ends, forming a cord that runs selvedge to selvedge.

The simplest piqué (**8.7**) has horizontal ridges that run straight from selvedge to selvedge. The first two shafts are alternated to start the plain weave, and then a soft, squishy wadding weft that will not show on the face is inserted *under* the face warps and *over* the stitching warps on shaft 3. In our draft **8.7** the wadding pick is inserted halfway through the weaving of the face fabric, which positions it nicely in the center of the cord. Be careful about the color of the wadding weft (for both Bedford cord and piqué): it must be colorfast so that it won't bleed onto the face of the fabric; if the face is quite light in value, the wadding weft will be less likely to show (as a sort of shadow) if it is light-colored, too. The stitching warps float on the back of the fabric. With three shafts, that is our only option. This structure is called a **loose-back piqué**.

With four shafts, we may weave into the stitching warp, which is called a **fast-back piqué**. Draft **8.8** shows the simplest example. The face of this cloth looks just the same as the face of **8.7**, but the back is plain weave, which makes the cloth more stable.

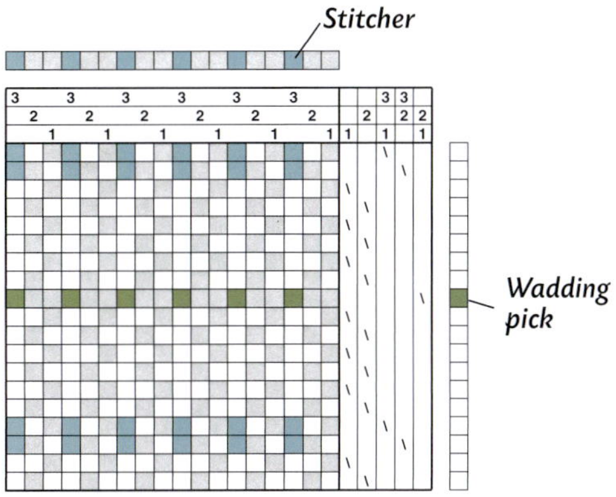

8.7 Simple piqué. This piqué makes horizontal cords. The first two shafts create the plain-weave face of the cloth. The third shaft carries the stitching ends.

As it is woven, a wadding pick is inserted into the cloth under the face ends and over the stitching ends to pad the cloth halfway through the weaving of the face. Both the face and backing picks weave together at intervals to join the two warp groups and form the characteristic furrow in the cloth.

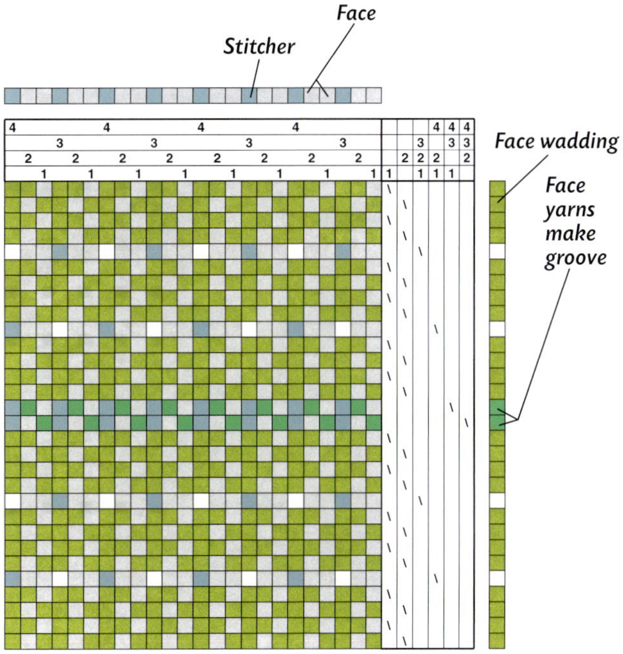

8.8 A very simple fast-back piqué. Four picks are woven to make the face of the cloth and then both face ends and one stitching end are lifted for a wadding pick. After four more face picks, both face ends and the other stitcher are lifted for a wadding pick. The wadding pick (white weft here) has made plain weave on the back with the stitching ends.

The furrow is made by lifting both stitchers with one face end for one pick and then both stitchers and the other to weave a firm groove into the cloth (shown as dark green here although in practice the same weft color would be used as for the face).

The addition of more shafts makes it possible to change the piqué so that the furrows zigzag. Draft **8.9** makes a dramatic waved piqué with eight shafts. The first treadling (I) is a fast-back piqué. The stitchers are lifted for two face picks in a row to make them more prominent. The second treadling (II) is a loose-back piqué. The angles of the zigzag are sharper because of the number of face picks between the lifted stitchers. The third treadling (III) is a ribbed piqué, also loose back. A rib and a waved piqué can be combined in one cloth; perhaps three ribs and one wave followed by three ribs.

In drafts **8.8**, **8.9**, and **8.10**, the ratio of picks on the face to those on the back changes. In **8.8** the ratio is 4:1. In **8.9**, 4:1, 4:1, and 3:1 for the three variations. In **8.10**

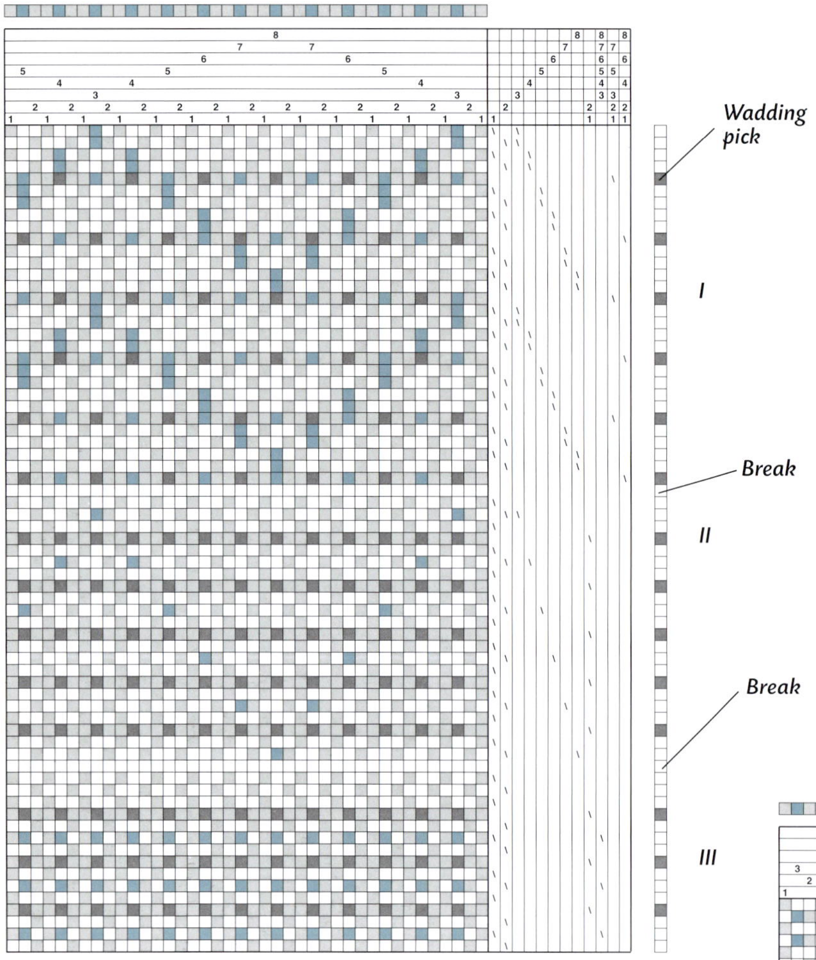

8.9 In this versatile threading we can weave:

I A zigzag fast-back piqué (each stitcher lifted for two picks to strengthen the effect)

II A steeper zigzag loose-back piqué (fewer face picks make the zigzag steeper)

III Deeply furrowed selvedge-to-selvedge ridge, no zigzag.

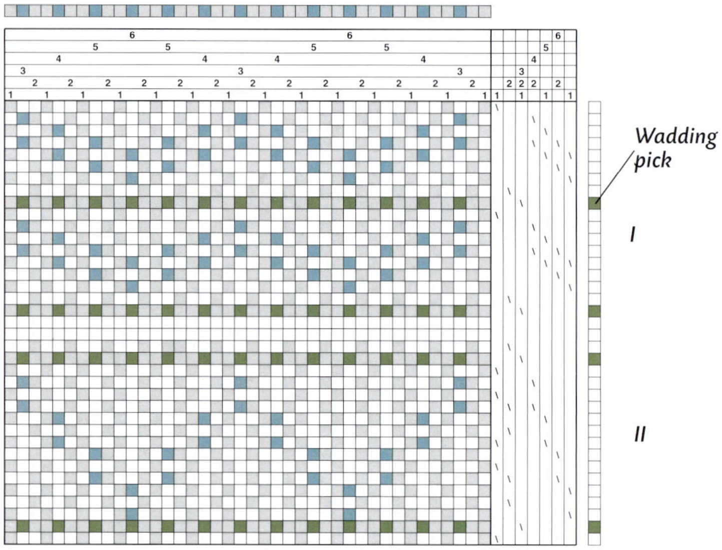

8.10 Six-shaft, waved, loose-back piqué. The wave in the piqué is relatively shallow in the first treadling, steeper in the second. Because each stitcher is lifted twice in both versions, the furrow that zigzags across the cloth is more pronounced. Give the wadding weft plenty of slack.

the ratios are 8:1 and 13:1. Fewer wadding picks make the cloth less three-dimensional when it is finished. Loose-back piqués are used when their backs are never exposed (as in upholstery), so the wadding picks can be large and squishy to make up for their smaller number. (They don't have to pass through heddles, after all.)

Besides forming straight or wavy lines, the stitchers may also be used to form isolated motifs in the cloth.

Draft **8.11** shows a piqué with two diamond shapes arranged in a half-drop; that is, in the second row diamonds appear *between* those in the row above and in the

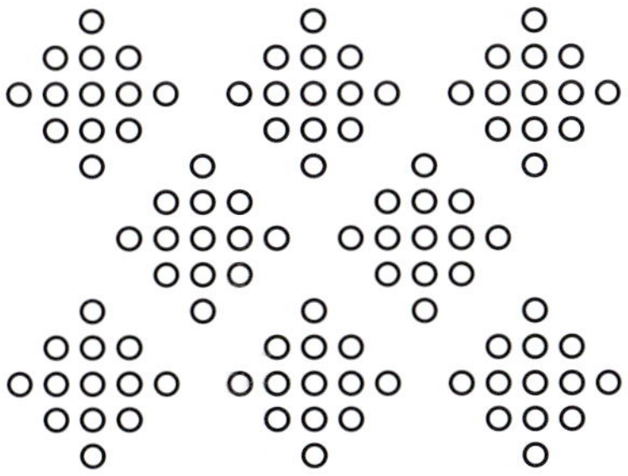

row below. To determine an appropriate sett, figure the sett for the face warp and add the stitchers to it. For example, if the sett for the face is to be 20 e.p.i. and there are two face warps to each stitcher (as has been the case so far), then there will be ten stitchers per inch in addition to the 20 ends for the face. When sleying the warp, do not give the stitchers their own dent; to do so would create a gap in the face of the cloth except where the stitches comes to the surface. Instead, add the stitchers to the dents of the face ends.

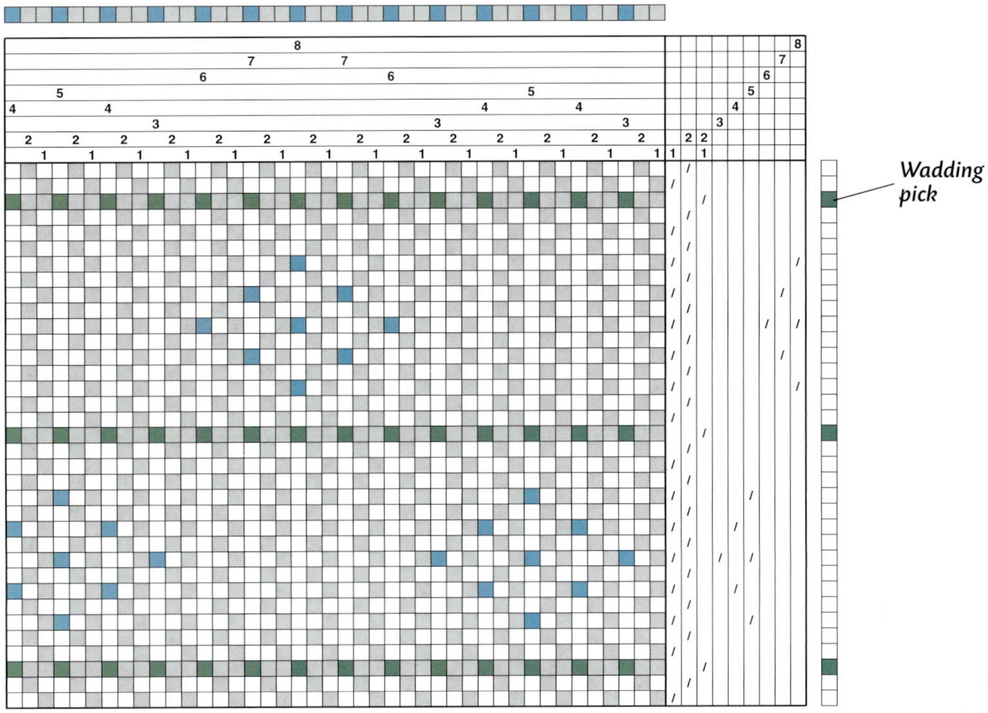

8.11 Piqué with two diamond-shaped motifs arranged in a half-drop. This example is shown as a loose-back piqué and is padded.

For example, for a face warp sett at 20 e.p.i., a 10-dent-per-inch reed could be used with two face ends per dent. The stitcher warps would be added, making three ends per dent: two for the face and one stitcher.

Because the face and stitcher ends require different tensions, it's convenient to beam them separately. If you don't have two warp beams, you can beam the ends for the face and then weight separately the few ends for the stitchers (see page 69).

Washing the fabric enhances the three-dimensional appearance of the piqué, and three-dimensionality is the whole point of piqué, so be sure to wash it!

Two loose-back piqués woven of very fine, heathered single, woolen-spun wool. The wadding pick is plainly visible on the back. The blue-green cloth was used as upholstery on an antique stool for a little pump organ.

9

Loom-Controlled Pile Weaves

Some of the most beautiful pile fabrics in the world, hand-knotted rugs, are woven by slowly and painstakingly knotting each tuft; some rugs have in excess of 300 knots per square inch. Much as I admire—indeed, covet—these textiles, they are not the focus of this chapter. Rather, we will consider the methods of making pile cloths that do not require hand knotting.

Pile may be either cut or uncut; that is cut pile or loop pile. In fact, both cut and uncut (loop) pile may appear in the same cloth.

Pile may be formed by the warp or the weft. Warp piles require two warps that are beamed and tensioned separately. Velvet and terry are two warp piles, the former cut and the latter uncut. In both cases, the warp that forms the pile often passes over a wire or a rod that establishes the height of the pile; the pile is then is woven securely into the ground cloth, and the wire or rod is ultimately removed. (If the pile were not woven into the ground, then the tufts would fall right out of the cloth.)

If the warp loops are formed by picking them up with the fingers, they may be of different heights—sculpted, if you will. Such hand manipulation is outside the scope of this book, however.

In either case, the pile warp is threaded onto shafts different from those holding the ground warp. The pile shafts will be lifted with the ground shafts to anchor the pile. To form the pile, only the pile shafts are lifted. If the pile is to be cut, the pile warp is usually distributed over more than one shaft, which allows the weaver to lift half with one pick and the other half with the next pick, thus distributing the pile more evenly. If loops are to be left, all of the pile warp may be lifted at once, making rows of loops more evident.

Pile formed by the weft is our main concern in this chapter. Only one warp is needed, although two shuttles may be required if the pile yarn and the ground yarn are to be different.

The weft pile structures here are made by weaving a firm ground cloth which varies from plain weave to 1/2 twill to 2/2 twill, depending on the desired effect and the number of available shafts. The pile is formed by weft floats that are cut as the weaving progresses *while the cloth is held under loom tension.* With the exception of pile rugs, the cloth is typically washed (wet finished) after being removed from the loom. The tufts of pile are most vulnerable after the pile is cut but before the cloth is washed; handle it carefully at this stage. Washing not only tightens the ground cloth as it shrinks, but also allows the cut pile to become fluffy. The lushest weft piles are made of materials that open or bloom during wet finishing, making the tufts of pile thicker and thus more securely held in the ground cloth. A woolen-spun pile weft performs very well in this regard.

If a shaggier cloth is the goal, the floats may be lifted with the fingers to form loops and thus a longer pile. This approach is more practical for single- and double-corduroy rugs where the floats are long enough to lift easily than for corduroy woven for clothing or upholstery where the floats are quite short.

Corduroy

The pile of corduroy fabrics is usually cut as the weaving proceeds, while the cloth is still under tension. The easiest way to weave corduroy is by using a single weft that weaves both the ground cloth that supports the pile and the pile itself. The structure of the ground determines how luxurious the pile will be and how many shafts will be required to construct it. The ideal, exemplified in traditional corduroy fabrics, is a cloth with warpwise ribs of pile in which the length of the pile varies **in a regular fashion.** If there are three lengths, then the longest tuft stands highest in the center, pile of middle height flanks it, and the shortest pile is at the sides of the cord. The cord thus formed is rounded in cross section.

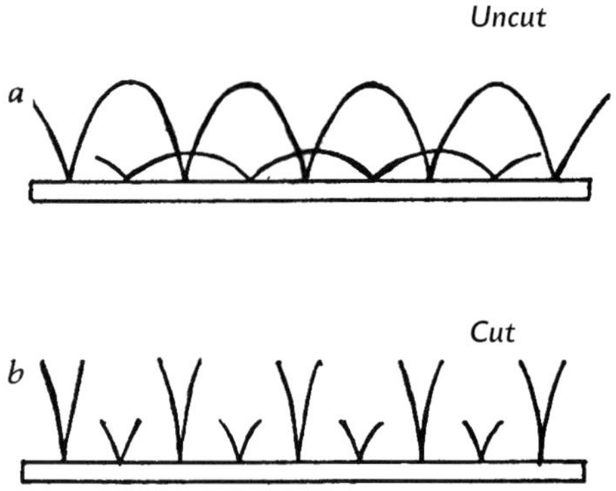

Figure 1 Pile length can be varied by pulling weft floats to different heights.

If the pile is to stand upright, there must be an abundance of pile threads sticking up out of the cloth. The more crowded they are, the better they support one another. At the same time, the ground structure—which holds the cloth together—must be woven firmly. There will therefore be many picks per inch.

The simplest corduroy is woven on a plain-weave base (**9.1a**). The first two picks create floats on the surface of the cloth (the pile-to-be), the third pick weaves plain weave, the next two picks weave floats again, followed by the second plain-weave pick. Weave corduroys with a heavy beat because the stability of corduroy pile depends on a firm ground cloth.

The floats in **9.1a** are all the same length when cut. Although they will produce a pile fabric, the corduroy will seem fuller and more

Corduroy pillow fabric. The added colors are made by inlaying lengths of contrasting yarns in the pile sheds. Cloth woven by Dixie Straight.

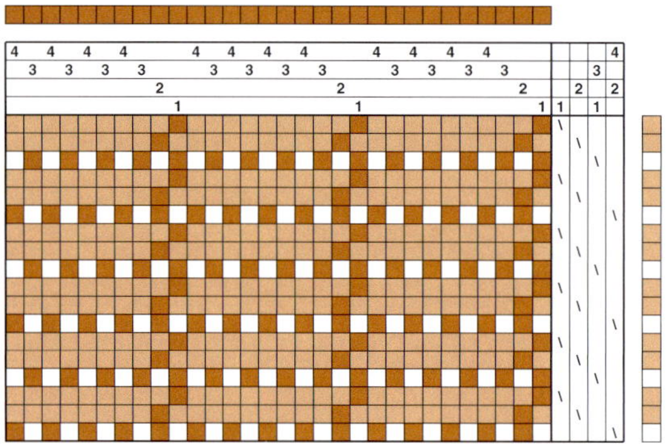

9.1a The simplest corduroy. The ground cloth is plain weave (there are two pile picks to one ground pick). The pile picks create floats in the cloth, which are cut after they have been woven. The pile picks are shown as a contrasting color here to make them easier to recognize.

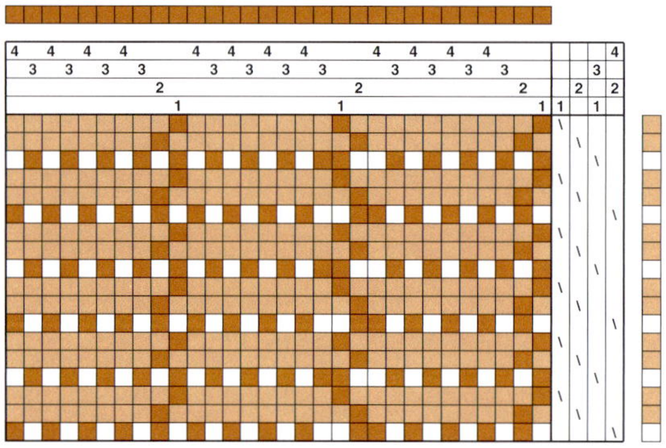

9.1b This corduroy uses the same number of shafts as in 9.1a, but because it is threaded slightly differently, the corduroy produced has more depth. Notice that the weft floats are two lengths: an 8- and a 10-end float. Because they are cut right down the middle, the cut pile is made up of different lengths.

Two novelty corduroys woven with a fine singles woolen-spun weft on a 2/20 worsted wool warp. The upper example is striped. The lower one is cut in some places and uncut in others, forming right triangles in the cloth.

uxurious if the floats are of different lengths so that they stand up at different levels. Draft **9.1b** makes floats that are eight and ten ends long; when these are cut, the pile has two lengths and seems fuller than that produced by **9.1a** but is achieved without adding extra picks or shafts.

Using either draft, it is easy to see the places where it is to be cut: right down the middle of long warpwise ribs of floats. I strongly recommend that you cut the floats while the cloth is still under tension on the loom. My preference is to weave about 2 inches (5 cm) of cloth, set down the shuttle, cut the floats, advance the warp by 2 inches, and begin to weave again. Use scissors with very slender blades that are very, very sharp— sharp right to the tip.

Once you have cut one line of the floats, cutting the next rib with thick-bladed or dull scissors can pull the cut wefts out of the cloth; so insert the blade of your slender, sharp scissors gingerly, making cuts of about a ¼ inch (6 mm) at a time. It doesn't pay to hurry this procedure, because if you cut through the ground cloth, the fabric will have a hole at that place. When I've cut the pile, I cover it with a piece of muslin or a tea towel to prevent dislodging the cut wefts as I lean against the breast beam while weaving. There is no doubt that cutting the pile in the corduroy is tedious, but the result is a very luxurious cloth. My favorite handwoven corduroy has a woolen-spun singles weft woven across a worsted wool warp: the warp needs to be strong, and the cut wefts "bloom," making them softer and fuller than the yarn is before cutting.

Corduroy woven on a plain-weave base is nice, but using a base of 2/1 twill or 3/1 twill makes it even more luxurious. Look back

This six-shaft corduroy was woven on a warp of 2/20 worsted wool sett at 24 e.p.i. Now, that is not excessive, but the weft count of 50 p.p.i. decidedly is!

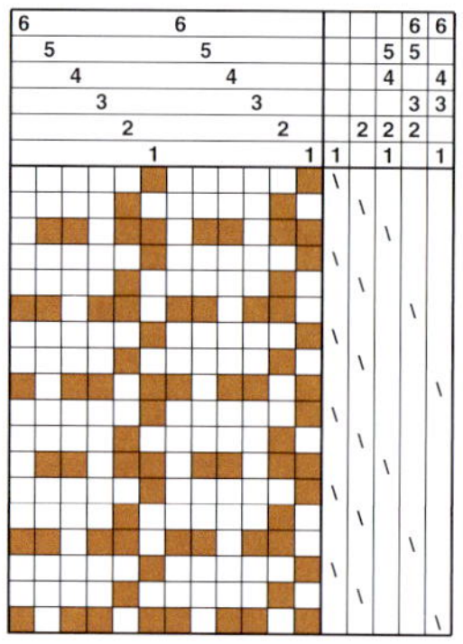

9.2 Corduroy based on a three-shaft twill.

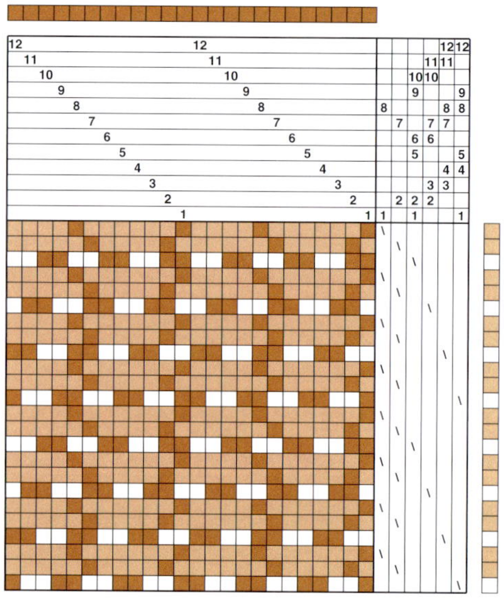

9.3 Corduroy with a four-shaft twill ground. Two pile picks are thrown between each ground pick. Notice that each pile pick weaves two different float lengths in the same pick, and that these alternate between the first pile pick and the second in the pair. The tan picks are pile wefts, and the white picks weave the ground.

at **9.1a**, the first plain-weave version, and notice that the wefts that float on the surface are all the same length and originate in only two places in the cloth (to the left and right of the cutting line). When you cut the pile right down the center of the float, the cut ends originate from those two places on either side of the cut and are the same length.

A corduroy with a three-shaft twill base results in a denser base cloth, which allows us to pack in more wefts, thus creating more pile (**9.2**). But the fullness of the pile in this version is only a little greater than that of the corduroy woven with a plain-weave ground. On the other hand, a corduroy woven with a four-shaft twill ground makes a lush, well-rounded cord. Draft **9.3** is the draft for such a cloth. The first pile pick weaves a six-end float and a four-end float. The second pile pick weaves a four-end float and a six-end float. This alternation within the same pick staggers the float lengths and allows the longer floats to make tufts that stand higher in the cloth than the shorter ones, forming a rounded shape. The four-shaft twill ground permits a denser cloth than either the three-shaft twill or the plain weave, making the cord even plusher.

Draft **9.4a** shows a dramatic corduroy woven on sixteen shafts. The pile is longer than those of the preceding versions although the base is still a four-shaft twill. Draft **9.4b** produces the same result with twelve shafts.

Just for the fun of it, I worked out the draft for the dramatic corduroy, which moves on the diagonal woven on a four-shaft ground cloth (**9.5**). Because it requires thirty-six treadles on a sixteen-shaft loom, it clearly would have to be woven on a dobby or table loom rather than a treadle loom.

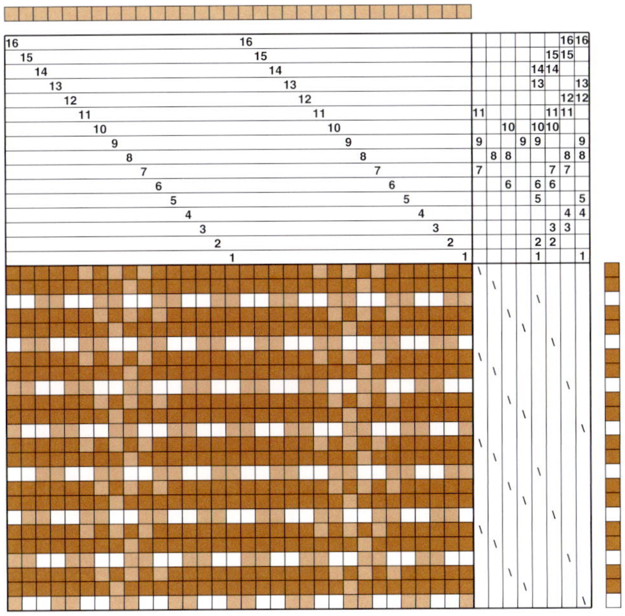

9.4a This corduroy has a four-shaft twill ground but has a much longer pile. The cords are farther apart, producing a sort of "wide wale" corduroy.

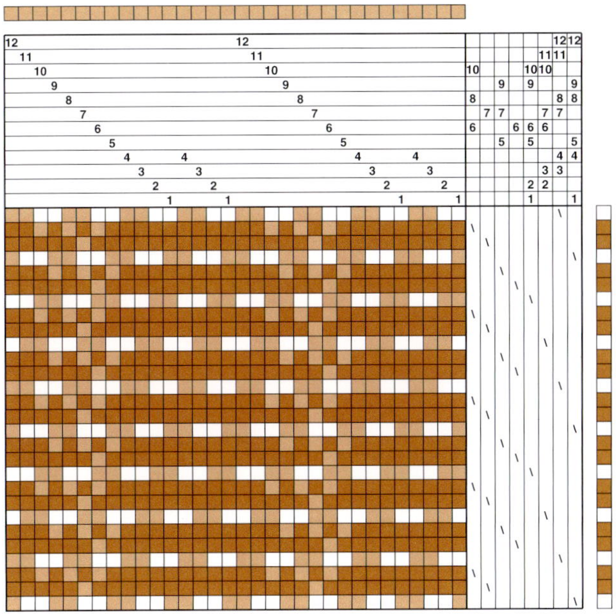

9.4b Twelve-shaft version 9.4a.

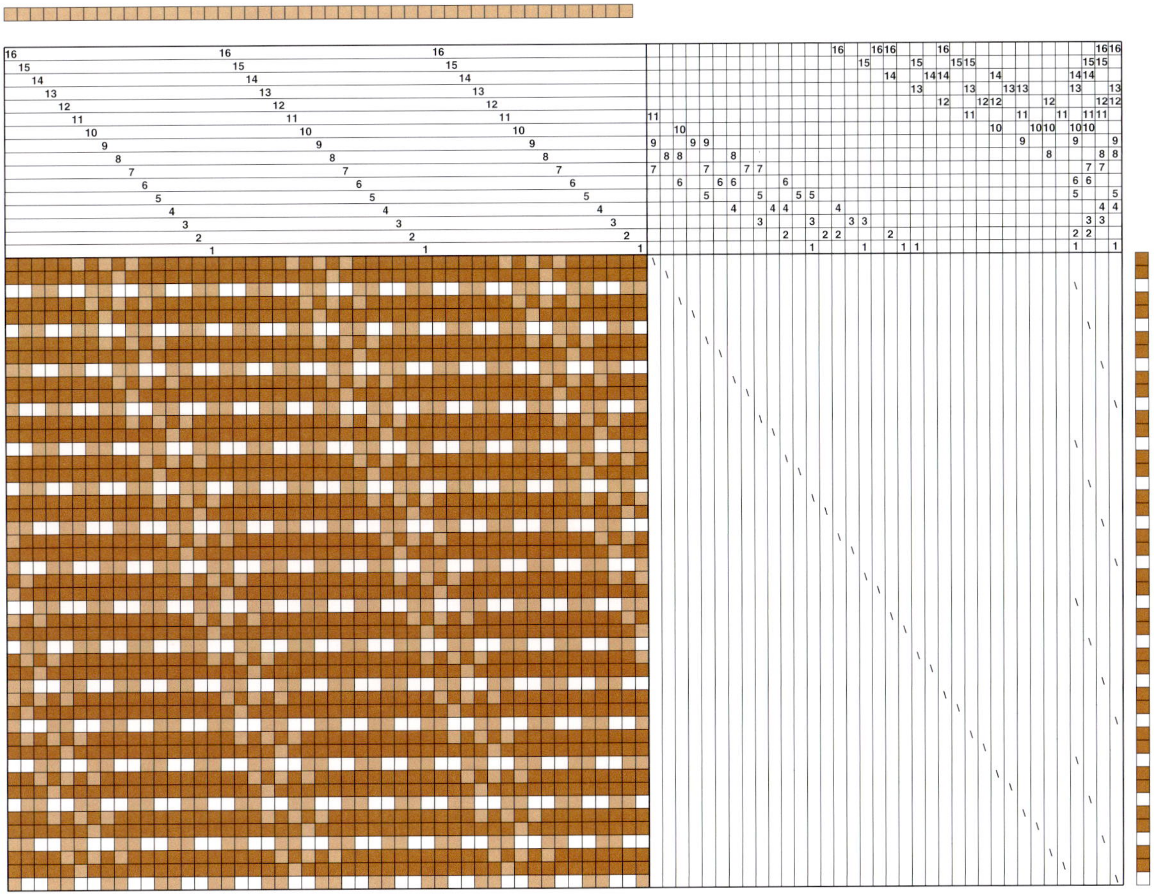

9.5 A diagonal cord with dramatic pile. How do we cut it? Very carefully!

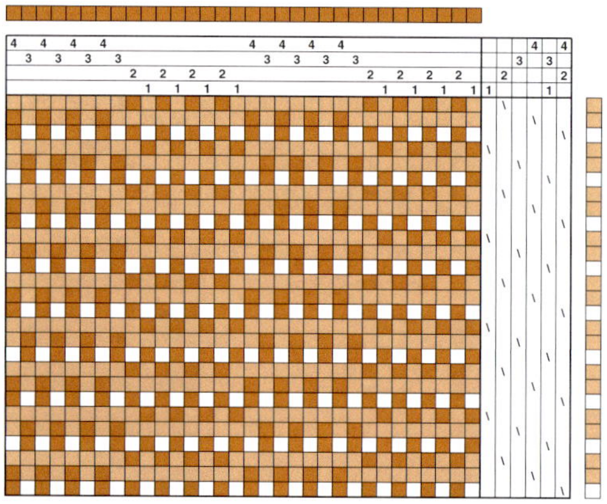

9.6a Four-shaft single corduroy. Two pile picks are thrown for each ground pick (plain weave). The structure forms two vertical columns of floats, which are cut by hand at intervals during the weaving.

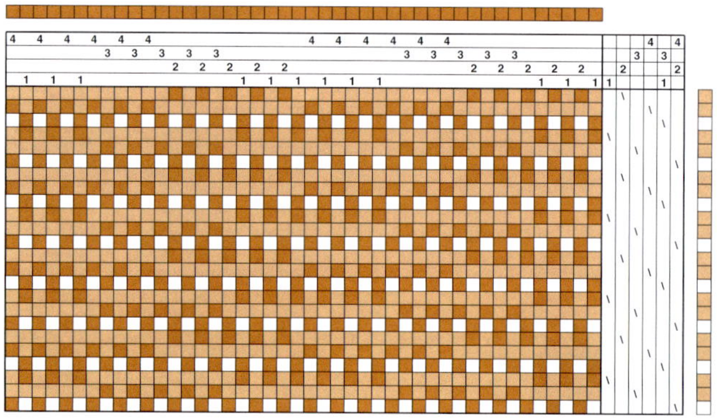

9.6b Four-shaft double corduroy, in the style of Peter Collingwood. There are two pile shots to each ground shot. The columns of floats are cut down their centers. Notice that the columns are offset so that the pile is fuller when cut.

Another kind of corduroy, originally devised by Alistair Morton, threads the warp in two blocks on four shafts: 1, 2, repeat and 3, 4, repeat. Plain-weave and pile picks alternate with pairs of pile picks which weave in one block (1, 2) and float in the other (3, 4). Then the pile floats in the first block (1,2) and weaves in the other (3, 4). The pile floats line up in parallel rows and are cut down their centers to form rows of tufts that parallel the selvedges (**9.6a**).

Double corduroy, Peter Collingwood's invention, was devised to create a fluffier pile for rugs than the one just described. The floats in this structure are staggered so that the center of the pile floats in one pick are offset from the pile floats in the next pile pick (**9.6b**).

Just as in the smaller corduroys described at the beginning of this section, the floats that become the pile are cut after a few inches have been woven and then the weaving continues. Cutting pile floats while the rug is held under tension makes the process a lot easier and the ground cloth less at risk of accidental cuts.

Velveteen

Velveteen is a cut-weft pile fabric (unlike velvet, which has cut-warp pile). It is woven with a plain-weave ground. Draft **9.7a**, a velveteen woven with four pile picks to one ground pick, uses half the shafts to tie the pile wefts to the cloth. These picks nestle into one of the plain-weave sheds but stand opposite to the other one. The back of the cloth resembles a rib more than it does plain weave.

A better solution, perhaps, is **9.7b**, in which the first four pile picks nestle with the first plain-weave shed and the second four pile picks, with the second plain-weave shed. Because it is possible to pack in more picks than is possible with **9.7a**, the pile produced is fuller.

Draft **9.8a** shows a velveteen in which the pile wefts are caught by more than one shaft, making the pile more secure. As in **9.7a**, the pile is caught by half the warp ends, and its back looks like a rib. Draft **9.8b** bears the same relationship to **9.8a** as **9.7b** does to **9.7a**: that is, all warp ends are used to tie down the pile wefts. The pile weft is thus more secure, and it is possible to pack in more picks per inch than is possible in the **a** version.

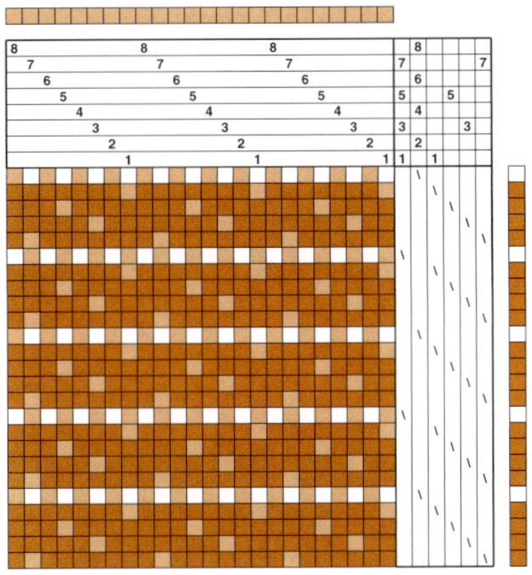

9.7a In this velveteen draft the pile is caught by half the warp ends.

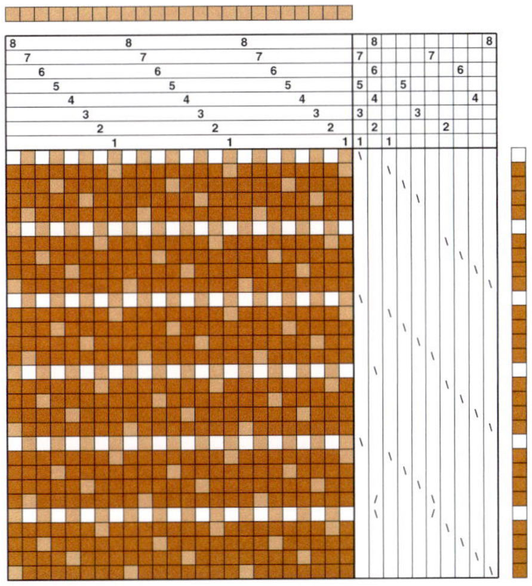

9.7b Here, the pile is caught by all of the warp ends. The cloth packs in more closely than in draft 7a.

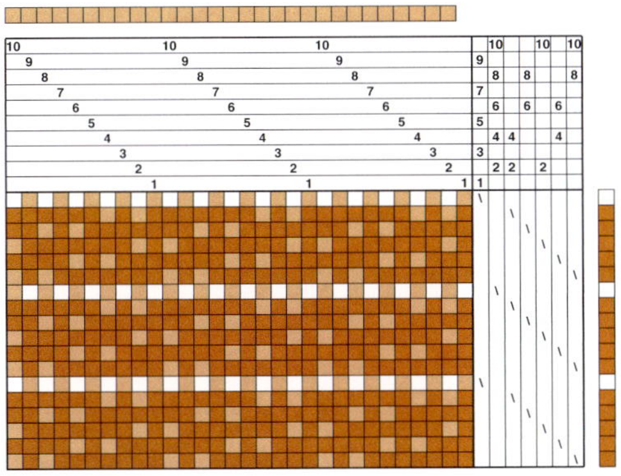

9.8a In this one, the pile weft is caught more securely than in 7a and 7b. The pile picks are caught by more than one warp end. Because the same combinations are used over and over, the back resembles a rib more than plain weave. The pile is secured only by half the warp ends.

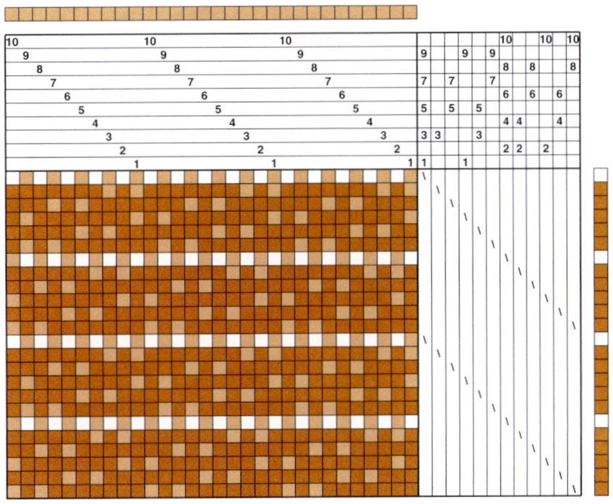

9.8b Here, the stitching of the pile weft is more evenly distributed. The back of this velveteen looks like plain weave.

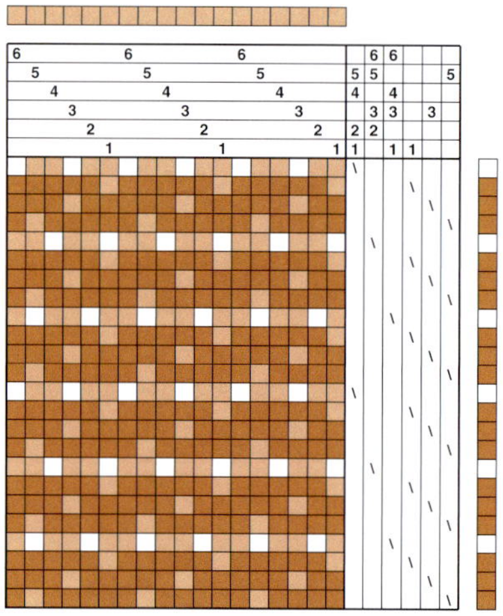

9.9 Velveteen with three-shaft twill ground. There are three pile picks to each ground pick. Notice that the pile pick just after the ground pick is caught by one of the shafts just lifted for the ground pick. The third ground pick is made by lifting a shaft that will be lifted for the next ground pick. The intermediate pick is not as securely bound.

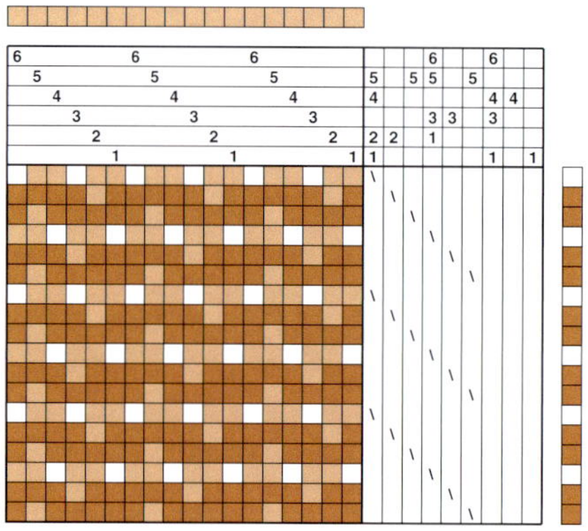

9.10 Velveteen with a three-shaft twill base and two pile picks per ground pick. This structure is set more closely and beats in more closely (2/1 twill compared with plain weave). Notice that the pile picks nestle into the ground pick that precedes them.

A velveteen with a three-shaft twill ground is shown in **9.9**. In this structure, there are three pile picks for each ground pick. Notice that the first pile pick following the ground pick is caught by warp ends on one of the shafts lifted for the ground pick. The third pile pick in the sequence is caught by lifting one of the shafts that will be lifted in the next, a ground pick. These pile picks are very secure; however, the second pile pick, which is located farthest from the ground picks, will not be as securely held.

A possible solution to the problem of a less-secure pile weft like the one described above may be seen in **9.10**. Here the ratio of pile picks to ground picks is 2:1. In this case, the pile picks nestle into both the ground picks before them and the one that follows. While the ratio here, 2:1, is less than the 3:1 ratio in **9.9**, the density of the pile will be about the same because the pile picks pack in so neatly.

When a more rigorous velveteen is desired, one in which the pile picks are more secure, we can use **9.11**. The pile picks are woven into the ground by passing under one end, over the next, and under the third. The ratio of pile picks to ground picks is 5:1. Because of the extra stitching of the pile wefts to the ground cloth, you might expect that the pile would be stubby. In fact, because the draft requires ten shafts, the float is actually seven ends wide compared to five ends in **9.10**.

Draft **9.12** is a velveteen based on a four-shaft, 2/2 twill. The ratio of pile to ground picks is 2:1. This pile won't be as luxurious as that produced by **9.11**, but the density of the cloth (2/2 as compared to 2/1 twill) will be high enough to make a nice velveteen.

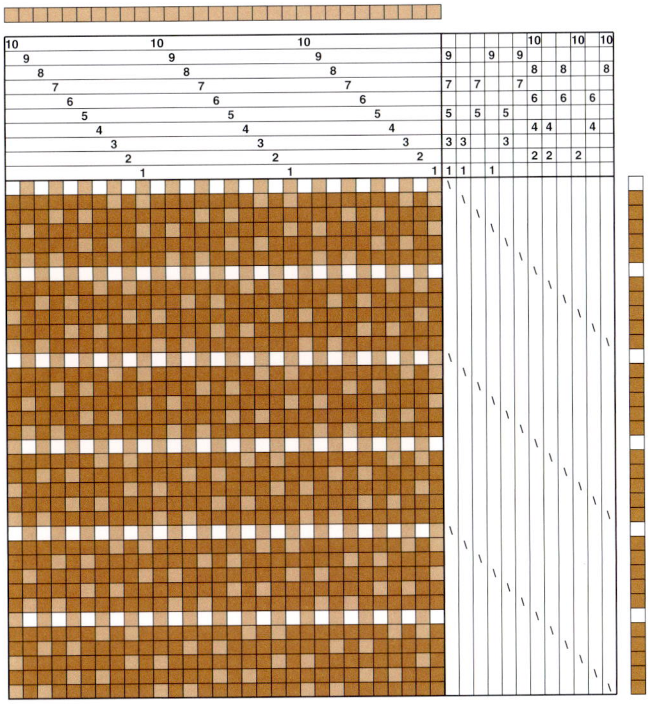

9.11 Velveteen woven into a plain-weave base. The pile picks are caught by three warp ends. Notice that the stitching points in the five picks after the first plain weave pick nest into the plain weave pick. The five pile picks woven after the second tabby "fit" into it as well.

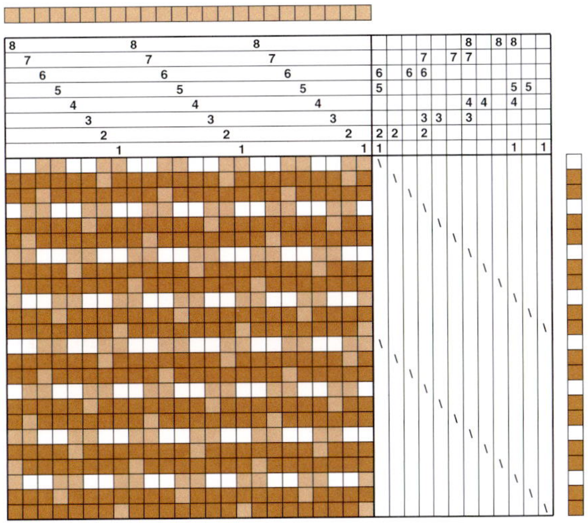

9.12 Velveteen based on a 2/2 twill. The ratio of pile to ground picks is 2:1. Each pile pick nests into both the ground picks preceding it. The second of the pair nests with the following ground pick as well.

It is simple to see how to cut the floats in a corduroy, but how to cut velveteens is more perplexing. It is useful to look at how the cutting of pile floats, both for corduroy and velveteen, are handled in industry. A V-shaped length of metal with a very sharp knife blade mounted at its tip is is inserted into the ladder of floats, cutting them.

In earlier times, the uncut pile wefts of both corduroy and velveteen were covered with slaked lime and dried over a hot roller; then flour paste was painted on the back of the cloth, which was again passed over hot rollers to dry. This stiffened the fabric so that the pile wasn't as likely to come out during the cutting.

In the 1880s, the same sort of V-shaped device was used to cut velveteen. The knife had to be run parallel to the selvedges more than once because the floats originate at different places in the cloth. In a traditional velveteen, the pile is uniform; in other words, it doesn't create a pattern in the cloth. This requires scattering the catching points so that the pile-cutting knife must be inserted at several points. This procedure is more tedious than cutting corduroy, but the results, of course, can be quite lovely.

10

Crepe Weaves

Crepe fabrics, sometimes called "crape" or oatmeal weaves, are characterized by a somewhat rough surface, even when they are woven from smooth yarns. The fiber and yarn style used in their creation has a great deal to do with just how rough the cloth will be to the touch. Crepe is the only structure considered in this book without a readily identifiable threading system. (For example, Bronson lace uses the threading 1, X, 1, X, 1, 2, where X stands for the number of the shaft used to make the pattern.)

There are two ways of obtaining a crepe fabric. One way is to use very highly twisted yarns woven in plain weave, set openly enough to allow them to collapse and crinkle when the cloth is wet-finished. I think of these as "physical crepes." The other way is to use a structure that gives rise to a small, overall pattern that is not readily "understood" by the eye: we look at the cloth but don't discern a particular pattern, just a jumble of short floats in both warp and weft directions. I think of this sort of crepe as a "structural crepe." It doesn't require specially spun yarns to construct it.

Physical crepe is most effectively made by weaving an open plain weave. A series of experiments I made on **tracking**, the name given to creating a crepey fabric when you don't necessarily expect or want it, showed that if the highly twisted yarns were set very closely, tracking did not occur. (The threads had no room to collapse.) The more open the sett (woven to square so that ppi=epi), the more dramatic the tracking was. Tracking was strongest when plain weave was used. To make a twill track even a little required such an open sett that the cloth was sleazy and at great risk of snagging. Our focus, here, is on structural crepes.

All crepe fabrics have floats in the warp and weft directions. The more random they look, the better. But creating a convincing

A physical crepe woven of fine wool. The structure, plain weave, was woven so there was room for the highly spun yarns to collapse when wet finished, creating diagonal "tracks" in the fabric.

crepe with a surface that is a little rough and that has relatively short floats running in both warp and weft directions so that the repeat isn't obvious is not possible on just four shafts. Using only four ends, it is not possible to make something that looks truly random. Draft **10.1**, a broken twill, and **10.2** are both examples of crepey structures using just four shafts.

Most crepes are threaded using a straight draw. Construction of stripes in either direction is to be avoided because you will lose the uniformly unstructured surface appearance that characterizes a crepe construction. Each end in the cloth needs to interlace to the same degree as the others. To weave a traditional crepe, we need to avoid interlacing some warp ends a lot and others more rarely because the former will become tight and the latter slack, and the resulting cloth will lack the uniform surface that we associate with this weave. In addition, we want about the same number and length of floats on each side of the cloth, making it reversible. The thread count is equal in both directions; that is, the number of picks per inch is equal to the number of ends per inch. Finer yarns and a single color for warp and weft are used, as a general rule in commercial production.

In drafts **10.2** and **10.3**, the crepes are constructed so that the tie-up is divided into four quadrants by drawing a line vertically and horizontally through the middle of the square that makes the tie up. In **10.2**, a quadrant consists of a 2 × 2 square; in **10.3**, a 3 × 3 square. The starting unit in **10.2** looks like this, where the circles represent a rising-shed tie-up:

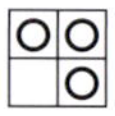

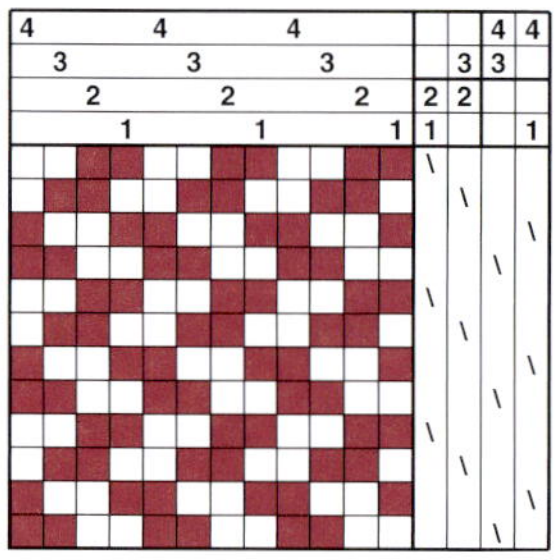

10.1 Broken twill. A 2/2 twill woven so that no diagonal rib appears. It is not a crepe.

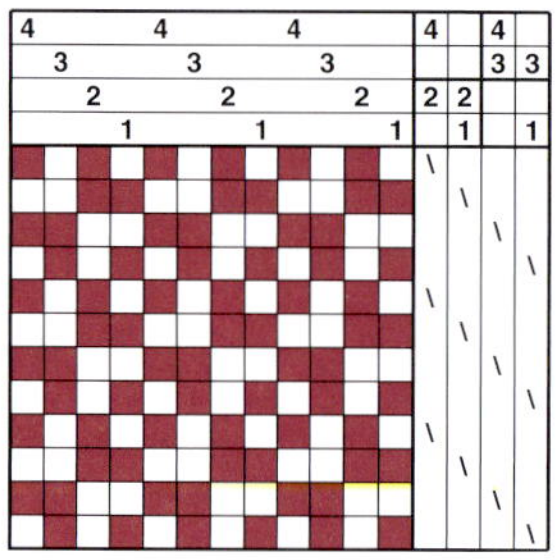

10.2 A structural crepe using four shafts. Notice that there are short floats in both the warp and weft directions. Four shafts do not allow the construction of a dramatic crepe.

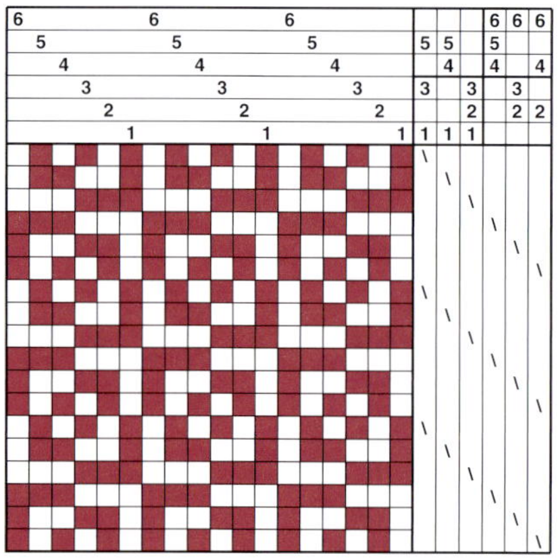

10.3 This six-shaft crepe weave is more dramatic than the four-shaft structure in crepe 10.2 and is related to it.

Notice that the pattern appears in the tie-up. The tie-up is constructed by entering the shafts to be lifted in a 3 × 3 square (the bottom left quadrant), and then reflected as its negative in the top left quadrant. Then the entire left half is reflected as its opposite in the right half of the tie-up. Some sources describe this sort of construction as a "diced weave."

Two eight-shaft crepes. They are woven of 10/2 pearl cotton using contrasting warp and weft. An even beat is critical when weaving fabrics like these, because the eye quickly spots any unevenness.

Two crepes woven of 10/2 pearl cotton in yellow-green across white, and a 2/20 worsted wool crepe. The foreground cotton fabric and the wool one are woven on eight shafts, and the remaining cotton cloth is woven using 4. Notice that the four-shaft crepe is less randomly textured.

Reflected to the right, and entered as the negative, we see this:

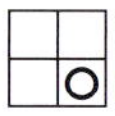

If this arrangement is reflected upward as its negative, the tie-up shown in **10.2** is the result. (Clearly, this method of constructing a crepe is limited to drafts woven on an even number of shafts.) Structures created this way are sometimes described, particularly in British texts, as being "diced."

Draft **10.6b** is constructed by interleaving a four-shaft crepe (**10.6a**) with a 2/2 twill. The two tie-ups are side by side so you can more easily see how they were used. When designing a crepe this way, you might have to try starting one or the other of the structures in different places until you come up with something that looks as though it will work. In this case, the treadling for the twill was reversed.

Drafts **10.7**, **10.8**, and **10.9** are all six-shaft crepes constructed by playing with shapes. The first is easy to see; in the second, the tie-up contains L-shaped pieces rotated, with a few extra ties to avoid long floats. In the third, the organization of the bottom three rows of the six-row by six-column square is reflected into the upper three rows so that filled places in the lower three rows are empty in the upper three, and *vice versa.*

An almost-curving trellis or vine-like shape is used in **10.10**. All shafts are lifted for the same number of picks; this is also true for **10.11**, **10.12**, and **10.13**. Draft **10.14a** is a tie-up for $\frac{1\ 1\ 1}{1\ 1\ 3}$ twill, which is rearranged to create the eight-shaft crepe, **10.14b**. The numbers above the tie-up for **10.14a** show the order in which the sheds were used. Starting with the first shed, we drop back one and then move to the next pair: 1, 8 and 3, 2 and 5, 4 and, finally, 7, 6, until all eight sheds have been used.

So, there are schemes you can try when designing a crepe structure. Sometimes they work and sometimes they don't, but they all come down to this: short warp and weft floats, each warp end lifted about the same number of times, and no stripes or easily discerned pattern in the cloth. The use of eight or more shafts, as usual, provides more options for breaking up a possible pattern than four or six shafts do.

The same characteristic—the tendency for floating ends or wefts to move toward each other—that makes lace weaves possible is responsible for the shifting that makes crepe weaves look, well, "crepey."

Crepe Variations

These are but a few of the possible ways to weave crepe on a four-shaft straight draw, varying the tie-up and treadling.

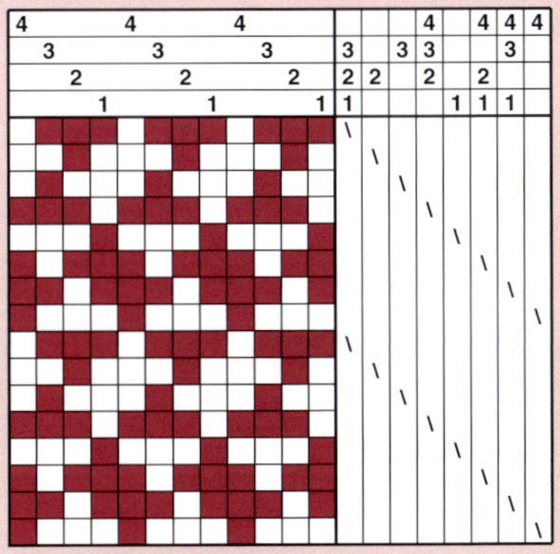

10.4a A four-shaft crepe. Written this way, eight treadles are required.

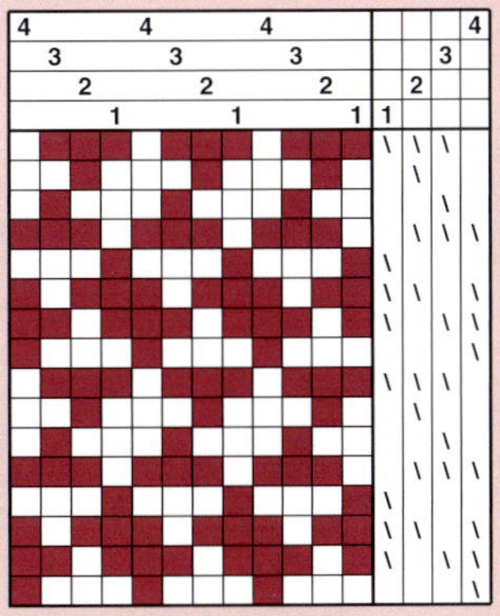

10.4b The same crepe written with a direct tie-up. Only four treadles are required, but you must use both feet.

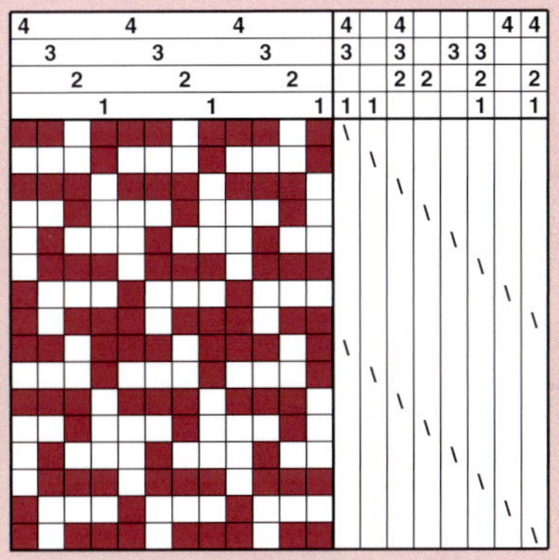

10.5a Another four-shaft crepe. Written this way, eight treadles are required.

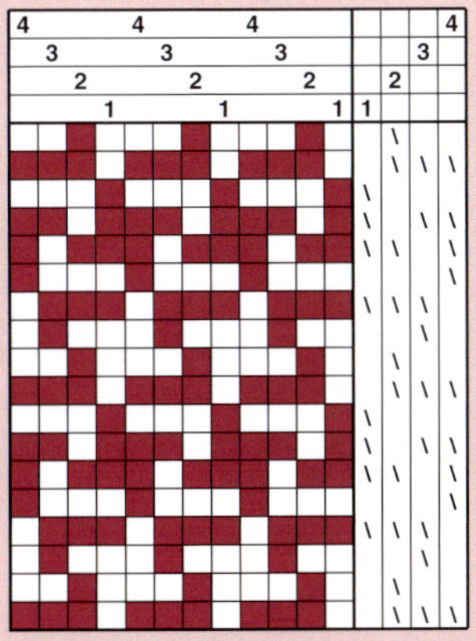

10.5b The same crepe using a direct tie-up.

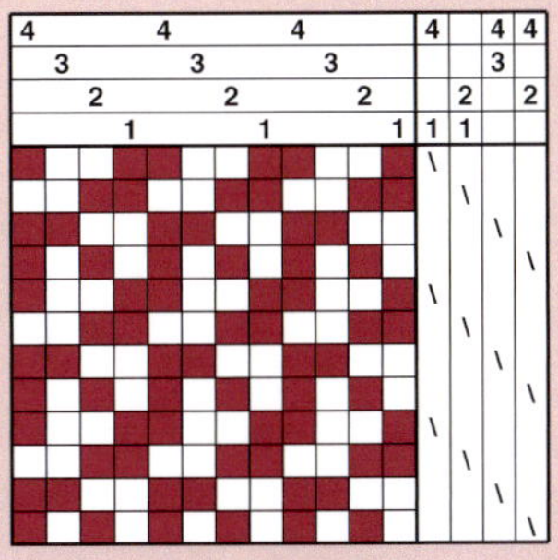

10.6a Yet another four-shaft crepe.

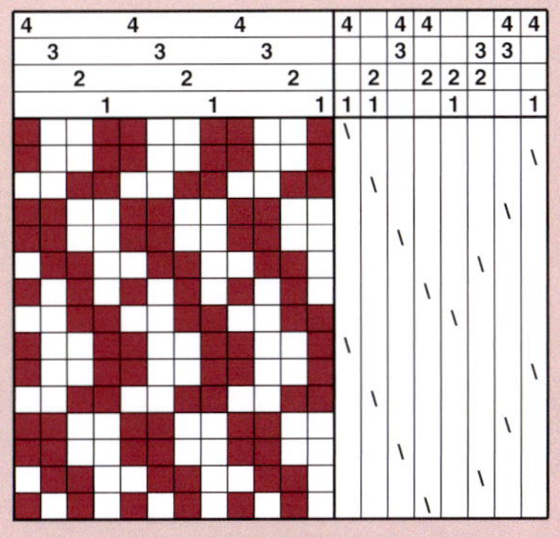

10.6b The same crepe is now interleaved with a 2/2 twill. Notice that the order for the sheds is different in the two halves of the tie-up (crepe on left, 2/2 twill on right).

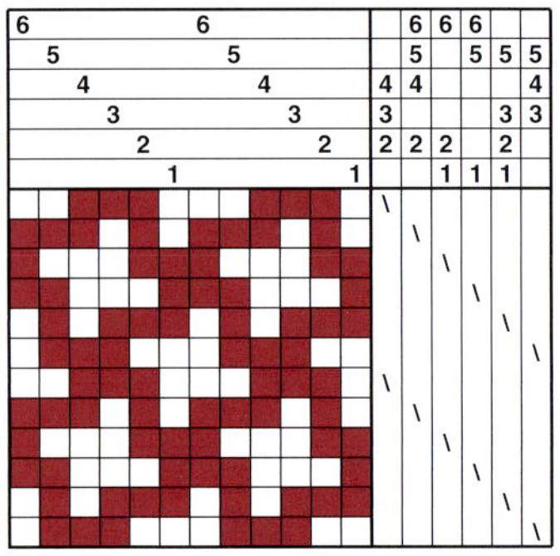

10.7 A six-shaft crepe. On paper it is a charming little pattern of pinwheels, but when removed from the loom and washed, a crepe is the result.

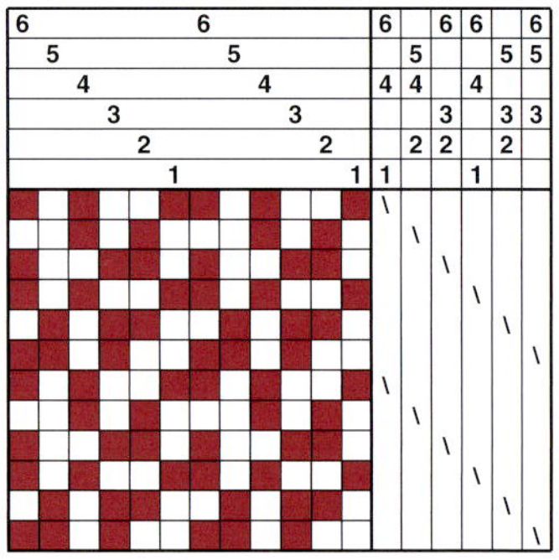

10.8 Another six-shaft crepe.

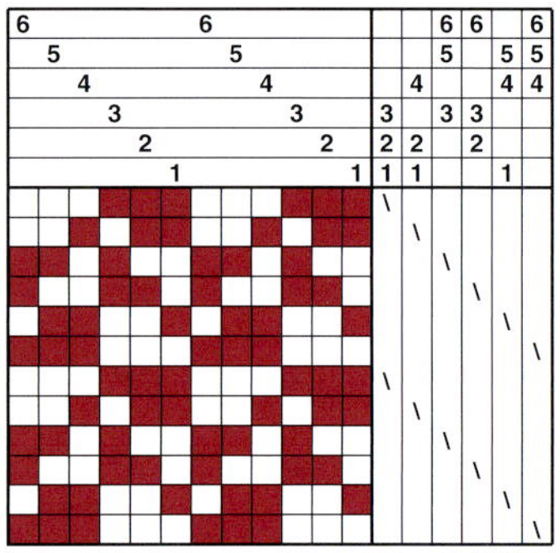

10.9 Another six-shaft crepe. The lifted threads in the first three rows of the tie-up box are reflected (as their negatives) to make the upper three rows.

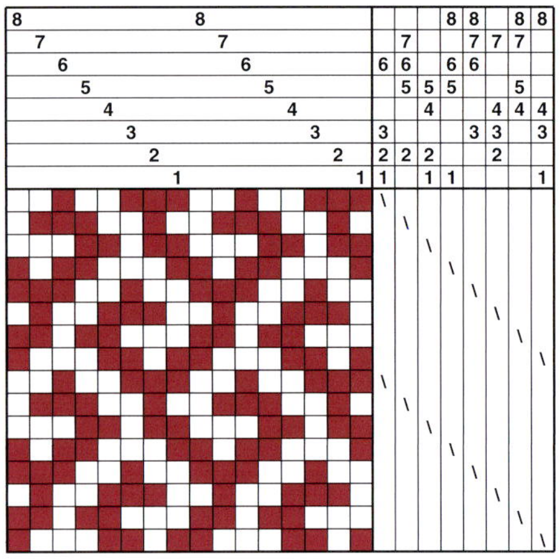

10.10 Although it looks like a trellis, this pattern, woven and washed is an eight-shaft crepe.

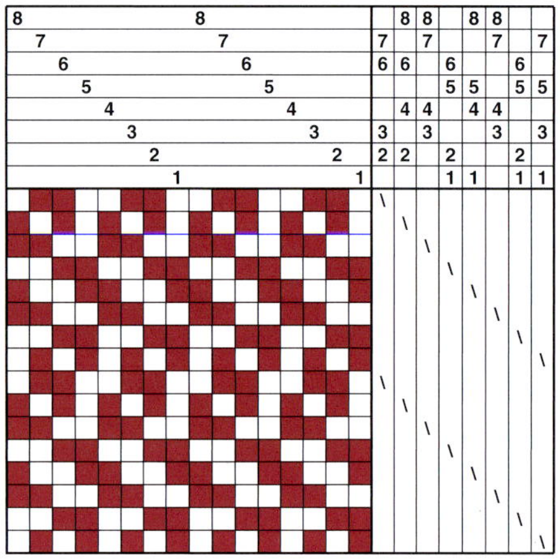

10.11 An eight-shaft crepe. The tie-up consists of sheds for 2/2 twill, rearranged (two sheds used twice and two just once), with two picks of plain weave added. The system used to rearrange the twill is not evident; the longest floats in either direction are over/under two ends/wefts.

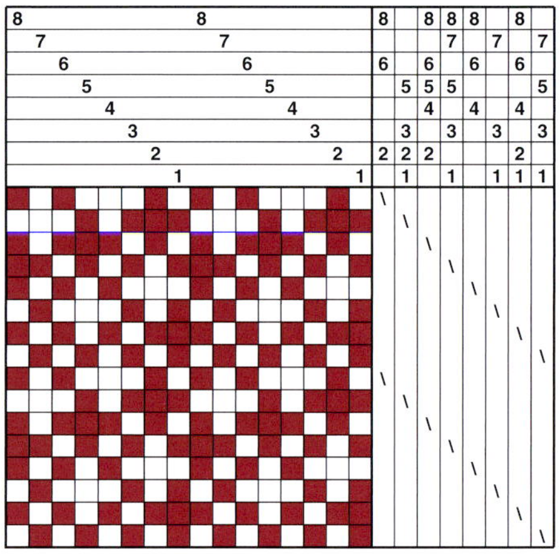

10.12 An eight-shaft crepe. No particular rule was used in its construction other than maintaining an equal number of warp and weft floats with each end intersecting about as much as all the others.

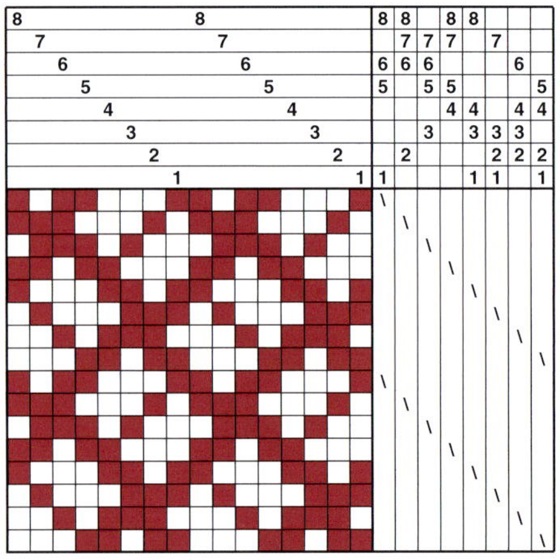

10.13 On paper this design looks as though it would be interesting and graphic, but woven and washed it forms a crepe. (Can you see the pattern in the tie-up box?)

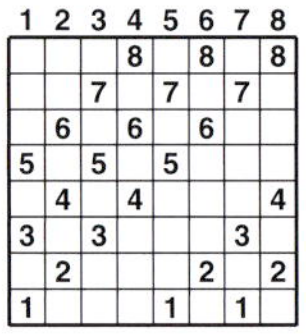

10.14a This is the tie-up for a $\frac{1\ 1\ 1}{1\ 1\ 3}$ *twill, which is rearranged to produce 10.14b.*

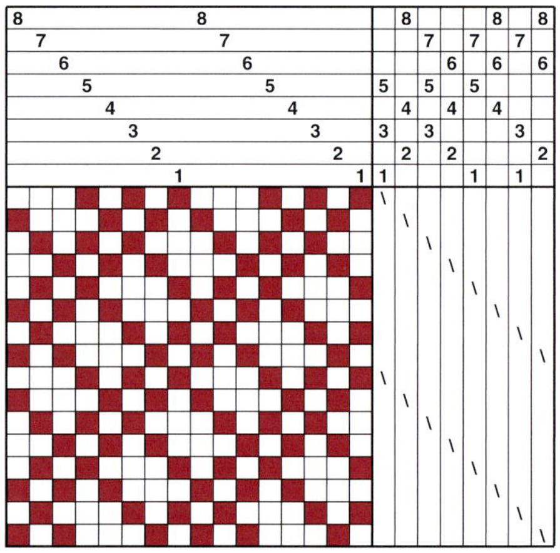

10.14b Once again a crepe on eight-shafts. Each end is lifted the same number of times. This tie-up is a rearranged $\frac{1\ 1\ 1}{1\ 1\ 3}$ *twill.*

11

Some of This, Some of That

Weavers can construct any number of interesting structures that don't fit naturally into any of the chapters above but aren't important enough to be the focus of an entire chapter. Because these structures have little in common, here are a little of this and a little of that. Take these for what they are—a handful of a host of possibilities that spring up outside the "boxes" of the classic structural systems.

Combined weaves

Different structures may be combined in a single cloth. One of the simplest combinations begins with a ground of plain weave and a vertical stripe of some other structure (**11.1–11.5** next page). Drafts **11.1** and **11.2** combine plain weave with a warp rib. Draft 11.1 is woven plain weave where ends are carried on shafts 1 and 2. The ends on shaft 3 are up for four picks, with those carried on shaft 4 on the back. Then the ends on shaft 4 float on the face for four picks, with those carried on 3 on the back. If the colors for the threads on shafts 3 and 4 are the same, this structure will look the same on both sides and be reversible. If they are of different colors, the cloth will still be reversible, with the stripe itself striped transversely. Draft **11.2** is shown with the ends carried on shaft 3 lifted for nine picks and down for one. The front and back of this cloth will look different. Notice that the ends between those on shaft 3 alternate between shafts 1 and 2 so that the rhythm of the plain-weave ground is maintained and the cloth is stable in the striped area. The ends carried on shaft 3 must be sleyed with the plain-weave ends; if the plain-weave area is sleyed with two ends per dent, for example, where the rib falls, the warp will be sleyed four per dent (a 1:1 ratio of ground ends to rib ends).

11.1 Plain-weave ground with a rib weave stripe. The threads carried on shafts 3 and 4 would be set at about twice the density (e.p.i.) as those carried on shafts 1 and 2 to keep the ribbed stripe firm.

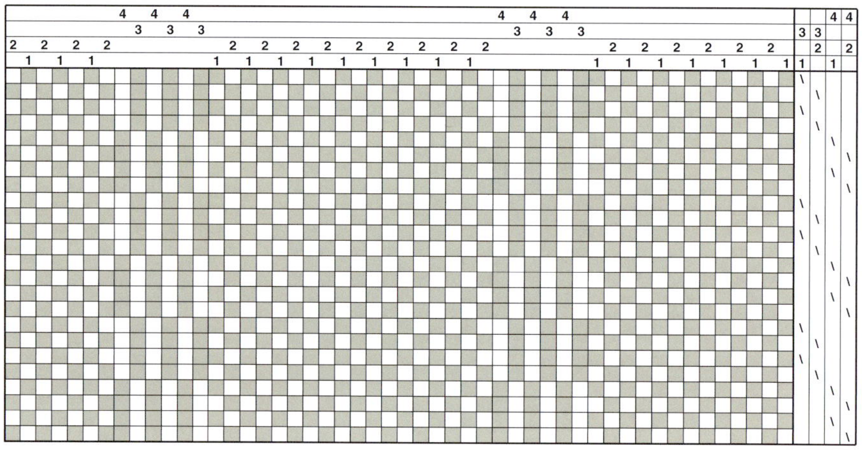

11.2 This draft makes another sort of rib stripe set into a plain-weave ground. The warp ends that float on the face of the cloth may be a different color so that they will stand out. Notice that the warp ends between the rib ends weave plain weave relative to each other so that the cloth is stable in the striped areas.

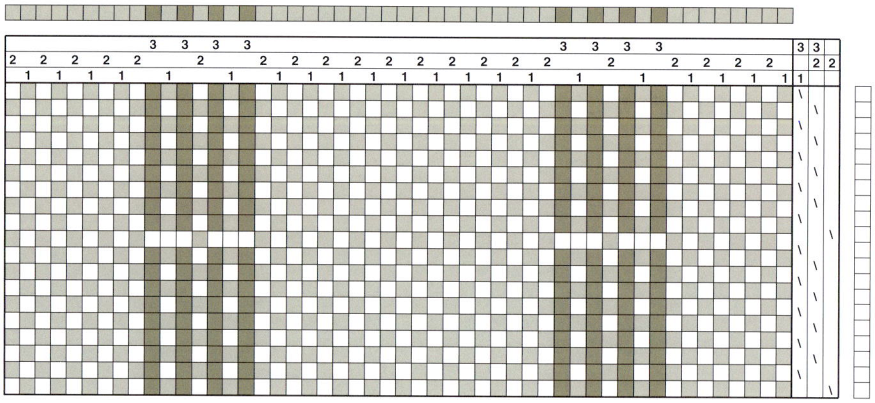

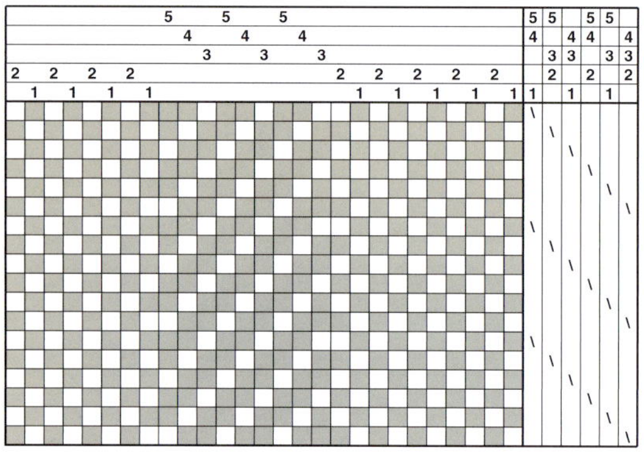

11.3 This time six treadles are used, one at a time for a 2/1 twill stripe in a plain-weave ground. Six are required because the twill repeats in 3 picks and plain weave in 2.

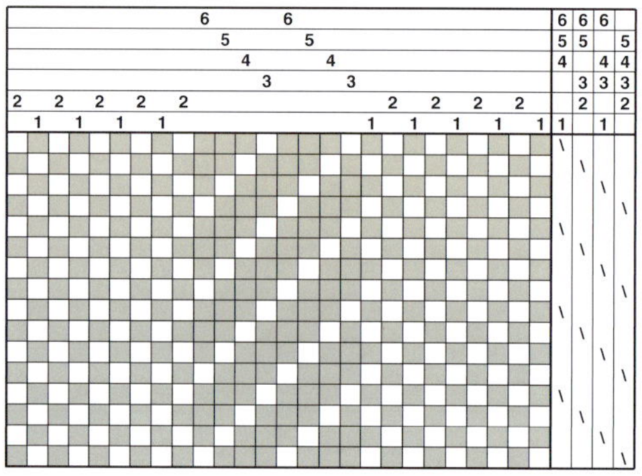

11.4 Four-shaft twill, 3/1, has been inserted as a stripe in a plain-weave ground. Only four treadles are required because the weave repeats in four picks.

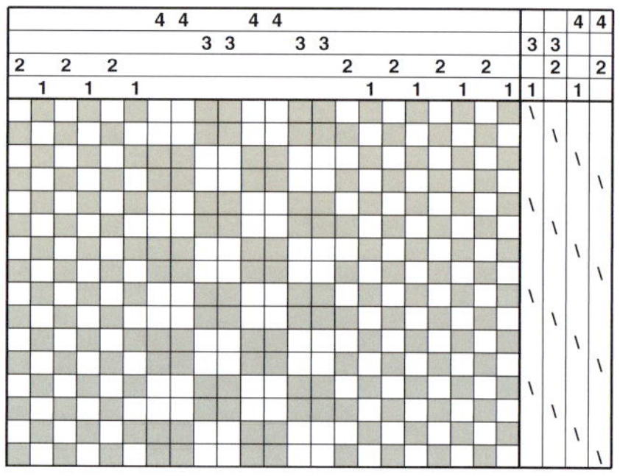

11.5 Basket-weave stripe in a plain-weave ground. The lack of a clean break at the edges of the stripe is very evident in the drawdown.

A 2/2 twill with 2/2 basket weave stripes. The yarn is woolen spun at about 1,900 yards per pound, tan in the warp and red tweed in the weft.

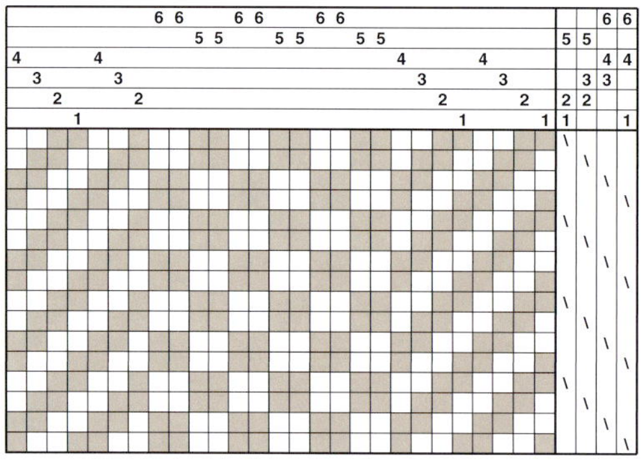

11.6a Basket weave stripe in a 2/2 twill ground. Notice that there is a clean break where the two structures meet. Draft 6b shows a more economical way to weave this cloth.

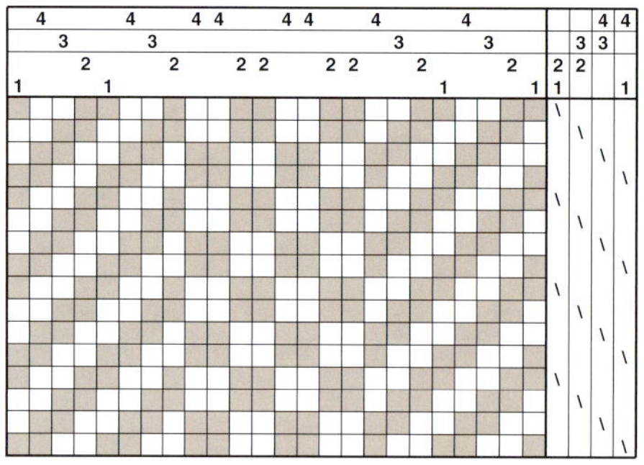

11.6b Basket weave stripe in a 2/2 twill ground. Notice that there is a clean break where the two structures meet. The threading is altered by deleting an end threaded on shaft 1 at the beginning of the twill area to maintain the break.

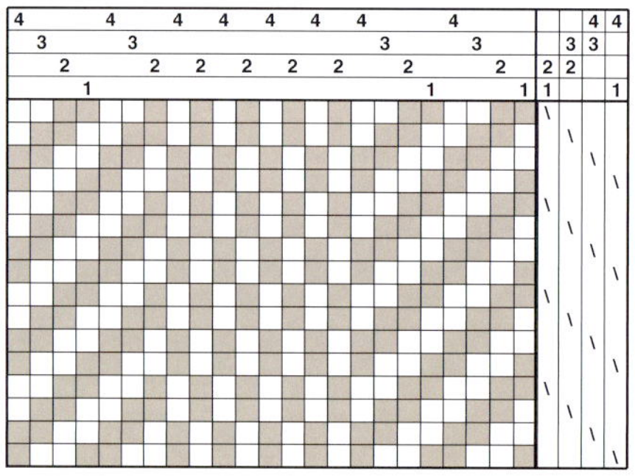

11.7a Rib stripe in a 2/2 twill ground. Clean breaks are maintained.

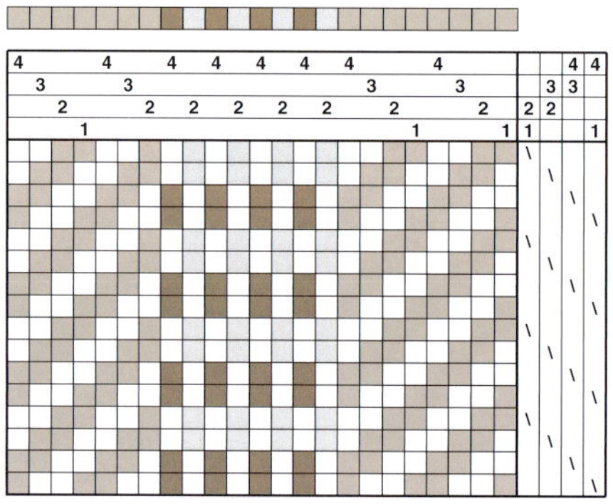

11.7b Rib stripe in a 2/2 twill ground. Clean breaks are maintained. The alternation of colors in the warp where the rib is threaded creates an interesting effect in the cloth.

Drafts **11.3** and **11.4** combine plain weave with warp-faced twill stripes. Draft **11.3** combines plain weave with a 2/1 twill; draft **11.4** combines plain weave with a 3/1 twill. There cannot be a clean break between the plain-weave and 2/1 twill. For both, the sett must be more dense in the twill areas to maintain the same firmness throughout the cloth.

Draft **11.5** combines plain weave with a 2/2 basket weave. The basket weave repeats in four picks and the plain weave in two, and so it is impossible to maintain a clean break between the two areas. The weft goes over or under three ends at a time where the plain weave and basket meet. There is no way to avoid producing these floats.

To maintain a clean break, we can combine two structures that each repeat in four picks, such as a 2/2 twill and 2/2 basket weave (**11.6a** and **11.6b**). In **11.6a**, we have simply added two shafts to the four required for the twill to make the basket. So far in this book, that is the way that this kind of draft has been constructed, but in this particular case, it is possible to write the draft more economically: in **11.6b**, four shafts and four treadles are used to weave both structures at once. The sett is the same for 2/2 basket weave and for 2/2 twill, which makes sleying the cloth easier because it isn't necessary to keep track of the threading at the same time.

Clean breaks are also maintained with the combination of 2/2 twill and the rib shown in **11.7a** and **11.7b**. Four shafts and four treadles are required for this structure. Although the sett formula (see Appendix C) suggests that the sett for the rib be the same as that for plain weave, I would set it the same as the twill surrounding it so that the rib will be more warp-faced. If the rib consists of two colors alternating, and the twill were a third color and the weft the same, , an interesting effect can be produced.

Draft **11.8a** combines plain weave with a pair of ends (carried on shafts 3 and 4) that are lifted to float on the surface for three out of four picks. The pick that catches one of the lifted ends goes under the other. The wefts that tie the ends on shafts 3 and 4 lie two picks apart so that attention is focused on the threads that are floating instead of on how they are caught. Weaving both under the same pick would produce a small horizontal line, which would be more noticeable (**11.8b**) than either structure in **11.8a** or the small diagonal that results from catching the floats in successive picks (**11.8c**). If you are aware of how the manner in which the ends in the little stripe are tied down affects their appearance in the cloth, you may choose the look you want. One time you may prefer one, another time another.

Nothing keeps us from making the warp floats longer except our concern for how practical the cloth will be. If yarns are relatively fine, the float can go over more than three picks, of course. Draft **11.8d** shows how the cloth would be woven if the two ends are permitted to float over nine picks each. If the number of picks per inch is large, then the float can be a practical length; if not, the float will be long and will snag easily. For example, at 36 p.p.i., the float will be only ¼ inch long, but at 12 p.p.i., the float will be ¾ inch long. This sort of structure permits us to put a very expensive or scarce yarn right up on top of the cloth where it can be seen for nearly its entire length.

A variation on this idea—and do you see how the variations are practically endless?—is shown in **11.8e**, in which sateen replaces the plain weave as the ground and the ends

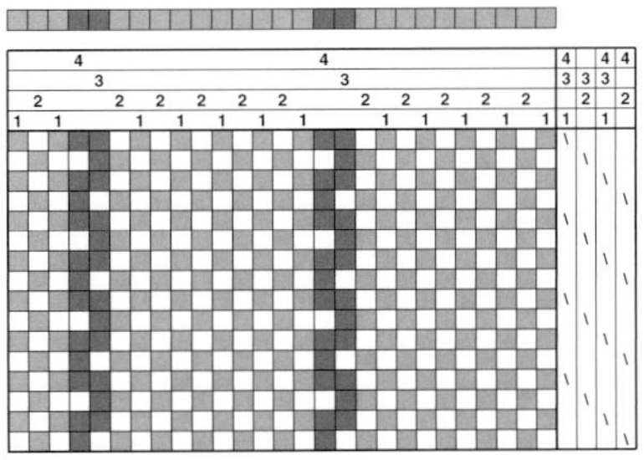

11.8a In this four-shaft structure, two ends are floated on the surface of a plain-weave cloth. They are caught by one out of four wefts; the stitching points are staggered.

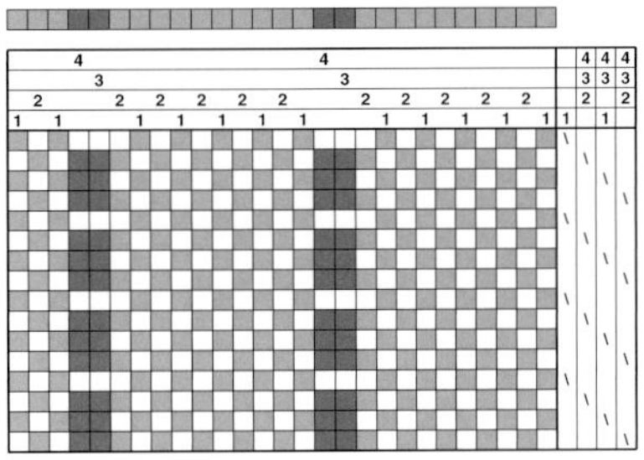

11.8b In this four-shaft structure, two ends are floated on the surface of a plain-weave cloth. They are caught by one out of four wefts; both are stitched by the same weft in this version (only three shafts would be needed to weave this).

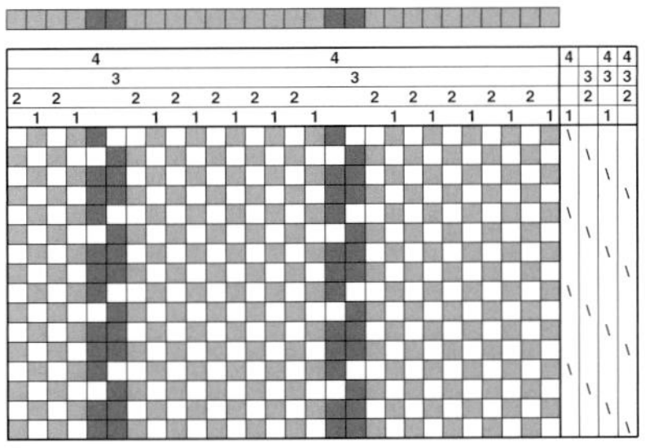

11.8c In this four-shaft structure, two ends are floated on the surface of a plain-weave cloth. They are caught by one out of four wefts; they are stitched one after the other, creating a little diagonal.

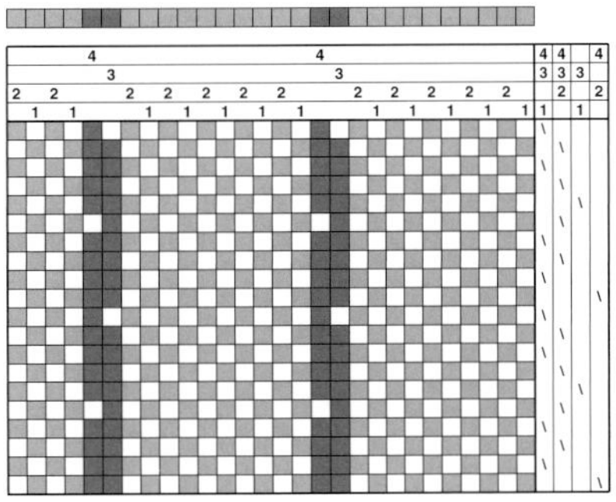

11.8d In this four-shaft structure, two ends are floated on the surface of a plain-weave cloth. This time the ends are permitted to float for nine picks—just to make the point that we can choose the length float we wish. Of course, the number of picks per inch is crucial here. If we weave 36 p.p.i., the float is ¼" long (quite acceptable); if we weave 8 p.p.i., then the float is well over an inch (almost surely not acceptable).

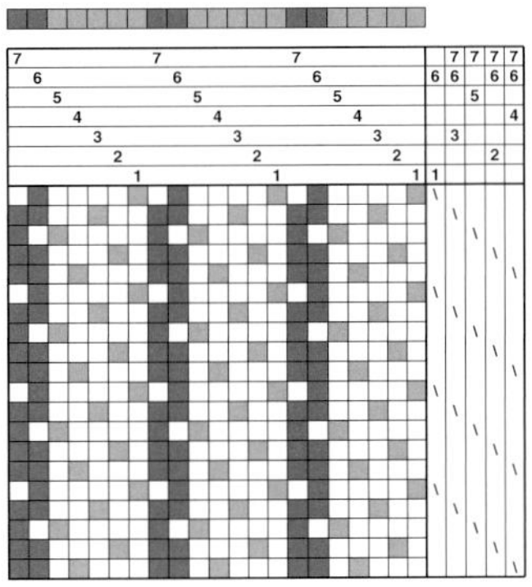

11.8e Here is the same idea with a sateen ground. The warp floats pass over four picks and are caught by the fifth. As in 11.8a, the floating ends are stitched so that the midpoint of the float, for one is the stitching point of the other.

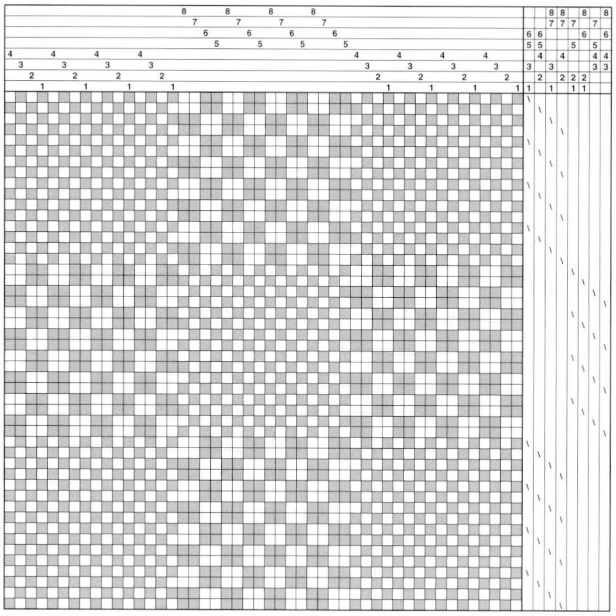

11.9a A combination of plain weave and 2/2 basket weave, woven as a checkerboard.

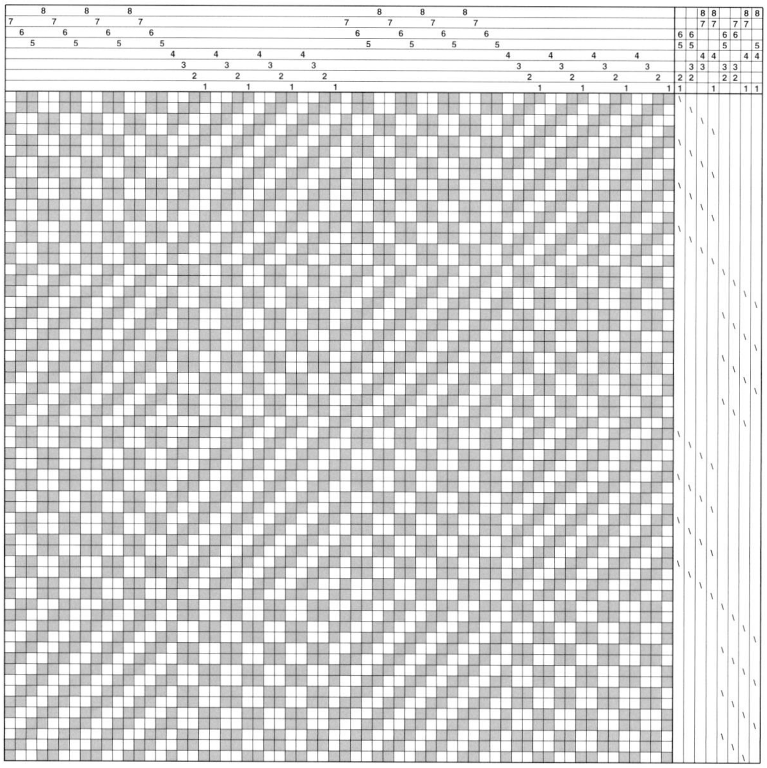

11.9b A combination of 2/2 twill and 2/2 basket weave, woven as a checkerboard. To maintain clean breaks, an end is omitted on shaft 8 (end 32 here), and a pick is omitted in the same place in the treadling (pick 32). The same alteration occurs at the end of each repeat.

that float do so with a clean break with the ground.

In **11.9a**, a combination of plain weave and 2/2 basket weave is woven so that the areas reverse as the weaving goes along, forming a checkerboard. The setts required for plain weave and basket are different; the basket weave is sleazy—or weft-faced—if woven at a plain-weave sett. Because all of the warp weaves plain weave and basket, switching from one to the other, it is a good idea to set the entire warp more densely than would be required for plain weave and beat it to square.

In this structure, unless the yarns are very sticky, the plain-weave area tends to spread out a little into the basket weave that surrounds it. With a denser sett, this effect is magnified. Plain weave, to anthropomorphize, seems always to be looking for more room and will spread out into any area that doesn't resist. Interesting effects may be obtained this way. By using a 2/2 basket sett and weaving the areas to square, the plain-weave areas will spread out to form nearly circular shapes.

Faced with the rectilinear grid formed by the intersection of weft with warp at right angles, it is easy to see why from time to time every weaver longs to make a circle. We have seen curves in Chapter 5, Distortions of the Grid, and in the discussion of undulating twills, but the creation of circles by loom-controlled means is possible in M's and O's, honeycomb weaves, and this combination of plain weave and basket weave. The basket weave does not move diagonally as twill can; its stability allows the plain weave to round out nicely.

Draft **11.9b** uses the same threading, altered by omitting end 32 so that the repeat is thirty-one ends long, the tie-up makes a checkerboard alternating 2/2 twill and 2/2 basket. The omission of one pick allows us to maintain clean breaks throughout the cloth.

Except for the checkerboard patterns, we have shown these combinations as vertical (warpwise) stripes. By turning the draft (see Appendix A), we can make the same cloth with the stripes running weftwise. The number of shafts required will be the number of sheds used in the original draft and the number of sheds, the number of shafts used before. If the pattern you wish to make requires more shafts than you have but uses fewer sheds, turning the draft may be the answer. For example, **11. 4**, which requires six shafts and four sheds, when turned becomes **11.10**, requiring four shafts and six sheds.

11.10 The structure shown in 11.4, turned so that it may be woven on four shafts instead of six.

We can put stripes into the cloth in both directions at the same time, forming a structural plaid. Draft **11.11** is 2/2 twill with an overcheck of rib weave. Only four shafts are required for this structure. Clean breaks are maintained throughout.

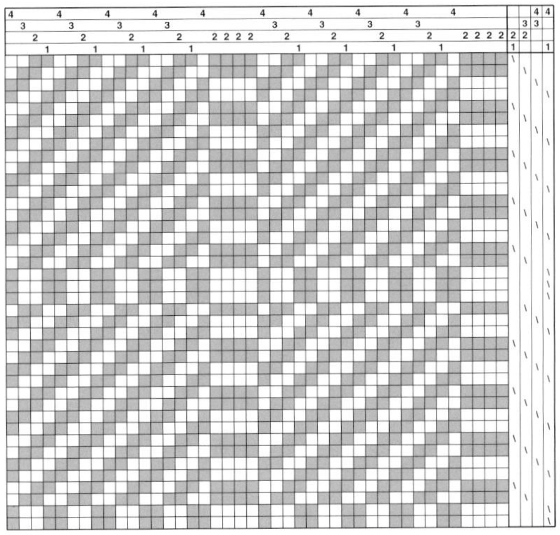

11.11 Two structures are combined in this example to create a structural plaid. The rib weave runs vertically and horizontally in a 2/2 twill ground. Only four shafts and four treadles are required.

More familiar, perhaps, is **11.12a** (next page), plain weave with a four-shaft twill overcheck. In this draft, the warp and weft stripes would typically be of the same color. Drafts **11.12b** and **11.12c** might be woven with warp stripes in one color and weft stripes in a second. In **11.12b**, the weft stripes appear to go over and under alternating warp stripes. In **11.12c**, twill stripes interlace as if they were twill ribbons woven plain weave over the ground.

All the drafts with the twill overcheck will be sleyed for plain weave in the areas threaded on shafts 1 through 4 and sleyed for twill everywhere else. The weft-faced twill areas when beaten will balance the twill nearly automatically.

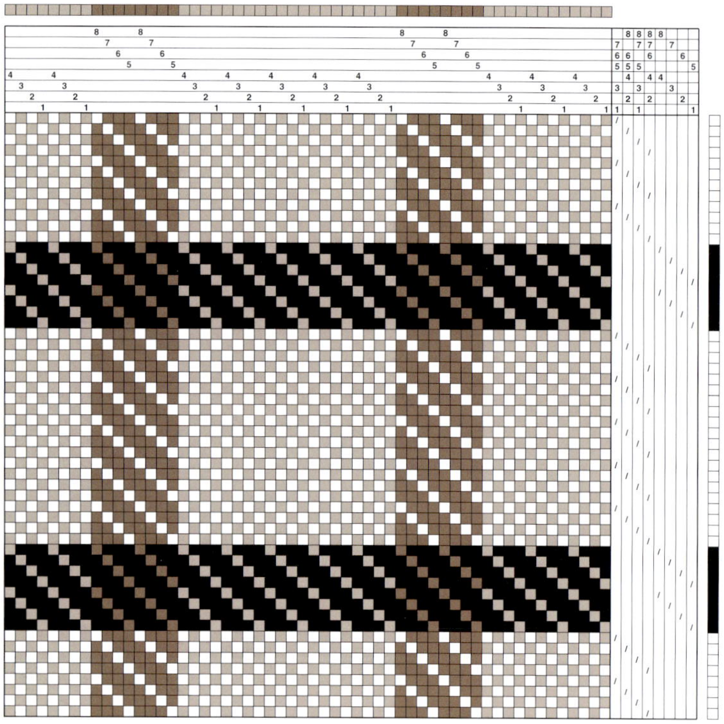

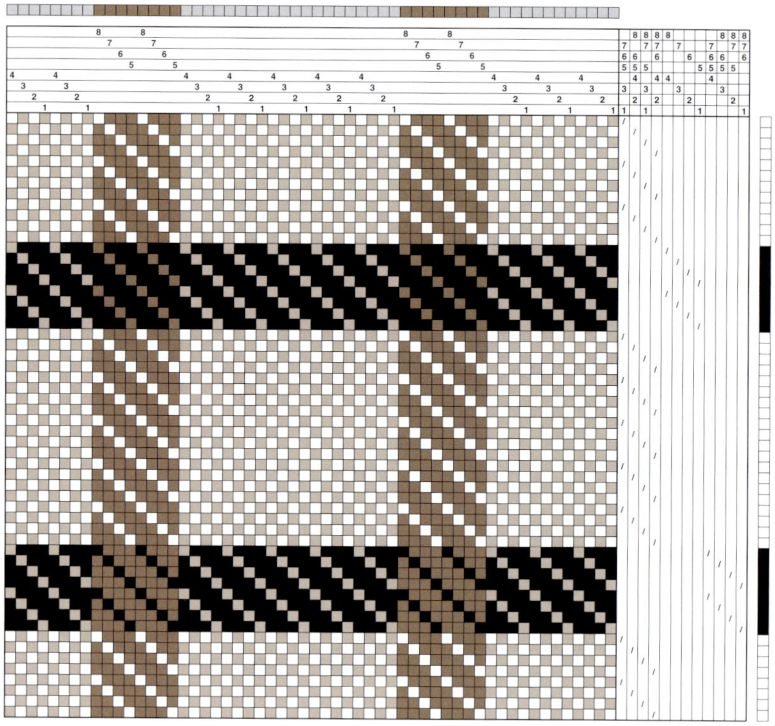

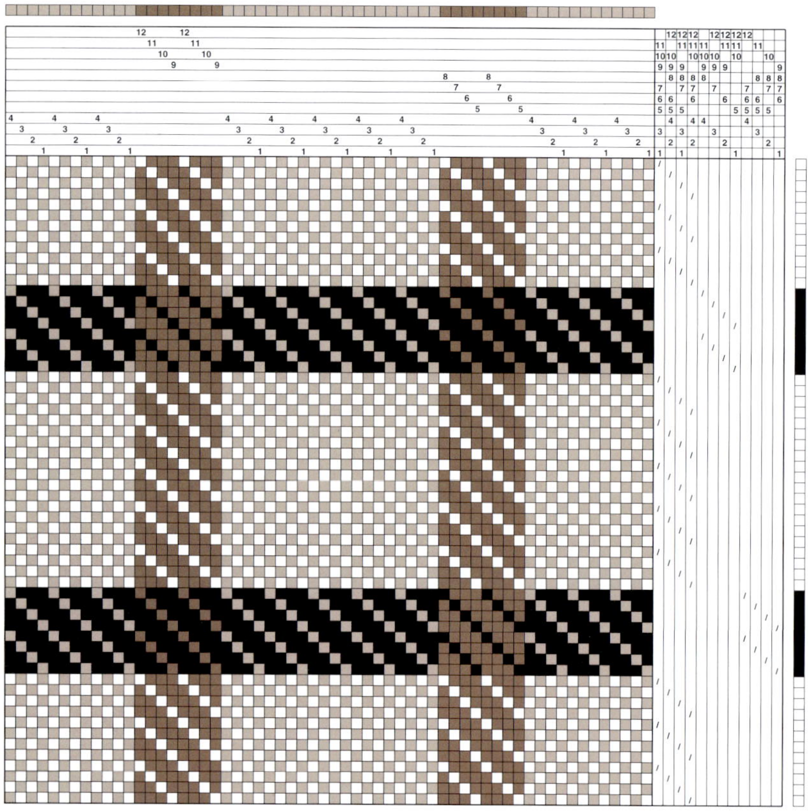

11.12a In this structural plaid, the twill stripes in the warp are woven as a 3/1 twill and the weft stripes as 1/3 twill. Notice that the twill line continues smoothly into the weft stripes without changing direction or creating a discontinuity.

11.12b In this variation, the vertical twill stripes appear to weave under and then over the weft stripes.

11.12c In this draft, the vertical twill stripes appear to weave under and then over the weft stripes, and the horizontal twill stripes do the same.

Silk twill stripes on a 2/20 heathered worsted wool plain-weave ground. Variation of draft 11.12c.

Creating these structural plaids is addictive, the only excuse I can give for including yet another one (**11.13**). Here, a 2/2 twill ground has an overcheck of 2/2 basket weave and may be woven on just four shafts using just four treadles. Using one color for the warp and a second for the weft shows off the structure and can, if you choose close colors and values, be subtle or, with complementary colors and contrasting values, splashy.

By making the stripes in the warp and weft equal in width and doing the same for the overchecks shown in drafts **11.11**, **11.12**, and **11.13**, checkerboard designs are made. We have seen checkerboards made by alternating 1/3 and 3/1 twills (Chapter 2, Twills) and two-block doubleweave (Chapter 7, Loom-Controlled Doubleweave), but they are only the beginning. We can alternate plain weave with Bronson lace using just four shafts to make lacy checkerboards. We can use two blocks of double plain weave to make doubleweave checkerboards or, if we have enough shafts, alternate blocks of plain weave on the face with twill on the

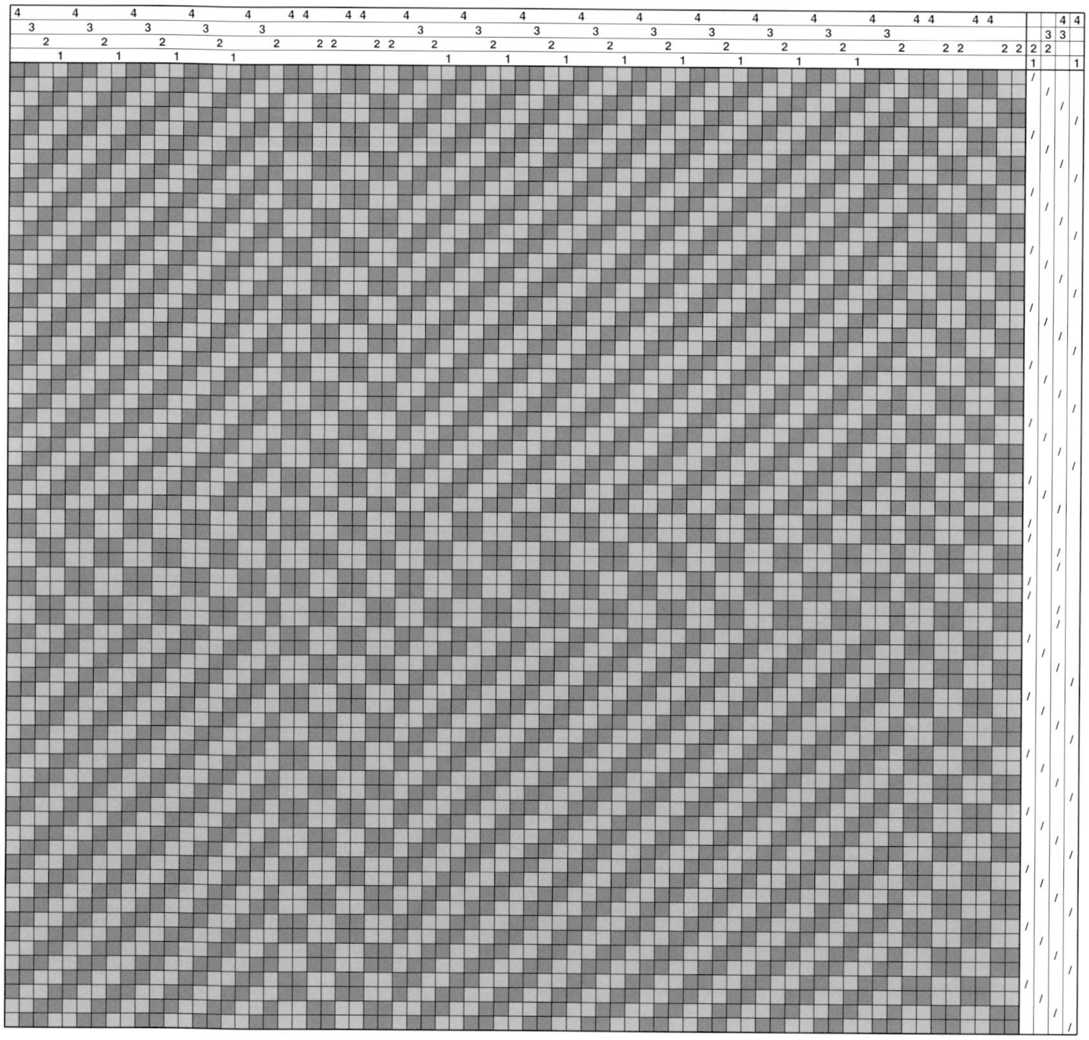

11.13 This structural plaid is made with a 2/2 twill ground and 2/2 basket weave overcheck. The repeats are arranged so that clean breaks occur at each change of structure, in warp and weft directions.

back with blocks in which the position of the two structures is reversed. We can combine satin with sateen to make a different checkerboard pattern. As you can see, the possibilities go on and on.

Supplementary warp/weft or broché fabrics

Sometimes we add threads to weave in a special way that has nothing to do with the basic structure of the cloth but simply to ornament it. They may be in the warp, the weft, or in both. A cloth with extra ends or picks that appear consistently but do not form its ground is sometimes called broché. If it is possible to put the extra threads in the warp, the fabric will require fewer shuttles, which makes the weaving quicker and allows a better weaving rhythm. On the other hand, the structure may require a second warp beam and possibly more shafts than are available.

When designing a cloth with extra threads embellishing the face, it is necessary to begin with the structure of the ground cloth. Good choices include plain weave, twills, satin or sateens, and crepes. If the extra threads are in the warp and they spend most of their time floating, they will have to be tensioned differently from the regular warp. If the extra threads are in the weft, the cloth can usually be woven using a single beam.

Draft **11.14** begins with a 2/2 twill ground cloth. The supplementary ends are placed four ground warps apart. The supplemental or broché ends are carried on five shafts, 5 through 9. They are lifted for four picks, dropped for two, raised for two and finally dropped for four before repeating. Each of the five supplementary ends starts this sequence at a different place, following a five-shaft satin stitching order: 5, 7, 9, 6, 8, repeat. Because they interlace less frequently than the ground warps, these ends will have to be tensioned separately. The supplementary warps are added to the ground warp in the reed, not given their own dents.

When double cloth is woven with supplementary warps and/or wefts, the floating threads, whether in the warp or weft, are usually sandwiched between the two layers of cloth. Drafts **11.15 a–11.15c** (next page) show a possible sequence for a cloth that is 2/2 twill on the face and plain weave on the back. Just to make it interesting, there are two face ends and picks for each back end and pick. Draft **11.15a** shows the two layers being woven at one time but separate and not stitched together. Draft **11.15b** shows the same cloth, but here the plain-weave picks, numbers 2 and 8, stitch the two layers

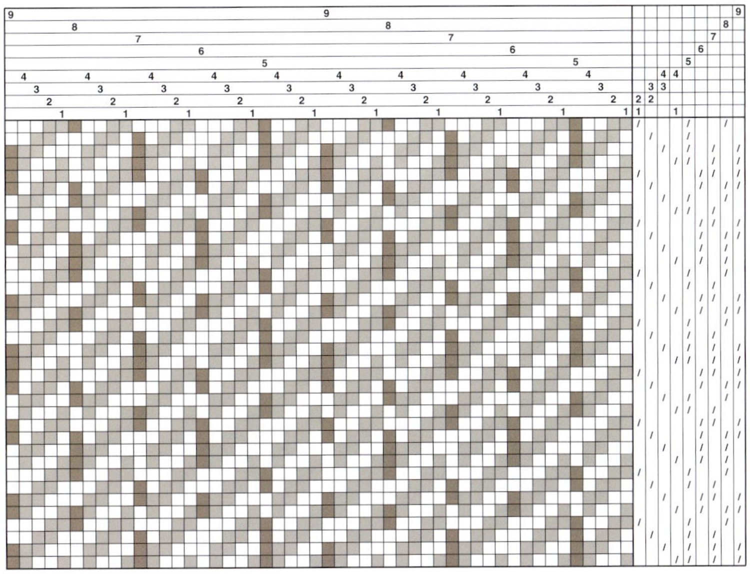

***11.14** 2/2 twill ground with supplemental warp ends weaving in and out of the cloth. The face and back of the cloth look the same because the supplemental ends float up 4, down 2, up 2, down 4, up 2, down 2, repeat, making the same pattern on both sides.*

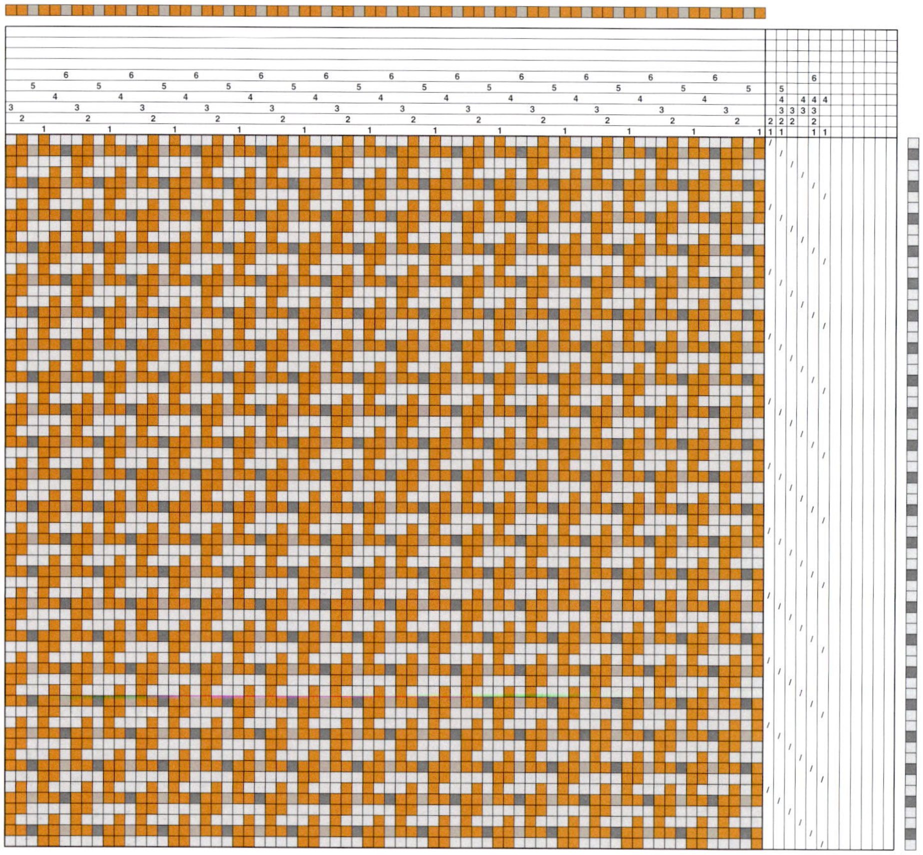

11.15a This draft weaves 2/2 twill on the face and plain weave on the reverse. As shown here, the two layers are not stitched together.

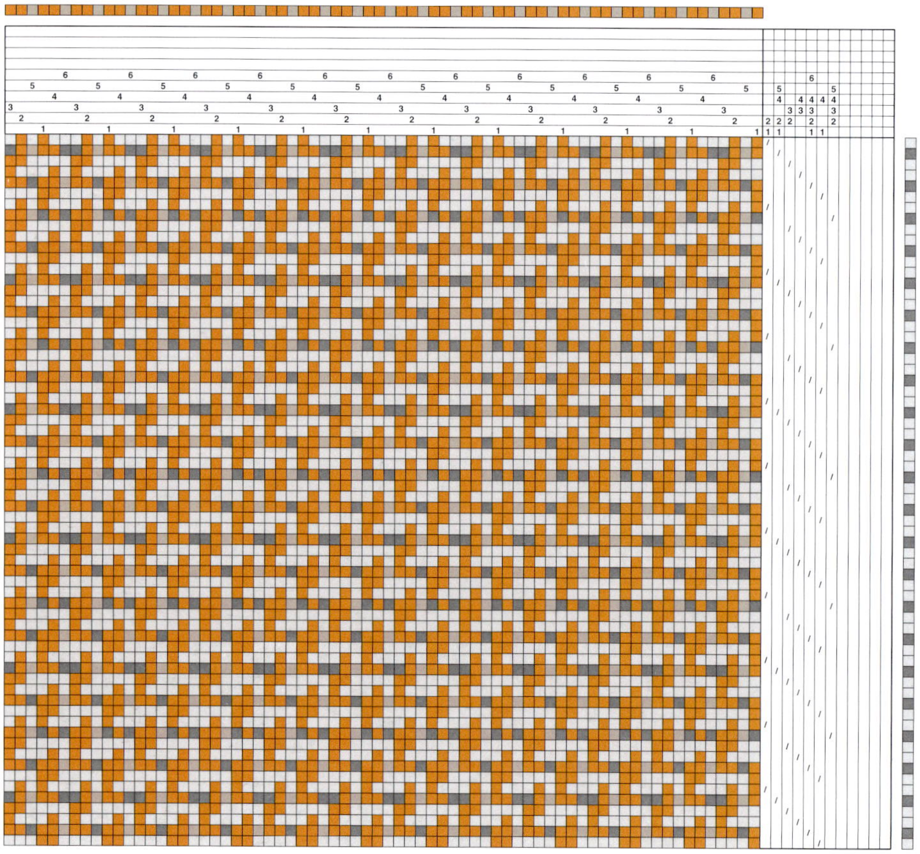

11.15b This draft weaves 2/2 twill on the face and plain weave on the reverse. The two layers are stitched together in the first plain-weave pick (pick 2) and the third plain-weave pick (pick 8). The stitching is accomplished by dropping one of the face warps so it is caught by the plain-weave weft but the stitching is hidden by the twill float from the face side.

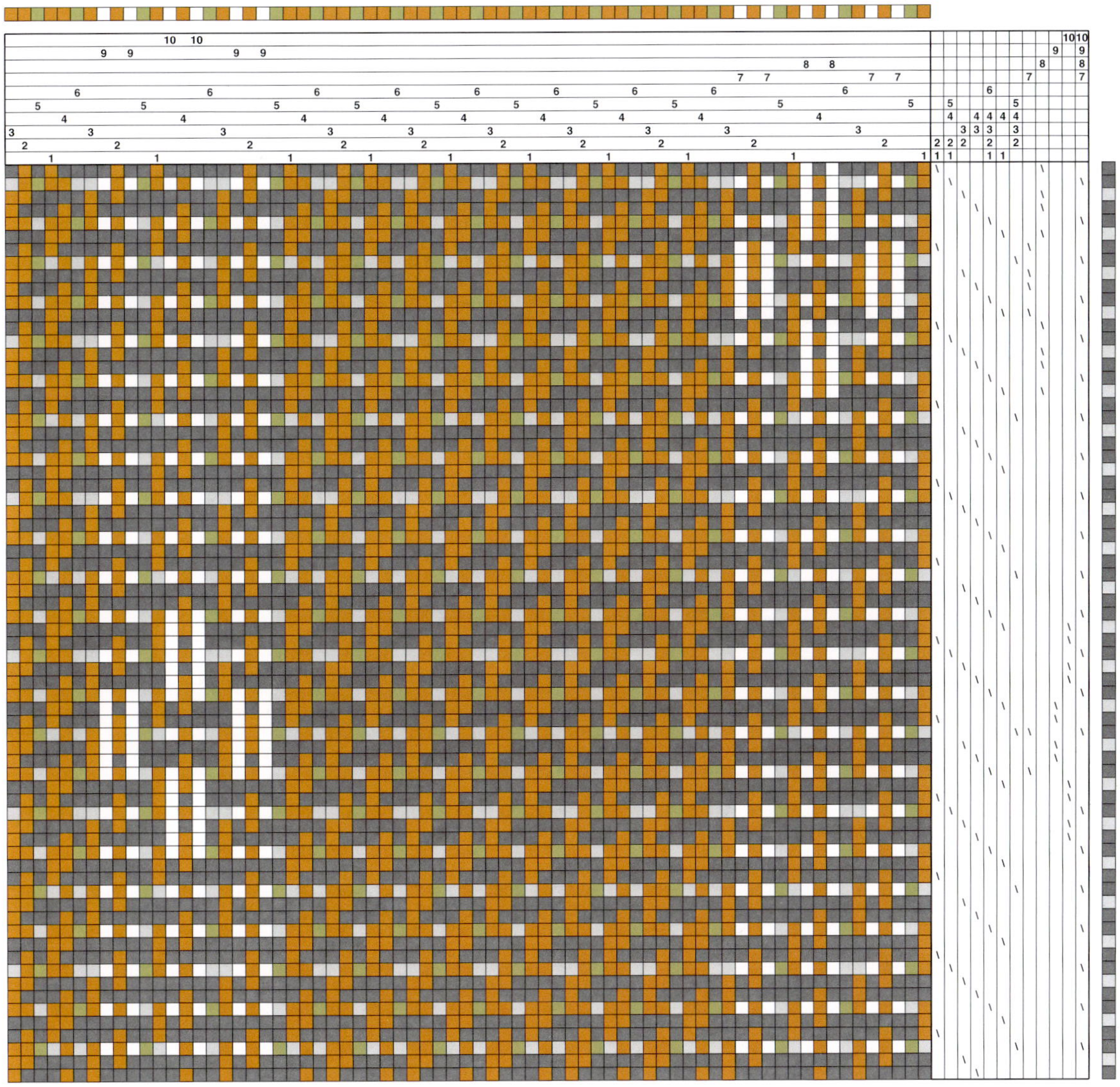

11.15c The supplementary warps have been inserted between the ends on shafts 1–6. Those for one figure are carried on shafts 7 and 8, the other on 9 and 10.

The treadling has been changed to lift the supplemental warps at intervals to form the pattern on the surface of the cloth. When they aren't sitting on top of the cloth, the supplemental warp ends are under the twill ends but over the plain-weave ends, carried on 5 and 6. To reduce the number of treadles needed, two feet are used at once to control the supplementary ends.

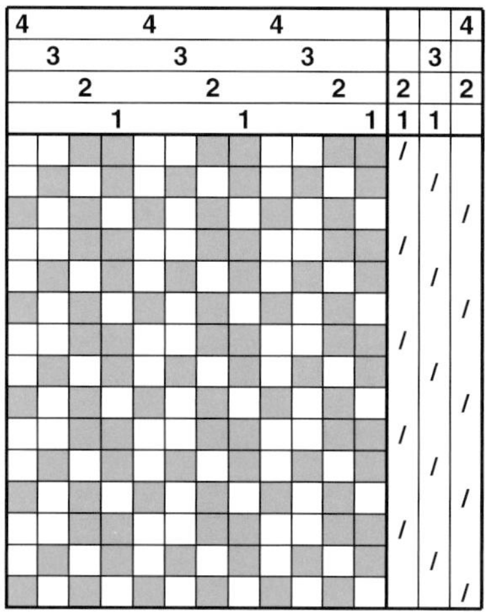

11.16 *Four-shaft tricot weave. The first two ends are lifted two out of three shots and the third and fourth ends are lifted one of three shots.*

If the first two ends are S-twist and the next two Z-twist and so on, the vertical rib is more pronounced.

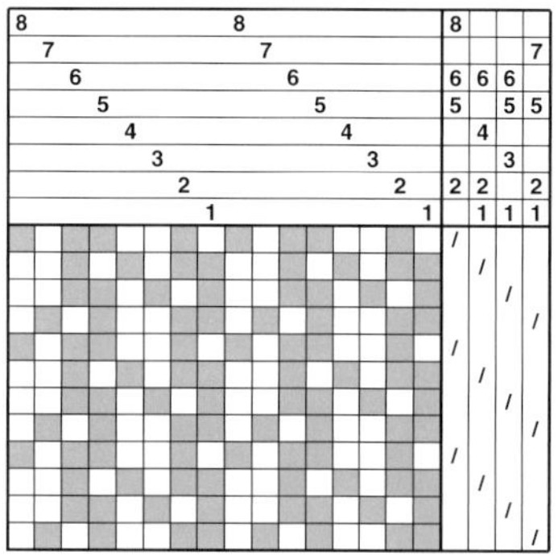

11.17a *Tricot weave with furrows in the warp direction. It resembles a knitted cloth.*

together. They stitch the cloth together by dropping one of the twill ends (so that the plain-weave weft passes over it) where the twill float conceals the stitch from the face of the cloth. (There is no place to hide stitching from the plain-weave face because there are no floats there.) The two layers are stitched together using two warp ends alternately so that one end is not stressed too much.

Draft **11.15c** includes the supplemental warp ends. The tie-up has been altered to lift the ornamental ends over the upper layer to form the design and then lift them over the plain-weave picks that weave the back of the cloth. The supplemental ends never appear on the back; when they aren't on the face, they are sandwiched between the layers. Four shafts have been used, bringing the total shafts to ten, so that the figure appears in two different places in the cloth in a half-drop placement. If only eight shafts are available, only one figure can be made; it will appear in a row both vertically and horizontally In this case, too, the supplementary warps are sleyed in with the ground warp, not given their own dents.

Tricot weaves

It is possible for weavers to create fabrics with ridges like those found in stockinette knits in either the warp or the weft. These fabrics look slightly crepey but are very evenly furrowed.

Draft **11.16** is a simple tricot weave using four shafts and three treadles. The first two ends weave up for two picks and down for one. The next two ends weave just the opposite: up for one and down for two.

Draft **11.17** is similar to **11.16**, but here the first two warp ends weave three picks up, one down, and the next two, one up, three down. This alternation of two warp-faced threads with two weft-faced threads makes the furrows that are characteristic of this structure. The stitchers are 1, 3, 2, 4, a repeat of four for warp-dominant ends and four more weft-dominant ends. It takes just two sets of two to complete the repeat in the weaving of the warp-dominant ends and two sets of two for the weft-dominant ends. The whole structure repeats neatly in eight ends and four picks. If this draft were turned, it could be woven on four shafts using eight sheds (**11.17b**).

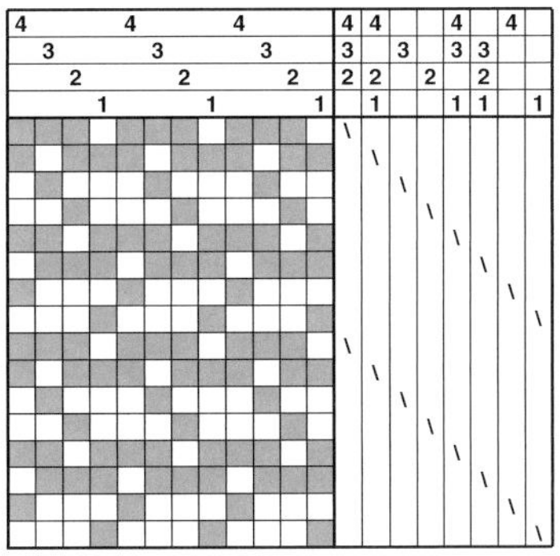

11.17b Tricot weave with furrows in the weft direction. It resembles a knitted cloth. This draft is 17a, turned. It requires eight treadles.

Draft **11.18** is based on four ends up, one end down plus one end up, four ends down. This structure requires twenty shafts to weave because the stitchers are arranged in a satin order: 1, 3, 5, 2, 4, repeat. If the first two warp-dominant ends stitch 1 and 3, respectively, then the next two stitch 5 and 2; the next two, 4 and 1; the next two, 3 and 5; the next two, 2 and 4. It takes ten of the warp-dominant ends to get back to the beginning of the repeat, and it will likewise take ten of the weft-dominant ends that lie in pairs between them to complete the repeat.

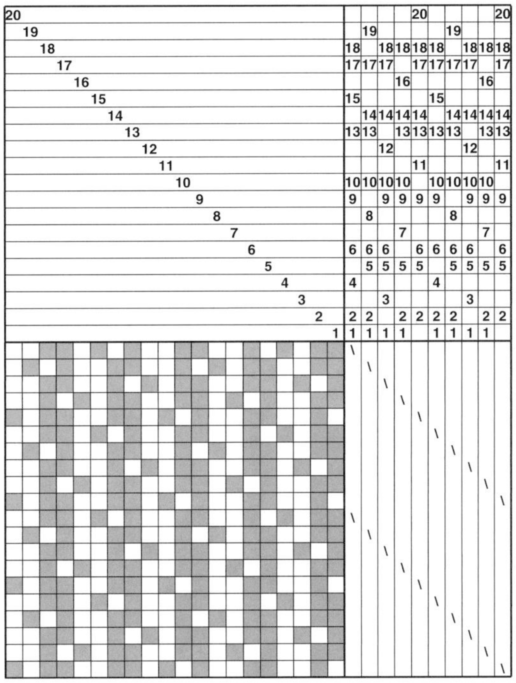

11.18 This tricot weave is based on two threads woven over four, under one, then two woven under four, over one. Twenty shafts are required to weave this pattern. If the draft were turned, ten shafts and twenty sheds would be required.

Stabilizing structures with an inner supporting fabric

In Chapters 1 (Plain Weave) and 2 (Twill), I advised avoiding certain constructions (4/4 basket and 4/4 twill) for functional fabrics because they aren't stable. These structures look luscious on the loom, with generous floats that show off the yarns, but once removed from the loom and finished, the threads shift, clump together, and go into general collapse.

The good news is that there is a way to retain the appearance of the cloth without experiencing the collapse. We may weave a sort of armature or internal structure that

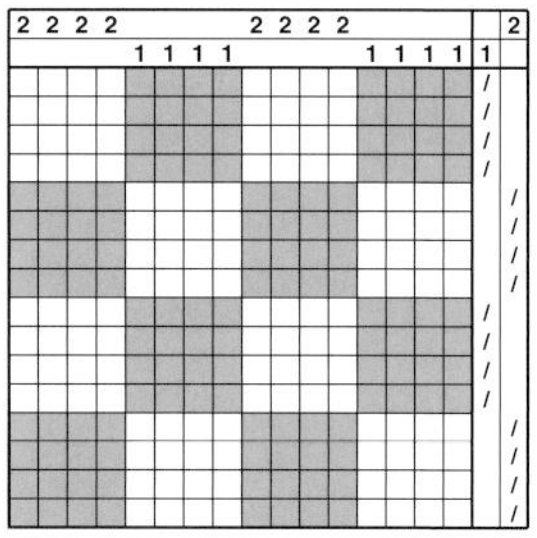

11.19a *This is the 4/4 basket weave we want to weave as a more stable structure.*

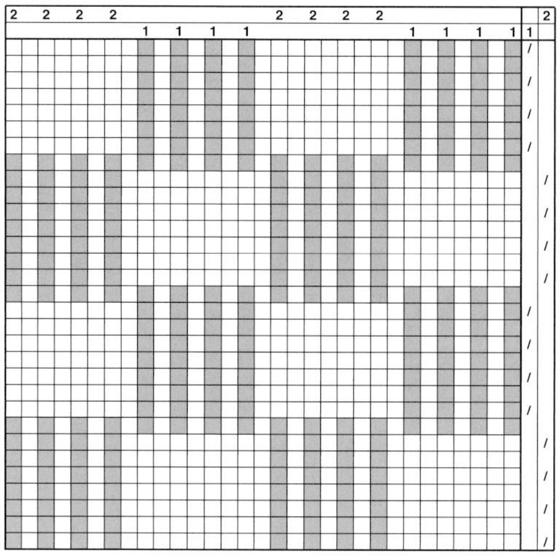

11.19b *This is the 4/4 basket weave we want to weave with spaces added for the supporting ends and picks.*

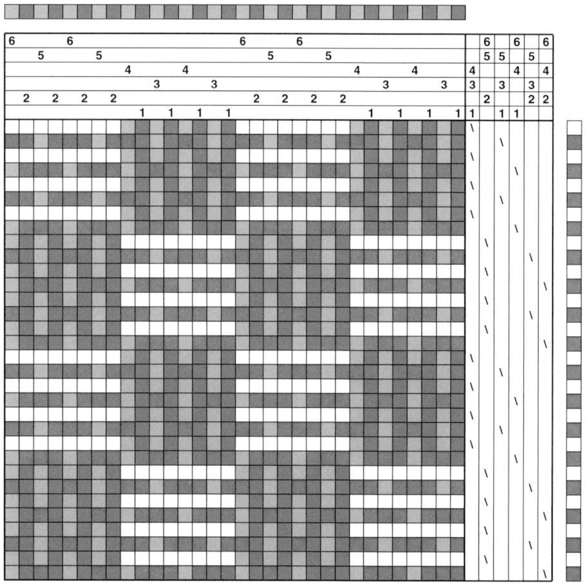

11.19c *The 4/4 basket weave with the stabilizing ends and picks in place. Notice that when the stabilizing picks are woven, the warp ends that are up for the basket weave are raised to keep them from being caught by the plain weave inside.*

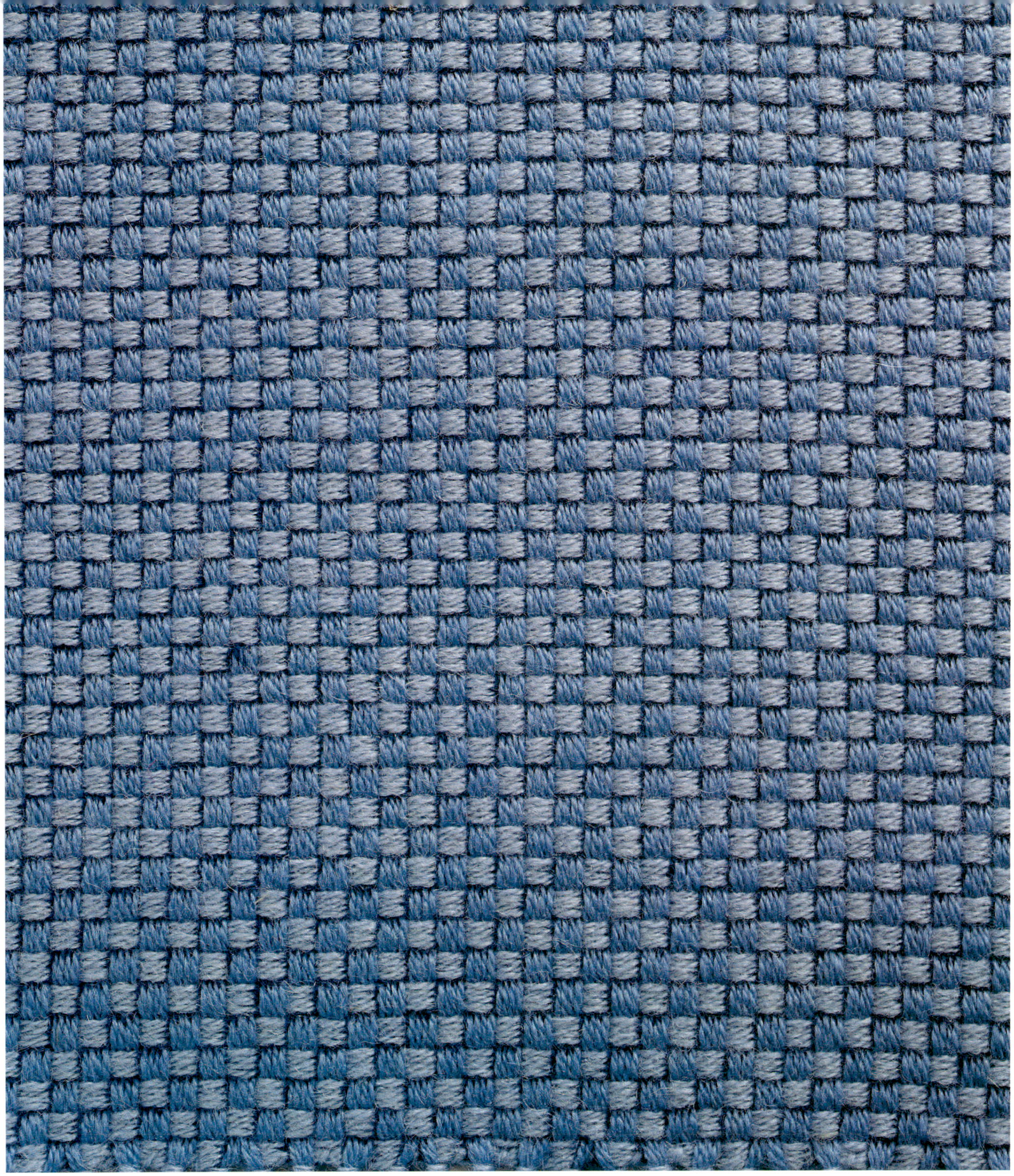

A 4/4 basket weave, woven with woolen-spun yarns at about 1,800 yards per pound, with an "internal fabric" of navy 2/20 worsted wool to maintain stability. See 11.19c.

11.20a 4/4 twill

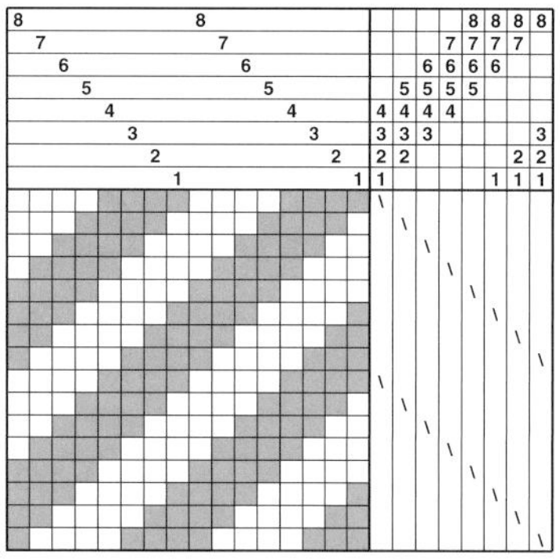

11.20b 4/4 twill with spaces added.

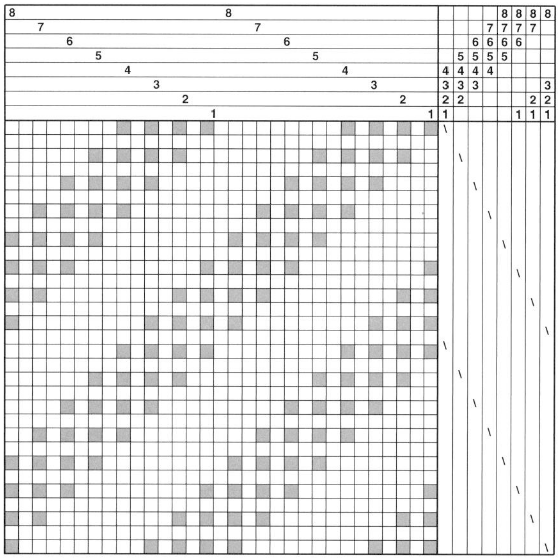

11.20c 4/4 twill with plain-weave inner fabric added to the draft. Notice that two treadles are depressed when the plain-weave picks are thrown.

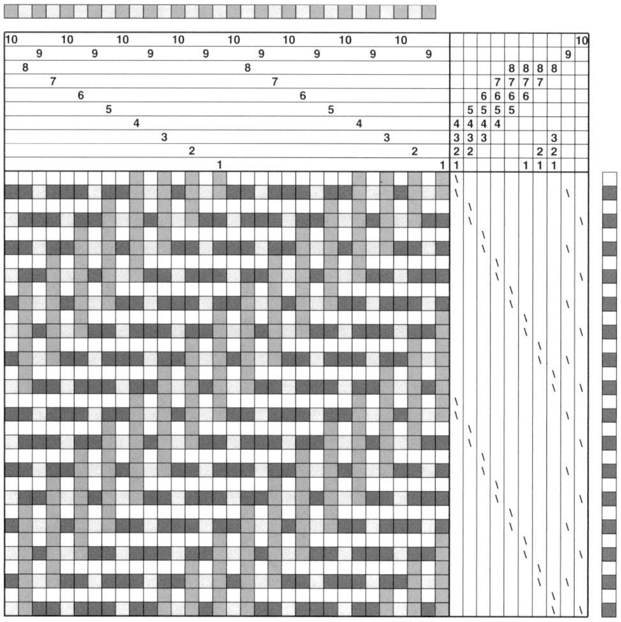

supports what we see on the face and back. The most stable structure is plain weave, which also requires the fewest shafts and fewest ends and picks per inch.

Let's begin by graphing the structure we want to make. Let's start with 4/4 basket weave. Draft **11.19a** shows just the ends and picks that weave the basket weave. In **11.19b**, the draft has been expanded to leave spaces for the ends and picks that will stabilize the structure. The plain-weave picks have been added to create the internal structure in **11.19c**. The ends and picks are shown in a contrasting color to make them easily visible. It would be a good idea to choose the same color for the plain weave as that used for the surface and back so that it won't show through. If the plain-weave ends and picks are the same color as the larger threads but a darker shade, then the visual depth of cloth is enhanced. Notice that the supporting wefts are thrown under the floating basket-weave ends and over the other basket-weave ends.

The supporting ends and picks can be the same size as the face and back yarns or finer. If they are bigger, the supporting structure will be revealed. Drafts **11.20a**, **11.20b**, **11.20c** and **11.21a**, **11.21b**, and **11.21c** on the following page show the same steps with other weaves that will benefit from this treatment.

If more support is needed (as in the case of very slippery face and back yarns), two ends and picks may be inserted. If less support is needed, the supporting ends and picks may be added at a ratio of one inner thread to two outer ones.

It would appear that cloth, just like people, can take strength from within!

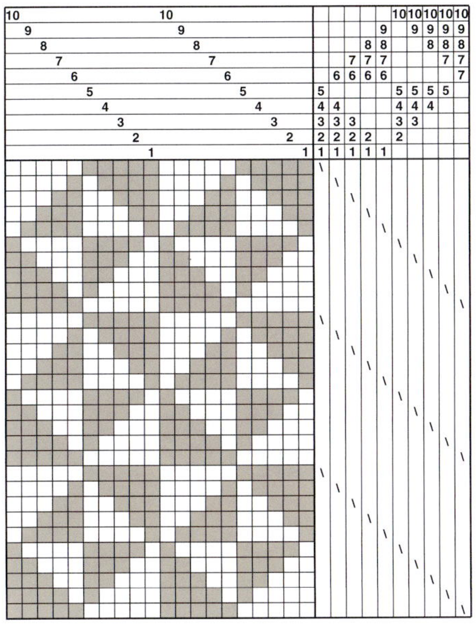

11.21a This interesting figure would not be stable as shown because of the lengths of the floats.

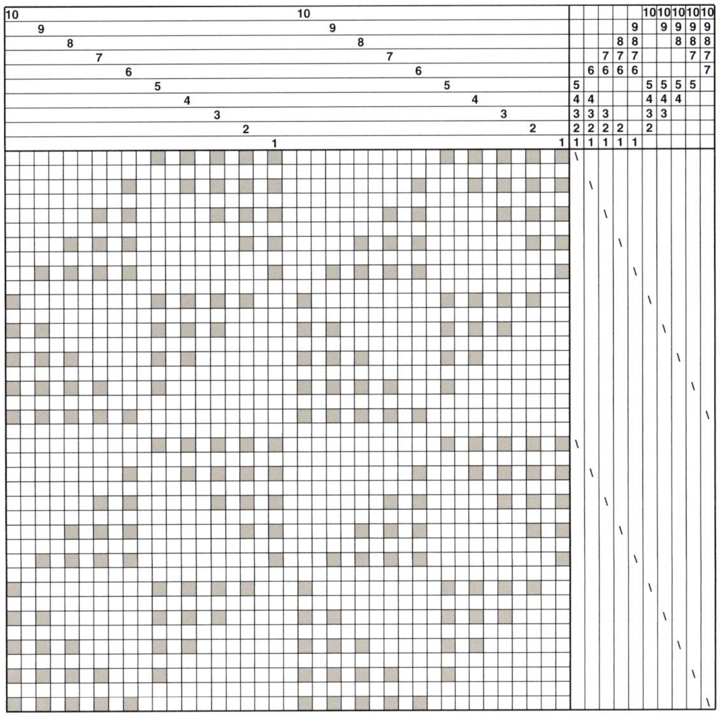

11.21b Spaces added to draft 11.21a.

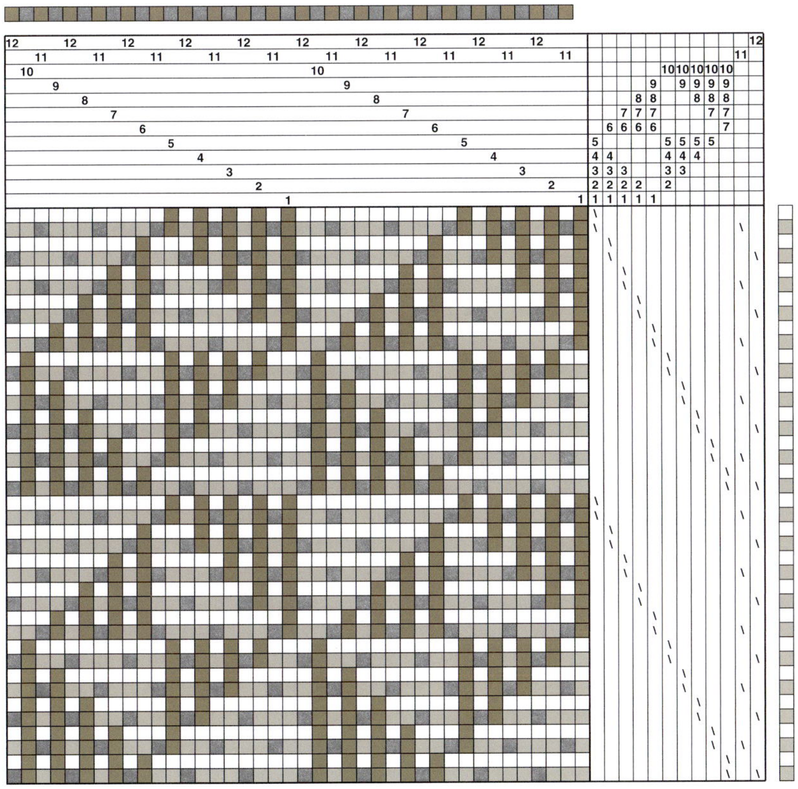

11.21c The figure from draft 11.21a is now drafted so that the inner, plain-weave cloth makes it stable. Once more, two treadles are depressed when the shuttle carrying the weft for the supporting, inner cloth is thrown.

12

Inventing Your Own Weave Structures

Have you ever imagined a cloth that looks like no cloth that you have ever seen or read about? It has floats in some places and not in others; they may move or switch from being warp floats to weft floats or do something else entirely. Must you conclude that yours is an impossible vision? Fortunately, no. There are ways to realize it, and they are far easier than you might imagine.

Handweavers today have an array of computer programs at their disposal. Although many of these are very effective in generating drafts and drawdowns, I continue to take great pleasure in designing with pencil and graph paper. Somehow this methods seems to require a kind of mental engagement that I miss when I use a computer for all my problem solving and creative play. So I will share with you here three approaches that I like to use when inventing weave structures.

Turning an idea into a draft

Having an idea is the beginning for everything. Once I decide which features I would like to have in my cloth, I make a sketch. It doesn't have to be pretty, exactly right, or fancy. All it needs to do is show where I would like to have plain weave or twill or floats or other features in my imagined cloth.

Figure 1 shows one such idea:

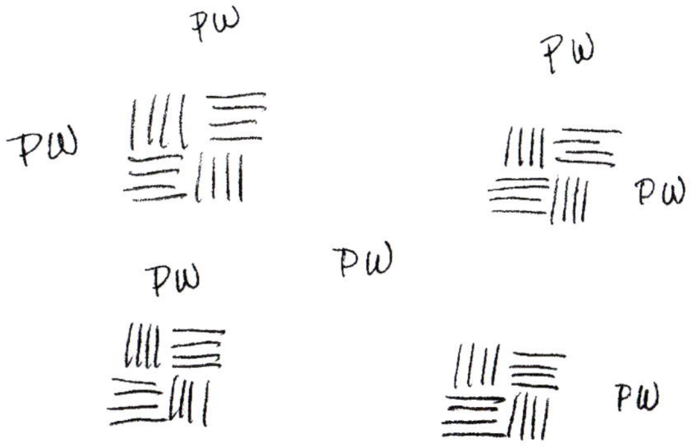

Figure 1. Here is a rough sketch of a fabric I have in mind: areas of vertical and horizontal floats surrounded by plain weave.

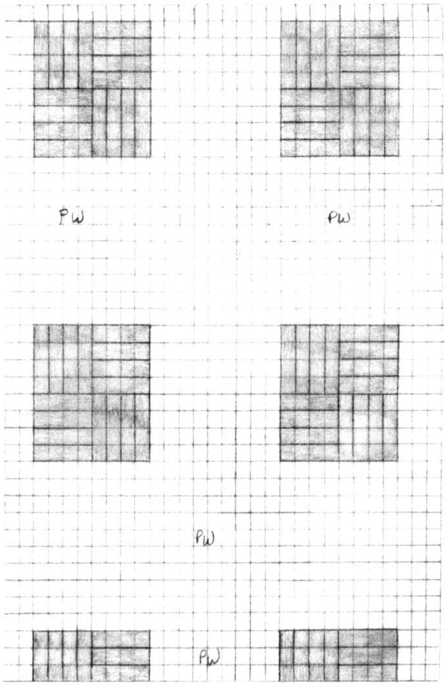

Figure 2 Here is my fabric concept transferred to graph paper.

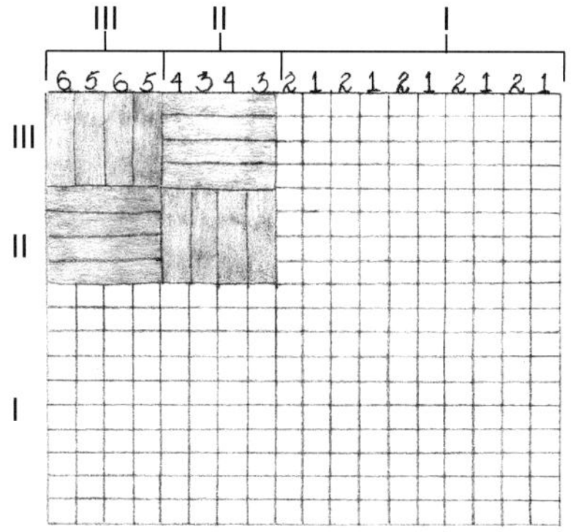

Figure 3 Here, I have delineated the three different areas and then assigned a pair of shafts to each.

The abbreviation in the diagram, "pw" means that I want the ground around the figures I have drawn to be woven "plain weave." The vertical and horizontal lines indicate the warp and weft floats, respectively, and show how many threads I want to have floating at one time.

Next, I move the drawing to graph paper so that I can be more specific about the placement of the parts of the structure. In my rough sketch, the floats do not line up exactly, and I need to refine my drawing a bit. *I don't start with graph paper because the looser I am as I approach a new idea, the easier it comes. I find that editing during the first stages can shut down the design process.*

Transferred to graph paper, the design above becomes **Figure 2**.

You will notice that rather than drawing in the plain-weave part, the letters "pw" are put down in the plain-weave areas. I reason this way: I understand plain weave very well and know how it looks. I am interested mainly in the figured areas.

My next step is deciding what part of the diagram makes one complete repeat. *It is essential that the initial drawing on graph paper include more than one repeat in all directions.* If it does not, it is possible to miss parts of the design.

Now I determine the threading. Knowing the number of shafts required for the design is critical: if it requires more than I have available, I need to rework my original idea. I need to know that number before I go further.

Figure 3 is one complete repeat. The figure is in the upper left part of the rectangle with the rest of the diagram in plain weave. The area to the right of the figure weaves plain weave from top to bottom. I know that all it takes to make plain weave is two shafts, so I will assign it to shafts 1 and 2. With that, I am on my way to making the draft.

The figure consists of four ends that are raised together for four picks beside four ends that are lowered together for the same picks. The first four picks do the same thing at the same time; for the next four picks, the first four ends are lowered together. All four ends could *all* be carried on the same shaft if that were all they did, but they also weave plain weave before and after they make the figure, and that requires two shafts. I therefore assign these ends to shafts 3 and 4.

The four threads to the left of the first four act together in the figure but do not do the same thing as the threads carried on shafts 3 and 4. Like these ends, however, they weave plain weave, and so they require two more shafts. These four ends are assigned to shafts 5 and 6. The completed threading draft is shown in **12.1**.

In writing the threading over the threads in **Figure 3**, I have divided the diagram into three sections according to what the threads

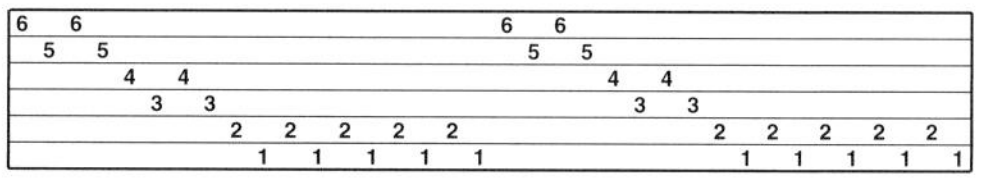

***12.1** This is the threading we have worked out for the fabric I sketched.*

are doing in each section. In section I, all of the threads weave plain weave all the time. To understand what is going on in a complex structure, break it down into very manageable little bits, in this case, two shafts at a time. Think about the ends carried on shafts 1 and 2. For the first pick, you lift shaft 1, and for the second pick, you lift shaft 2. Similarly, you lift the ends threaded on shafts 3 and 4 separately to make plain weave: 3 and then 4. And likewise, the ends threaded on shafts 5 and 6 also alternate to create plain weave. Put the little bits together, you'll

Woven in 2/20 natural worsted wool, the bottom fabric is similar to the design worked out on the opposite and following pages. The top fabric, also 2/20 worsted wool, has the same figure in a half-drop with more plain weave surrounding the little figures. This fabric requires ten shafts to weave. (Can you see why that would be?)

lift shafts 1, 3, and 5 followed by 2, 4, and 6 to weave plain weave all across the cloth.

In section II, the ends carried on shafts 1 and 2 are still weaving plain weave while those carried on shafts 3 and 4 are down for all four picks. I put "—" into that part of the diagram. It means, "yes, I thought about it and no, nothing in this section is lifted." The ends carried on 5 and 6 are up for all four picks, so I enter these shaft numbers in the table under 5 and 6. In section III, the ends on shafts 1 and 2 continue to weave plain weave, the ends on shafts 3 and 4 are lifted for four picks, and those on 5 and 6 are not lifted at all. The small table below is made to reflect the threading in each section from **Figure 3**.

Transferring the information from this table to a draft produces **12.2**. Now all you have to do is decide what yarns and sett you will use.

This method is just as simple as it appears here. Anyone can use it.

Section	1 and 2	3 and 4	5 and 6	combination	repeats
I	1	3	5	1, 3, 5	alternate 5 times
I	2	4	6	2, 4, 6	
II	1	–	5, 6	1, 5, 6	alternate twice
II	2	–	5, 6	2, 5, 6	
III	1	3, 4	–	1, 3, 4	alternate twice
III	2	3, 4	–	2, 3, 4	

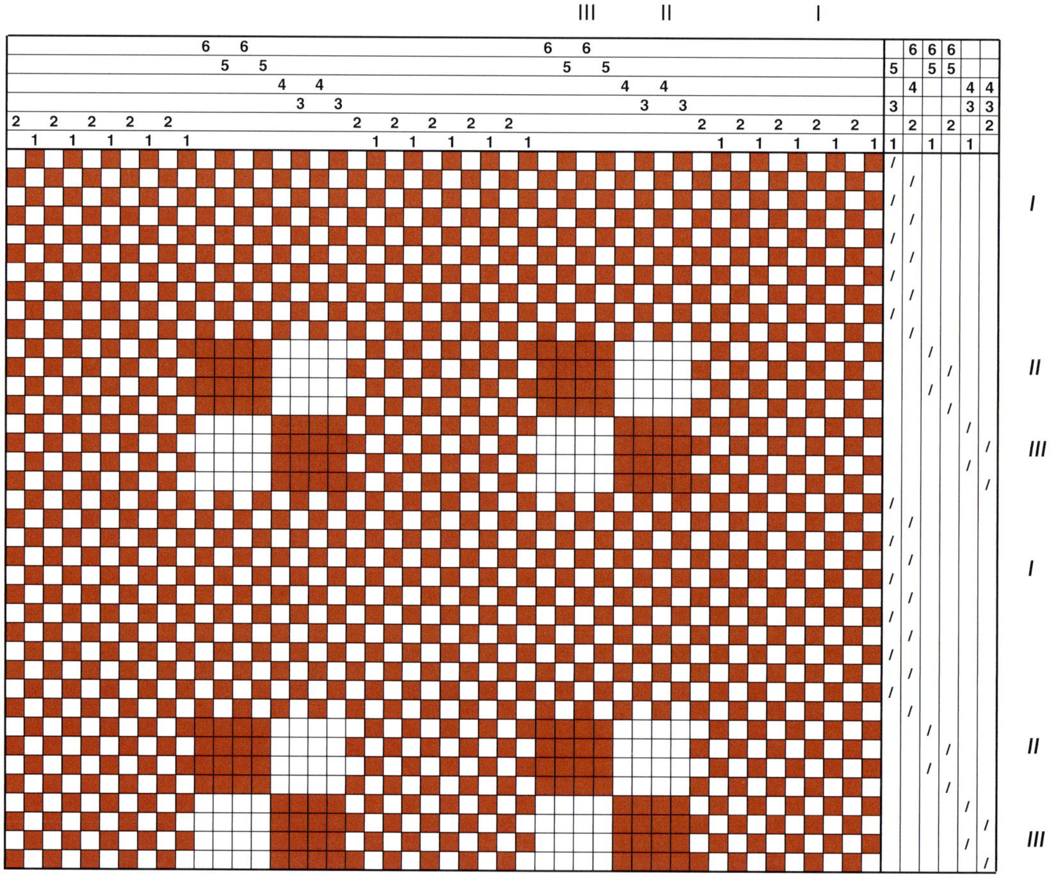

12.2 Here is the completed draft.

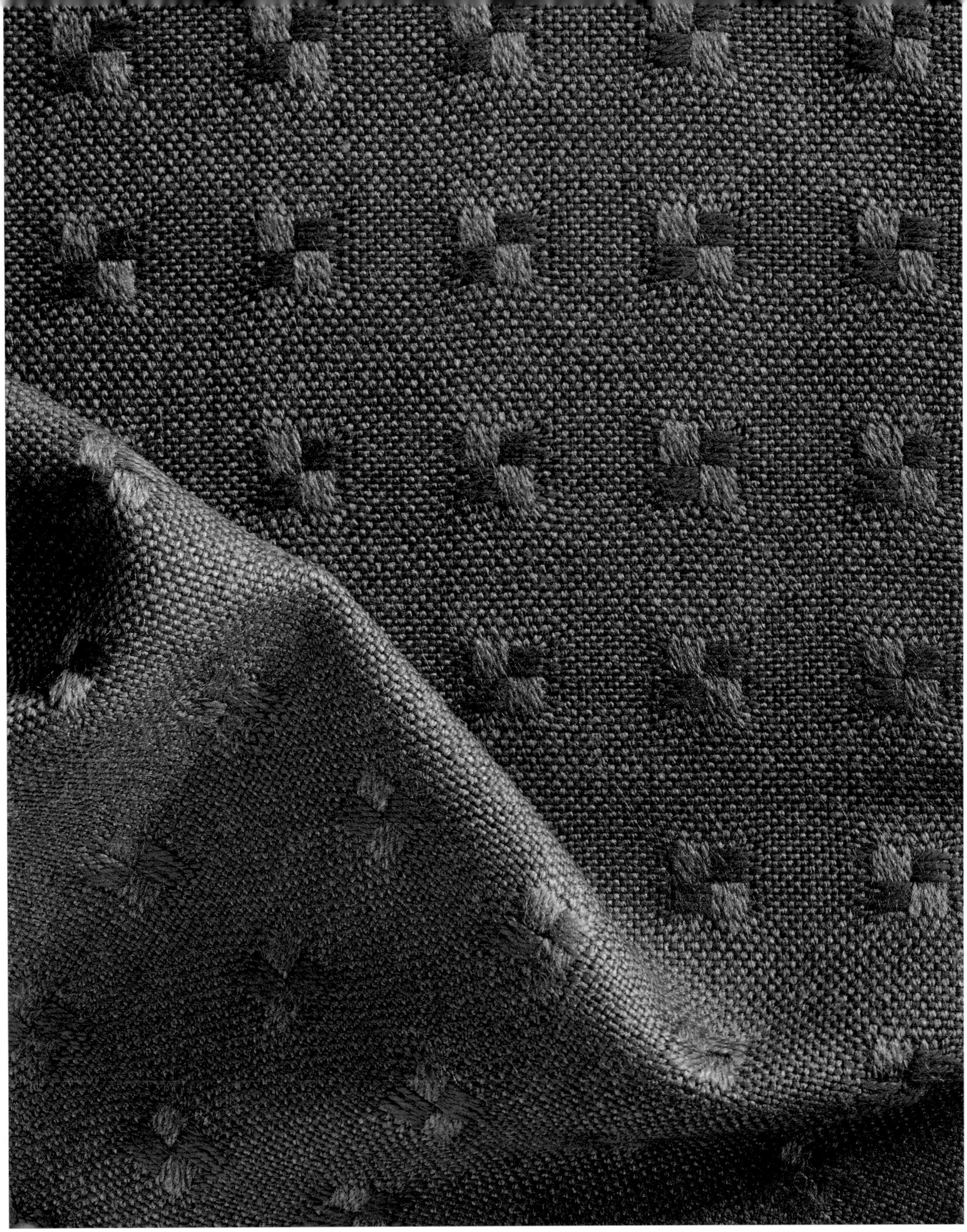

This is another version of the design worked out at the beginning of this chapter. The warp is 2/18 silk/wool; the weft is all silk for the added luster, clearly visible here.

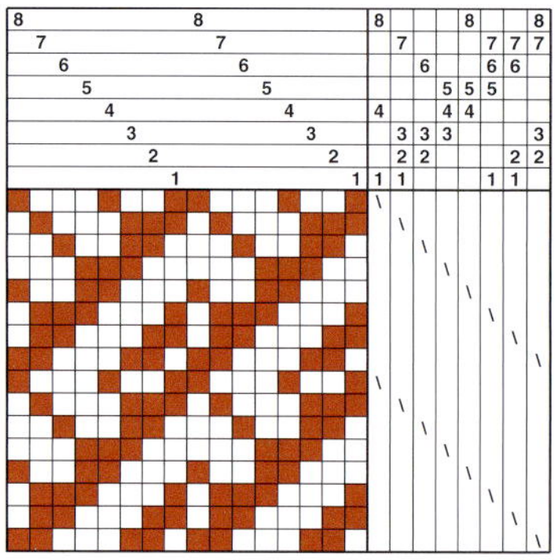

12.4a The tie-up produces this pattern when a straight draw and straight treadling are used.

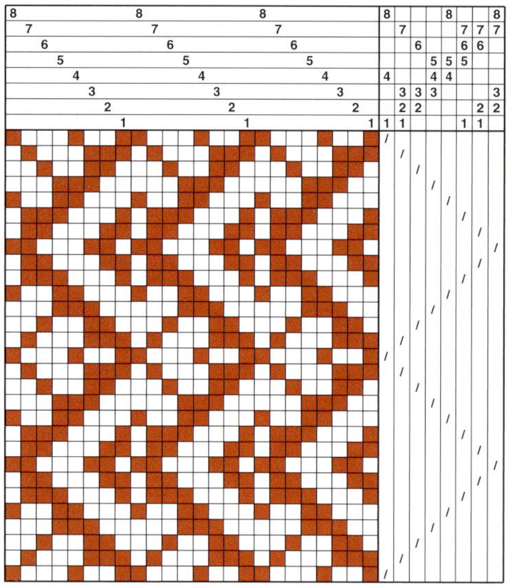

12.4b The same threading and tie-up are woven by reversing or pointing the treadling.

Working from the tie-up: another approach

I sometimes start designing with a familiar straight draw and treadling. A whole range of interesting fabrics can be derived just by experimenting with the tie-up.

This method of designing a structure works best when you have more than four shafts. With a straight-draw threading and the treadling repeating from left to right, we can focus on the tie-up area alone. **Figure 4** is the tie-up for an eight-shaft example:

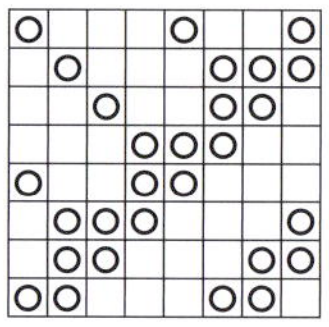

Figure 4

When this tie-up is applied to a straight threading and used with a straight treadling, **12.4a** is the result. When the treadling is reversed, the pattern looks more orderly (**12.4b**). When the threading and the treadling both reverse **12.4c**, the pattern is formal looking, very orderly, indeed.

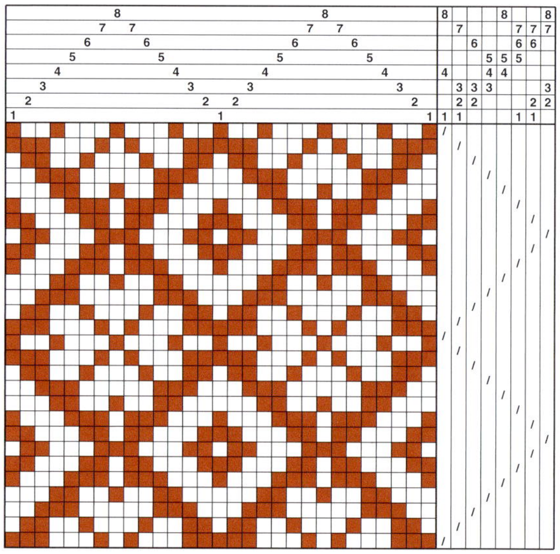

12.4c If the threading and treadling are reflected to make a point threading, this is the result.

Draft **12.5a**, straight threading and treadling, produces a continuous pattern because the tie-up is designed to make the diagonal lines meet. Notice that the lower left-hand corner of the tie-up (where the first pick of the repeat and shaft 1 coincide), a diagonal begins. The next pick (second treadle) lifts shafts 1 and 2, the next raises 2 and 3, and so on to the eighth treadle. Where the diagonal originates, both shafts 1 and 8 are lifted, and so the diagonal is two ends wide everywhere. The areas of plain weave in the tie-up also create a diagonal of plain weave because of their position within the tie-up.

Draft **12.5b** shows how the same tie-up affects a pointed threading and treadling: a neat and rather formal pattern is formed. Note that the columns at the left and right side of the tie-up box are the axis of reflection: they appear once, at the centers of the treadling points. Likewise, the top and bottom rows are axis of reflection for the places where the threading points. Their implications will be discussed below.

These examples are woven using eight shafts. Using more shafts offers even more scope for creating interesting weave structures. Draft **12.6a** (next page) shows a sixteen-shaft design with a tie-up that I constructed as I did the previous one. First, I made a diagonal line running from corner to corner. Because a line that is only one thread wide does not show up well in the cloth, I made this one much bolder: three threads wide.

I filled in the upper half of the tie-up to make a radiating pattern. The single-thread diagonals cut the weft floats in the cloth, making them three ends long.

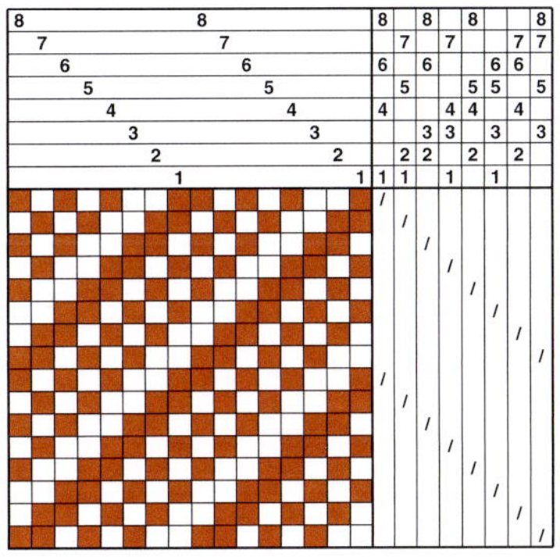

12.5a This tie-up has been designed so that the pattern produced is continuous. The repeat occurs in just eight ends and picks.

12.5b The tie-up from 5a is combined with a pointed threading and treadling to make a very formal pattern with a larger repeat (fourteen ends and picks).

I filled in the lower half of the tie-up to make a basket weave that will open up when the fabric is washed, producing a lacy diamond in the cloth. The basket weave is a 3/3 basket because nothing else is possible the way the pattern is reflected. The closest we can come to a 2/2 basket, for example, is shown in **12.6b** (next page).

Because the top and bottom rows and the left and right columns of the tie-up are not repeated as the cloth is woven, a 2/2 basket that repeats neatly as the 3/3 basket did in **12.6a** isn't possible: There is no central thread in a 2/2 basket as there is in a 3/3 basket. So it shouldn't surprise us to find that a 4/4 basket doesn't fit, but a 5/5

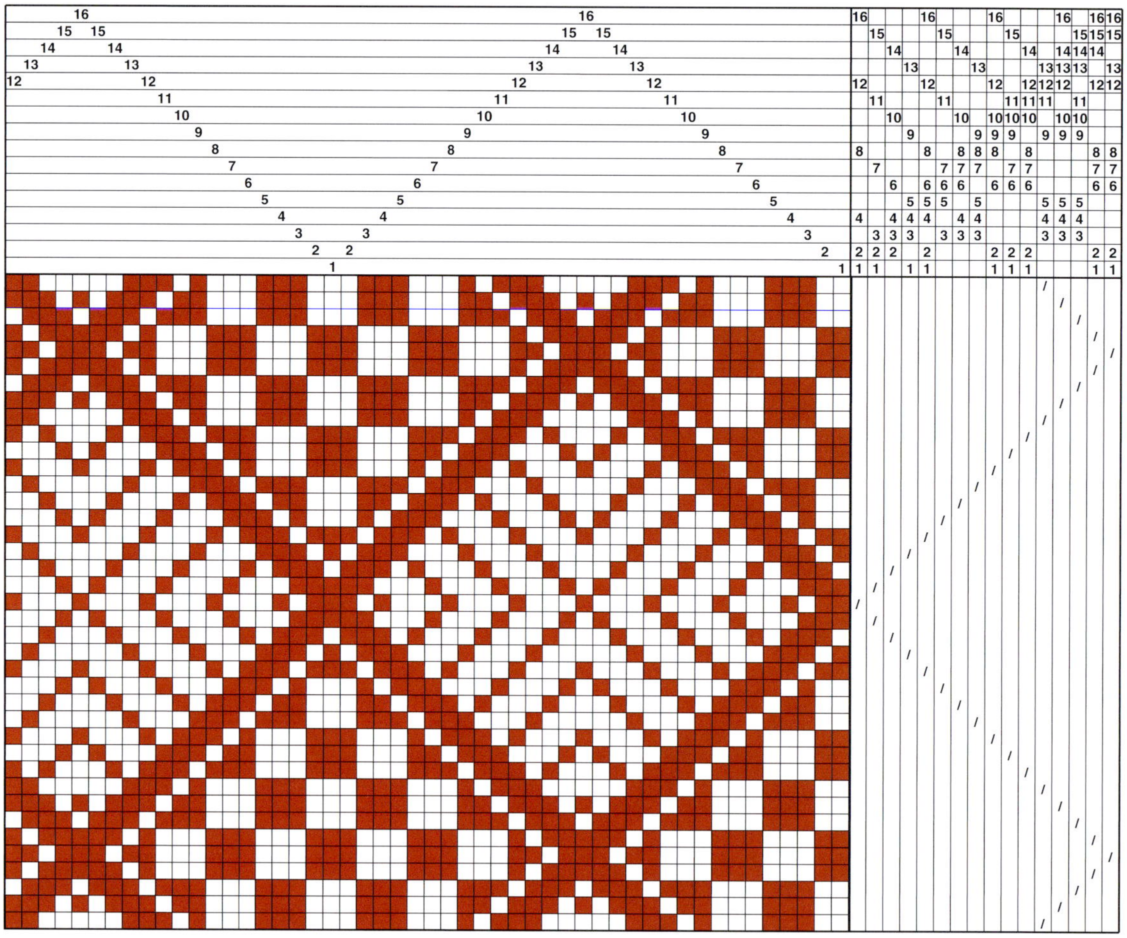

12.6a With sixteen shafts, we have a 16 × 16 square in which to work. A diagonal line in the tie-up starts the design, dividing the pattern into quadrants. What lies above the line is reflected to fill one diamond, what is entered below the diagonal fills the other diamond. The pattern repeats in thirty ends and thirty picks.

basket will. A 5/5 basket takes up a lot of room, though, and unless the threads are very small and sticky, the cloth would probably be pretty soft in the area where the basket weave is woven. Draft **12.7**, on twenty-four shafts, shows one such possibility. The basket weave is in the lower part of the tie-up. The addition of several rows of plain weave, forming a frame for the radiating pattern, similar to those in **12.6a** and **12.6b**, helps to stabilize the cloth. Even when the cloth is woven to square with a firm sett and a beat to match, the plain-weave areas are necessary to make the cloth more stable.

The possibilities for making these neat, formal little patterns are many. I love them woven in white crossing white—to my eye, one of the few times when color adds little to the end result. If you are willing to tie and retie treadles or have a loom with a dobby mechanism, a single long warp can produce a variety of patterns on the same point threading.

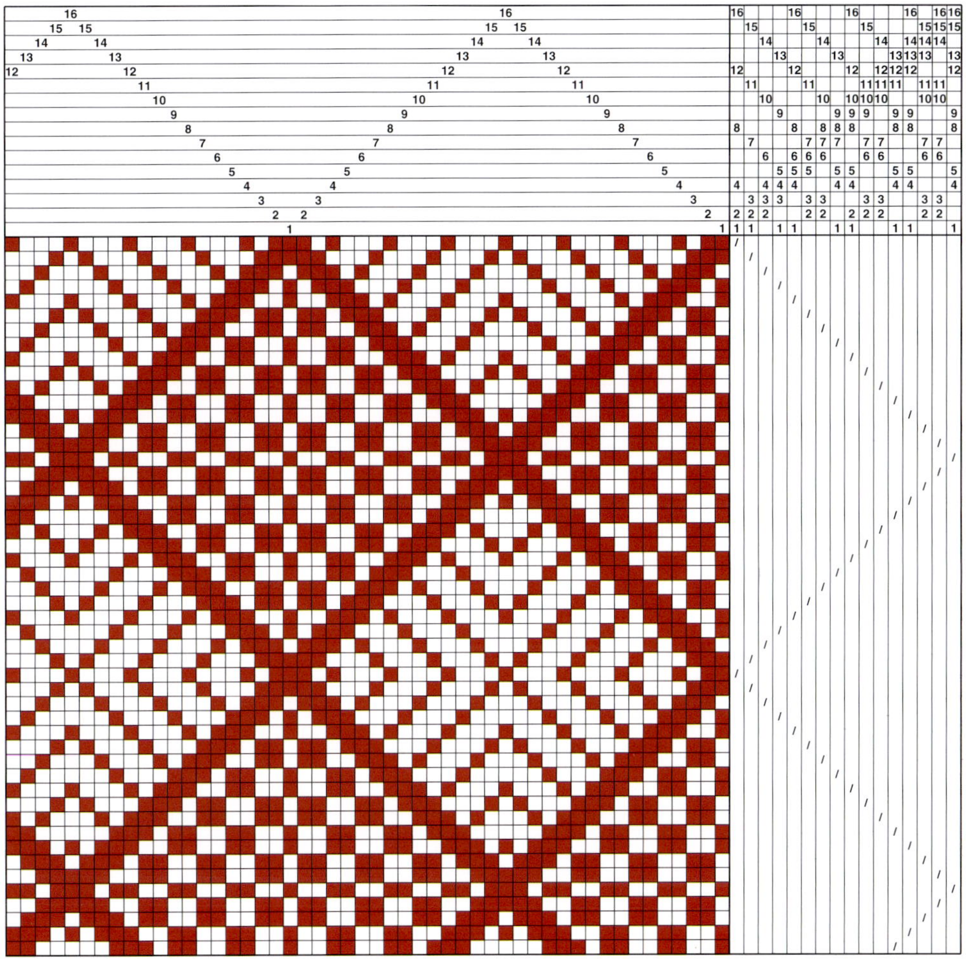

12.6b This is the closest we can get to a 2/2 basket weave using a point threading and treadling.

A third way to construct the cloth structure you want

Sometimes I know just how I want the cloth to be constructed, down to every detail, but don't have the draft. In that case, I draw the pattern I want on graph paper, making a cloth diagram in effect. (This is also a way of figuring out how to reproduce the structure of an existing cloth.) Once I have drawn that diagram, I can work out the threading and then the treadling. Let us consider the chart on page 238, where "X" means that the warp is on top in a given spot and an empty square means that the weft is on top there.

12.7 5/5 basket weave in one diamond.

Five variations woven on sixteen shafts, designing from the tie-up. These designs were all woven on the same warp using 40/1 linen.

The pattern we want to explore is shown in **Figure 5**. One area weaves plain weave,

1	2	1	3	4	5	6	2	1	2	1	2	Shafts to be lifted
X		X		X		X		X		X		1, 4, 6
	X		X	X			X		X		X	2, 3, 4
X		X	X	X				X		X		1, 3, 4
	X				X	X	X		X		X	2, 5, 6
X		X			X	X		X		X		1, 5, 6
	X		X		X		X		X		X	2, 3, 5
X		X		X		X		X		X		1, 4, 6
	X		X		X		X		X		X	2, 3, 5
X		X		X		X		X		X		1, 4, 6
	X		X		X		X		X		X	2, 3, 5

Figure 5

and another area contains a little figure made up of floats. The first step is to assign shafts to the various columns. When there is a column that weaves exactly like another, it is assumed that the threads that each column represents are on the same shaft.

The threading, reading from left to right, appears at the top of the diagram. Notice that when we come to a column that doesn't weave exactly like the ones we have already assigned to a shaft, we assign it to a new one.

Once we have established the number of shafts and the order in which they are to be used, then we can figure out what sheds need to be made. The shafts that must be lifted to make this cloth are listed down the right side of the diagram. Put into draft form, it becomes **12.8**.

Of the three methods described above, the first is the one I use the most. Try them all, but do experiment with creating your own designs.

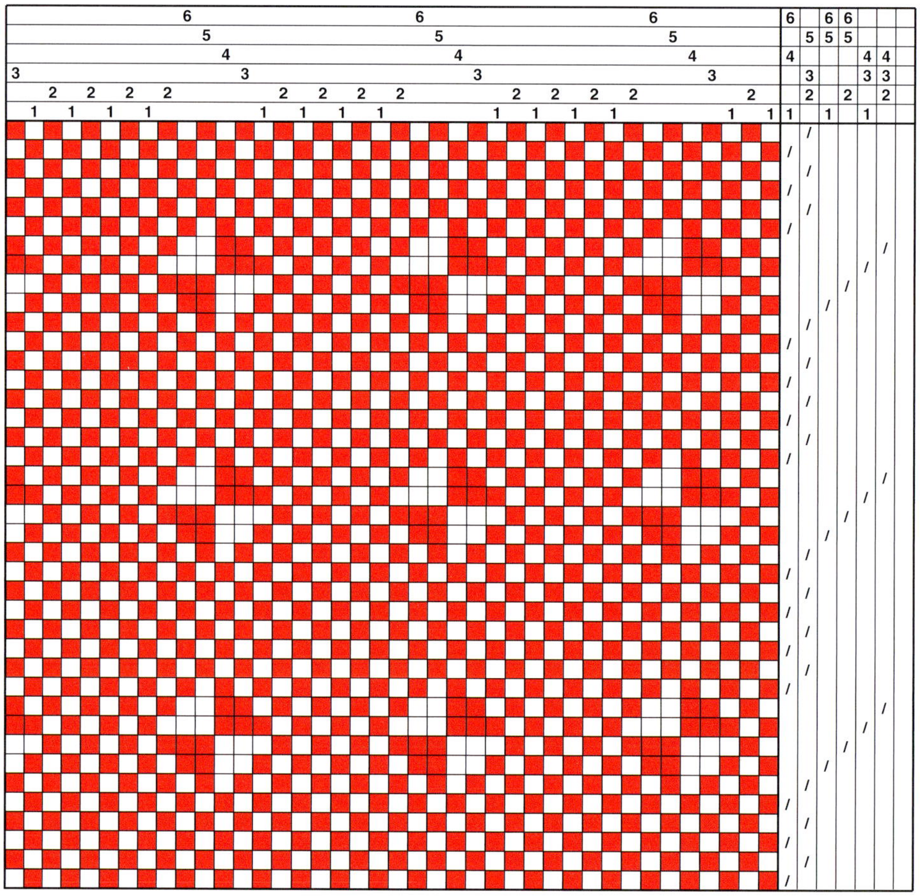

12.8 This is the draft for the idea worked out from a draw down.

A sixteen-shaft cloth of 2/36 natural wool, woven on a point threading with a point treadling. It is very light and airy.

Three of these fabrics (two upper right and one lower left) were designed as upholstery fabrics. The warp for all three is 2/20 worsted wool, with two ends—one dark green and one dark blue—used as one and threaded on a straight draw on sixteen shafts. The weft is two red 2/20 worsted wool yarns used as one. All three structures were worked out by designing from the tie-up, the method described on pages 232–235. The upper right one makes counterchange right triangles.

The second fabric from the upper right is also a counterchange pattern—a pinwheel woven in 3/1 twill on a ground of 1/3 twill (or the reverse, depending on your point of view—which is what makes it a counterchange pattern).

The design on the lower right is either red with blue diagonals and dashes, or the reverse on the other side.

The remaining fabric was woven of 2/8 worsted wool with loop mohair decorating both sides. The ground fabric is 1/2 twill (2/1 on the other side) woven with a bluish red on an orange warp. One side is red, the other orange. The equal-arm crosses of deep indigo loop mohair appear on both sides and are the same size on both sides. This cloth was designed by the first method described in this chapter.

Woven on a straight draw on sixteen shafts, this experimental fabric was designed from the peg plan. Recall that a peg plan is used with a dobby loom or can be used on a table loom. I wanted to see what a strong, steep diagonal crossed by a curving line superimposed on a 1/3 twill would look like. Because it repeats clear off the bottom of the page, the peg plan is quite long.

Both of these fabrics have square spots woven into them. In both, the ground cloth is 2/20 worsted wool, woven in plain weave. In the bottom cloth, the dots are a tweed yarn that interlaces with the ground weft. The ground requires two shafts, and the warp spots require 2 more. They float for three picks maximum, and are caught by one pick before floating again. The rest of the time, the tweed yarns float on the back, making the take-up different from that of the ground warp—so the warp for the spots must be beamed separately.

The cloth with beige dots on a middle gray ground is also constructed with two warps. The beige dots are made of warp floats that float for five picks. Unlike the bottom fabric, the spots here are not placed so that they line up in both the warp and weft directions—on the corners of imaginary squares. These dots are placed according to the stitching points for a five-shaft satin.

The ground cloth, woven plain weave even under the dots, requires two shafts; the dots, where all the warp ends for a particular dot are carried on the same shaft, require five more.

Both of these all-silk fabrics are constructed of two ends of 60/2 silk used as one in both warp and weft. Both fabrics were threaded in a point threading on sixteen shafts and woven following a point treadling and repeat in thirty ends and thirty picks. They were designed from the tie-up.

The weft colors are a little different from those used in the warp so that the slight color difference emphasizes the weave structure. I wanted to avoid creating a design that was diagonal.

The left cloth is a pattern of interlocked, hollow diamonds on a plain-weave ground. The two patterns visible in the lower part of the right-hand cloth consist of diamond grids, one with a little figure (X, O) in the center, and one plain.

13

Summing It Up Where to Go From Here

Now that you have a lot of information about weave structures, what do you do next? The answer is very simple: whatever you like.

I am very serious about that. You have my permission—my encouragement!—to do whatever you like at your loom. If no one else does it the way you are considering, don't worry about it. As long as you keep in mind that your object is to make beautiful cloth that will do what it is asked to do, you may go about that in any way that works for you.

I hope that you will have fun designing and weaving your beautiful fabrics and that you will understand how much power you have to bring a new idea or a re-working of an old idea into being. Just think of all the wonderful cloth you can make. Get started!

Appendix A
How to Turn a Draft

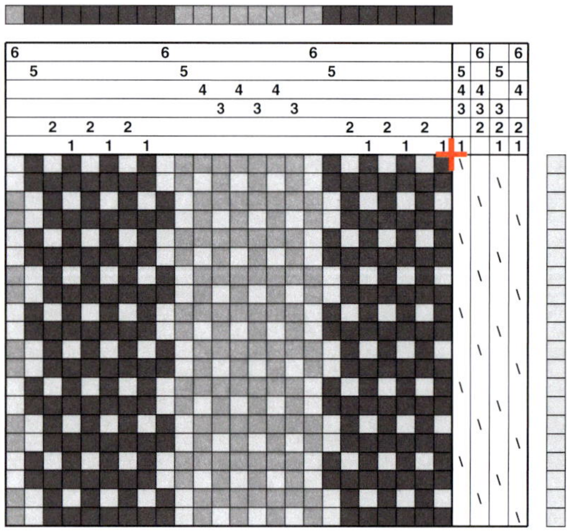

A.1 Draft to be turned. We begin with a draft that requires six shafts and four treadles.

There are three situations in which turning a draft can be helpful: when the design or motif runs crosswise and you want it to run lengthwise, when the draft you want to use requires more shafts than you have but fewer different sheds (treadles), or when you are tired of throwing multiple shuttles and would rather throw one.

When a draft is turned, the warp becomes the weft, the weft becomes the warp, and the number of ends per inch becomes the number of picks per inch, and vice versa. In effect, the cloth is turned 90 degrees.

The place to begin is with the original draft. Be sure that you start with a complete draft; if you are turning an overshot, for example, the tabby shots must be included in the original draft. The draft we will turn is shown in **A.1**.

First, put a big, red plus (+) right at the point in the draft (**A.1**) where the threading, tie-up, treadling, and cloth diagram come together. This marks the starting point for all of the changes we'll make.

Next, prepare the area for the turned draft; the number of treadles used in the original draft becomes the number of shafts in the new one and vice versa (**A.2a**).

Enter the treadling order from **A.1** into the new threading area, and the threading order from **A.1** into the new treadling area. Enter the warp color order from the original as the weft color order in the new draft, too. Likewise, add the weft color order in the warp color order area. The result is **A.2b**. Finally, working from the + and thinking of the spaces in the tie-up as either being "full" or "empty," transfer the information from the old tie-up's horizontals to the new tie-up's verticals. I may actually chant aloud as I read the first row from the old draft: "Full empty full full." I repeat the chant as I enter the marks in the first column of the new tie-up (**A.2c**). In far less time than it takes to tell about it, the draft has been turned.

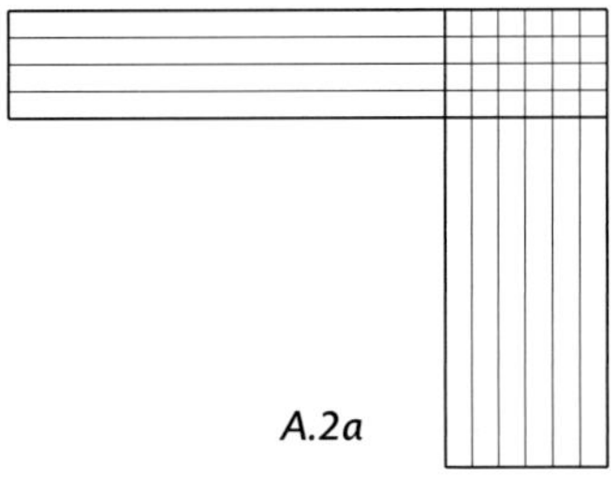

A.2a

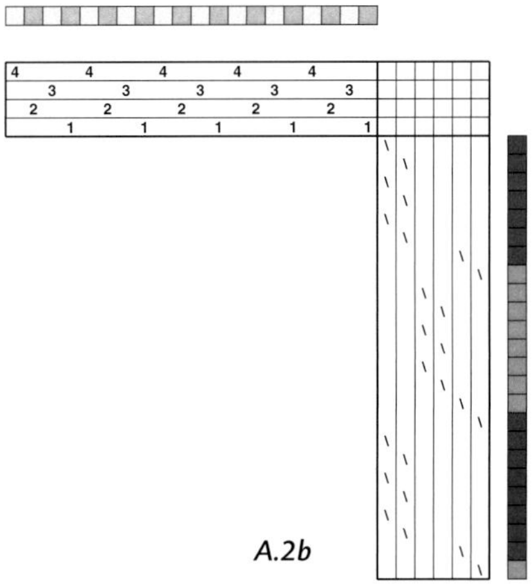

A.2b

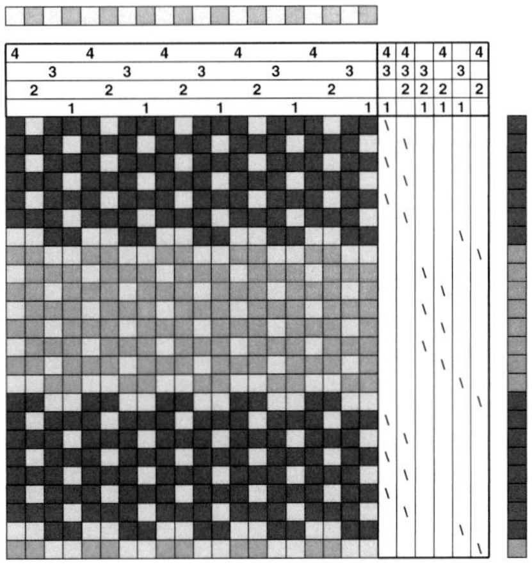

***A.2c** This is the draft in A.1, turned. Notice that the treadling order working from the + is what was the threading order. The threading order was the treadling order. The color order for the warp is, here, the color order for the weft (more convenient, too) and the color order for the weft is now the color order for the warp.*

Appendix B
Deciphering Industrial Drafts

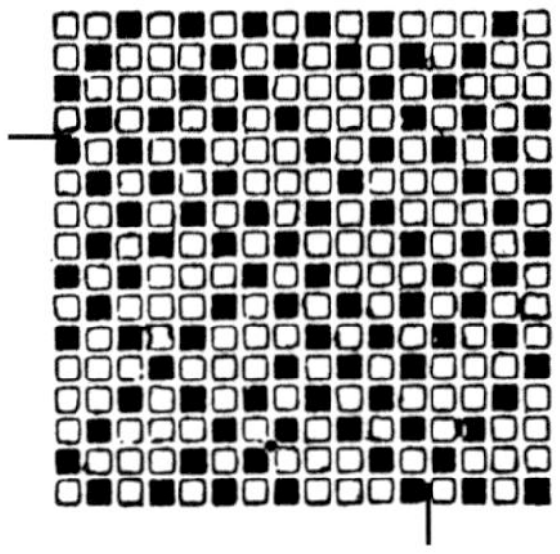

B.1 Original draft

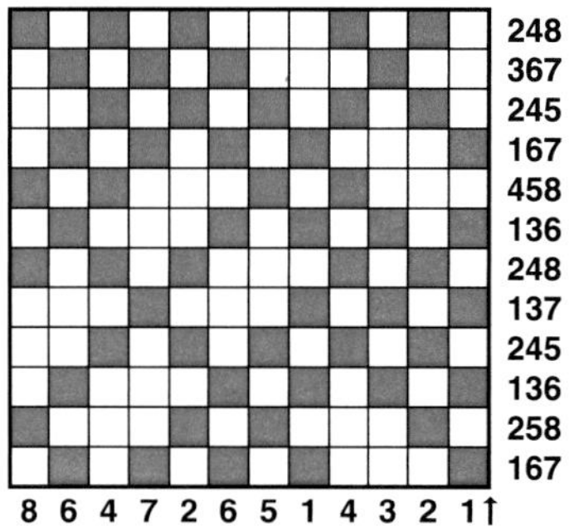

B.2

Several very useful books, most of them written at the end of the nineteenth and beginning of the twentieth centuries, were intended originally for use by designers in textile mills. Except for one, they are long out of print and thus available principally in libraries. The exception is *A Handbook of Weaves,* written by G. H. Oelsner in 1915, translated and revised by Samuel S. Dale in 1952, and reprinted in 1952 by Dover Publications.

At first glance, a novice weaver finds the book is baffling—at least I did when I bought my copy. All the information we need to use its many drafts is there, but not in the form familiar to beginning weavers. Instead, the structures are presented as cloth diagrams. But despite their unfamiliarity, getting from those to the sort of drafts most handweavers use is not difficult at all.

Many of the diagrams, grids of filled-in and empty squares, have a little mark on the left side and one at the bottom. Realizing that the mark at the left signifies the end of one repeat and the start of another in the weft direction and the mark along the bottom, the same for the warp direction was the key that unlocked this book for me.

Counting the number of squares in each direction tells us the number of picks and ends, respectively, used to make the structure represented by the grid. These numbers can be misleading, however, as it is always easiest to thread a straight draw, and that is the way looms are threaded in industry. The use of a straight draw is implied throughout the book, but you may be able to weave some of the structures on fewer shafts than indicated by the repeat marks. For example, Oelsner's figure 675 on page 147 (Figure 1) is marked as a twelve-shaft, twelve-treadle weave, but close examination will show that fewer shafts are required. Figure 2 shows a single repeat from Oelsner's figure 675, and shows how to figure out the threading, tie-up, and treadling in our conventional format.

Here's how to decipher it. The numbers at the bottom of the diagram represent the shafts. Each ■ denotes a point on the cloth where the warp shows (is on top of the weft). To obtain the threading, start with the first column on the right and assign it to shaft 1. The second column, because it is different from the first, is assigned to shaft 2. The third column starts out like the second but is not exactly the same—which it would have to be if they were carried on the same shaft, and so we assign it to shaft 3. We keep adding shafts until we find a column (the fifth one in this case) that duplicates an earlier one. In this case, the fifth column is the same as the first, so we assign it a 1.

Note that we could just as well have started assigning from the other side; while the number assigned to a particular column would have been different, the resulting cloth would have been the same.

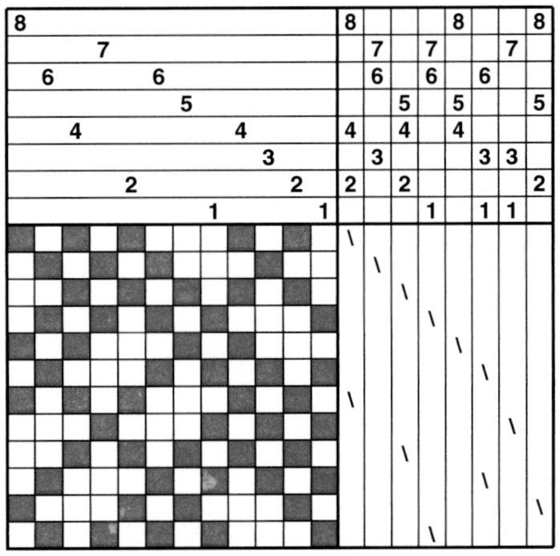

B.3 Standard draft notation for figure 675, page 147 from A Handbook of Weaves. *As presented in the book, the draft required eleven shafts and twelve treadles, but when analyzed, it turns out to require eight shafts and eight treadles, but is no longer threaded on a straight draw with a straight treadling.*

Once we have established the threading, we can see what sheds are required. We do that by considering each row (horizontal) and writing down the number of the shaft to which each column with ■'s in it is assigned. With this information, we can write the draft in the usual format (**B.3**) or work directly from the diagram.

If you were working in the textile industry at the time Oelsner's book was written, you would find the warp threaded on a straight draw, and the diagram would be a pegging plan for a dobby loom. It could also be used as the tie-up for a treadle loom.

With the key to this book and others like it, you can figure out how to use any industrial draft you encounter!

Appendix C
Calculating Setts

Sett, usually expressed as ends per inch (e.p.i.), describes the density of the warp ends, that is, the number of ends that occur in an inch of warp width. It is easy to predict that you can put more tiny threads and fewer big ones in an inch, but the size of the threads is not the only factor that enters the calculation of the sett of a warp.

Consideration of the weave structure as well as the size of the warp threads is also essential in determining setts with a high degree of accuracy.

Calculating the sett helps to limit the number of samples you need to make as you perfect a design. In any case, the calculation will be only an estimate. The proof of the calculation is the cloth itself.

The simplest way to calculate the sett is to apply this formula, which is actually a sentence abbreviated to make it more concise. The formula is

$$S = \frac{T \times R}{(I+R)},$$

where S is the sett, T is the number of times you can wrap the warp yarn around a 1-inch (2.5-cm) rule, R is the number of ends in one repeat, and I is the number of times that the weft intersects the plane of the cloth in one repeat. Thus, the sett, in ends per inch, is the number of wraps of warp yarn in an inch times the number of ends in one repeat, all divided by the sum of the number of weft intersections and the number of ends in one repeat.

Wrapping the yarn around a ruler to obtain T is an art that practice will make more consistent. Leave no spaces between consecutive wraps, but keep them in a single layer. Wrap stretchy yarns under as little tension as possible because we want a measure of its relaxed size, the way it will be in the finished cloth.

R is self-explanatory, and in many cases, it may be simpler to determine than you might predict. For example, all the structures that are based on plain weave—three-element weaves with plain-weave shots or tabbies and lace weaves, should be set as if they were plain weave, making the calculation very simple.

I, the number of intersections per repeat, is best shown with a cross-sectional diagram. The diagram opposite shows one repeat plus one end each for plain weave, 1/2 twill, 1/3 twill, 2/2 twill, 5-shaft satin, 8-shaft satin and $\frac{3\ 1}{2\ 2}$ twill.

You will notice that I is always an even number, and that makes perfect sense: if a repeat begins with the weft yarn above the plane of the cloth (indicated by the dotted line in the diagrams), it must also end above the plane of the cloth. If it ends up on the other side of the cloth, then we have either left out part of the repeat or added more than we should have. That is, after all, what a repeat means: the thing that just occurred starts all over again at the beginning of the next repeat.

In our diagram, the weft begins above the plane of the cloth and one full repeat plus one more end is included in the drawing. You will notice two little vertical lines in each diagram. Those indicate the starting and ending points, respectively. The number of times that the weft line intersects the plane of the cloth is the number of intersections in one repeat, or I.

When we are figuring the sett, we must have not only room for each of the warp ends but also room for the weft to pass from one face to the other.

This formula is made with some assumptions that may or may not be true. It assumes that the sizes of the weft and the warp are comparable. It assumes that we want a balanced weave, that is, as many picks as ends per inch. It also assumes that the yarns in the warp are all the same size. Some special cases require adjustment of the calculation above. If, for example, the warp is made up of a mixture of yarns, we will need to use an average for T: Here is how you do that: wind at least 2 or 3 inches on the ruler using all of the yarns that will be in the warp in the proportion in which they will be used. If you wind 3 inches, count how many ends fit into that space and divide by 3 to obtain the average. When you have calculated the sett, choose a reed with fewer dents per inch so that the larger threads will not be crowded. For example, if you calculate a sett of 18 e.p.i., choose a reed with 6 dents per inch, not one with 18 dents per inch. At 3 ends per dent in a 6 dent/inch reed (to obtain 18 e.p.i.), there ought to be plenty of room for the larger ends to pass through the reed without abrasion or sticking. Some

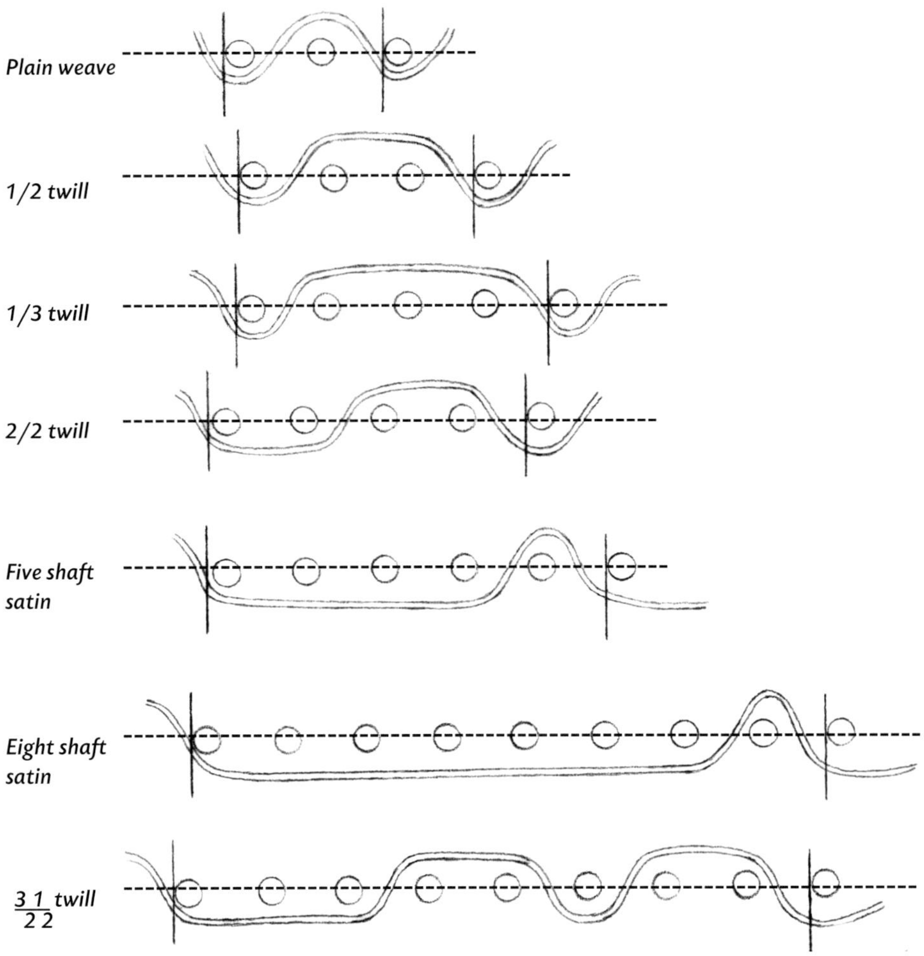

fabrics need to be firmer in their construction than others. Upholstery fabrics require firm setts and firm beats to make them stand up to the wear to which they will be subjected. Use the formula to calculate the sett and then add 15 to 20 percent to the result. Use this figure for the sett for your preliminary sample.

Slippery yarns need a closer-than-usual sett to prevent slippage, and thus instability, in the fabric. If the weft slides along the warp, or if the warp slides along the weft, the cloth will not be stable. First, calculate the sett according to the formula and then add 10 to 15 percent to the result. Exactly how much you add depends on how slippery the yarn is. When you have the sett, make a sample and adjust the sett further as necessary.

Some fabrics, such as scarves and shawls, must drape well to conform to the body of their wearer. The structure can help with drape (twills and satin weaves drape better than plain-weave fabrics), but to ensure that the cloth will drape, calculate the sett by the formula and then reduce it by 5 to10 percent. Be aware, however, that if you are making a scarf out of a very slippery silk, subtracting 5 percent for better drapability and adding 15 percent to compensate for slipperiness will produce a sett that is 110 percent that of the calculated number.

When you are choosing yarns to weave a tapestry, it is very likely that the sizes of the warp and weft will be different, and the basic formula given above does not apply. Figuring the sett for a tapestry is quite simple, though. Wind one end of the warp yarn and one of the weft, alternating as you go, until you have filled an inch with no overlaps or spaces. In this case, the sett will be the number of warp ends in that inch. When setting a warp to weave tapestry, you need to leave enough room for the weft to pass between the warp ends—not more, not less.

When there are two or more structures across the warp, figure the sett for each and then select a reed that will allow you to set each part of the warp appropriately. For example, let's suppose that you want to weave a cloth with warp-faced twill stripes set into a plain-weave ground. If T for your yarn is 30 wraps per inch, then for plain weave the sett is 15; for the 3/1 twill stripes, it would be 20. If you use a 10 dent/inch reed, you can sley the twill stripes 2 per dent and the plain-weave ground 1/2/1/2, alternating 1 and 2 per dent.

The last special case is warp-faced structures. Common sense tells you that a rep (warp-faced) weave would be set so that S is equal to T. I have found, however, that using that sett practically guarantees that the weft—which is supposed to be hidden in a rep weave—will show. If you add 25 percent to the number of wraps per inch, however, you will have good coverage.

Above all, remember that this formula is intended only to estimate the sett. It is a place to begin. Weave a sample at least 8 inches (20 cm) wide, wash the cloth (or block a tapestry), and then decide whether the sett was right for your purpose. If you keep records of your experiences with each warp, it won't be long before you will have an excellent reference that you can consult as you design new work. I think of my own records as a way of sending information to my "future self." I feel kindly toward Sharon-in-the-future and don't want her to work any harder than she must to complete a particular job.

Bibliography

Anderson, Clarita, Judith Gordon, and Naomi Whiting Towner. *Weave Structures Used in North American Coverlets.* Olney, Maryland: Anderson, 1979.

Black, Mary E. *The Key to Weaving.* 2nd. Rev. ed. New York: Macmillan, 1980.

Barrett, Clotilde, and Eunice Smith. *Double Two-Tie Unit Weaves.* Boulder, Colorado: Weaver's Journal Publications, 1983.

Davison, Marguerite Porter. *A Handweaver's Pattern Book.* Rev. Ed. Swarthmore, Pennsylvania, 1971.

Emery, Irene. *The Primary Structures of Fabric: An Illustrated Classification.* Washington, D.C.: Textile Museum, 1966.

Oelsner, Gustaf Hermann. *A Handbook of Weaves.* Translated and rev. by Samuel S. Dale. New York: Dover Publications, 1952.

Strong, John H. *Fabric Structure.* New York: Chemical Publishing, 1947.

Sullivan, Donna L. *Pique: Plain and Patterned.* Jacksonville, Florida: Sullivan Publications, 1988.

Tovey, John. *Weaves and Pattern Drafting.* London: Batsford; New York: Reinhold, 1969.

Van der Hoogt, Madelyn. *The Complete Book of Drafting for Handweavers.* Coupeville, Washington: Shuttle-Craft Books, 1993.

While these are the books I used as I wrote this book, I routinely read everything I can find about weaving, color, and design, so perhaps a lifetime of reading ought to be listed here—an impossible task!

INDEX

Page numbers listed in **boldface** indicate a draft. Page numbers listed in *italics* indicate a figure.

A Handbook of Weaves 248, 249
Atwater, Mary 152

backed weaves 173–175, 176, *174* **174**, *175* **175**, **176**, 178
balanced weave 4
basket weave 10
twill 26, **29**
basket weave *8*, 8, 10–13, **10**, **222**, **236**
half basket 10 **10**
Bedford cord 179–183, 184, *179, 180,* 182, **184**
beiderwand 152, **154**, 155 **155**, 156
bibliography 253
blocks *30* 30, **79**
clean breaks 29
block weaves 77–78, 81
twill 29 **29**, 30–32
bobbins 47, **47**
braided twill 62 **62**
Brighton honeycomb 90 **90**, 92 **92**, 93
broche 217, **218**
broken twill 28 **28**, 29, 32, 34, **202**
Bronson lace 107 **107**, 108 **108**, 147 **147**

canvas weave 104 **104**, 106
cloth
diagram 5
loom state 4
collapse weave 221, 223–225, **222**, **224**, **225**
color
variations 4, 5, 6
value 6
twill 61
color-and-weave effect 22, 24
log cabin **23**, 24
Collingwood, Peter 196
combined weaves 207–216, 217, **208**, **210**, **211**, **212**, **213**, **214**, **216**
compound weaves 123–156, **123**
beiderwand 152, **154**, 155 **155**, 156
crackle 152, **153**
dukagång 124, 146
inlay 123 **123**, **124**, 126 **126**, 127 **127**
monk's belt 140 **140**, **141**
Moorman technique 124 **124**
overshot 129, 130–144, **132**, **135**, **136**, **137**, **138**, **139**, **140**, **141**, **142**, **143**
doublewidth 171–172 **172**, 173
pile 148, **148**
summer and winter 145–151, **145**, **146**, **147**, **148**, **150**
cords 10, 14
Bedford 179–183, *179, 180,* **182**, 184 **184**
hair 14
corduroy 190, 192 **192**, 194 **194**, **195**, **196**, *200* 200
corkscrew twill 48 **48**, 50
crackle 152, **153**
crepe weaves 201–206, **202**, **205**, **206**
crystal twill 36 **36**

Dale, Samuel S. 248
damask 68, 69, 70, 76–78, **76**, **77**, **78**, 81 **81**
false 32 **32**
twill 32
Davison, Marguerite 106, 131, 132 **132**, **133**, **136**, **137**, 138 **138**
design 227–243, *228*, **230**
draft *227, 228,* **229**, **230**, **232**, **233**, **234**, **235**, **236**
diagram, cloth 5
dimension 8
distorted grids 95–122, **96**
Bronson lace 107 **107**, 108 **108**, 147 **147**
canvas weave 104 **104**, 106
honeycomb 110 **110**, 113, 114, 138, 147 **147**
Brighton 90 **90**, 92 **92**, 93
huck 96 **96**, 98 **98**, 100–102, **101**, 103 **103**
leno 103 *103*, 106
mock 104 **104**, 106
linear zigzag 118 **118**, 120 **120**, 122 **122**
M's and O's 114 **114**, 116–117, **117**, 118
spider weaves 118 **118**, 119, 120 **120**, 122 **122**
Swedish lace 106 **106**, 107
dobby looms 5
peg plan 86
dornick twill 35 **35**, 36
double-faced twill 42–43, **42**, **43**, 44 **44**
doubleweave, loom-controlled 157–178, *158* **158**, *159* **159**, *160* **160**, *164* **164**, **165**, *166* **166**, *170* **170**, **171**, **172**, **175**
backed weaves 173–175, 176, *174* 174, *175* **175**, **176**, 178
double-width cloth 160 **160**, 161, 166, 170, **171**

overshot 171–172, **171**,173, **172**
matelassé 176, 178 **178**
double-width cloth 160 **160**, 161, 166, 170, **171**
drafts
design *227, 228,* **229**, **230**, **232**, **233**, **234**, **235**, **236**
industrial, understanding 248 **248**, 249 **249**
profile 79 **79**, **100**, **102**
structural 5 **5**
turning 246–247, **246**, **247**
drape, fabric sett 252
dukagång *see* compound weaves

edges 29, 30 *see also* selvedges
Emery, Irene 21, 36, 123
ends, cutting 180 **180**, **182**
ends per inch 4
even twill 26

Fabric Structure 21
Fairchild's Dictionary of Textiles 3
fiber *see* yarn
flaws 4
floats 25, 45, 46, 94
length 52

granite weave 29
gray goods 4
grids *see* distorted grids

hair cord 14 **14**
half basket 10 **10**
halftones 140 **140**, **141**, **142**, **143**
Handweaver's Pattern Book 106, 130–131, 132, 133, 136
herringbone 34 **34**, 35
honeycomb 110 **110**, 113, 114, 138, 147, **147**
Brighton 90 **90**, 92 **92**, 93
huck 96 **96**, 98 **98**, 100–102, 103, **100**, **101**, **103**
huckaback *see* huck

inlay 123 **123**, **124**, 126 **126**, 127 **127**
interleaving twill 46, 48, 50–55, **50**, **51**, **53**, **54**, **55**, **205**

King's Flower **132**, **133**, **172**

leno 4, 20 *20,* 103 *103*, 106
mock 104 **104**, 106
log cabin 22 **22**, **23**, **24**
looms, dobby 5
loom-state cloth 4

matt weave 10
matelassé 176, 178 **178**
monk's belt 140 **140**, **141**
Moorman, Theo 124
technique 124 **124**
Morton, Alistair 196
move numbers 64
degenerate case 64
M's and O's 114 **114**, **116**, 117 **117**, 118

Oelsner, G. H. 248, 249
overshot 129, 130–144, **132**, **135**, **136**, **137**, **138**, **139**, **140**, **141**, **142**, **143**
doublewidth 171–172, 173, **171**, **172**, **173**

patterns 16
symmetry 34, 35
pegs 86
picks per inch 4
pile 148 **148**, 189, 190
pile weave, loom-controlled 189–200, *190*
corduroy 190, 192 **192**, 194 **194**, **195**, 196, *200* 200
velveteen 196–200, **197**, **198**, **199**, **200**
piqué weave 179, 184–188, **185**, **186**
fast back 185, **185**, **186**
loose back 185, **186**, **187**
pirns *see* bobbins
plain weave 3–24, **4**, **14**, **225**, **230**
unbalanced 21
warp-faced 21
weft-faced 21
ply *see* yarn
point threading, treadling 235–236, **235**, **238**, 237–243
Primary Structures of Fabrics, The 21, 36, 123

rearranged twill 51 **51**, 52, **55**
rep weave 21, 22
imitation 21, 22 **22**
repp weave *see* rep weave
rib weave *see* rep weave
samples, making 14
sateen *see* satin
satin 63–82
damask 69, 70, 76–78, **76**, **77**, 81 **81**
double-faced 70, **71**, 72 **72**, 73 **73**, 74
false 28
intervals 64
irregular 68 **68**, 73
regular 64
sateen 63, 64, **65**, **66**, **68**, **71**, **74**, **76**
satinette 73
stripes 74, 76
satinette *see* satin
selvedges 47 *47*
floating 45
setts
calculating 250–252, *251*
drape, for 252
stability, for 252
variations 18, 20
shadow plaid 16

shadow stripe 16
shafts
2-shafts 4 **4**
basket weave **10**, **222**
hair cord **14**
half basket **10**
plain weave **4**
3-shafts 25, **43**
combined weaves **208**
mock leno **104**
piqué **185**
twill **25**, **43**
4-shafts 10 **10**, 38
basket weave **10**
Bedford cord **180**
Bronson lace **107**, **108**
canvas weave **104**
combined weaves **208**, **210**, **211**, **213**, **216**
corduroy **192**, **196**
crackle **153**
crepe **202**, **205**
doubleweave **158**, **159**, **160**, **171**, **172**, **175**
honeycomb **110**
huck **96**, **98**, **101**, **102**
inlay **123**, **124**, **126**
King's Flower **132**
linear zigzag **118**, **120**
mock leno **104**
monk's belt **140**
Moorman technique **124**
M's and O's **114**, **116**
ornamental weft **127**
overshot **132**, **135**, **136**, **137**, **138**, **140**, **141**, **142**, **143**, **172**
piqué **185**
spider weave **118**, **120**
summer and winter **145**, **146**, **147**, **148**, **150**
Swedish lace **106**
tricot **220**, **221**
twill **28**, **34**, **35**, **36**, **39**, **42**, **43**, **50**, **55**, **56**
waffle weave **84**, **87**
5-shafts **39**
damask **77**, **78**, **81**
combined weaves **208**
sateen **65**, **71**, **74**, **76**
twill **39**
6-shafts **238**
basket weave **222**
Bedford cord **180**, **182**
combined weaves **208**, **210**
corduroy **194**
crepe **202**, **206**
doubleweave **178**
M's and O's **117**
ornamental weft **127**
overshot **135**
piqué **186**
plain weave **230**
sateen **68**
sponge weave **93**, **94**
supplemental warp/weft **218**
velveteen **198**
waffle weave **86**, **94**
7-shafts
combined weaves **211**
sateen **71**, **76**
twill **48**
8-shafts **59**, **62**, **66**, **232**, **233**
backed weaves **174**
Bedford cord **182**, **184**
beiderwand **154**, **155**
combined weaves **212**, **214**
crepe **206**
doubleweave **164**, **165**, **170**, **172**, **174**, **176**, **178**
huck **100**
M's and O's **117**
ornamental weft **127**
overshot **139**, **140**, **141**, **142**, **143**, **172**
piqué **186**, **187**
sateen **66**, **74**
satin **77**
summer and winter **150**
tricot **220**
twill **29**, **32**, **44**, **45**, **48**, **51**, **59**, **60**, **62**, **224**
velveteen **197**, **199**
waffle weave **87**, **88**, **90**
9-shafts
supplemental warp **217**
10-shafts
Bedford cord **184**
linear zigzag **120**
plain weave **225**
spider weave **120**
sponge weave **93**
supplemental warp **219**
twill **224**, **225**
velveteen **197**, **199**
waffle weave **90**, **93**
11-shafts
huck **103**
12-shafts
combined weaves **214**
corduroy **194**, **195**
overshot **142**
plain weave **225**
sateen **73**
twill **225**
14-shafts
damask **76**
satin **72**
sponge weave **93**
16-shafts
basket weave **235**
corduroy **195**
doubleweave **166**
linear zigzag **122**
overshot **143**
spider weave **122**
twill **53**, **54**, **234**
waffle weave **87**, **88**, **92**
20-shafts
tricot **221**
24-shafts
basket weave **236**
shuttles 47 *47*
simple weaves 123
skip 4

skip dents 18–20
spacers 20
spider weaves 118 **118**, 119, 120 **120**, 122 **122**
sponge weave 93 **93**, **94**
stability, fabric 221, 224
  sett 252
staggered twill 28, 29
stitchers 64
stitching 176
stitching points 64
straight twill 26
stripes 6, 8, 74, 76
Strong, John H. 21, 22
summer and winter 145–151, **145**, **146**, **147**, **148**
Swedish lace 106 **106**, 107
symmetry 34, 35

table looms 5
texture 8, 14, 15
thread
  count 4
  size 14
threading 5
  as drawn in 136, 137
  doubleweave 171 **171**, 172
  on opposites 138, 139
  straight draw 34
  trompt as writ 136
threads, crowded 4
tie-up 5, 30
  design 232–234, 235, **232**, **233**, **234**
  skeleton **150**, 151
  treadle looms 5
tracking 201
treadling 136–138
  as drawn in 136, 137
  doubleweave 170, 171 **171**, 173
  order 5
  rose fashion **136**, 137 **137**
  shadow fashion 136, 137
  spider fashion 136, 137
  star fashion 137 **137**
  trompt as writ 136
tricot weave 220 **220**, 221 **221**
trompt as writ 136, 137
tubular cloth 161, *162* 162
twills 25–62, **25**, *26*, **28**, **29**, **32**, **34**, **35**, **36**, **39**, **45**, **48**, **50**, **51**, **53**, **54**, **55**, **202**, **224**, **234**, **235**
  balanced 26, **29**
  block 29, 30–32
  braided 62 **62**
  broken 28 **28**, 29, 32, 34, **202**
  corkscrew 48 **48**, 50
  crystal 36 **36**
  dornick 35 **35**, 36
  double-faced 42–43, **42**, **43**, 44 **44**
  even 26
  granite weave 29
  herringbone 34 **34**, 35
  interleaving 46, 48, 50–55, **50**, **51**, **53**, **54**, **55**, **205**
  movement 26, 34
  rearranged 51 **51**, 52, **55**
  sett 26
  staggered 28, 29
  straight 26
  undulating 56–61, **56**, **60**, **62**
  whipcords 48
twist 14, 16 *16*

undulating twill 56–61, **56**, **60**, **62**
units *see* blocks

value, color 6
velveteen 196–200, **197**, **198**, **199**, **200**

waffle weave 83–94, **84**, **86**, **87**, **88**, **90**, **92**, **93**, **94**
  Brighton honeycomb 90 **90**, 92 **92**, 93
  honeycomb 83
  sponge 93 **93**, **94**
warp 3, 4, 47
  advancing 18
  beam 69
  extra 127 **127**
  hit or miss 16, 17, 18
  mixed 16, 17, 18
  supplemental 129, 217 **217**, **218**, **219**, 220
Weaving as an Art Form 124
weft 3
  ornamental 126, 127 **127**, 129
  supplementary 217, **218**
whipcords 48

yarn
  abrasion 18
  bed 16
  novelty 18
  ply 16
  problems with 17, 18
  selection 4, 5, 6
  twist 16 *16*
  variations in 14

zigzag, linear 118 **118**, 119, 120 **120**, 122 **122**

Weaving Notes